the devil's disciples

the devil's disciples

makers of the salem witchcraft trials

Peter Charles Hoffer

The Johns Hopkins University Press
Baltimore & London

▼

Johns Hopkins Paperbacks edition, 1998
9 8 7 6 5 4 3 2 1

The Johns Hopkins University Press
2715 North Charles Street
Baltimore, Maryland 21218-4363
The Johns Hopkins Press Ltd., London

FRONTISPIECE: Seventeenth-century woodcut, redrawn by John
Ashton, 1887, depicting the devil at night with his disciples. From
Notestein, *Witchcraft in England* (1911), 271.

*Library of Congress Cataloging-in-Publication Data
will be found at the end of this book.*

A catalog record for this book is available from the British Library.

ISBN 0-8018-5201-3 (pbk.)

For Bill and Pat Stueck,
true friends

BOY   You are not going to say Old Marina isn't a witch, because you can't.

ANDREA   No, I can't say she isn't a witch. I haven't looked into it. A man can't know about a thing he hasn't looked into, or can he?

BOY   No! But THAT! (*He points to the shadow.*) She is stirring hell-broth.

ANDREA   Let's see. Do you want to take a look? I can lift you up.

BOY   You lift me to the window, mister! (*He takes a slingshot out of his pocket.*) I can really bash her from there.

ANDREA   Hadn't we better make sure she is a witch before we shoot? I'll hold that.

The BOY *puts the milk jug down and follows him reluctantly to the window.* ANDREA *lifts the boy up so that he can look in.*

ANDREA   What do you see?

BOY   (*slowly*) Just an old girl cooking porridge.

ANDREA   Oh! Nothing to it then. Now look at her shadow, Paolo.

The BOY *looks over his shoulder and back and compares the reality and the shadow.*

BOY   The big thing is a soup ladle.

ANDREA   Ah! A ladle! You see, I would have taken it for a broomstick, but I haven't looked into the matter as you have, Paolo. Here is your sling.

Bertolt Brecht, *Galileo,* scene 14

Contents

Preface

ON SEPTEMBER 13, 1710, a farm laborer named William Good begged the government of Massachusetts to listen to his troubles. He lived in Salem, where nearly two decades earlier his family was destroyed "upon the account of supposed witchcraft." He reminded the lawgivers: "1. My wife Sarah Good was in prison about four months & then executed. 2. a suckling child dyed in prison before the mothers execution. 3. a child of about 4 or 5 years old was in prison 7 or 8 months and being chain'd in the dungeon was so hardly used and terrifyed that she hath ever since been very chargeable haveing little or no reason to govern herself." The colonial assembly offered him thirty pounds to patch what could never be made whole.[1]

For more than a year between January 1692 and May 1693, the men and women of Salem, Massachusetts, and its neighboring towns lived in imminent fear of witches and their master, the Devil. Hundreds were accused, many of whom languished in jail for months. Nineteen men and women were executed, and one was pressed to death. Neighbor turned against neighbor, children informed on parents, and ministers cast out members of their congregations. When the crisis was over, almost as suddenly as it had begun, its survivors tried to make amends for their rush to judgment. Within a decade of the trials, two of the judges had publicly renounced their part in the affair, and one entire jury panel apologized en masse for its verdicts. On August 25, 1706, the most persuasive of the accusers, Ann Putnam Jr., whose vivid testimony as a twelve-year-old "victim" convinced grizzled magistrates and learned clergymen that their neighbors were secret agents of Satan, stood before the congregation in Salem Village and asked pardon of all those she had hurt.[2]

Fourteen years after her testimony had convicted many of the accused, Ann Putnam felt compelled to explain what had happened as well as to confess her errors. Surely the Devil had been among them and had deceived them, she offered. Samuel Parris, the minister whose sick child Betty was the first of the girls "bewitched," later acknowledged that God had "suffered the evil angels to delude" him and his neighbors.[3] Putnam and Parris honestly believed that the Devil had snared them. To almost all who lived through those days of judgment, such an explanation seemed the most obvious. As Thomas Fisk, foreman of one of the Salem trial juries, subsequently admitted, "We confess that we ourselves were not capable to understand the mysterious delusions of the Powers of Darkness, and Prince of the Air . . . whereby we fear we have been instrumental with others, tho ignorantly and unwittingly, to bring upon ourselves and this People of the Lord, the Guilt of Innocent Blood."[4] But why?

Was it God's wrath on those who had strayed from His way? Puritans saw themselves as the center of God's plan for His world and searched for His purposes constantly.[5] For the men and women who witnessed the events in Salem, confession and apology went hand in hand with the explanation that God was testing His chosen people and had found them wanting. As the Reverend Samuel Willard preached on November 27, 1692—after watching the trials closely and grieving aloud that innocent people had gone to the gallows—"There is a voice in every turn of providence which passeth over men, and it speaks to them, signifying what it is that God requires of them at such a time, and it highly concerns them to hear it, that so they may practice accordingly."[6]

Providence spoke to the people of Salem that year in fire and brimstone. Eastern New England was besieged by misfortune. A brutal, lingering war on the frontier with France and France's Native American allies had already cost both sides many more lives than were lost in all the witchcraft trials held in Britain's American colonies. Accompanying the conflict was a crisis within Massachusetts's government, a veritable revolution in which a party of local patriots had overthrown royal government but not been able to replace it with a stable provincial system. Partisan factions waited upon the will of a new English king and the arrival of a new charter of government. A more subtle but equally disquieting religious predicament gnawed at the very marrow of Puritan worship. Attendance at services was falling away, as was the Puritans' desire to seek full membership in their churches. The latter required an attestation of grace before the congregation which many churchgoers were unwilling or unable to provide.

Parris and Willard shared the faith that God had singled out New England, but His will was not plain. Was all the suffering a test of faith or a proof that God had hidden His face from His people? Emotionally and intellectually drained by their involvement in the events but determined to give answers to their fearful congregants, ministers like Parris and Willard became students of the Devil's wiles. Like the ordinary folk who knew all about witches and magic, the ministers became the Devil's disciples.

By trying to probe the meaning of the crisis, the men and women of New England became its chroniclers. Indeed, much of what we know about the tragedy comes from the pen of another minister, Cotton Mather, whose role in the events was critical, and a merchant, Robert Calef, whose barbed accusations of Mather's misconduct have become classic examples of early American nonfiction.[7] Later generations of New Englanders, burdened with guilt, retold the tale in various ways to cast aspersions or exculpate their ancestors.[8] Nathaniel Hawthorne, a descendant of one of the magistrates who interrogated the suspects and sat on the court that condemned them, pleaded the cause of the accused in *The House of Seven Gables.* In our own century, writers living through another era of unfounded suspicion and unprovable charges recast the Salem trials as a metanarrative of persecution. The most haunting of these latter-day adaptations, Arthur Miller's *The Crucible,* remains a moving indictment of McCarthyism and the Red Scare of the 1950s.

The story of the witchcraft accusations in 1692 still chills audiences three hundred years later, for the trials have become icons of superstition and credulity, hysteria, and injustice.[9] Mere mention of them calls up the specter of unproven and unprovable aspersions, the presumption of guilt, and the destruction of family and community. As one former president of a major state university recently wrote of his own plight, "In our attempts to show rightful outrage over genuine instances of sexual misconduct, let us not produce a 1990s version of the Salem witch hunts. The accused and their families suffer tremendously from over-zealous 'trials' in which due process is thrown out the window. We must remember that just as victims have rights, so do the accused."[10] Even our vision of the future is haunted by the specter of the Salem witch trials.[11]

Part of our fascination with the witchcraft trials at Salem comes from a feeling of moral superiority, a rush of relief that we are not so super-stitious, so gullible, so intolerant, as those men and women who be-lieved that their neighbors flew through the air on poles to a secret meet-ing on Thorndike Hill, at the back of Reverend Samuel Parris's home, and there carried out satanic rites. Yet behind that smug certitude lurks our fear that we are as prone to rumor, panic, and insinuation as Salem's denizens. On January 28, 1994, with the Philadelphia area blanketed by snow, fears of continuing bad weather brought rumors of a terrible storm approaching: "Psst. Have you heard? There's a storm coming in. A big one this time. A huge one, in fact. A massive, gigantic, humon-gous, cataclysmic, mother-of-all-blizzards storm. It'll be three feet this time. Maybe five. Maybe seven. Where'd we hear this? Uh, in the check-out line. In the barber shop. At the exercise class. At the gas pumps. At work. At school. Somebody said . . . Thus goes the great blizzard rumor of this icebound winter of '94."[12] The story is humorous, but the under-lying group dynamic is not. Made uneasy by the unpredictability of the weather and diverted from familiar patterns of work and domesticity by its severity (just as the American Indian raids of 1691–92 a few miles away frightened people in Salem and disordered their lives), modern city dwellers grasped at false reports and elevated them into dire omens.

Such rumor panics can open the door to our fears of hidden forces. Choose at random from the available late-twentieth-century examples of the same process—pressure exerted on ordinary people living in an ordinary community to come to grips with the horrifying disturbances of modern life—and we find rumor leading to fears of a conspiracy. In the winter of 1993–94, gripped by dread of a crime wave, people in Saint Louis turned the fact that two girls had been abducted and slain into a grisly (and untrue) tale of satanic rites of dismemberment.[13] Every year at Halloween in Stull, Kansas, in our nation's heartland, ordinary peo-ple break into the town cemetery, hoping to catch a glimpse of the Devil—for it is rumored that the burial ground is one of the two gates to hell. The other can be found in Salem.[14] The root of our obsession with Salem's tragedy is more basic than curiosity about an event distant in time and mentality from our own. It is the need to know why people turn upon their neighbors and kin, the need to know about our other, feral, side.

In recent years historians and archivists have recovered and published original legal and local records to help a new generation of young people understand how men and women in Salem saw their world and made decisions about their neighbors.[15] There are first-rate full length studies of the crisis and the place where it occurred.[16] Beside these stand superb scholarly analyses of witchcraft in Massachusetts.[17] Still, our appetite is not sated, for a new generation of doctoral candidates, descendants of the participants, and authors of children's books have found more to say.[18]

All of these accounts share a genuine empathy for the people who lived in Salem, yet none really explains the events. And we need—we demand—some explanation. But the events cannot be dismissed as the work of the Devil, though there was deviltry in some people's hearts, or as an excess of local family animus, or as a struggle for the means of production. We cannot categorize the Salem cases as a provincial example of the great European witch hunt, for Salem's agony was entirely out of step with the declining curve of prosecution for witchcraft in the Western world. In fact, the witchcraft trials of 1692 and 1693 were an abnormality in the larger context of English and New England history. There had only been thirty-four prior cases in eastern New England, and only three of these came after 1680. Two of those ended in acquittal, following the pattern of most of their predecessors.[19] The Salem outbreak was thus unprecedented in New England's history. What was more, by 1690 the number of cases in England had sharply declined, and convictions had become all but impossible. Learned judges pressed juries to find a verdict of not guilty.[20] Salem was an exception in its time, a throwback to the witch-hunting crazes of a much earlier time in continental Europe and England.[21]

The task for the historian today is to see these events as contemporaries saw them but to interpret them using the tools that three hundred years of academic scholarship have produced. Our goal is "to produce an interpretation of the way a people lives which is neither imprisoned within their mental horizons, an ethnography of witchcraft as written by a witch, nor systematically deaf to the distinctive tonalities of their existence, an ethnography of witchcraft as written by a geometer."[22] We want to explain the story in our words but tell it in theirs. In the present volume I have relied upon new and striking findings on child abuse, recovered memory, and the psychology of girls in dysfunctional settings to revisit the motives of the accusers and the accused. I have reframed the story in a new and broader spatial context, relying upon an "Atlantic Rim" model of the human landscape of the late-seventeenth-century West. West Africa and the Caribbean were then vital parts of a world on whose edge Salem lay, and the diversity of peoples and cultures in that world infuses my story.

Although I have relied upon modern scholarship and social science research to explain the course of events, I wish the people who lived those events to be seen for themselves and to speak in their own words. If any tale could "carry itself,"[23] it would be a narrative of Salem's travail. Perhaps that is another reason why we are attracted to these sad occurrences. There is human longing, fear, animus, righteousness, sorrow, and mischief in abundance. But what was it like to live then, in fear of witches and their mischief?

Seeing comes first: we must try to view their world through their eyes. Fortunately, the Essex Institute/Peabody Museum in Salem and the Danvers Historical Society have managed to preserve or restore much of the physical context of Salem and Salem Village in the late seventeenth century. In the historical district of Danvers, once Salem Village, one can still walk the lanes and cross the meadows that the accusers and the accused traveled. The dimensions of buildings have not changed, and many stand in situ. The summer air is filled with pollen, insects, and the barking of dogs, and the winter is cold and wet, just as they were three hundred years ago; urbanization has not changed the landscape all that much. The roads are paved, but they still run along the courses of the old paths. The rhythms of sunrise and sunset still mark the passage of the day, and the night is just as dark and ominous.

The historical record of the events in Salem survives in written form, much of it taken down for use at the trials. Like the Catawba of the Piedmont who in these same years yearned to know how the South Carolina traders among them magically communicated with one another using only ink marks on paper, we need to "make paper speak."[24] We want to turn dry written records into lively human voices, to treat the printed words in the historical record as remnants of talk among various groups of people, to recapture the swift riposte and earnest entreaty of private conversation, the solemn reading aloud of sermons in church and depositions in the courthouse. The men and women of Salem exchanged words and gestures and silences that were pregnant with meaning. They chattered and argued, cried out and stood dumbfounded. We must become "epireaders" of the historical documents, "transposing the written words on the page into a somehow corresponding human situation of persons, voices, characters, conflicts, conciliations."[25]

I start with names, for names are the beginnings of most conversations. Tituba's name reveals to us her origins, allowing us to follow her from Africa to Barbados. There she met Samuel Parris, and with him she traveled to New England. For us the appearance of names in these scattered, fragmentary, elusive records, like a blip on a radar screen, tracks a journey that comes to its end in a tiny settlement on the edge of a forest frontier: Salem Village. There Parris's voice was often heard and his words recorded in the village records and the church book. He left us notes of his sermons, a dialogue between him and his congregation, his "auditory."[26] We watch and listen, straining to see and hear what he said and how his listeners responded, sensing the growing animosity between him and a portion of his flock.

The legal record is another set of conversations, this time among suspects, accusers, witnesses, judges, and spectators. Today these exchanges are formal, almost ritualized by complex rules for criminal procedure and standards for the admissibility of evidence. Then, there were few curbs upon what could be said, and rumor and reputation dominated the dialogues. The controls upon belief were not dictated by legal regulations but by social understandings. Speakers and audiences understood their relationships to one another. Meaning depended upon who spoke to whom and on the social distance between individuals.[27]

In these testimonies we rediscover the oral culture of rural Essex County, a world of servants, farmers, and children in which the folklore of witchcraft flourished. There we find the seeds of unrest, suspicion, and panic in Salem that winter of 1692. Tales of Indian massacres, occurrences of witchcraft, and other omens and prodigies that people shared with one another came together and were magnified in times of stress. An oral, vernacular folk culture of ordinary Puritan farmers and craftspeople, homemakers and parents, absorbed and transformed an official, elite, text-driven culture of law and theology and elevated whispers of suspicion into official inquiries and trials.

When we visualize the setting and recast the written documents as conversation among social actors, we begin to reconnect the social and the legal stories. Perhaps under the assumption that only lawyers can decipher legal records, many historians regard court records and procedures as bewildering and dull, but anyone who has sat through a criminal trial knows that from start to finish it is action, a multiform conversation among many parties. What happens in that courtroom is the very stuff of life, framed (if sometimes denatured, it is true) by conventions of polite address and rules of admissibility of testimony. Then as now, contests of law created expectations and framed conduct.[28]

Although the first half of this book is concerned primarily with social relationships and the second half with legal events, the two subjects are inseparable, as the conversation in the records makes plain. Parris owed his employment to a legal agreement; the village itself struggled for a legal identity; and the social nature of witchcraft belief overlapped the legal definition of witchcraft. The accusations, confessions, trials, and pardons that constitute the legal story in the second half of the book are also signs of changing social values, the beginning of a world in which the Devil surrendered pride of place to other, more human sources of evil.

Where to start, then? With Salem itself? Perhaps with witchcraft in England? Or with the Puritans and their laws? But for one woman, an outsider, the "Other," there would have been no witchcraft crisis in Salem. She is Tituba, and by beginning our story with her, she gains a voice, and we gain an "alternative perspective" on the people who became the Devil's disciples.[29]

Acknowledgments

HOW TO THANK the many kind and helpful people who contributed their time and effort toward the completion of my work? I am grateful to the staffs of the Danvers Historical Society, the Essex Institute in Salem, Massachusetts, the Folger Library in Washington D.C., the Rare Books Rooms at the Columbia University Library in New York City, the New York University and University of Pennsylvania Law Libraries, the African Studies Institute at the University of Pennsylvania, and the Library System of the University of Georgia. The Ethel Wolfe Institute at Brooklyn College, the Columbia University Seminar in Early Modern History, the patrons of the Rorschack Lecture and Harold Hyman, at Rice University, Bill Nelson and his happy band of seminarians at New York University, and the program committee of the American Society for Legal History permitted me to offer parts of this book as lectures under their auspices. I acknowledge also my debt to John Baker, Tim Breen, Mike Briggs, Bob Brugger, Natalie Hull, David Konig, Mike McGiffert, Bill Nelson, Richard Ross, David Schoenbrun, and Mike Winship, who commented on pieces of various drafts. Elaine Breslaw, Daniel Mandell, Tony Phillips, and Mike Winship shared with me unpublished material that was immensely

Acknowledgments

informative, and Warren Alleyne gave wise counsel from far away. David McGee checked the citations. Grace Buonocore copyedited the manuscript. Bob Brugger and the rest of the wonderful people at the Johns Hopkins University Press have taken another chance on me, and my obligation to them cannot be fully repaid. I gratefully acknowledge permission from Indiana University Press to reprint a portion of Bertolt Brecht's *Galileo*, © 1952.

the devil's disciples

prologue: tituba

MY ACCOUNT of what happened in Salem is one of an overlapping set of stories scholars are just beginning to tell about the Atlantic Rim in 1692. The older narratives of witchcraft in Salem spanned the ocean from England to the Puritan colonies in North America and stretched in time from the statutes of Elizabeth I which criminalized witchcraft to the beginning of the eighteenth century, when witchcraft prosecutions all but disappeared. It was a Euro-American story, with English-speaking heroes and villains. What if one were to begin the story in a different place with a different character?

Salem Village might have been an isolated farming community on the edge of English America, but it was tied to the whole Atlantic world by riverine and transoceanic trade. Over those watercourses moved goods and people, including a woman, Tituba.[1] However she came to serve among the Puritans of Salem Village,[2] Tituba's presence and her role could hardly have been predicted. Tituba's story teaches the contingency of history. A slave woman, displaced and diminished in the vast commerce of human cargo, changed a great many lives in unanticipated ways. All the great forces that transformed the Atlantic world, strong vectors of capital and trade, mentality and people, converged like so many lines in the single vanishing point of an individual's life. The motion of that point moved all the great forces in new directions.

Tituba also reminds students of our early history that everyone matters. Though multitudes were in motion crossing vast spaces, life in the village was intimate, in tune with the seasons and cycles of planting and harvesting. New faces—strange faces—were cause for comment, and in times of trouble, for suspicion among neighbors, but even the most dependent of women and men could act in their own behalf. Though she was an object in the stream of commerce, Tituba had the power to resist her oppressors, and by resisting, to change her world.[3] Her story is proof that the imprint of culture cannot ever be wholly eradicated by distance or suffering, for there are always connections to the lives of others in the life of a single one.

Tituba's story would not have intersected with Salem's story without the avarice and ingenuity of others quite unlike her in their beliefs and ways. The Puritans of eastern Massachusetts were many things besides pious Christians. They were sailors and shipmasters, cloth makers and homemakers, merchants, child rearers, farmers, teachers, midwives, ministers, and soldiers. When they first came to New England, they sought self-sufficiency and failed, but they could not allow themselves to believe that God wanted them to falter, so they went into the forests and onto the oceans. Some of the most enterprising of their number became overseas merchants and benefited handsomely from trade with that farthest flung of English Caribbean possessions, Barbados. They sent their sons and nephews to deal in cane sugar and slaves, and Barbados's profits became the currency of Puritan Salem's salvation. To work the sugar plantations the English turned from indentured servants drawn from the home islands to slaves from West African lands. Among these were the lush forests along the tidal basin of the Niger River and the coast as far west and north as what is now Senegal. In the center of the market for slaves was the "slave coast" from Dahomey to the Igbo country in the southeast of present-day Nigeria—Yorubaland. That is where this story begins, with a young girl named Tituba. Tituba was a female house servant of minister Samuel Parris of Salem Village, the western farming portion of the chartered port town of Salem. Tituba told Parris's daughter Elizabeth and her friends about worlds on the other side of the ocean. Tituba tied the Niger riverine trade in the Bight of Biafra to Salem's busy port, for *Tituba* is a Yoruba name.

Prologue: Tituba

In Yoruba, *Tίtί* means "endless," "never ending." It is a common part of female names in Yoruba. *Uba* is not so common, but in names, *oba*, "kingship," is ubiquitous. The two sounds are easily confused, and *A tί tό oba* (we are as good as the king) and *tίtί la oba* (kingship is forever) could easily have been rendered as *Tituba*. *Tituba* is also a verb root that means "to atone" or "to apologize." It is possible that some family, needing to show submissiveness, so named a female child, as an offering to whoever had to be assuaged. Thus the name becomes a sign of obedience that reestablishes the harmony of a village or a clan. Even more intriguing is the possibility that *Tituba* was a hybrid name, a name that the girl gave herself in slavery; *Tίtί Yoruba,* "the Yoruba live on; Yoruba is everlasting; I am Yoruba and will remain so, whatever you do to me, wherever you carry me."[4]

3

Today, the Yoruba have complex naming systems and ceremonies. The child has many names—one for the clan, one for public use, and often a nickname. The first is a secret name, but in slavery there were no secrets. The secret name describes the soul of the child and predicts that child's life's course. The souls of children are part of a clan's communal spiritual existence, as the child will be watched over by the spirits of ancestors. Thus the past, present, and future are linked in a name. In life, the child will usually be known by one name. Yoruba names are always sentences; the predictive power of the name has a declarative force. There can be worlds of pathos in names. If a mother wanted a sickly child to live, she could call him Onwumbiko: "death I implore you." Were that infant to die young, she might name the next Ozoemena: "may it not happen again." The precise meaning of Tituba's name cannot be recovered from European alphabetic text, however, for Yoruba is an inflected language, a tonal language, and we do not know whether the *ti* was high, middle, or low in tone. Nevertheless the name speaks volumes, for it deflects the story, pulling it inexorably toward the African shore of the Atlantic world.[5]

What's in a name?[6] For the Yoruba, the name, given after divination, was a beckoning, an omen, a prophesy. It spoke to its owner, of course, predicting life course and personal character. One's name also spoke to others who knew the language and its naming conventions. Thus another Yoruba would know much about Tituba even before she appeared. What would happen when Tituba found herself in a setting in which her name was just a phoneme, a set of sounds? The burden would then be placed on her to introduce herself, to create an identity,

Among people who did not speak Yoruba, Tituba would have to adapt or disappear.

The Yoruba lands stretched across the whole of the slave coast, and the people (who called themselves the Lucumi, for *olu cumi*—"hello my brother")[7] and their Oyo kings engaged in the slave trade on a large scale.[8] Slaves were a kind of currency—a legal tender of war and domination which Africans created and Europeans exploited.[9] African elites controlled their end of the trade. Unawed by Europeans, in command of price and commodity negotiations, they extended a longstanding internal market in slaves to new buyers, in return for luxury items and other foreign goods.[10] Indeed, by the end of the 1670s, the balance of trade clearly favored the African slave providers over their European consumers, and the former received more value per slave than in previous years.[11] Yet the exchange was never fully elaborated in the language of either the West African or the European, for on the middle ground where slave traders of all colors met, Africans who were taken in war or had "pawned themselves" became, in the hands of Europeans who neither understood nor cared about West African customs of dependence and deference, mere objects of commerce.[12]

The Oyo kingdom, at the center of Yorubaland, provided many of those slaves, and they were carried by local agents to the foreigner's fortress-warehouses on the slave coast. The English maintained such factories along the coast from Senegal to the Niger, and one of these, at Quidah (Whydah to the English, Igelefe to the Yoruba),[13] had the usual garrison and "trunk" for slaves awaiting shipment across the ocean.[14] There, supercargoes working for British merchants, primarily the Royal African Company, put together cargoes of slaves for the English settlements in the West Indies.[15] From the slave coast they took 5,000 souls away in the 1670s. By the 1680s, the sugar revolution and the demographic catastrophes that together changed Barbados from a white to a black colony led to a massive demand for and influx of slaves. Royal African Company slave cargoes averaging 230 men, women, and children crossed the ocean to the English island 72 times in the 1670s and, with slightly smaller average loads, 121 times in the next decade. On average, about 12 percent of the "cargo" died en route, sometimes from disease, sometimes from simply not wanting to live. Suicide was always a problem. In the factories, in reality forts along the coast, Europeans also succumbed to disease. The average span of life was one to two years, but some died sooner and a few survived. On board the ships, the sailors and officers also died of disease, further human cost of the trade in human lives.[16]

There survives a detailed first-hand account of enslavement in Yorubaland and the middle passage from the eighteenth century. Its author was male, which distinguishes his experience from Tituba's, but he was a child of roughly her age when he was carried from his home. Olaudah Equiano, an Eboe of Benin, was "kidnapped" as a boy of eleven in 1756. Equiano recalled that he lived far from the sea, in a compound that his father, a respected elder, helped rule. Olaudah's name meant "vicissitude or fortunate; also, one favored, having a loud voice and well spoken," and children were expected to live up to their names. Along with the elders, society was ordered by priests or wise men. These "magicians" were doctors as well, trusted herbalists, and diviners. They could tell from the corpse of the murdered dead who had committed the crime.[17]

Into this paradise came a serpent: "stout-mahogany colored men from the South west of us . . . [who brought] fire-arms, gunpowder, hats, beads, and dried fish." At the markets in Benin these "Oye-Eboe"—"redmen [who] lived at a distance"—traded with Equiano's people, sometimes in slaves, for the Oye-Eboe always brought slaves with them, and Equiano's elders also had slaves: "but only prisoners of war, or such among us as had been convicted of kidnapping, or adultery, and some other crimes which we esteemed heinous." To these Oye-Eboe the children of Benin were a temptation, for they could be stolen from their compounds and sold to West Indian planters who preferred the slaves of Benin for their "hardiness, intelligence, integrity, and zeal."[18]

So in truth Equiano's world was never peaceful—much like Tituba's world a hundred years before. In times of famine or the wars between neighboring states which plagued Benin, his people went to their fields armed. Children playing near their homes always posted a lookout, for the raids were accompanied by capture of anyone for sale or use as slaves. Equiano made clear that slavery was not a European imposition upon the Africans but a part of West African customs, and war brought enslavement to many. Captured on one such raid, Equiano and his sister were taken from their homes. He was sold to a family whose head was a blacksmith, and was treated well but pined for home. Sold again, he was carried to the coast. At last, he was sold to Europeans, horrible men with loose red hair who chained the slaves aboard great ships and carried them away from their homes. The stench below deck was almost insufferable, and many fell ill. Equiano despaired until he found in the hold people from his own land. True to his name, he soon began asking questions, absorbing information, adapting to his new situation. The suffering was palpable, and a few of his new companions attempted suicide, but the voyage came to an end at last. "We came in sight of the Island of Barbados, at which the whites on board gave a great shout and made many signs of joy to us."

For the crew, captain, and mates, the voyage was a success; for the slaves, it was only a transition to another form of degradation. On board came the merchants to assess the value of the cargo, one of the many lying at anchor in Bridgetown harbor. The slaves' dread was allayed by the arrival of older slaves from the island who explained to the newcomers their fate. They were not to be eaten but sold as field hands. Equiano joined the coffle as they filed from their pens on the wharf to the yard, where the auction began, and buyers departed with their new purchases. New shipboard friends were parted just as families had been separated on the far shore and carried off to different plantations.[19]

Another hundred years later the story was continued by another young man, like Equiano carried away from his home by the slavers. In 1821, in the Egba region south of the old kingdom of Oyo, Samuel Ajayi Crowther was captured and sold for the overseas trade. Crowther was fortunate; he was rescued from a Portuguese slave ship by a British squadron cruising the coast of West Africa for that very purpose, a complete reversal of the colonial powers' roles whose causes are much debated but whose effect on the young man was electric.[20] Brought to Sierra Leone, Crowther was to become a bishop in the Church of England, return to his home, and convert many to his new faith. He left a memoir of his travails which demonstrates unequivocally that slaves were commodities on an international market. He was in his early teens, a member of a well-to-do family in a market town, when the armies from the north swept down upon them. Women fled the carnage, clinging to their children, and were caught in nooses like cattle. Gathered up by their conquerors, led past the smoking ruins of their former abodes, they were carried off into slavery. "Farewell, place of my birth, the playground of my childhood, and the place which I thought would be the repository of my mortal body in its old age," he recalled thinking when he had to flee the carnage. One imagines that Tituba thought much the same, if not in Victorian prose. Crowther was bartered for a horse "that very day" and began his travels, like a bill of exchange, endorsed by its successive holders. Later owners exchanged him for tobacco and rum, other commodities in the stream of commerce.[21]

The slave ship was a great funnel through which poured the many nations and peoples of West Africa, so perhaps it does not matter where along the slave coast Tituba got her name or whose culture among the many of West Africa it signifies.[22] So many slaves came together in the trade because slavers made it their business to buy in small lots from various jobbers. Too many slaves in a cargo from the same clans meant increased danger of resistance or rebellion. It was better to make up a cargo from many nations. The English slavers favored the Bight of Biafra, but the plantations on Barbados and Jamaica were melting pots for "Coromantees" from the Ashanti kingdom of modern Ghana, Mandingo from the interior of Senegal, and Congolese from south of the Niger.[23]

Slaves faced with this veritable babble of voices began to piece together a pidgin, a common tongue from the many, but they did not lose their own tongue. Each language group clung to large fragments of its mother tongue, because it had power, the power to help the slaves remember and cope. "Cornered like this, their deepest prayers and desires were expressed through their mother tongue. It was, and still is, explicitly stated that Yoruba is more powerful than a European language. So grandparents blessed their grandchildren on Christmas Day with Yoruba prayers. Morning and evening prayers for safety and success were uttered in Yoruba. The dead needed Yoruba songs to despatch them properly."[24] Later, when settled in the colonies, slaves would turn pidgin into Creole, stable compound languages that blended many local dialects and dominant European (masters') tongues into a vernacular language, and with it a vernacular culture. Thus *Tituba* stands for the many who came, found ways to survive, and left their names in the historical record.[25]

The first port of call for the English slavers was always Barbados, 150 miles to the east of the other sugar islands and thus closest to the West African coast. In the 1650s and 1660s, Dutch and English slavers brought cargoes to the wharfs at Bridgetown, the capital of the English colony. In 1672, the Crown chartered the Royal African Company to regulate the slave trade and tap into its profits. Those Africans who survived the middle passage on the Royal African Company ships were greased and blackened to look healthy for buyers and then paraded on the shore. The slaves were auctioned, the best traveled sold to plantations inland, the worst for wear put back aboard ship for sale on one of the other English islands to the west. On those wharfs, Tituba arrived as a girl, perhaps one of the twenty-one whose prices were recorded in the slavers' ledgers for the early 1670s. A healthy girl cost between sixteen and eighteen pounds.[26]

Tituba may have been purchased first by Samuel Thompson, whose estate, including the slaves, was leased to others and finally broken up and sold away. A list of slaves owned by Thompson, leased to Edward Prideaux and later signed over to John Hothersall, may have contained Tituba's name. On that inventory are the names of nineteen "negro . . . children," probably under the age of fourteen, the youngest of whom was "Tattuba." It is impossible to determine how an Englishman might have heard the Yoruba tonalities of "Tituba." Above Tattuba is a "Tity," obviously an Anglicization of Titi, another Yoruba word, and possibly a fragment of another child's name. Perhaps the two girls shared the slave deck in the middle passage from the fort at Quidah or were taken aboard ship farther east along the slave coast—two children, separated from their kin and culture, who whispered to each other in the same language and were sold to the same master. The English merchants preferred young, healthy slaves, and African slave traders were so informed. On the Thompson inventory, among the other young Negroes, was a Hannah, a Jack, and a little Betty. Tituba kept her African name, but it was becoming less than it had been, for she was among those who did not know its meaning.[27]

Whatever the particular composition of the labor force on any given plantation, for the slaves community was a matter of necessity. On Barbados Tituba came to a miniature village, a composite of African building styles and cultures, composed of many peoples, gathered around the plantation house. It was on those plantations that the island's economy, and its value to the empire, depended. Masters provided some basics of clothing and cooking ware, housing and seed, but the slaves themselves rebuilt their lives from within their experience and desire.[28] Visitors often remarked that the slave quarters resembled African villages, and they did, down to the domestic division of labor.

Tituba came into not only a new and untested Afro-Caribbean quarter with a babble of tongues, it was also an island under siege. Barbados, conceived as an outpost of English military aspirations and commercial enterprise, had by the 1670s become something else entirely. In 1624 English adventurers, later joined by British and Irish indentured servants, occupied the island. Just as tobacco was failing as a crop, the planters, with Dutch help, were able to shift to sugarcane production. Slaves were transported from South American sugarcane-growing areas to join with indentured European servants. The face of the island, once rich green from dense woodland, gradually became bare as timber was consumed by the face load to feed the fires that boiled down the sugarcane. Wood for building and fuel had to be imported from New England. By the 1660s, a second revolution was changing the human face of the island, from white to black. Slave importation from Africa increased, slave gangs became the rule, and local landlords gradually left the island and the duties of overseeing planting to younger relatives or hired managers.[29]

As more and more Africans were brought together in these great sugar factories, cultural hybrids emerged. Hybrids are coping mechanisms, ways in which different peoples try to make whole what has been riven. The process began, again, with language, conversations in gestures and loan words on the ships lying at anchor off the coast of West Africa, conversations continued below and above decks on the voyage, perfected in the slave quarters, the fields, and the English towns, as slaves learned to talk to one another. Language restated social relationships, creating, if necessary (and it generally was), fictive kinship networks, uncles and aunts who were not blood kin but performed the nurturing and socializing roles of biological parents.

Magic and divination practices from different parts of West Africa were typical of these hybrids. In Barbados Tituba was exposed to a more Creole version of folk arts the Yoruba knew so well—to divine fortunes with shells and heal sicknesses with herbs and incantations. Folk healers mixed and matched the preparation of all sorts of potions—brewed, boiled, stirred, and baked.[30] With each potion went incantations, more language, recalling the powers of Gods left in Africa who, disembodied, made the voyage to the New World with their acolytes. Song, dance, and conversation came together, as these rites were performed in public and became a social glue holding the community together. Among the many practitioners of forms of worship and healing, witches were the most potent and the most feared. A witch used her powers to harm people, but the very same power—the power to see into the heart of darkness—

had to be employed by diviners and healers of those possessed by witchery. The line between the two was thus blurred, or rather was crossed in both directions by women and men.[31]

It is hard at this distance to recover the language of incantation, but its tone and impact are not lost. Some of the Yoruba still practice Ife divination, for to them Ife is all knowledge. Animal sacrifices, part of Yoruba popular religion, were combined with Christian elements of worship. In other Yoruba communities in the Caribbean, these rituals became "Santeria." The propitiation of the old gods in the Africans' new world was a stirring and emotionally charged event, impenetrable and frightening by turns to European observers. Of course, then, far more than now, witches were also feared, but they could be asked to turn their powers upon the white oppressor.[32] At the same time, slaves considered the masters to be witches, for they inflicted pain and used malign spells. Against them, countermagic was needed.[33]

There was much for a young Yoruba female to learn. The first lesson was the hardest: Tituba found herself away from home, far from familiar faces and places. For a Yoruba, family close at hand and home ground underfoot meant safety, for family networks provided material and spiritual sustenance, and native land was sacred. Earth was power and strength. Earth was precious and dear. Everything smelled of earth—the houses, the pots, the utensils. The women who worked in the fields smelled of earth. In losing the familiar, Tituba's experience was similar to that of the increasing number of West Africans taken by force from their homes and transplanted to Barbados. Their coping strategy was to re-create community, but for each new arrival, fitting into that community was no easy matter.

In these new surroundings, pools of pathogens waited everywhere. Diseases drawn from many parts of West Africa, such as yaws, elephantiases, and sleeping sickness, came with the pests that accompanied the slaves. To this mix were added the infirmities and infections the masters and indentured servants brought with them, killers like influenza, bubonic plague, and smallpox. Chicken pox and measles were not usually fatal to the English, Scots, and Irish, but they were to the Africans, who had no resistance. So, too, were the tropical parasites the newcomers found on the island. Some Africans had inherited immunities, for example to malaria, but the mosquito that carried the malaria parasite did not come to Barbados until the eighteenth century. Other diseases, principally yellow fever, affected everyone on the island. So did a variety of stomach and intestinal ailments. Every malady was accompanied by fever, discharges, skin lesions and eruptions, and lethargy. There were doctors of all kinds, with remedies of all sorts, most of which made the sickness worse. Africans preferred their own medicine, although providers of folk remedies faced new diseases and had to adapt to a new flora. Tituba must have watched with horror as maladies unknown in Africa struck down her new companions. That she survived was a statistical victory—for on some plantations the turnover of slaves was complete every two years—and a sobering one. It taught her to put a high premium on survival, for life was never a given.[34]

The second lesson was the barbarity of New World slavery. West Africans knew slavery, but its regime was not the same as slavery in the West Indies. In Yorubaland, bondage was as much a cornerstone of political and domestic systems as it was a form of property. This is not to say that slavery in West Africa was benign or beneficial to the enslaved. Slavery was, rather, one of many clusters of situations in which individuals found themselves disadvantaged—"dependence without recourse."[35] In most West African cultures, slaves were outsiders, marginal members of the community, and could not claim the protection of kin. They lacked the status, the power to inherit, the ability to marry, and the mobility of free persons, but they were human beings, could aspire to incorporation in their masters' society, and were never reduced to being mere property. Equiano's father had many slaves, but they were part of the household. Slave women could marry their masters or their masters' children. A slave woman had no kin nearby with any rights to protect against maltreatment in such marriages, nor could she return to her parents' village if the marriage failed, but her children did not share her lack of protection. They became part of their father's kin. Slaves could claim rights to sustenance, and over time, slowly, the line between free and slave blurred.[36]

On Barbados—in the eyes of the law and the lawmakers—slaves were chattel, movable property. The English on the island made a clear distinction between free and slave. Crossing from the latter to the former through manumission was uncommon, for colonial law erected barriers to humane sentiment and personal compassion. The slave code of 1661 clearly defined bound and free persons, the end result of earlier efforts by the planter legislature to control unruly servants. Martial law, with its uncompromising vision of discipline, may have been another source of inspiration to the planter-lawgivers, but the Barbadian legislators could claim the distinction of providing a model of slave law adopted in the rest of the English West Indies, Virginia, South Carolina, and the other mainland slave societies.[37] In all of these jurisdictions, following the Barbados model, slaves were denied the procedural privileges of free defendants in criminal cases as well as the basic civil liberties of English subjects. Merely offering a gesture of violence to a white person was grounds for a severe whipping. Fomenting rebellion was treason. Slave homes were to be searched every two weeks for stolen goods or weapons, and slaves were not to bang drums or blow horns, lest the music reveal itself as a signal for revolt.[38] The discretion given the master class in the slave code of 1661 enabled masters not only to discipline slaves but to buy and sell slaves easily, a basic requirement of the marketplace. After all, to be free literally meant that one could hold property against the claims of others or the state. Slaves, by contrast, were not free, had no property, even in themselves, and could not maintain such a claim against a free person.[39] Thus any free person could discipline a slave without fear of legal liability, except when the master brought a civil suit for destruction of his property.

Custom and good sense among the masters dictated that children not bear the burden of work which adults bore, but slave children were soon put to work, first in the "grass gang," then in the "second gang." There was little of the fraternization with free children characteristic of later plantations on the mainland of the British colonies, for there were very few free children.[40] Even young slaves soon realized that they were never to be free. The law captured this essential truth: the children of slaves were to be slaves for life as well. The lesson would be reinforced by the brutal treatment of slaves on many plantations. The misdeeds of bad masters and brutal overseers were carried in tales from plantation to plantation over an oral network that sent its messages in pidgin. Runaways, visiting or hiding out, served as the town criers of the black underground. Statutes condemned slaves leaving the plantation without a pass, and masters offered informers one hundred pounds of sugar to identify these "wandering negroes."[41] Tituba may have come to Barbados just before the abortive rebellion of 1675, which grew out of such mistreatment, but every slave knew what had happened to the ringleaders. Even good masters, an oxymoron endemic to the slave system, routinely inflicted corporal punishment on unruly bondsmen and women, but it was the system itself that brutalized. The slave code of 1661 was harsh, reflecting both the relentless demands of the labor market and the pervasive, insidious racism of the master class.[42]

As sugar prices declined throughout the 1660s and 1670s, lesser planters were gradually driven from the field and larger planters committed more of their land to sugar production. Ever larger labor gangs became the rule, which required a larger number of slaves, at the same time that increasing density of slave population increased the likelihood of malnutrition and the risk of disease. Overcrowding and increasingly inhumane conditions in the slave quarters made the slaves' lives harsher but did not deter masters from increasing the importation of slave laborers. Many masters ordered what amounted to a speedup in production. Not only did such labor practices further burden the time and energy of the slaves, but they also made plain to every slave that he or she was a cog in a machine rather than a person.[43]

Although market forces drove the system as a whole, the decision to enslave Africans, to import more slaves, and to treat them harshly was not solely a dictate of the "invisible hand" of supply and demand—quite the contrary, as the code of 1661 amply demonstrated. Race played a key role, for slaves were black, and Englishmen believed that black was the color of inferiority.[44] The laws used "negroe" as a synonym for slave, as when "no master or owner of Negroes or other slaves" might allow them to parade about on Sunday without a pass, and "negroes [could] be sued for, and recovered by, personal actions."[45] *Negro* was merely the Spanish word for black, but color mattered to the English master class—the lawgivers—of Barbados. The likelihood that a slave would be allowed to move about freely, gain competitive skills, or even win his or her freedom was tied to race—for mixed race was one potential ticket out of bondage.[46] Tituba, an African, bore the full burden of her blackness. Indeed, as the number of African slaves increased, the value of any one of them declined, a fact that the slaves must have recognized.

Slaves adapted to the conditions imposed on them. As the number and size of the plantations grew, the slaves extended their network of communication along paths between the plantations. Some slaves used these paths to absent themselves from their quarters for a time or to try to escape from a particularly abusive master or overseer. Other slaves met on these tracks to plot open resistance. Most slaves mastered the art of negotiation with masters and overseers, a species of bargained-for exchanges. An ongoing process of dickering over terms and returns of

13

labor regulated this relationship. Some slaves made themselves experts in key portions of the production process of refining the sugar, increasing their value to the planter and simultaneously expanding their autonomy, or became managers of the labor of other slaves. "The most valuable slaves were also exempt from the field gangs. Craftsmen, head watchmen, head carters, and skilled workers ranked with the drivers of the great gang as the chief men of the negro community."[47] Drivers were indispensable intermediaries between owners or their agents and the slave workers. By joining the managerial ranks, such slaves might have broken ranks with their fellow slaves, but everyone knew that slavery still bound even the most respected driver or foreman. When negotiation failed, slowdowns were possible, as was breaking tools and machines, a technique that English agricultural workers mastered when new agricultural machines replaced men and women in the fields of that island.[48]

Tituba had a third burden: she was female. Gender does make a difference, and the difference is only partly biological. Of course her story is part of "women's history," but it was lived in a world of both men and women.[49] Such relations are often asymmetrical, and nowhere more so than in slavery. Men could rise within the truncated hierarchy of slavery through skill, personality, and perseverance. Women rarely escaped the field gangs. Even in resistance to authority, women and men did not have the same opportunities. African men demanded autonomy and resisted openly when it was constrained or ignored, sometimes joining with white male indentured servants in rebellions.[50] In 1675, the entire colony erupted in such an insurrection. A house servant informed on the plot, and the ringleaders were captured. Six black men were burned alive, and eleven others, beheaded, were dragged through the streets of Speightstown, where the rebellion had its focus. Thirty-five Africans were executed in one way or another before the governor was satisfied that a salutary lesson had been administered, but smaller uprisings again shook the colony in 1683, 1689, 1692, and 1702.[51]

African women fought enslavement in other, more subtle ways. Women slaves on Barbados adopted West African childbearing and rearing techniques, featuring long lactation periods, or prevented childbirth with abortifacients and birth control devices, infuriating their masters. Slave mothers devoted themselves to their small children, re-creating West African domestic priorities in the face of the planters' demand that women work in the fields. Indeed, by giving their children highest priority,

14

they forced planters to concede the primacy of African family styles within the plantation. On smaller plantations, women maintained their own special roles in agricultural production. African women were able as well to reestablish some of the specialized professions of their homeland, particularly as dispensers of folk remedies. After 1670, as large-scale sugar production and absentee ownership came to dominate Barbadian plantation life, these areas of female autonomy contracted. For slave mothers before and after 1670, life expectancy was short.[52]

We do not know if Tituba became pregnant or had a child before she was purchased by Parris, or if she had children afterward. The later record indicates that Tituba had a Barbadian consort, sometimes described as a husband, when she lived in Salem, which strongly implies that Parris purchased him in Barbados. The manservant, named Indian John (or John Indian), was probably not African. The name is syncretistic but not uncommon. American Indians were almost always given English names and very often had the eponym *Indian* supplied to indicate that they were not English, despite their English forename.[53] We cannot reconstruct Tituba's relations with Indian John. Yoruba men did not consider women as objects or mistreat them, for Yoruba respected the female line, but Indian John was not Yoruba. Moreover, once in Barbados, female slaves were subject to mistreatment both by male slaves and by masters and overseers. Cases of miscegenation were rarely pursued by authorities—the Barbados code did not mention miscegenation, and there was no punishment for it—but it was commonplace, if one takes the number of mulattoes as a measure of sexual relations between blacks and whites.[54] Sometimes, masters or managers took care to see that their illegitimate black offspring were well cared for or given their freedom, but this was hardly the rule.[55] Tituba must have witnessed miscegenation but may have been too young to suffer it.

Tituba had one tool for coping which her masters might have appreciated, for it was a tool that Europeans were adopting as well in these years: the fabrication of a mask to conceal her inner self. She had learned already that Yoruba have two layers of identity, a public one, a persona or mask, and a private one, an inner self. The naming ceremony began the teaching of this doctrine, but a Yoruba folktale further instructed the people in the importance of this mechanism. Such folktales were devices for socialization of young people as well as entertainment for everyone.[56] In this Yoruba tale, the king invited the animals to a great feast and offered a prize to the best dancer. All the animals danced, but the king surprised them by awarding the prize to the tortoise. Why, they asked? Because only the king could see the tortoise dance, he said, for "his dance is entirely within him." The tortoise was honored for keeping separate the exposed public person and the withdrawn and hidden self. The persona, the mask, may be seen by others, but the self is best hidden. Only the king could see the tortoise dance, for only the king could see the self behind the mask.[57] If Tituba could wear her mask well, she could protect herself from the demeaning rigors and foreign demands of the masters. Yet the act was a costly one, costly because the self remained secret, yearning for a time and place far away.

Tituba endured in Barbados a crash course in survival, learning to cope on many fronts. She could not know that she would have to deal with another, even more extreme change of scenery. She was to be a household servant to a merchant. If this prospect were not novel enough, what would happen when the merchant left Barbados, with its tropical climate, and moved to Boston, dry and hot in summer and icy cold in winter? There she would walk dirty, crowded streets among a sea of unfamiliar, pasty faces. There would be few like her there and probably no one who spoke her mother tongue. Instead, for the first time, Tituba would be surrounded by Europeans. Familiar rituals of worship would be replaced, at least in public, by Puritanism. And the women she worked with would be white, with very different prospects from her own. Adaptation to such a world would be difficult, another test of survival. What did the merchant, Samuel Parris by name, say to Tituba, and she to him? How did they converse? We do not know, but we can surmise that she was never fully human in his household, never the equal of his other women, his wife and daughters, and that was the root of the tragedy, for arbitrary or forced inferiority breeds distrust and suspicion.

samuel parris

BARBADOS WAS an island of immi-
grants. Though the slaves like Tituba were African, the master class was
English, among whom were the Parrises. Father Thomas and son Samuel
had come from London's prosperous middle class, eager to profit from
England's new empire. Samuel was born in England and taken, in his
youth, to Barbados by his father. From the island Samuel's father sent
him to Cambridge and Harvard College. Recalled to Barbados to settle
his father's estate, he lingered for a time and then took himself to Boston
and a merchant's life. Later came the call to the ministry, but it did not
bring peace of mind. His travels taught lessons in loneliness. He never
stayed long enough to form the attachments that give a child a sense of
security and make a man comfortable in the customs of a place. During
the witchcraft crisis, like Tituba, he was an outsider in Salem Village,
without the network of kin and long-term friends which can sustain a
person in times of trouble. Even after he left Salem, Parris would never
really settle down.[1]

One senses that convivial conversation did not come easily to Parris,
that he found small talk difficult. He was suspicious of others' motives
and rigid in his relations with them. Contacts became contracts or es-
trangements. Although others may have had unsavory motives for ac-

cusing their neighbors of witchcraft, Parris truly believed that the Devil had made converts in his own congregation, had insinuated himself into Parris's own family, and had done it to reduce the minister's life to a living hell.

Samuel Parris's father, Thomas Parris, had made and lost a fortune in real estate and shipping on the island. Eager to escape the risks of sugar planting and the vagaries of sugar prices, he borrowed heavily, invested in slaves, and failed again. His younger son watched. An older son was already established as a nonconformist minister in England, married, with children. Samuel's mother had come to Barbados but predeceased Thomas and was buried, probably in the burying ground off James Street, for she and her husband were nonconforming Protestants, "Puritans," and the churchyard of St. Michael's was not for them.[2] Although he decided to rent out his remaining plantation lands and move to Bridgetown permanently, the elder Parris still had connections in England, New England, and Barbados. Before Thomas died, he gave to Samuel the gift of an education at Harvard College. There the younger son traveled in 1670, accompanied by his father's friend, John Oxenbridge. Oxenbridge would minister to souls at Boston's First Church; Samuel would study in Cambridge, at the college that had already produced two generations of ministers for New England pulpits. Unfortunately for Samuel, Harvard in the 1670s faced a crisis. The number of students had declined, the physical plant had decayed, and the students were in open rebellion against President Leonard Hoar, who tried to stem the college's failing fortunes by strictly enforcing its rules. Samuel did not stay the course in any case, for in 1673 he received word that his father had died and he returned to Barbados.[3]

Samuel's stint in Cambridge had disrupted the life of a young planter, but there is no evidence that Samuel had come to doubt the values or methods of the planter classes. The vicissitudes of life on the island notwithstanding, he had left a station near the top of Barbadian society to journey to a place where he had no roots. Barbados was the richest of the European colonies of its day, and planters there had achieved a remarkable degree of freedom from English oversight. By contrast, Cambridge was cold and harsh, and the rigors of Harvard under President Hoar were far from the privileges that a master's son had on the island.[4]

Yet Samuel Parris's return was not paradise regained. If he was like New England's Puritan sons sent to Barbados, he yearned for the comforts of family and church, and if he did not reject the materialism of the counting house, he regretted the demands it made upon his spirit.[5] Smaller planters like his father were being inexorably squeezed from their land, and Thomas Parris had already sold off all but one of his farms by the time he died. Disease continued to carry off the Europeans. Slave rebellion, two years in the future, was already feared, and hurricanes had already struck, though the most damaging would come in 1675. Many young men like Parris were leaving the island, seeking their fortunes in England or its North American colonies.[6]

But the island was never far from its expatriates' thoughts, for there were fortunes to be made from its sugar and rum. Denuded of timber, with a labor force too large to be fed by native hands, Barbados needed flour, lumber, and fish.[7] Puritans like the Parrises need not be sugar producers to get rich; they could become middlemen and merchant factors. The whole web of this trade rested upon credit, and that is how young men like Parris got started. Family and friends provided risk capital— though when payments from consignees did not come in, failure, bankruptcy, and disgrace lurked in the blank pages of the ledger book.[8] Life was precarious, precious, and contested. There was danger and uncertainty everywhere.

Young Parris, however, had a future on the island if he managed his affairs with care. He tried his best. Selling off his father's remaining holdings in the countryside, he set himself up as a merchant in Bridgetown. A woodcut from 1695 shows the waterfront town dominated by wharfs and jetties. A later map illustrates a maze of streets stretching almost a mile and a half in a crescent along the southwestern, lee shore of the island, between a swamp on the east and a gravelly slope on the west. The climate was tropical, wet, fly filled in the day and mosquito ridden at night, but the wharfs were crowded with ships, and others waited in the ways to dock and carry off their cargoes of sugar. In the taverns and the counting houses all classes and races of people mingled.[9] The plantations began at the town's edge, and life on them was hard, but in Bridgetown the Europeans re-created a thriving, if precarious, European settlement. There traders gathered, gossiped, and prayed that the trade winds would bring their ships safely home and blow the monstrous storms of summer far from their little island.

For merchants and planters, slaves provided a hedge against failure. They were mobile capital and could be sold or carried to another, safer clime. Parris purchased young Tituba and the man who later was styled her consort, Indian John, as house servants. One scholar called Tituba "ageless," suggesting that she was into middle age (when age ceased to matter), thereby giving her a haglike visage appropriate for a witch. If Tituba was in her teens when Parris bought her, around 1680, she would have been twenty-something in 1692—hardly ancient, although her features might have been prematurely aged by a life of forced travel and hard labor. Parris would have intentionally bought his slave young, for New Englanders wanted "to train the [slave] children entirely within their own families so that the children would grow up anticipating their masters' wants and needs, likes and dislikes."[10] When, within three years of arriving, Parris had made up his mind to leave, he took the two slaves, Tituba and Indian John, and sailed for Boston.

His travels thus far were not unusual. Many young men had fled the island for the mainland. Boston was a natural destination for him; not only did the Parris family have dealings there, but other Barbadian merchants had used Boston as a depot for their wares.[11] In effect, London, Boston, and Bridgetown formed a triangle for the traders. If most of his fellow emigrants became planters in the southern mainland colonies, Parris was already determined to be a merchant, and his ties were with New England. He was not, however, a New Englander, but, for the better part of his life, a Barbadian—a member of the white, monied, mercantile, master class of that island.

Late-seventeenth-century Boston was bigger than Bridgetown, if no more opulent. In it were about one thousand houses and six thousand people, living on a peninsula of three hills connected to the mainland by a neck of land. Most Bostonians crammed into small dwellings on narrow streets, perpetually in shade, for few of these houses had more than a window or two (glass was so expensive), and candles were precious items. The kitchen was the only warm room in the winter, and no room was cool in summer. Water had to be doled out, and lumber for building and wood for fuel were costly and had to be brought by ship from Maine. Open sewers and rickety outhouses left a permanent miasma in the air, and food soon spoiled if it was not cooked, smoked, or salted.

With all its inconveniences Boston was healthy enough, if one could avoid the pox and other epidemic diseases, for the town was safe from Indian raids and foreign enemies, at least most of the time. The inhabitants worked hard, prayed to find in themselves signs of God's grace, and worried about the future, for children still died without apparent cause, rumors of war made the rounds of the taverns and open markets, and wise people knew that the Devil had not forgotten Boston. Three churches, all Congregational in form of worship, served the godly, and the houses of God were full on the Sabbath and active throughout the week. Down King Street from the First Church one could find the counting houses and the wharfs of a busy port; it was a short distance from piety to commerce. The town, a tiny way station on the vast coast of an even vaster wilderness, was tied to the Atlantic world just as Barbados was, by bonds as strong as the rigging of its ships and as frail as the tissue of credit.[12]

By the time Parris arrived, Boston's merchants had freed themselves from some of the constraints of the narrow, agricultural mentality that had dominated the colony in its earliest years. Leading businessmen argued that the region depended not upon its self-sufficient farms but upon its success in commerce. The same men claimed credit for transforming Boston from a backward settlement on Shawmut peninsula to a port city. They brought the wood, the rice, the rum, and the manufactured goods that made life a little sweeter.[13] By the early 1680s, these arguments had gained sufficient weight to give the town's merchants a secure political foothold in the colonial government, climaxed in 1686 when Joseph Dudley, a merchant, was named to lead the colonial council. Although the sway of the merchants was interrupted by Dudley's displacement in 1687, they remained a force in politics henceforth.[14]

In Boston, Parris married Elizabeth Eldridge, an older woman (she passed away in 1696, in her forties). They had a son, John, who died in his teens after the witchcraft episode was over (he never took part in it); a daughter Elizabeth, called Betty, in 1683; and another daughter, Susannah, born in 1688. Parris also took charge of his niece, Abigail Williams, a common arrangement among New England families. Then he rented a shop and borrowed from creditors to begin trade once again.[15] Sometime in this period of his life, Parris had his portrait painted, a miniature. In it he is dressed as a man of modest means, sober, a not quite handsome man, with a long face, full but tightly set lips, large eyes and a straight but prominent nose. He appeared wary, almost weary, but the face was still unfinished—a man midway through life, seeking its meaning perhaps.[16]

A year later, he was bogged down in lawsuits for his unpaid bills. Fighting these off made him suspicious of law and wary of trade, but he was still moderately successful.[17] Perhaps he saw the similarity to himself in the travails of John Bunyan's pilgrim "Christian," who stood trembling at the foot of the hill leading to "Legality's" house and learned from the Evangelist that fear was well founded: "ye cannot be justified by the works of the law, for by the deeds of the law no man living can be rid of his burden."[18] More important, Parris knew that he could not rival some of his near neighbors, and this may have galled him, because he had experienced exactly the same disparity between aspiration and achievement in Bridgetown. Boston's merchants had grown in power, just as in Bridgetown, but the growth was uneven. The result of success was a growing inequity in wealth and influence within the mercantile set: the rich got richer. At the same time, he had a family to support, and an unstable business in an insecure field was not a recipe for serenity.

Sometime in the mid-1680s, he began to explore a career in the ministry, for which he had trained during his stint as an undergraduate at Harvard College. His father had been an avid churchgoer and a strong supporter of nonconformity; his older brother was a minister in England. Samuel had already become a member of the First Church of Boston, sponsored by its minister, James Moody, successor to Oxenbridge, and accepted by his fellow congregants. There is no record of his giving offense to the church or to the town. He had been involved in lawsuits, but what merchant had not, and he had either settled or withdrawn them, surely a more Christian act than pursuing litigation to its conclusion. Parris did not have the academic attainments to compete for the better pulpits, but ministers were always in demand in frontier villages and hamlets. He tried his hand as a supply minister, preaching first in Stow in the summer of 1685, and then, when that relationship ended, he attended church meetings, giving talks to private groups and waiting for the opportune opening.[19]

Until he discovered his calling for the ministry, Parris's world had been mercantile. Puritans believed strongly that a good man diligently devoted himself to his calling—professions, whether of faith or of enterprise, were taken seriously. The successful merchant nevertheless ought to have qualms about success. Had he turned from God to spend too much time in the counting house? A true vocation in the business world might be a virtue, but for the Puritan such worldly virtues were a balancing act on a high wire. Less successful, envious rivals might censure too successful a merchant. The true Puritan merchant must be conscious of such dangers—the danger of envy, or covetousness, of things for their own sake. So the man had to constantly examine his motives—

why was he engaged in trade? The good Puritan also examined his ledgers just as he examined his soul for evidence of God's pleasure or ill will. Parris was never really successful; did the lawsuits and the unpaid bills prove that his mission lay elsewhere? Even afflictions were useful—scourging the soul from within, purifying it.[20] Did Parris turn to the ministry to save himself?

So far away in time, no one can know what in Parris's heart led him to the ministry. He was at Harvard before the great reform of 1679–80, which in some quarters brought the opening of the churches to those who sought Christ in a variety of ways. The "federal" ministry, led by Increase Mather, of Boston's Second Church, still fought to retain a semblance of uniformity in worship and belief, but Mather and his friends' objections to Solomon Stoddard and other reformers led not to renewed orthodoxy but to even more diversity in religious practice. Parris, returning to Boston in 1681, came back to just what he had left in 1673: Puritanism divided into factions.[21]

It was thus far more likely that Parris heard the quarreling of ministers than the voice of God, even though Puritans believed that their covenant was with the Lord. Had Parris seen his calling in the caviling of the clergy? In later years, he seemed drawn to controversy, but he never liked factiousness in others, however often he succumbed to it himself. What might have attracted him was the majesty and the drama of the ministry. When he was admitted to membership in Moody's church, Parris had to narrate an experience of grace. Such admissions of sin and redemption in a Congregational church exhibited some of the characteristics of ensemble acting, with professions of faith questioned and countered. The drama of confession was scripted, but in each congregation on each occasion there was improvisation. In these performances ministers played a leading role, directing the entire cast and leading the examination. Ministers also led by the words they preached and the counsel they gave. The great Puritan sermonizers, and there were many in Parris's day, raised the sermon to an art form, the measure and symbol of high culture. When he gained a pulpit, Parris worked hard to duplicate their feats. Perhaps he chose a career in the church because he admired the ministers he knew.[22]

How the church committee from "the farms" of Salem Village, at the western edge of the town of Salem, obtained Parris's name cannot be determined, but obtain it they did, and they pursued him. Perhaps members of the Putnam family who lived in the village and had dealings in Barbados recalled his name when he began to preach in Stow. Perhaps he had sent out feelers. First the elders, led by Captain John Putnam Sr., one of the patriarchs of the village and a selectman for the town, and then a committee of younger men sought him out and invited him to preach. He came in the spring of 1688 and returned in the fall. From November 15, 1688, through April 1689 committees of young and old from the village courted Parris and he listened. Finally he consented.

Negotiations with the Salem Village deputation had the quality of a mercantile exchange, for Parris, whose piety was unquestioned, wanted his new parishioners to contract themselves to support him. In this, he was not being entirely mercenary. The Puritan Church was "gathered," a compact among worshipers and their minister. In a later deposition, Parris recalled the terms of the agreement: a salary of sixty pounds a year, part in money, part in kind, and when money became "more plenteous," the money part to be paid him would "accordingly be increased"; fixed price on the in-kind part of his salary, a hedge against inflation in the price of corn and other provisions; contributions and fees from outside the village not to count against his income; his own choice of the provisions to be given him as part of his remuneration, so that no one could simply dump surplus or spoilage on him; free firewood (or six pounds more to buy it, later rescinded by consent); two men chosen each year as special collectors to insure that he was fully paid; and an escalator clause for salary raises.[23]

It was a hard bargain, but given the treatment John Higginson had lately received from his parishioners in Salem, and he the grand old man of the Essex County ministry, Parris had to be cautious.[24] After further discussion, the village committee gave him two acres of meadow, the parsonage—changing their prior rule that no minister was to own that property—and a barn, but they hardly could guarantee their promise of raises.[25] Parris was no starry-eyed neophyte, and his business sense did not desert him. With others, he purchased additional lands in the town and received rent for them. He still had property in Boston and Barbados. After all, no minister with a family could be expected to live on his salary.[26] And was not everyone else—everyone of importance at any rate—in Salem involved in a variety of business enterprises? Bartholomew Gedney was a merchant who also practiced medicine and ran a tavern on the side. Jonathan Corwin, whose father George was the biggest fish jobber and one of the biggest merchants in the town, became a merchant himself but also operated a drinking establishment. On a lesser scale others diversified; for example, John and Elizabeth Proctor (or Procter) ran a small farm with their children and their servant Mary Warren and opened a tavern on the Boston Road. They all paid regularly for their licenses.[27]

Why did he take the job? We will never know. The village committee had courted him for more than a year, but he hesitated. Perhaps in the end he was as motivated by what happened in Boston as what might happen in Salem. Throughout 1689, Boston seethed with unrest. Governor Andros, the placeman of King James II, was James II's choice to rule the Dominion of New England in the days before James was deposed. A chameleon of cunning and calculation, Andros exuded charm and exercised ruthlessness by turns, making friends with patronage and enemies with high-handedness. When news reached Boston that King James had been driven from his throne, Andros was pursued, captured, and imprisoned. No one knew what this act of lèse majesté would bring. The town's leading minister and one of its leading merchants, Increase Mather and Samuel Sewall, were already in England attempting to persuade royal authorities to reinstate the colonial charter, with little success. No one could calculate the response of the new king, William of Orange, to the Bostonians' act of rebellion. Parris might have found the precariousness of life in Boston enough motivation to seek the stability of a parish in western Salem.[28]

With him, in September 1689, traveled his slaves, his wife, his son and daughters, and Abigail Williams. Within this small family circle, he was master—all Puritan men were. The bond he had with his wife cannot be traced, for she is a shadowy figure in all the records, but the prescriptive literature all directed the husband and wife to love and honor each other. They were not equals—such a thought defied Scripture and reality—and they had different roles, but they were to be sturdy mates and fellow travelers on the path of right living.[29] Trouble came to marriages when individual differences or family conflict entered the home, but there is no evidence that these vices disturbed the Parris domicile, for the Eldridge family did not contest whatever land or chattels Elizabeth brought with her to the marriage, and the Parris clan was far off and quite content. Relations between husband and wife might have become distant or brittle, but nothing in the historical record indicates domestic discord. When Elizabeth Parris died, Samuel extolled her as

"Best Wife, Choice Mother, Neighbor, Friend."[30] Yet women were still the descendants of Eve, and Eve had tempted Adam to eat the fruit of disobedience. Parris believed that from such sin grew all human opposition to God's will: "As long as there is a contrary seed, a Seed of the Woman, and a seed of the Serpent, there will be opposition, more or less, open or secret."[31]

Puritan parents spent time and effort on their children, and Puritan literature abounds with imaginative concern for the well-being of little ones.[32] One may suspect that from the tenor of his sermons Samuel Parris was a caring, intrusive, moralistic father of a sort common among the middle classes of his circle. As he later told his congregation, "[The church must be] watchful of sin, even as parents, seeing their young children over bold with Fire, or water, they bring their children neer to the fire, and hold them over the water, as if they would burn them, or drown them whereas they intend nothing less, only to awe them and fright them, that they may hereafter keep farther off."[33] Far more important for Betty and Susannah was their relationship with their mother, about which the records are almost entirely silent, although for girls the maternal bond is more important than the paternal one.[34] If "few tangible traces survive of what mothers taught daughters and mistresses their serving girls generation after generation,"[35] clues to the strength of the bonding marked the pages of mothers' diaries and daughters' letters.[36]

Parris's road to Salem was hardly straight and narrow, but he had chosen the way himself. Elizabeth, his wife, and his three children dutifully accompanied him; that was what was expected of them. Tituba and Indian John came as well. They were slaves and had no choice. They must have comforted each other, both strangers in this strange land, but soon their paths would divide. Tituba remained a house servant, but Parris, still the merchant, would hire Indian John out to work. There were a handful of other black people in the village to which Parris traveled, some brought directly from Africa, others from the West Indies. Some were house servants, like Ann and Candy. Others worked in shops and fields, like Wonn, Tony, and Hager. Some were married, like Daniel and Judith. They were not supposed to congregate after hours, as the white servants did, at ordinaries or taverns, but male slaves could be found drinking or playing games of chance alongside other working people. Isolated, Tituba was drawn toward the children, and they to her, at least for the time being.[37]

Like Tituba, Parris was much traveled. He was used to sea travel and may have made the journey from Boston to Salem town, some thirty miles, by coaster. The village committee had put up the money to bring Parris's predecessor, Deodat Lawson, by boat from Boston to Salem.[38] Shallops moved up and down the shore regularly carrying passengers and cargo, but they had only one mast and were risky in bad weather. Schooners and ketches, more substantial two-masted sailing ships, were regular visitors at Salem harbor by the 1680s and took on passengers.[39] The road from Boston to Salem was far rougher than passage on a coaster. Two-wheeled oxcarts were slow and backbreaking; a carriage was too expensive. If Parris and his family came by the Boston-Ipswich road, they hired a wagon. Parris had gone to Salem Village to preach on a temporary basis in the spring of 1689; by the time he brought his family and servants form Boston, in the fall of 1689, he knew the way well.

Salem town was not much different from Boston—a port of entry into the hinterland for the products of the world, a place of debarkation for the produce of woods, fields, and gardens of New England. On Salem's wharfs squealing pigs and stolid cattle milled about as sweating seamen rolled barrels up gangways into the holds of ships. Into the ocean-going vessels the dockmen hauled bushels of peas, corn, and oats and barrels of turnips and Indian squash. Onion was much prized in Africa; apples and pears were welcomed in Jamaica. Fish caught off the shore and in the shallows were salted and packed in the holds as well. Salem was prosperous, busy, and confident, but the wealth that spewed across the wharfs was built upon poverty—the ramshackle two- and three-story housing for the laborers, cartmen, and fishermen sprawling from the port to the banks of the North River a quarter of a mile distant. Families of sailors and fishermen were jammed into one- and two-room shanties filled with old, rickety furniture and worn wooden eating utensils.[40]

From Turner's wharf on the South River or perhaps another farther along the curve of the harbor, Parris would have traveled with his family up the shallowly graded side street (for Salem was but four feet above sea level) to Main Street (now Essex Street), past shops, inns, and the marshy commons, to the southern edge of the North River, and over the bridge that led to the farms. The houses along the high street were impressive, two and sometimes three stories high, heavy timbered, with red, yellow, or green painted clapboard siding and cedar shingles, overhanging upper floors, dormers, and gables, and a multitude of small, diamond-latticed windows. Salem was, after all, the oldest of the Puritan towns and prided itself on its town spirit. It was no longer a lonely outpost of yeoman farmers, although their descendants still lived in the wards to the south, west, and north of the peninsula. Now, densely populated streets were shared by fishermen, artisans, laborers, merchants, and shopkeepers, whose interests diverged from those of the men and women of the village, where Parris was bound. The inhabitants of English's and Phelp's wards on the peninsula looked ahead, to a more secular, materialist world. Philip English, who owned warehouses and wharfs up and down the harbor, where his fourteen sailing vessels berthed, filled his dockside mansion with imported silver and elegant furnishings and commanded a large workforce. He and his peers were men on the make, quietly abandoning the mores of the hinterland, at least those that the leaders of the farming communities publicly espoused.[41]

Parris would have left Salem along the Lynn road, climbing up from the North River at the edge of the town, passing Trask's Mill and then turning north at Read's Hill. Behind him, if he turned, he could see the port; ahead were the farms. The village center was four miles and some before him. All along this part of his route lay the salt marshes; at Trask's they became freshwater marshes, a fringe of estuary that stretched north of the road, where the Frost-Fish, the Endicot, and the Bass Rivers all emptied into the bay. Marsh grass had supported the first cattle of the town and succored extensive herds still. The hay grass was cut, laid out and turned to dry for a number of days, bailed and carried by barge to the road edge, and finally hauled by cart to the farms beyond.[42]

Everywhere the Parris family looked, people worked hard—labor-intensive agriculture in the lands to the west kept Salem's port fed. Farmers' houses lined the road, their fields a patchwork stretching back from the lanes, over the hills. The Endecotts (or Endicots), scions of the first governor, had parcels in the "north fields" to the right of the highway. The extensive and well-to-do Porter family and its kin owned lands nearer the village. In and beyond the village, much of the arable land was worked by Putnams of various generations. Overall, however, there were no latifundia, no great patroonships as there were in neighboring New York Colony. Families lived on their holdings and worked them, or rented plots to other families.[43]

The road ahead was not long—only five miles to the village center, the parsonage, and the meeting house—but it was already a road beset by controversy. The villagers were legally residents of the town of Salem, but they had gradually loosened the ties that bound them to the older coastal settlement. In 1667, many of the homesteaders in the village petitioned the General Court in Boston, the legislature of the colony, for an exemption from the watch duties that every head of family had to fulfill. The men of the village explained that they lived from five to ten miles from the watch house in Salem town and had to march those miles fully armed, leaving their families prey to Indian raids. Assembling the village contingent took time, for the houses were dispersed, some a mile away from the center of population and the training ground in the village, and marching to the town consumed still more time, while the sickly and weak at home were left unprotected. The village troops comprised but three dozen, coming to the aid of the town watch three hundred strong— a misallocation of force, given the danger of those times for the frontier towns. King Philip's War lay nearly a decade in the future, but the General Court recognized the justice of the villagers' plea and granted them the exemption from military service in the town. Three years later, the villagers again approached the general court, seeking permission to erect their own meeting house and select their own preacher, rather than travel the road to Salem on the Sabbath day. In 1672 the general court gave them the right to build a house of worship and to name a committee to gather funds for a minister who would reside among them.[44]

Going down that road, Parris entered a new world. He had traveled the seaways from London to Barbados, then to Cambridge, then back to Barbados, then to Boston, and finally to Salem. He had always lived by the ocean, his livelihood linked to the commerce of the Atlantic Rim. Now he journeyed back into a more primitive way of life, ruder, less accomplished, more suspicious of strangers, part of the same empire in which he grew to manhood but tied by looser strings.

Crossing the Ipswich road, he left behind the families who had the strongest connection to the town, the Porters and their kin. Israel Porter had a mill on the Crane River, little more than a creek, but the mill made money, and others along the road had established small mercantile or manufacturing enterprises. As Parris followed the road past Phillips' Tavern, he left behind the river traffic and the shops and followed narrower, less frequently traveled lanes. The pine clapboard of the farmhouses was no longer painted but weathered, for paint was too expensive and perhaps too gaudy for some of the denizens' simple tastes. The distance between farmhouses was greater.

Along the road were fences of timbered wood or stone gathered from the fields.[45] The boulders and stones were a relic of the glaciers. Slate, granite, and limestone deposits marked the retreat of the wall of ice.[46] Other fences were fashioned from split rails. A good stone wall—the craft of laying boulders in a ditch, then building up smaller stones so the fence would not crumble in the cold or topple in the wind—proved to any passerby that the fence builder was an able man, skilled in the ways of husbandry. The best stone walls demonstrated even more than craft, for they required a substantial workforce. Farmers of means employed a gang of servants and day laborers, sometimes including Native Americans and Africans.[47] Knowing how and where to fence the land encompassed a culture, as well as demonstrating craft, for fences marked boundaries between fields, cattle runs, and livestock pens, and boundaries were important signs of one's status. Disputes over fences crowded the dockets of the Essex County Quarterly Court and sometimes led to threats of violence.[48]

Did Parris also notice how similar these farmhouses were, how little differentiated them one from another? The New England saltbox was an architectural model capable of lateral and vertical expansion, but it never lost its rectangular solidity and regularity. The Puritans disparaged ostentation, although they did not glorify plainness like the Quakers. The farmhouses on the road did vary in scale, however, and sheer size sent a message. The bigger the house, the more substantial its denizens. The good steward wanted neighbors to know that God's command to be fruitful and multiply had been fulfilled. The open spaces between the houses—for the village was not a nucleated town like Salem itself or even Boston—made the differences in scale of buildings even more obvious.

Traversing the road, Parris and his family had entered the overlap of two distinct geopolitical zones. To the east was the ocean, always dangerous and filled with England's mortal rivals but chartered and known. To the west stretched a vast expanse of land and timber, full of promise but inhabited by Native Americans whose pathways the English did not follow and whose folkways the English did not fathom. At the confluence of the two regions, husbandmen and laborers transformed forests and parkland into farms.[49] The sounds and sights of this edge culture were striking. In the daytime, the road ahead was visible and reassuring. Though it was two oxcarts wide, a fully loaded wagon would have nearly filled it. Parris and his family could reach out and touch the fences and brush, for the fields came to the edge of the road.

The human buzz of the town here gave way to the cacophony of the countryside, as pigs, dogs, oxen, cattle, horses, and sheep came to the fence to stare at the loaded wagon. The farm animals were all carriers of ticks, fleas, and other parasites. These insects were joined by the dragonflies and deerflies of the forest and swamp, for no place in the village was more than a quarter of a mile from one of the marshes. The insects would have been out in force near the end of the summer. The night was different, for wolves, bears, and wildcats preyed upon the browsing and grazing animals, and the predators' grunting and howling could be heard throughout the dark hours. The darkness itself was unrelieved, broken only by flickering candles in the farmhouses, and these were extinguished early.[50] Parris had traveled a road like this when he went to Stow and knew that the western edge of the Puritan world was different from its eastern border. In this light, the stiffness with which he pressed his demands during the negotiations becomes clear—he wanted guarantees that the vicissitudes of his new home would be mitigated, for it was greatly different from what he left behind.

The farmers must have known that Parris was coming, and some no doubt waited by the road to greet him as he passed. The hallos were more leisurely than a man from Boston would expect, but the stares were harder than in Boston, for in the country the minister was a man of great importance. He was teacher, counselor, consoler, and conduit to God.[51] Most of the population of Salem Village, five hundred souls altogether,[52] congregated in the center of the village, perhaps by the training ground, or at Nathaniel Ingersoll's inn, which stood at the crossing of the road from Salem and the meeting house road, to greet the new preacher and his family. Ingersoll was a substantial farmer and local businessman with ties to the many Putnams in Salem Village. His inn was two stories tall, with its front on the meeting house road and its back facing the meadow belonging to the parsonage.

An imposing building in its setting, the inn would not have impressed Parris, but its great room, the large front parlor, was a tavern and a local gathering spot.[53] (Inn, tavern, public house, ordinary—all had slightly different legal meanings, for all required licenses, and different connotations to the locals). Visiting dignitaries tarried there, but its habitués were the farmers and their hired hands, the servants (though they were not supposed to idle at the tavern without their masters' permission), and women, who were not supposed to be there at all. Men and women ate and drank cider, wine, and beer, talked, and perhaps danced or played at shuffleboards. The latter game had been banned by the General Court in 1646 but was a favorite nonetheless, for it allowed gambling on the skills of the players. One of the charges laid against Bridget Bishop of Salem by the Reverend John Hale of Beverly during the witchcraft trials was that she encouraged young people to stay up all hours at her house playing "shovel-board."[54] Taverns were also the sites of illegal and dangerous horse races and impromptu fisticuffs.[55] In nearby Gloucester, townspeople petitioned the court in 1674 against "the great inconvenience of having a tavern so near the house of God": "[S]everall do say that some do very much indispose themselves for the worship and service of God [by excessive drinking]."[56] Public drunkenness was a misdemeanor in law and was presented at the quarterly sessions of the peace by the grand juries, but that was no balm to Parris or his more pious and respectable parishioners.[57]

Parris knew that Ingersoll was one of his supporters, but the tavern must have been a daily trial to the minister. Whether he was working in his study or preaching in the meeting house, he could hardly miss the fact that his parishioners spent part of their time carousing in the tavern, because the tavern stood between the parsonage and the church. He could hear the raucous shouting and see the tipplers when they spilled out onto the steps of the tavern. The quarrels and imprecations that arose in these precincts were the antithesis of Parris's own sermons, the sacred and the profane inextricably mingled. When they got excited, defamers called down the Devil himself upon their adversaries or accused those who offended of being an "old witch, old wizard."[58] Parris was no innocent, however, and he accommodated himself. He had seen the excesses of the planter class in the West Indies; he knew what sin looked and smelled like.

If the tavern marked the irrepressibility of the profane, the parsonage and the meeting house symbolized the physical vitality of the sacred. They stood just off the crossing of the major two roads in the village and gave the cluster of homes and shops its collective identity. The village had no legal standing as a chartered town, but with its own meeting house and minister, it could hold its head up alongside the other fully established towns, for in all of them the church was the center of activity.

Parris and his family were to live in the parsonage built in 1681 for George Burroughs, one of Parris's predecessors, and later occupied by Deodat Lawson, Parris's immediate precursor. Parris knew that it

32

was owned by the village, and he bargained hard for transfer of title. Throughout the summer of 1689, the village did nothing to accommodate his demand, but in October the village meeting agreed that he should have the property.[59] The structure was a two-story clapboard with a central chimney and four fireplaces. The house sat on a half cellar. Forty feet by twenty feet in dimension, it was a substantial home. If it followed the typical house plan, and there was little variation in these, it had four rooms, two on each floor, laid out opposite an entryway and narrow, wooden stairs. A lean-to kitchen, commonplace on farms, completed the parsonage. The house was surrounded by two acres of meadowland, and a path across part of the meadow took Parris to the meeting house without having to walk past the door of the tavern.[60]

The parsonage rested on stone driven into the earth. The foundation had a story to tell repeating the tale of the stone fences on the road. The rocks were a glacial remnant left to test the will of New Englanders. Stones had to be removed to till the fields. The Puritans improved upon the stones, however, using them to build fences and foundations. The stones became markers of the Puritan commitment to cultivate time and place, not to make it more comfortable, although they were not averse to comfort, but to make the world more fruitful, fulfilling God's command.[61] But the stones were still hard, stark reminders that life could be harsh and a livelihood had to be wrested from the very bowels of the earth. It was a solemn lesson to the London/Bridgetown/Boston–bred man that the hearts of the villagers had to be softened before they would turn to him, or to God.

The meeting house stood on a small rise, facing the road. Completed over a five-year span between 1672 and 1677, it was an unimposing building, resembling more than anything else a large farmer's house. Boxlike in shape, twenty-seven by thirty-six by twenty-eight feet high, with two windows on each side and a small entry porch in the front, it was already in need of repair after fifteen years of New England winters and summers. Parris would eventually convince the committee to fund improvements and maintenance.[62] The windows were small, latticed with diamond-shaped glass. Little light came through them, but that was unimportant, for light was supposed to come from the pulpit. The house of God was an auditory, a place to listen, its interior designed so that everyone who came faced the preacher and could hear his words. There was no nave, no transept, no mystery to the building directing the worshiper's spirit on and up, for the minister's "plain style" of preaching required a plain style of building. Nothing was to detract from God's word. The congregation occupied the pews according to a combination of age and economic status, the best people in the front pews. Children sat with their parents or on the stairs. Servants and slaves were welcome, but they stayed in the back. Sitting in someone else's pew was a finable offense, assuming the village had the same rules as other congregations.[63]

The communion table, where the bread and wine were given to the deacons for redistribution to full members of the church at the Lord's Supper, stood at the side of the building. The pews and the pulpit were subtly ornamented with natural motifs cut into the wood. The serving vessels were simple pewter or brass, and Parris found them inadequate, too poor for the sacrament of the Lord's Supper. Sometime before Parris's arrival the pulpit was raised and a gallery added. The meeting house was probably not painted outside, and its pine clapboards already had a weathered look when Parris arrived, though other meeting houses in the area were painted red or yellow. Inside, the walls were whitewashed.[64]

In the meeting house Parris gave his ordination sermon. For the Puritan ministry, the sermon was crucial, for in it the minister became the Lord's messenger.[65] The sermon preached by a minister at his ordination, the gathering of the church, was the most important sermon of all, for at this service the ministry itself was reconsecrated, the covenant of the minister and his flock with God renewed and the Godly community established. At Parris's ordination sermon, Nicholas Noyes came from Salem town, John Hale journeyed from Beverly, and Samuel Phillips traveled from Rowley to join with the worshipers of Salem Village. All three men would play a role in the witchcraft trials, but now they were unaware of the later uses of the meeting house or the travails of its new incumbent. Phillips, the oldest at sixty-three, laid on the right hand of fellowship, "with beautiful loveliness and humility."[66]

Public preaching in the house of worship brought minister and flock together, and if the contact between them was shaped by ritual and convention,[67] Parris had finally found a place in which his speech mattered. He had three audiences that day, and for hours he spoke to all of them. The first audience was the three other ministers present, his peer group. Their expectations and reports of his performance were important to him, particularly so as he was not a graduate of Harvard or one of the colleges at Cambridge. In all communities of professionals, the expecta-

34

tions of one's peers shape what one says and does.[68] Perhaps with this small but vital audience in mind, Parris termed his sermon "poor and weake," although he had obviously spent time and energy on it.[69] The densely reasoned, formulaic character of his sermon was not meant to please the visiting clergy with its erudition, for it was no more or less scholarly than the typical published Puritan sermon, but the careful reasoning, the sequencing of argument from naming the scriptural text, through explication, to lessons and application, reassured them that Parris was familiar with the conventions of Puritan preaching.

The second audience was his congregation. With them, as he wrote in the church records for that day, he began a conversation in piety and mutual love. "We whose names . . . are hereunto subscribed, lamenting our great unfitness [for such] an awful and solemn approach unto the Holy God and [deploring] all the miscarriages committed by us, either in the days [of] our unregeneracy or since we have been brought into acquaintance with God in the communion of his churches . . . yet apprehending ourselves called by the Most High to embody [ourselves] into a different society . . . this day give up ourselves one unto another in the Lord. . . . We resolve uprightly to study what is our duty, and to make it our grief, and reckon it our shame, wheresoever we find ourselves to come short in the discharge of it, and for pardon thereof humbly to betake ourselves to the blood of the Everlasting Covenant." Ingersoll signed, as did Nathaniel and John Putnam Sr., the committeemen who had brought Parris to the village. Thomas, John Jr., Edward, Jonathan, and Benjamin Putnam added their names, as did Henry and Benjamin Wilkins and their father, Bray. Others joined.[70] Notably absent were the largest landholders and richest men in the village, the Porters, for they were members of John Higginson's church in Salem, but they sat in their pews to hear the ordination sermon.

Parris had chosen as his text Josh. 5:9: "And the Lord said unto Joshua: This Day I have rolled away the Reproach of Egypt from off you." This was the divine promise for those who were within the covenant, and for those who did not subscribe to it, there was only danger, for the Lord warned the Egyptian and the Canaanite and all rebels from Heaven that they would be rooted out from the earth and their land given to others. Was this not the fate of New England's Native Americans, who would not bow to the manifest truth of the Lord's chosen people? Parris did not make that lesson explicit but could have assumed all his congregation could make the connection, particularly after "King Philip's War" in 1675–76 had led to the decimation of many eastern Massachusetts Indian bands, for the Lord's covenanted few, obstacles were removed, the Jordan rolled back, and the enemy defeated.[71]

36

This doctrine he thought "exceedingly useful" for such "unbelieving days." Too many who should have been members of the church in the village ignored their religious duties until too late. Sinners, they imagined that they had time enough, but it was almost too late. Prosperity came to those who walked in the path of piety, Parris promised, recalling the language of his other, former life, and Joshua was proof of the proposition. Joshua was "a type of Christ Jesus," a forerunner of the true Messiah. Joshua led the Israelites into the wilderness and, with God's aid, made that wilderness God's kingdom. God then restored Israel, removing all "reproach, contempt and disgrace from the people." Instead, the people stood in honor and dignity, just as he would do for the regenerate among the Puritans in the wilderness of New England. Parris here employed a convention of Puritan rhetoric called typology which established relationships between Old Testament and New Testament or contemporary events or persons.[72] Massachusetts was a new Israel, for its people made a covenant with God, just like Abraham's seed, and the prophets of the Old Testament foretold the coming of the Christian Messiah, just as Parris preached the Word in the meeting house. His congregation stood in Israel's place, but to receive this blessing they had to renew the visible and sacramental communion with God. Then the eyes of the blind would be opened to the joy of God's care; Christ in His majesty would be present in the church.

Puritan sermons often ended with the application of doctrine, and Parris closed his with a personal message to his congregation. "Much work is laid, or like to be laid, upon my weak shoulders. . . . I am to carry it not as a Lord, but as a servant. . . . I am to labor that my doctrine may burn, and my conversation may shine. . . . As I am to give Cordials to some, so I must be sure to administer corrosives to others." Heavy was Parris's burden; his congregation had to help: "You are to pay me that Reverence which is due to an Embassadour of Christ Jesus. You are to bear me a great deal of love. . . . You are to obey me (at least) so far as I watch for your souls. . . . You are to pray for me and to pray such and fervently always for me, but especially when you expect to hear from God by me. . . . You are to endeavor by all lawfull means to make my heavy work as much as in you lies light and cheerful . . . and not . . . to make my life among you grievous, and my labor among you unprofitable."[73]

The tenor and content of Parris's concluding message suggest a third audience for his sermon—the author himself. He wanted from his parishioners a contract similar to the one he had negotiated with the village committee. They must help him. Such a contract echoed that between God and His chosen people, and Parris referred to the higher covenant by reminding his listeners that he was Christ's emissary on earth. Parris wanted more than help, however; he wanted, indeed he needed, affection. Ministers often manipulated their congregants' emotions—their desire to gain the minister's approbation—in order to reach their hearts and enable them to seek God, but Parris's requirement went the other way. He demanded that his flock love him.[74]

True, Parris's appeal for the affection of his parishioners was a "use," an application, of the doctrine he found in his biblical text. Although he did not spell out the connection himself, he touched upon two of the basic themes of church polity. The first was that the gathered church was based upon a contract, a willing exchange. Without voluntary adherence, the gathered church would fail. Such adherence included submission to the wisdom of the minister and assistance for his labors. More telling, he built his argument upon the likeness between a gathered church and a Puritan family. The minister, he hinted, is the father, to whom the other family members owe obedience. Parris was already the father of three children, and the church-family parallel suggested itself. In law, he was master in his own home. He could not command the love and obedience of his church members as he could his family members, but he could ask for it.

Such uses were part of the formal, fixed structure of sermons, but his discourse on the relationship between minister and flock was too intense, almost desperate, to be mere convention. He knew that Salem Village had a history of trouble with its ministers and that the village was not unanimous on his nomination to the post. His call for loyal service was personal. He had traveled a long way from London and Bridgetown. He was a merchant's son, used to the ways of a plantation society on a island colony, accustomed to being obeyed. His sojourn in Boston had allowed him to sample the ministerial life but had not changed his habits of mind. In addition, he wanted obedience and love from his congregation because he needed it. There was no family—no network of kin, save a distant brother and his family—to supplement his reserves of spiritual strength or reassure him in time of need. Nor was there a connection that passage of time and mutual care had woven between him and other ministers in his cohort. In Salem, he was as isolated in heart as he was in body.

Parris's demands were reasonable on their face and to him critically important. To insure the future of his small brood, he had to make a Devil's bargain—not with the mysterious dark stranger that some saw in the winter evening's shadows—but with the faction of the village which promised to pay him his salary. To them he could and did speak candidly in his house and by the way. But he, no less than Tituba (though she more visibly), remained an outsider in the village. He had traveled far from home, leaving one calling for another to answer the summons of the villagers. And there was the irony, for in the place where Parris sought peace and fulfillment, neither would be found. In these days, Salem was suffering its own trials, and they would soon sweep Parris and his household into a flood of recrimination.

salem village

▼
2

IN 1689, the town of Salem no longer
represented the peaceable kingdom that Puritans sought and valued.[1]
There were times in its earlier history when a more compact settlement,
led by families to whom everyone else deferred, adhered more closely to
the ideal of one church–one community, but by the 1680s, that town
was gone.[2] Salem had become a congeries of distinct wards or precincts,
each with its dominant interests, only coming together on church days
and funerals. Even the comradeship of muster days, when militiamen
trained together, had vanished, as outlying wards sought and gained
permission from the selectmen of the town to police and patrol their
own districts. The town offices themselves, once the pride of civically
responsible farmers, now went unfilled. Few could be found to serve as
constables. Social order itself was unraveling. The General Court of the
colony bid town selectmen name "tithingmen" from among the freemen
to watch over the children, insuring that they learned a trade, their catechism, and the criminal laws of the colony and did not live in dissolute
ways. In Salem, evidently, parents and masters failed in this duty, although in this delict, Salem was hardly unique. Still, how could men
and women practice their devotionals when children ran up and down

the stairs of the church and played with their dogs in the streets during the sermons?[3]

A spirit of mercantile hardness had crept into the town. As John Higginson, one of Salem's first settlers and its minister for more than a half century thereafter, wailed in 1663, "My fathers and brethren, this is never to be forgotten, that New England is originally a plantation of religion, not a plantation of trade." Higginson staved off a movement for a second church led by a group of newly arrived merchants who cared not for his strict views on church communion. Although he won the battle, they won the war, for the unity of old Salem ruptured, lost in the struggle between new and old residents. Higginson watched helplessly as the neighborhoods of Salem lost their coherence and town spirit flagged. He compromised, baptizing children of churchgoers who were not in full communion, but he could not prevent the decline in church membership.[4]

The town also faced the threat of physical dismemberment. The selectmen had not resisted when the freemen of Beverly and Marblehead gained permission from the General Court of the colony to form their own towns. Throughout the 1670s and 1680s, however, the town's leaders refused to concede to similar demands from some of the residents of the village. The latter were determined to have their own fully chartered town, but the General Court would not grant their petitions without the consent of the selectmen of Salem, and the village leaders could not gain a majority in the town council. In part, the town resisted because it needed the tax rates and the manpower of the "farms." In part, the village could not gain autonomy because its leaders repeatedly divided among themselves. One cause of the split mirrored the transformation of the town as a whole. The other cause was a growing rivalry between two great families in the village whose hostility made collective political action impossible.

Salem villagers played out on their smaller stage the same drama of farm against trade, declining unity and growing factionalism, and dispute over churchgoing as troubled the whole of Salem. The village, a ward of the town and isolated in some respects, experienced the pains of transformation but lacked the resources that the town had to cope with change. For coastal Salem, the shift to market relations could be accommodated, for it went hand in hand with capital accumulation, diversification of investment, and the rise of new and successful types of enterprises. For the village the same innovations could not be accommodated as easily, because the villagers lacked the capital, labor, and skills to partake of the advantages of the market and because the factionalism of two families, created in part by the economic changes, split the villagers over the course to follow in response to novelty.

For the entire town, no single family's strategy for coping with change was vital to the success of the process of adaptation, for Salem was too diverse and there were too many important families in it. Not so in the village. Originally, the farms had been a neighborhood, a group of families starting out more or less even in the quest for land and power, as in other settlements in the frontier arc.[5] As the farms were more thoroughly settled and the land passed to second and third generations, some families proved more successful than others. What emerged was a rough hierarchy maintained not by force but by deference.[6] Village marriage patterns created a network of kinship which reinforced this hierarchy. The fortunate families added to their wealth and status through astute unions and long residence in the area.[7] Over time kin became clan, and clan loyalty stretched across generations became a surrogate for political party in local contests for office. Had a single family emerged or remained the controlling force, the political geography of the village would have resembled that of Springfield, to the west, where the Pynchons ruled land and town. This was not so in the village, where two families, once friendly rivals and sometime allies, grew to distrust each other.

The Putnams appeared in Salem in the early 1640s. The patriarch was John Putnam, who emigrated from England to Massachusetts in his sixties. By 1662, at the age of eighty-two, he had amassed more than eight hundred acres of land and had three surviving sons, Nathaniel and two known locally by their militia ranks, Lieutenant Thomas and Captain John. To them, before he died, the elder Putnam gave lands in the far west of the township. They, in turn, provided land for their children, dividing what had been a substantial holding into smaller and smaller parcels. The children of Nathaniel and Captain John married into other village families—the Hutchinsons, Ingersolls, Sibleys, Walcotts, Houltons (or Holtens), and Buxtons.[8] Hutchinson, Ingersoll, and Holten owned large parcels around the parsonage. Sibley and Walcott had their house lots even closer to the meeting house and the minister's residence. Like a ring of outworks, lots owned and worked by the third generation of Putnams—Jonathan Putnam, James Putnam, Joseph Putnam, John Putnam Jr (the son of Captain John)—and Nathaniel Putnam (II) surrounded the church and parsonage. To the west on the road lay Topsfield and lands disputed by (Sergeant) Thomas Putnam Jr. (Lieutenant Thomas's son) and a number of Topsfield families.[9]

Lieutenant Thomas Putnam died in 1686, but before he passed, he prepared a will that divided his farms and pastures among his children. His sons, Sergeant Thomas and Edward, received parcels of land. Ann, who married William Trask but predeceased her father; Deliverance, who married Jonathan Walcott; and the four other daughters got monetary settlements. The largest portion went to Joseph Putnam, the elder Thomas's son by his second wife, Mary Veren, and to Mary. They received the family farm. Sergeant Thomas married Ann Carr, child of a wealthy family, but acquired nothing of her inheritance, a sore point. Joseph married Elizabeth Porter, daughter of Israel Porter, a far more advantageous marriage than any made by Joseph's brothers, for it linked Joseph to the only family whose wealth could rival his own. Faced with a demographic squeeze in the third generation, the Putnams tried their hand at West Indian commerce, ironmongery, and land speculation but were not successful. Politically, they had no better luck. Captain John maintained the family's voice in the town councils well into the 1680s, but his son John Jr. and other Putnams in his son's generation were unable to retain the family's political influence at the center of power. The younger sons did play an increasing role in local governance, dominating the meetings of the villagers. The family was litigious as well, often coming to the county court to defend its interests in land.[10]

The Porters first came to Salem in the 1640s, led by John Porter, an English immigrant in his forties. Before his death in 1676, he owned more than two thousand acres, in addition to mills, inns, and other enterprises. According to the first tax census in Salem, completed in 1681, the Porters were richer than the Putnams. Four sons—John, Joseph, Benjamin, and Israel—outlived their father. John and Benjamin never married, but their brothers had large families. Instead of seeking to amass lands in the west, they looked to the east and commerce. Porter children married into the mercantile elite of Salem, including two of the richest men in the county, Daniel Andrew and Thomas Gardiner. As Putnam political fortunes in the town waned, Porter opportunities waxed. By the 1680s, Israel was a perennial member of the selectmen, joined occasionally by his brothers-in-law Andrew and Gardiner.[11]

The idea that the village was divided by clans, like the borderlands between England and Scotland, cannot be taken to an extreme. There were plenty of householders who knew the Putnams and Porters well, had dealings with them, but were not affiliated by marriage or bonds of loyalty. These included some of the older families like Giles and Martha Cory (or Corey), George Jacobs Sr. and his children, the Towne sisters—Rebecca Nurse (or Nourse), Sarah Cloyse, and Mary Esty (or Easty)—and the Proctors. Some of the latter, like George Jacobs, had a long history of abusing others, fighting, and getting into trouble with the justices of the peace, while some, like Francis and Rebecca Nurse, were men and women of admirable charity, who took in the orphan and cared for the sick.[12] The village also had its marginal members, moving from household to household, doing odd jobs, sometimes begging for aid. Some of these people were young laborers, for whom the peripatetic lifestyle was a stage in their life course. For others, it had become a career, like Sarah Good, whose begging was by 1689 a matter of general irritation.[13]

The Putnams and the Porters were the most visible lay people in the community, and status brought with it obligation. They were expected to provide political leadership. They served in the town council as selectmen and went to the General Court representing the town. Their own interests, however, pointed them in slightly different directions when it came to matters of policy. That is, rather than speaking for a united village, they came to speak for factions that they themselves led. The crucial test in this growing contest for power was the two families' ability to provide the people of the village with a plan for the future. They may have adopted slightly different styles, the Putnams more open, the Porters more secretive,[14] but their task was the same: to respond to the challenge that faced their neighbors.

The Putnams worked hard after 1670 to sever the village from the rest of the old town.[15] They tried a direct approach, seeking permission of the selectmen; they tried to get around opposition in the other wards of the town by appealing to the General Court; they assayed a nibbling approach, seeking reduction of rates. So ordered, replied the General Court, but the selectmen of the town only grudgingly conceded the point, "to demonstrate to all mankind how favorably [they would] deal with them."[16] What was the Putnams' motive? Surely a resentment of the increasingly commercial policy of the new generation of the town's leaders entered into their calculations, but the Putnams valued the advantages of commerce, and the village benefited from the commercial success of the harbor wards.[17] Salem Village was still overwhelmingly agricultural, but its men and women went to town often enough, and the Putnams had no desire to build a wall on the village side of the Ipswich road. Try as they might to bring about separation, the Putnams failed, but not because mercantile interests trumped the aspirations of the farmers in a head-on contest of wills. The merchants could not prevent the separation without the assistance of farmers from elsewhere in the town.[18]

The Putnams believed that village interests differed from the rest of the town not because commerce flourished on the east side of the Ipswich road and faltered on the west side but because most of the villagers looked to the interior of the colony, a vast space potentially filled with family farms, while eastern Salem's farms and farmers fit into a coastal region of more diverse living patterns and occupations. Given that the political structure of Puritan Massachusetts was framed by towns, and towns selected their own governments, the Putnams reasoned that they must have independence to pursue these aims. The obstacle was their own town's government, but from its decisions appeal always lay to the General Court, which could not only set aside local ordinances but create new towns.[19] The wishes of the Putnams and their allies in Salem Village merely echoed those of the leaders of the village's neighbors to the north and west, Lynn, Andover, Topsfield, Wenham, and Beverly.

Independence had a price. The Putnams had to establish—financially sponsor if necessary—institutions of local government and worship which an independent community wanted and needed. They argued for and won a freeholder-based system of choosing and maintaining a minister, giving the franchise to the many small farmers whose interests lay closer to home than to the harbor and its ships. From this perspective, the Putnams' desire for autonomy was again not so much an attack upon the mercantile ways of Salem town or a covert assault on the Porters as an attempt to play a nurturing, supportive role in the village's maturation.

The Porters, for reasons of their own, stood in the way, for complete independence would put them at the mercy of the village majority, still primarily agricultural, and the Putnams. The Porters did not withdraw their interest in village affairs but instead quietly undermined the Putnams' plans for the village's acceptance into the western arc of agricultural towns. The Porters' alternative to the Putnams' efforts was to fashion closer ties to the rest of the town, based not on unity of belief or common worship but on buying and selling in the market. The Porters had done this in microcosm, marrying into mercantile families. Perhaps this was a truer vision of Salem's future than the Putnams possessed, for such a market system came to the region in the next century, but for most of the villagers, this vision seemed fraught with danger.

As the two families began to develop a system of alliances based on marriage and patronage, disputes over land surveys and unpaid debts became tests of clan loyalty. As these disputes came into the courts, clan leaders could look to these alliances for support. When Nathaniel Putnam claimed that a piece of his land was wrongly occupied by another—and he was a veteran legalist—to his support as witnesses came his in-laws, his married and unmarried children, and his friends.[20] His opponent would find sureties for an appeal to the General Court in the opposing camp.[21] Such suits, as much tests of partisan fealty in the village as anything else, meandered their way from county court to General Court and back over a course of many years. Not every suit was waged along clan lines. Sometimes Putnams sued other Putnams, as when Captain John sued his brother Nathaniel for taking timber from the captain's land without permission. Fortunately for family harmony, the suit was dropped.[22] Many other suits that once would have been settled through traditional methods of arbitration by neighbors were now litigated to their conclusion.[23]

Suits dragged on, resolving little. Such litigation has as its motive not just material gain but the restatement of dignity. One's opponent has tried to get away with something, to break the rules that had, in former times, governed interpersonal relations. All the parties come to see the litigation as a way of making their claims public, speaking not only for themselves but for their communities, whose values they proclaim to be under attack.[24] These endless lawsuits did not resolve differences, clarify status, discharge animus, or reestablish dignity, however; the animus that spurred them festered unabated.[25]

Private civil suits for unpaid debts and unfulfilled obligations began to merge into and overlap more ominous legal proceedings as the Putnams' personal concerns became villagewide quarrels. The Putnams were no strangers to self-help, cutting down trees or ordering new surveys when their interests were threatened. In the 1670s they turned to the courts, however, to resolve a longstanding dispute with the town of Topsfield, over whose border some of Nathaniel Putnam's lands supposedly lay. To determine how much Putnam could claim, Topsfield appointed

45

Jacob Townes and John Howe (or How) to approach Captain John and "any other" Salem men and ask for the deeds to the disputed land, but the Putnams could not produce documents. Instead, they offered on their oath that the real estate was granted them by the General Court. Appealed to by the Topsfield men, the General Court tried to quiet the dispute over title to the lands, but even after the sites were resurveyed, the feud continued.[26]

By the 1680s, the conflict between the Putnams and the Hobbs-Esty-Howe-Towne-Wildes families of Topsfield was a fact of village life. In January 1687, the dispute took a new and ominous turn, for the Howes had gained powerful friends in Salem. Joseph Porter and his brother-in-law Daniel Andrew joined Topsfield's Isaac Esty as witnesses that Captain John Putnam had felled timber on land that did not, according to Howe, belong to any Putnam. The Putnams retorted by convincing a Salem grand jury to present Esty for "telling a lie in open court."[27] The dispute over timber and meadow remained on the court docket, for out of court animosities now ran deep. Some of these must have been expressed in subtle ways to the Topsfield women who lived in the village—Rebecca Nurse, Sarah Cloyse, and Mary Esty.[28]

The ministry inevitably became a focal point of these tensions, as a succession of ministers quarreled with important members of the leading clans, who, their dignity offended, insisted that the minister be dismissed. To the minister's defense in turn came other factions within the clan structure, in the process of which personal disagreements became public disputes.

Having received, after five years of agitation, permission from the General Court to build their own meeting house and name their own preacher, the freeholders of Salem Village hired James Bayley to be their preacher on November 11, 1672. A young graduate of Harvard College, Bayley was not an ordained minister, but the village committee gave him a salary of forty pounds. The next year the villagers asked Bayley to stay on, and a year later, of their own free will, Nathaniel, Captain John, and Lieutenant Thomas Putnam, with two others, gave the young man thirty acres of upland and meadow. Bayley would farm these as well as preach and teach. The land was a gift to induce Bayley to stay, but by 1679 he had done something to offend Bray Wilkins, a substantial farmer and close friend of Nathaniel Putnam's and John Jr.'s. Bayley admitted in a letter to the villagers, "There hath (as yourselves will know) some uncomfortable divisions and contentions fallen out among us here, and these divisions being about myself." Bayley asked to know what was in his parishioners' hearts, but the two Putnams and Wilkins did not explain their dissatisfaction, save to remark that Bayley had not been called to his post in the proper way. Instead, he was invited to the pulpit by those "that were not capacitated so to do."[29]

The Wilkinses and Putnams who rejected Bayley did not have to give an explanation. They behaved as though the office was their gift, like the land. Bayley served at their pleasure. But Bayley had friends in the Putnam clan, notably Lieutenant Thomas Putnam and his son Sergeant Thomas and Captain John Putnam. When the "petition" against the pastor came to their hands, they retorted that Bayley had been chosen "by the great consent and vote of the inhabitants." What could be more "capacitating" than the people? If Bayley had offended Bray Wilkins and his kin, the Wilkins family could hardly set itself up as judge and jury. Bayley's supporters insisted that outside authority be called to arbitrate the dispute, and their brothers and cousins and friends agreed. John Higginson, Salem's venerable pastor, investigated and reported that there was no truth in the rumors spread abroad that Bayley was inattentive to his domestic or his ministerial duties. Amen said Lieutenant Thomas and Captain John, along with thirty-eight other freeholders, including Joseph Porter. Bayley still wanted the job, and the villagers met and voted to retain him for the next year. Now Nathaniel and John Jr. swung into action, rallying support for an appeal to the General Court. The upper house of the General Court supported the Higginson report, but the lower house agreed with Nathaniel and John Jr. Bayley stayed for his year and then left. For severance pay, and to close ranks behind the departed outsider, Lieutenant Thomas joined with Nathaniel and John Jr. to give Bayley another thirty-one acres. The minister rented it out until 1700, when he sold it.[30]

Bayley's case did not pit Putnams against Porters, but it did demonstrate that personal slights could become public issues with speed and weight when the local magnates felt that they had been offended. As Bayley's case proved, the Putnams might not always agree among themselves, but when they did, they could control the nomination of ministers. They chose as Bayley's replacement George Burroughs. Burroughs graduated from Harvard a year after Bayley, in 1670, and preached in Falmouth, Maine, on Casco Bay, until King Philip's War devastated the area. With other Maine settlers, Burroughs relocated to Massachusetts, where the committee found him and offered him the village pulpit. He arrived in 1681 at the newly built parsonage, receiving the same salary of sixty pounds which Bayley had been paid in his terminal year and encountering the same troubles.

Burroughs' wife died that year, and he had to borrow money to pay for the customary funeral wine. Captain John Putnam was happy to help, but within a year dissention divided the two men. "Brother against brother and neighbor against neighbor" was how Jeremiah Watts put it on April 11, 1682. Unless Watts was being allegorical (a fair possibility; he also thundered, "This is the time of Antichrist's reign"; warned, "Now are witnesses slain"; and promised "to draw up the marks of the beast"), the brothers were again the elder Putnams. The court admonished Watts for his scandalous words, but the village committee was indeed unhappy with its selection. Most unhappy was Captain John, who had lent Burroughs money a year before but now held up the minister's salary. When Lieutenant Thomas hesitated about harassing Burroughs, Captain John grabbed his brother by the coat and convinced him to change his mind.[31]

Burroughs was in debt to Captain John, but it could easily have been "settled" or set off against what the village owed Burroughs in arrears. Burroughs had, however, offended Captain John by refusing to preach unless he was paid and was planning openly to leave. Captain John, joined by Lieutenant Thomas and Nathaniel, first petitioned the court to force Burroughs to stay. This failed, and Captain John then filed suit for the debt. When Burroughs appeared in the village to close his accounts amicably, Putnam arranged for the town marshal to seize the wandering minister. Nathaniel Putnam, with Ingersoll and Sibley, put up bail—perhaps hoping that Burroughs would change his mind. When the case came to court, in June 1683, witnesses deposed that Burroughs had ordered the funeral wine on Captain John's account, with the latter's permission, but as Burroughs answered, the village committee owed him far more in back pay. Burroughs no sooner answered their charges than the Putnams withdrew the suit—Captain John's honor satisfied and the power of his family to appoint and dispose confirmed.[32]

Enter Deodat Lawson, "son of a dissenting minister of Norfolk England." He came to Massachusetts in the 1670s and floundered around, until he was called to serve the village. All was quiet for a time, but in 1686 his supporters, seeking leverage in their effort to make the village and its church independent of Salem, pressed for his ordination.[33] Captain John and his son John Jr. led the effort, but by now a new group had emerged to challenge the Putnams' hitherto unshakable control of

48

the pulpit. Led by Joseph Putnam and Daniel Andrew, the dissenters wanted a full discussion of the ordination issue. Joseph Hutchinson, their ally, turned up the temperature of the debate by fencing in the land that he had given for the meeting house thirteen years before. Fences were always matters of contention in New England, and the act of fencing in common land was a symbolic attack on the Putnams as well as a practical insult to the village committeemen. Lieutenant Thomas Putnam hailed Hutchinson into court, but Hutchinson retorted that he never bound himself to surrender the land. To add insult to insult, he demanded that the court, in the name of justice, tell Thomas Putnam to stop pulling down fences on other people's property.[34] Again the village had to ask for outside help, this time from a town committee including merchants Bartholomew Gedney, John Hathorne, and William Brown Jr., only to discover that they were closer in interest to the dissidents than to the Putnams. The selectmen advised against ordination of Lawson, correctly reading it as a step toward the secession of the village, and he left shortly thereafter. In the meantime, village factionalism had become notorious throughout the colony.[35]

Behind the opposition to Lawson stood the Porters. The Porters were not members of the village church, but Salem town's, though they might attend meetings in the village on occasion. Membership in New England nonconforming churches did not automatically transfer when a communicant moved. Some churches routinely welcomed a newcomer who belonged to another church, but other congregations, including Salem Village's, required a new confession of faith in front of the congregation, followed by its favorable vote.[36] The Putnam ministers had upheld that rule, giving the Putnams the power to decide who could sit as full members of the church. The Porters had no objection to this arrangement until Putnam influence in the village became overbearing. The proposed ordination of Lawson forced the Porters to confront the implications of Putnam control of the pulpit. Thus the Porters, who had joined in the petition for a village meeting house and minister (it was a politically astute move, for most of the villagers supported the idea), dug in their heels when the holder was not to their liking.

Samuel Parris's appointment fell into this widening crevasse. The Putnams chose him, and over time anti-Putnam men became his opponents.[37] The clear lines of pro- and anti-Parris affiliation did not come until the witchcraft crisis was under way, however. It was not a clash of clans which made Parris's life so hard in the village; it was Parris himself.

49

Unlike his three predecessors, who, in varying ways, would have preferred to avoid controversy, he sided with those who supported him and preached against those who opposed him. The anti-Parris faction retaliated at a village meeting on October 16, 1691, when the Putnam-dominated rate committee was ousted and Joseph Porter, Joseph Hutchinson, Joseph Putnam (who had cast his lot with his wife's family, the Porters), Daniel Andrew, and Frances Nurse were chosen in their stead. Parris replied by summoning his supporters to a meeting in the parsonage and pleading for their aid. The breach widened but was yet bridgeable, for Nurse, Hutchinson, Porter, Nathaniel Putnam, and John Jr. that same week joined in an appeal to the town council to reduce the village's rates.[38]

Who was to resolve differences like these when they folded into the social antagonisms and the political rivalry of the great families? The village lacked a regular town government. The householders met and selected a committee whose decisions were binding on those who were willing to be bound, but appeals lay to the town and the General Court. All the towns in the colony were the creatures of the General Court, and in past years the village had petitioned for relief before the General Court. In these years, however, a new Dominion of New England had replaced the charter government, and most of the settlers suspected the motives of its leaders. No one could be certain what the future held for the towns or for the colony. In 1689, the politics of the colony passed from uncertainty to uproar. Learning that the hated King James II had been driven from his throne, a party of merchants and ministers ousted Governor Edmund Andros, Dudley's replacement, from his post and imprisoned him.

Where would the strife end? There were still courts—the Court of Assistants met, as did the local courts—and they maintained to some extent the sense of community which the fathers of the towns wanted. Nevertheless, Governor Simon Bradstreet was old and tired; his councilors (many of the same men who served Andros's Dominion, and before him, the first charter government), were uneasy. No one could predict what the new charter would say or mean. In England, Massachusetts's agent Increase Mather labored mightily to explain the ouster of Andros and lobby for a return of the original charter, but he must have known that the commonwealth would never regain its old autonomy. In the village, Parris seemed safe among the farmers, but a few miles off lay the port of Salem, and beyond it, unseen but felt, the frightening grip of an emerging imperial system. Left to themselves, the villagers turned the selection of a new minister into a purely factional issue. Porter dissent prevented the Putnams from exercising their authority and Parris from gaining the security he needed.[39]

In times of troubles like these, ministers reassured their congregants. When uncertainty short-circuited the official means of information dissemination, simple words of comfort from the pulpit outweighed whole libraries of learned tracts and cartloads of government pronouncements. In this, the minister had a special role to play. The congregation was his "auditory," eager for his teaching.[40] Now more than ever, Parris's role in the community went beyond formal pastoral and ministerial tasks, to make sense of a world coming apart. He preached twice on the Lord's day, and perhaps once during the week, in addition to leading lessons and counseling privately. He was the arbiter of disputes and the source of information.[41] His words were heard far beyond the pews.

Faced with growing local factionalism and colonywide disorder, Parris remained outwardly calm, though one can hear the strain of the self-discipline in his voice. On November 22, 1691, he began a series of lectures on the text of Psalm 110: "The Lord said unto my Lord, sit thou at my right hand until I make thine enemies thy footstool." The first two lectures, delivered that day, traced the importance of Christ's ascension to the right hand of the Father. He reassured his flock that the psalm was "made up of many pretious promises, that have a direct tendency to the consolation of the Faithful." Consolation was his theme and his purpose: for people—the implication was all people—are exalted next to God, and God would assert His rule over those who were the enemies of His faithful. He would subjugate their "consciences and inward parts," creating a reign of righteousness on earth. Parris had opened the door a crack to his yearning congregation to see Christ, wounded and humiliated, rise again to sit at God's right hand. Through this figurative elevation, for Parris did not want to fall into the trap of denying Christ's divinity, those who sought the Lord would be saved. Christ interceded and mediated for the sinner. He came before the Father and pleaded with all his sufferings as tokens of his earnestness: "The worth of souls is above all the world."[42]

These words of comfort came not from Christ, of course, but from his servant Samuel Parris. As he told his congregants in the second two lectures, given on the morning and afternoon of January 3, the role of the minister was essential in the gathered church. From within the flock of saints he gathered, Christ chose a few to preach the Word, and "for this purpose Christ hath given ministers" to his people, "by which means the dark minds of the Elect are enlightened and their hard hearts are softened." Even the elect must pay attention to the preaching of the minister, Parris reminded the stiff-necked in his congregation, for opposition to him was opposition to the Word. They too should fear the wiles of Satan, for proud hearts that resisted the ministrations of the preacher could not be open to God's grace. But Parris held out an open hand to those who would return to the faith of their fathers, for Christ was the healer, and the meeting house His home.[43]

The Parris who read these sermons strove to rise above faction. Because of his background, he had faced obstacles that others in his situation did not. He had not grown to manhood in New England, much less had intimate contact with the ministry there. His relative inexperience with the ways of the men and women of the farming interior had left him impatient with his parishioners and insensitive to their expectations. Whatever they might be, he was no provincial but a man of the Atlantic world, and some of his parishioners did not understand the sacrifice he made to live among them.[44] Nevertheless, Parris still walked the high road, restraining the arrogance bred in the scions of the plantation master class.

He found comfort in assembling bits and pieces from the Jeremiad model of sermonizing developed during the Restoration and honed throughout the 1670s and 1680s. Its formula was simple and attractive to him: recite the afflictions of the people caused by their falling away from their parents' covenant with God; rehearse God's quarrel with New England; show the way back to grace, warning the indifferent and stubborn what would happen if they lagged behind. If, unlike the masters of the Jeremiad, he did not trace his own lineage back to the founders of New England, Parris proved an adept pupil of their style.[45]

Bereft of parents and kin, without long-term friends, newly installed in a calling whose other professors were well established and more experienced than he, he coped. Caught in a longstanding feud between powerful political factions, he ministered to the souls of all and hoped for a day when all would present themselves for full membership in the church. From his first sermon to his last, that was his ideal—a fully covenanted community, wherein residence coincided with membership in the church. Parris resented the failure of the village committee to pay what they owed him, but he could contain that resentment so long as his pastoral duties went well. This was the winter of his third year in Salem. Sixty-one people had joined the church, and that was gratifying, although only one member came forward to seek full communion.[46] Parris insisted in orthodox fashion that the Lord's Supper was not meant to bring a person to grace—rather, it was reserved for those who had been chosen and could demonstrate to the congregation that they were ready for full membership.[47] So, too, under Parris's leadership, the congregation still rejected the more liberal implications of the "half-way covenant," allowing the children of churchgoers to participate in communion, though they had no personal experience of grace to relate.[48]

Throughout New England there was a crisis in communion—fewer were coming forward. This was certainly true in Salem town.[49] Perhaps the grandchildren of the founders were falling away from the faith of their fathers and mothers, a declension of disturbing implications. Ministers like Parris decried such backsliding.[50] He worried that many who were regenerate simply did not believe in themselves, and he begged them to come forward and join their fellows. He would not credit the idea that he was the cause of the decline in church membership, but he worried aloud that a malignity was abroad, some evil force that had crept into the meeting house and spread its wings of doubt and backbiting among his parishioners. Over time, the carping had grown more severe and may have kept some from coming forward. Too, there were always those who practiced a more relaxed version of Puritan worship than Parris demanded of his congregants.[51]

Early in January, after Parris preached his sermons on the intercessory care of Christ, a crisis of faith erupted in the village which made the division of the congregation unmistakably clear. Despite an opinion on the matter from the Essex County Quarterly Court delivered on January 17, 1692, ordering the village committee, still dominated by Parris's enemies, to collect funds for Parris's salary, the committee dithered. That rankled but did not surprise Parris, given the committee's prior position. If the records show no single episode that broke his will, the strokes of misfortune continued to fall. He had offered conciliation in the bosom of Christ and his opponents returned ill will and contumely. His supporters, particularly the Putnams, had other reasons to dislike and distrust Parris's assailants in the Village and probably stoked Parris's frustration and anger. The pattern of his earlier failures seemed to be repeating itself. He had decided to strike back at his, and God's, enemies.[52]

Parris finished his lecture series on the ascension of Christ on February 14, but the tone of this final sermon was entirely different from that of the previous four sermons. Instead of proving that men and women had a friend sitting at the right hand of the Father, Parris decided that Christ's ascension put one more judge of iniquity into the heavens. "It is a woeful piece of our corruption in an evil time, when the wicked prosper and the godly party meet with vexations." For Parris now saw a godly party beset with troubles: "and now we call the proud happy: yea, they that work wickedness are set up." He no longer consoled or sought unity. Instead, he condemned—and through him, Christ condemned—those who refused to help the minister do God's work. The reference to "the proud" and the "set up" alluded to the committee elected by the village. It was "set up" after a fashion. Parris sent an unmistakable message to Israel and Joseph Porter and their allies: "because stronger is he that is with us and for us, than he that is against us," the committeemen would pay, in the next world if not in this, for their iniquities. Christ, no longer the gentle mediator who pleaded with His own suffering for the salvation of souls, became the contemnor. Ministers in His service were to "endeavor a true separation between the precious and the vile, and to labour what in them [lay] to gather a pure Church unto Christ." Others they were "to refuse and reject."[53]

Parris's view of the prerequisites for church membership ran athwart the many compromises made since the first generation had passed from the scene, but he had clerical allies in his conservatism. If there is a distinctively sour note in these powerful sermons, it is not that Parris departed from conventional doctrine but that there is nothing in any of his writing which suggests he knew he was saved, no testimony of grace, no sweetness, no light bathing him and washing away his sins, no relief from the psychological vise grip of his own anxiety. The most telling attack upon a minister in Puritan Massachusetts was that he was secretly unregenerate, and ministers repelled such attacks with fury, as Anne Hutchinson and others learned early in Massachusetts's history. No one (on the record) accused Parris of being a secret sinner, but in these days of uncharitableness, all he offered his parched congregants was dry doctrine. One wonders if Parris had suspicions that he might be a secretly unregenerate soul. Such rebels from God misled themselves, and the potential was always there, even among the ministry. No one could really know the will of God.[54]

Thus far there were no witches in this dispute, only men with strong wills. Indeed, Parris's quarrel with some of his parishioners was not unusual, for there were often "conflicts between insistent or embattled ministers and their reluctant, hostile, or parsimonious townsmen."[55] The fear of witches came to Salem from beyond its boundaries, from the woods to the west and north. These witches rode the winds of war. What began in Europe late in 1688 as a dynastic struggle escalated into a world war over religion and power. The conflict exposed the colonies to stark, unrelieved terror.[56] Salem lay at the southern end of a region of marsh and wood thrown open by "King William's War" to human predation. To the north of Salem there stretched a line of towns, including Beverly, Ipswich, and Portsmouth, reaching up into eastern New Hampshire and Maine, like a picket line on a battlefield. These settlements lay in the path of raiding parties of eastern Abnaki, Huron, Ottawa, Canadian Mohawk, and their dreaded French allies.[57]

In the border towns, the fear of Indians was pervasive. News of renewed hostilities awakened a lightly slumbering memory of the carnage of King Philip's War, barely won a generation before. Then Salem had lost many of its sons in fighting at "Bloody Brook" outside Deerfield.[58] Although that war had ended in victory, nightmares from it remained. Everyone knew someone who had not come back from the ambush, yet in Salem Indians still strolled the lanes and drank at back porches or in the fields with laborers and servants. The county courts regularly heard presentments of men for giving liquor to Indians and punished Indians accused of misdemeanor. Only two years after King Philip's War, John Proctor of the village was presented by a Salem grand jury for selling "strong water" to an Indian.[59] There were few cases of suspected homicide of whites by Indians, and none came from Essex County, but rumor traveled long distances to reach the ears of the suggestible. To the villagers, Indians lurked in the dark corners of the imagination, like the fear of muggers in the modern city.

In war, the renewed stress upon a military hierarchy of captains, lieutenants, and sergeants had added to and reinforced looser status relationships based on landed wealth. The Putnam connection of 1689 was reforged by war. For the menfolk, the prospect of war on the frontier raised levels of insecurity and testosterone. They marshaled themselves, trained, and prepared to march off to defend the frontiers of the settlement. Women experienced war differently. Never warriors save in extraordinary situations, and never by choice, they did not go off to war but were its victims nonetheless. They too remembered what had happened to hundreds of women and children in 1675 and 1676. Many died in their homes or on familiar paths: no place was safe, and women were as likely to die in the fields and houses as men. The very young were even more likely to die, killed because they could not be carried on the long journey back to Canada. Even the women who escaped the raids watched their parents or children die, destroying the illusion that family was a haven. Girls over the age of eight were taken into captivity, to be sold to the French in Canada, and perhaps ransomed back or recaptured.[60] For these young women, sleep became dreadful, much like the tormented sleep of the sinner who feared the judgment of the Lord would fall in the night. Indeed, was not the Indian an instrument of a malign providence, another judgment of the all-seeing God?[61]

The dread of Indian raids was kept alive in tales of captivity the rescued or ransomed victims wrote and by ministers' sermons and narratives of the war. It was as close to a popular literature as any in New England, and it chilled its audiences as it touched deep layers of cultural and psychological need.[62] The women captives became archetypes in sermons and other forms of literature.[63] They were Deborah and Jael, slaughtering the enemies of the Israelites, heroic and stoic by turns, keeping themselves and their faith alive in hostile lands. They could express without fear of reproach violent tendencies that women had to conceal in normal times. Indeed, captivity tales hallowed violence. Hannah Dunston, captured by the Abnaki, slew ten of them in their sleep before she escaped. She was lionized in Boston for her feat, praised by brilliant young Boston minister Cotton Mather himself from his pulpit for conduct that would have been incomprehensibly horrific had she not acted against New England's foes. Women could also exhibit the strength of purpose in suffering which all good Christians were expected to exhibit in times of danger and woe.[64]

This burned-over region of raids and counterraids, in which the villages and towns of both Indian and newcomer were imperiled, would in 1692 include all of the major witchcraft areas, and not by accident. Although the incidents that brought a group of girls from Salem Village to Andover to hunt for witches there were a coincidence, an unforeseen and unforeseeable consequence of the witch hunt in Salem Village, the conditions under which their accusations were treated seriously were similar in Andover, Beverly, and elsewhere.

A modern parallel demonstrates the complexity of causation. In 1988 a region in northwestern New York no larger than that anchored by

Salem Village experienced a minor witch hunt of its own. Stories of ritual murders and other satanic rites spread through the towns and villages surrounding Jamestown, New York. There were no trials or executions, but the conditions were ripe for a witch hunt. What had happened? The region faced hard times; unemployment was rising; teen suicides seemed to point to a broader moral crisis. In the midst of these troubling conditions, an old warehouse was refurbished for use as a rock music concert hall and rented out to heavy metal musicians. At the same time, parents were watching network television shows that sensationalized stories of satanic worship. Rumors circulated among the teenagers through oral networks that were already established. Parents overheard bits and pieces of these reports and took their concerns to the police department in Jamestown. A group panic soon engulfed the community, centered on a tale that a blue-eyed, blond-haired teenage girl would soon be abducted and sacrificed in a satanic rite. With slightly different details, the same story circulated in all the towns in the region. The episode died when authorities reassured parents than no such plot existed—but had authorities believed more strongly in the underlying mythos of abduction or the active interest of Satan in the Lake Erie towns, the result might have been different.[65]

The Salem Village region was similarly gripped with panic and overrun with dreadful rumors in the winter of 1691–92. War stories circulated in the town, and the girls in it were frightened by what they heard. Merging the bits and pieces of stories from the north with their own imagined tales, they began to formulate a larger mythopoeic structure— a fantasy world for themselves. Parents overheard and misunderstood. In trying to make sense for themselves of the girls' stories, the parents reconfigured the elements of the story, making it a more conventional tale of witches and their victims.

Such conversations went on continuously, for most of the communication in this village passed from mouth to mouth. Far more than others in that day, the Puritans of New England enjoyed literacy, book reading, and sermons based on written texts, but ordinary people still trusted word of mouth and their own experience more than the distant authority of books. To this extent, popular—vernacular—culture resisted the encroachment of elite learning. Servants met servants on the roads; farmers visited the "ordinaries" and shared stories; goodwives gossiped over fences. There was much visiting, particularly when a child was ill. Older women dropped in on younger mothers nursing their children and shared folk cures. In these settings, the details of an untoward event or suspected atrocity changed, magnified, and spread outward with each telling. Stories of wonder, joy, and danger all passed through the village in this way.

58

In Salem that winter, there were many strangers with strange stories to relate. Salem was a way station on the road south from the beleaguered settlements. A steady stream of refugees fleeing Indian raids brought reports of massacres, first-hand accounts of fighting, and predictions of savagery to come. There was enough truth to the stories to make the refugees something of celebrities, but they carried with them a kind of germ, the symptoms of which were frightening. They had seen terrors and they terrified those who listened to them.

Rumors of violence on the frontier blended into tales of witchcraft, as a set of vernacular beliefs about witchcraft, including countermagic, merged imperceptibly at its edges into the fear that the French and Indians would drive down the coast and destroy Essex settlements. Indeed, some suspected that was the plan in the north,[66] but the mere fear itself made Salem people readier to accept supernatural explanations for illness and misfortune. When the witches were identified, the accusers grew in number beyond a circle of impressionable girls to include older men and women unrelated to the victims or the witches, save by contiguity and common tongue.

It was this tension more than any other which made rumors of witchcraft so real. They flowed into and out of other social pressures. For example, in Andover, on Salem's northwestern border, a population boom had put terrific pressure on what had been a well-functioning system of distribution of land. Too many sons and daughters overburdened customary gift and inheritance patterns, straining the social and emotional relationship that owning land reflected and reinforced. Andover was a patriarchy, with sons living well into their twenties on family farms. Using land, fathers controlled their children, and children accepted that control, for good behavior would bring a patrimony and the chance to start one's own family on one's own farm. Too many children living into adulthood threatened those ways. It was not by accident that so many of the witches accused in the Salem crisis would come from Andover.[67]

In Salem that winter, Parris thus found himself in the middle of a growing panic. It came in whispers, floating on the chill, damp air. Undistracted, he might have controlled it, but he was himself besieged by his enemies, and the evil crept into his own home. It began with the cold. Whatever the state of Parris's mind or the safety of his coming to the judgment day, winter was a hard time for ministers and their congregants. New England winters are severe, and this one was no exception. Even in the meeting house, the bitter cold crept through the walls and under the doors, reaching Parris in his raised pulpit. He wore a heavy gown and gloves, and his parishioners were bundled up; but there was no heat (there was no fireplace in the meeting house), and Parris often had to break off his preaching "by reason of the Cold."[68] The fields were frozen, and to go out one had to swaddle in cloth and wool, or fur, if one could afford it. To go indoors one had to dress warmly as well, for the only source of heat was the fireplace, and fireplaces in wooden homes were not efficient sources of warmth. Night came early, and with it, more cold. Without a ready supply of firewood (another of Parris's complaints), the parsonage was nearly as cold as the meeting house.

Parris carped that his house was cold. The cold sifted through the rooms and into his family's spirits. The worsening weather brought sore throats, fevers, and hacking coughs that could be heard throughout houses and passed from villager to villager. The refugees brought with them additional sicknesses. Infirmity was everywhere, but in Salem one child became uncommonly ill: Betty in the Parris household. Elizabeth Parris Sr. had her hands full with little Susannah. Neither mother nor younger daughter was strong; both would die within five years of the winter of 1692. Whispers that Betty's illness was not natural soon carried on the dense night air, borne by the same ether that wafted the rumors of death and destruction on the frontier. Surely the Devil was near.

witchcakes

IN LATE February 1692 Betty's stomach hurt, she claimed, and she began to behave oddly. Serious illness was not uncommon among the young in early New England; a mother and father could expect that more than one of their children would die before reaching adulthood. But Betty was not merely ill abed. She dashed about, lashed out, and dove under furniture. Her cousin Abigail followed suit.[1] A hellish, dire possibility must have occurred to Parris. The similarity of their behavior to that of the Goodwin children of Boston three years earlier, known to Parris, he was there, and retold in Cotton Mather's tract *Memorable Providences*, was striking. Word of mouth had heightened every detail of the Boston case, and it led to the execution of an old Irish washerwoman, Mary Glover, for witchcraft.[2]

Whatever the cause, Parris viewed the illness as a judgment upon him, and perhaps the village as well. The Parris parsonage was beset that winter with recrimination and animosity as Parris battled with his congregation. After meeting with his supporters in the parsonage parlor in January, Parris agreed to a new course of action: John and Edward Putnam and the other seventeen conveners were prepared to bring a lawsuit against the committee. The committee, led by the Porters, backed down for the time being, but the fragmentation of the village and the fracturing of the congregation was evident to all, even the little ones in Parris's household. Samuel Nurse and the other dissenters in the church had attacked Parris for asking Betty and Abigail who or what afflicted them.[3]

As Betty's illness persisted, the household became more tense. Parris's sermons already likened his sufferings to those of Christ and the ill will of the villagers who would not pay his salary to the vileness of the sinners who scoffed at God.[4] They were the enemy and his persecution their aim. The two-story framed house echoed with loud voices and even more ominous silences as winter grew colder and Parris, worried about firewood and souls, found enemies all around. Soon, other girls who came to visit and play with Betty appeared infected with her ailment. Eleven-year-old Ann Putnam Jr., whose father, Sergeant Thomas, and uncle Captain John were Parris's great supporters in his troubles, and Mercy Lewis, a servant in the Thomas Putnam household, were soon beset, as was Mary Walcott, who lived next door to the parsonage. The circle of contagion spread to other girls, including the village doctor's niece, Elizabeth Hubbard.

The girls undoubtedly knew about Samuel Parris's troubles. As in all these vernacular houses, the children's bedroom abutted the parents' bedroom on the second floor and stood directly above the first-floor parlor, a large room, where Parris met his parishioners, heard their personal stories, and admonished or comforted them. The floorboards of the upper rooms were single planks, filled with knotholes and badly joined. Through the cracks sand and dirt fell to the floor below and sounds traveled upward. One can see Betty and Abigail with their ears or eyes pressed to the cracks as Parris and his supporters rehearsed the travails of his ministry in the parlor below.[5]

Every morning, as the family prayed together, working its way through the two Testaments, Parris must have prayed with Betty for her recovery. He used the occasion to remind her that she should prepare herself for God's judgment. Fear drove Parris, fear for Betty, fear for the efficacy of his prayers, fear for the unregenerate among them whose souls were at stake. Yet prayer was no cure, and sometime the prayers of the godly went unanswered. Cotton Mather knew: "To see a Dutiful Child of God lying in the dust before Him, and begging for his mercies with an importunity, that pierces the very heavens, and relying on the Attributes and Engagements of God, and the merits, and prevailing intercession of our Advocate in the heavens, and hold on doing so; praying without ceasing, and still be denied; still complain, O my God, I cry in the Day Time, and thou hearest not, and in the night-season I am not silent."[6] Like Cotton Mather, Parris taught his children that they were to look to the savior of their souls for a lasting cure, but then Cotton Mather had lost all but one of his eleven children before they reached adulthood. The good parent not only instructed the child but provided an example of grace and perseverance in hard times.[7] But Parris's temper was frayed, and his family devotions must have crackled with the strain, just as his sermons showed his anger. A ministry that was supposed to rest upon the love between the minister and his flock had turned hateful.

He summoned his brethren to his side to pray with him, and John Hale, John Higginson, and other ministers came.[8] Nothing less was expected of them. Three years earlier, the Reverend Samuel Willard of the old South Church in Boston—who had seen many sick children and prayed with many sick parents—told his congregation that children were "lambs in the fold," a gift to their parents not to be regarded lightly: "If others in a family suffer want, and be pincht with difficulties, yet the Children shall certainly be taken care for, as long as there is anything to be had."[9] Willard's words of comfort circulated widely, and members of his congregation such as Samuel Sewall called on Willard to pray with them in times of illness. When Sewall's infant son Henry became ill a week after his birth, Sewall suffered agonies of grief, but Willard eased Sewall's burden. Friends and other ministers joined Willard in prayer at Sewall's side.[10]

Such prayers were more than supplications; they were confessions of human error as well. When Parris prayed, he not only sought the aid of God but was expected to admit his own sins.[11] In seeking divine assistance, Parris had to confess error. It must have occurred to him that some of his troubles were his own fault, the result of his stiff-necked, demanding personality. Thus Betty's illness forced Parris into a crushing psychological conundrum: to seek God's aid he had to ask pardon from men—the very men whose actions he deeply believed had caused all his troubles. Nevertheless, Puritans like Parris believed in the efficacy—and the necessity—of prayer to heal the sick. At the Wednesday devotional meetings in his parlor, under Betty's bedroom, Parris reached out to his neighbors and his congregants, seeking support in prayer.

Yet again prayer did not work; Betty grew worse. While some prayed, others performed more intimate rituals of healing. Neighbors visited to sit with the sick children and allow the family members some respite.

Lingering illnesses among children exhausted mothers, and neighboring women often were as concerned for the health of the mother as for the child. The visitors also observed closely, looking for symptoms, advising on cures, and watching for signs of the supernatural.[12] The rooms in which sick children were tended were crowded with helpers, but some neighbors stayed away from the parlor of the Parris home, just as they stayed away from the communion table at the village meeting house.

Little Betty could hardly have escaped the emotional terrors of a home besieged, for children perceive relationships in a painfully honest and direct way.[13] Worse, girls did not have the outlets for reduction of tension which boys had. The absence of alternatives to the few restricted roles available to young women in Puritan society not only confined the spirit of girls like Betty, but it also denied them a chance to undergo the annealing rigors of an identity crisis. Identified already as little mothers, they could only conform or rage against the only identity available to them.[14] Betty's pain was to her thus consuming and inescapable in a way that it would not be for a boy her age, which may explain why her older brother escaped her ailment.

More important for the events that would follow, her ailments were not diagnosed by women but by men. The gendering of medical diagnosis of ailments like hers was not confined to Puritan New England, of course. In 1616, John Cotta, an English doctor, had published his study of symptoms like hers, proposing to separate natural ailments from supernatural or spiritual infections. If nonnatural causes remained "hidden and infolded in mists and clouds of the unknown," he insisted that all symptoms ought to be viewed as part of a natural process of sickness and health. Even when witchcraft was suspected, the doctor was to proceed in the same diagnostic manner that he used to uncover any disease.[15] Cotta's subliminal message was that diagnosis was best left in the hands of doctors—men—not cunning folk or wise people, particularly the female conjurers and charm manufacturers ordinarily consulted by the common folk.[16]

Cotta's proposals were widely quoted by other doctors and ministers, for male authorities understood symptoms of dysfunction in women or girls according to male concerns. Such transformation of female experience was common in the diagnosis of hysteria cases. Trancelike states, numbness, and other physiological abnormalities were taken as symptoms of both hysteria and witchcraft.[17] Some modern medical observers still liken the Salem girls' fits to hysteria,[18] for hysteria has long been associated with being bewitched.[19] Hysteria among young women can present itself as unexplained somatic eruptions, palsy, rigidity, and awkward, repetitive body movements. It may also involve perceptual disorders, illusions, and visions, such as the specters of the witches which the girls later saw tormenting them, or watching their torments, with the witches' "familiars" alongside them.[20]

For doctors and ministers in the seventeenth century, Satan was a convenient and compelling explanation for mental distress of all kinds. When Bethia Hinkley of Barnstable assaulted her husband, neighbors agreed that she was "so furr left of God into the temptations of Satan and the corruptions of her own heart as greatly to dishonor God, and to give matter of just offense." Fortunately her church was able to intercede, and she came to her senses.[21] Hysteria does not come and go, however, with the ease with which the girls moved in and out of their symptoms.

Panic, which may be a part of hysteria, complicates certain medical conditions. The girls testified that they were choking. Such symptoms are common in hyperactive bronchial disease (asthma) patients and may be brought about by episodes of intense stress combined with physical exertion, pollution by mold spores or other airborne agents, or pathogens such as viruses. Sudden changes in room temperature may cause an episode. Often, there is no obvious cause and attacks come without warning. Children and teenagers are the most likely asthma sufferers, and their acute episodes may be a few minutes or much longer in duration. They cannot breathe, and to an observer they seem to be in mortal toil. If asthma played a part, it is not surprising that the girls' attacks of choking were common indoors, in damp and moldy houses, and in the evening, when fires were stoked, rooms became smoky, and temperatures increased. There was little that could be done for asthma then, although it is usually outgrown and is rarely fatal—facts that conform to the girls' later freedom from this symptom.[22]

A more severe diagnosis is the possibility that Betty suffered from epilepsy. It is one thing to read about epileptic fits or other forms of seizures in a book; it is quite another to watch them in person. Anyone watching epilepsy will be struck by the almost impossible contortions of the body and the pitiable, because uncontrollable, motions of the limbs. It is possible that Betty had a form of seizures. Years later Cotton Mather recalled how the afflicted were "horribly distorted and convulsed."[23]

64

Some of these symptoms correspond to petit mal,[24] but the seizures did not continue when Betty was removed from her house. Nor is epilepsy contagious, as the Salem girls' fits apparently were, although others might have simply copied her symptoms.

The fact that Parris removed Betty from the village soon after the examinations of suspected witches began may be read as evidence of his fear that the cause of her afflictions was human, not pathogenic or organic. Was she perhaps an abused child? Some of her symptoms fit the admittedly vague confines of the emotional maltreatment syndrome, including accusations against others and an overheated fantasy life. Betty acted out and by so doing vented her emotions on her caretakers. Her intractability and hallucinations fit the pattern as well. Who might have abused her? It is impossible to say, but Puritans were no slouches when it came to verbal abuse of each other. When committed by neighbors, these speech crimes were actionable in law, and spouses were brought to court for abusing each other so loudly that neighbors noticed.[25] Under the *Lawes and Liberties* of 1648 it was a felony for children to curse or disobey their parents, but no penalty was attached to verbal abuse of children by their parents.[26] Betty may have been a victim, but the verbal abuse syndrome is not infectious. Of course, its effects can easily be aped, especially by others in similar situations.[27]

Finally, it is possible that the root of the problem was not individual at all but collective. At times, the girls acted as though they were possessed.[28] Possession spreads rapidly through a community, affects women or girls primarily, and reinforces tendencies already present in a particular culture. In Salem Village that winter, surrounded by evil forces, some visible, others invisible, young girls who believed in the existence of demons and witches might easily succumb to possession neuroses. Some of the girls were already emotional tinderboxes, having seen their families destroyed by the visible red demon—the Indian. Future sufferers Sarah Churchill, Mary Watkins, and Mercy Lewis had all been orphaned by Indian raids in their native Maine.[29] Closing their eyes, they could see and hear the horror. Betty, Abigail, and little Ann might have been highly suggestible to such terrors.

Parris finally consulted William Griggs, a new doctor in the neighborhood allied to the Putnams by marriage, and Griggs decided that Betty's illness was not natural. Her pains were the work of the Devil. Unlike the ministers, who counseled one another to be cautious, Dr. Griggs preferred a supernatural explanation. He had much precedent. In the Glover case, which all London watched in 1602, two physicians testified that a child's fits were caused by something supernatural. After Elizabeth Kelley, the nine-year-old daughter of John Kelley of Hartford, Connecticut, died in 1662 under suspicious circumstances, Dr. Bryan Rosseter deposed that the cause of death defied medical knowledge.[30] Rumor had it that Griggs had used this diagnosis before, but he was not the only physician in Essex County to conclude, when his own nostrums failed, that his patient was bewitched.[31] In a deposition against Mary Bradbury, James Carr reported that some twenty years earlier Dr. Crosbe had treated Carr for fits with "visek" (physic) soaked in tobacco, and when that failed, Crosbe told Carr that he was "behaged."[32]

It was common knowledge that witches targeted children. Well over half the indictments against witches in England involved the sickness or death of children. Popular books on witchcraft described how witches used "oil of live infants stolen out of the cradle or dead ones stolen out of their graves" to make an unguent or jelly.[33] Acquitted of charges of witchcraft in 1651, Mary Parsons of Springfield, Massachusetts, acknowledged that she was guilty of infanticide. Her own child, sick and wasting, died in her hands. Neighbors suspected her of bewitching the child, but her act, confessed at last, was not supernatural at all. Nevertheless, when the tale was retold in popular imagination (and later written down by John Hale), it became a proof that the Devil hungered for the soul of the despairing mother so much that he took the form of the dying child to tempt Goody Parsons.[34] The deaths of otherwise healthy babies were attributed to the first Salem witch to be executed, Bridget Bishop. She was seen fourteen years before the Salem crisis in the rooms of infants, at night, after which the infants sickened and died.[35]

Parris was not yet convinced, but Betty grew worse, as did Abigail. Almost beside himself with worry, Parris still listened to his brethren in the ministry, prayed, and waited for some sign. If he read William Perkins, English Puritanism's foremost authority on witchcraft, he would have learned that witches could indeed hurt the innocent, and even the godly were not immune, though all cures came from the Lord. Later English Puritan writers such as John Bernard and John Gaule agreed that everyone was at risk, but the faithful were to put their trust in their Maker. Perkins' warning was echoed by Increase Mather, who reported cases of such affliction in Massachusetts, to which the only cure came from prayer, faith, and seeking protection within the covenant with God. On the scene, Hale told Parris to wait a while longer.[36]

Others were not so patient. Betty's travails had become public knowledge, a sign of greater evils than a small girl's distemper. While Parris fretted and consulted ministers and doctors—members of a professional, elite culture—his near neighbor, Mary Sibley, the mother of another afflicted girl, Mary Walcott, delved into the folklore of countermagic and acted. Neighbors had an obligation to assist one another in time of trouble, particularly when a child's health was at stake.[37] The Sibleys lived at the foot of Thorndike Hill, not a quarter mile from the parsonage. Mary was related by marriage to the Putnams and had been admitted to membership in the Salem Village church under the guidance of Parris in 1690.[38] With her neighbors' sickness unabated by the ministrations of concerned clergy and doctors, Sibley proposed an old English folk remedy to find the unnatural source of Betty's illness that Griggs had diagnosed. Tituba and her husband, Indian John, were asked to bake a rye cake with the urine of the victims and feed it to a hound, supposedly a "familiar" of the witch, an intermediary sent by the Devil to carry out the witches' commands.[39] Taking urine from supposed victims of witchcraft was a common practice in countermagic. The urine might then be bottled or otherwise prepared for testing or even fed to the suspected witch.[40]

Indian John was no baker—Tituba made the cake.[41] In joining in this enterprise, Tituba was entering a "middle ground" with her neighbors, in which her customs and understandings and their very different ways came together. The result was not a synthesis but a kind of pidgin countermagic, for finding or conjuring was regarded as an acceptable response to unnatural events among the English migrants and their descendants. In the notorious Mary Parsons case, both Mary and her husband Hugh were regarded as witches by their neighbors. He was the more quarrelsome partner, threatening those who did not pay him for his work or give him milk and wood when he demanded them. She bedeviled him at home, he averred. When a pudding fell from a bag and appeared to be bewitched at a neighbor's house, one of the men there took a piece and threw it into the fire. The official who took testimony, Justice of the Peace William Pynchon, did not mention the fact that this was countermagic, for the law had no place for folk trickery, but the neighbors expected the witch to appear at their door, summoned by the burning

67

of his or her work. They deposed that Hugh Parsons appeared without warning and for no reason shortly after the pudding was consigned to the flames. If Pynchon never explained why the testimony was relevant, the deponents knew, and undoubtedly so did he.[42] Throwing food associated with a witch into fire would not only identify the witch but harm her. Elizabeth Seager of Hartford was a suspected member of a ring of witches, but proof was hard to establish. The Connecticut court hearing her case admitted evidence that Seager was burned when a piece of a cheese she made was thrown into the fire by a neighbor.[43]

Sibley had crossed a line between being a good neighbor and practicing as a cunning woman, a crossing that brought her uncomfortably close to being a witch, but it was a line that New Englanders regularly crossed. In times of stress, formal religion, with its priests and books of prayers, may not comfort so much as older folk religions. The Puritans were not immune from this power to recall folkways, or rather, because Puritanism itself entailed a set of folkways, Puritans could call upon alternative, coexisting ways of managing life, illness, and death to those instilled by the teachings of their ministers.[44]

The line between medicine and folk cunning was blurred by the way in which "regular" medicine was practiced. Griggs' predecessor in Salem, Dr. Zerobabel Endecott, had in his notebooks a regimen for distraction "in a woman" which rivaled Sibley's recipe: "Tak milk of a Nurce that gives such to a male Child and alse take a hee Catt and cut of one of his Ears or a peece of it and lett it blede into the milk and then lett the sick woman drink it. Do this three times."[45] The prescription might work or not—for contemporaries the important consideration was that such a remedy was the conventional one. In this context, the witchcake was not a drastic departure from orthodox treatment.

Sibley and Tituba assumed that the best remedy to *maleficium* ("harmful magic") was countermagic. Their faith had deep roots in English and New England vernacular culture, as it had in African customs. Among the Yoruba, for example, one went to the *àjé* for help against witches, even though everyone knew that to counter the witch the *àjé* had to have the power of the witch.[46] Folk magic was widely practiced and quietly condoned in early modern England and New England—so long as it achieved a benign purpose,[47] even though the fear of witches literally came over on the first ships that carried English settlers to New England. Sailors nailed horseshoes to the masts when witchcraft menaced the voyage.[48] There were many who practiced divining, folk cures, and other forms of magic in the seventeenth century, in part because many more wanted and paid for such services.[49] Malevolent witches, that is, men and women who were so divorced from the life of the community or so furious at other individuals that they thought they could and actively tried to use their powers to harm others or others' property, also plied their craft. Such miscreants might gather in secret to plot revenge or mischief; contemporaries identified such groups in the forests of Pendle in Lancashire, the fields around Chelmsford in Essex, and the rocky coasts of Devon. Entire matrilineal lines—grandmothers, mothers, daughters, and granddaughters—were accused of witchcraft, to which many confessed.[50]

The broadsides and pamphlets in which these confessions appeared developed a formula to explain witchcraft: the witches were either weak-minded wenches easily misled by the Great Deceiver, or ill-tempered hags who asked the Devil for assistance.[51] The misogyny of the accounts was integral to their popularity. Old women were at risk of accusation at any time, as John Gaule only half joked in 1646: "every old woman with a wrinkled face, a furr'd brow, a hairy lip, a gobber tooth, a squint eye, a squeaking voice, or a scolding tongue . . . and a dog or cat by her side" was not a witch, though the opinion of the common people made them all suspects, for in truth, he opined, "the fittest subjects" for the Devil were "women commonly." Did they not revel in "infirmity, ignorance, impotence of passions and affections, melancholy . . . and vagrant lust"?[52] Richard Baxter, a Puritan divine cited with admiration by New England luminaries such as Increase Mather and Cotton Mather, was even more explicit about the gendered nature of witchcraft: "Lustful, rank girls and young widows that plot for some amorous, procacious design, or have imaginations conquered by lust . . . [there] Satan oft sets in."[53]

As galvanizing and cathartic for some as these rumors of secret gatherings of hags may have been, the stuff of witchcraft suspicion was much more mundane. For every case that came to trial, there were hundreds of rumors that circulated. Everyone knew how witches operated: they cast a spell or sent a familiar (some animal that was given them by Satan and had the Devil's powers), or they breathed on their victim, or cursed, or left something evil behind, or took something with them and used it to bewitch their victim, making a poppet perhaps. They killed and maimed livestock, spoiled cheese and butter, and caused meat to rot. A hard stare from a witch could cripple a cow, maim a horse, or sicken a grown man.[54]

During the pretrial witchcraft hearings in Salem, magistrates warned suspects not to look directly on the accusers, lest the former's evil eye afflict the latter anew.[55] More than one of the accused, confessing guilt, confirmed that they had the evil eye and used it. One may dismiss such fears as mere superstition, but in that time touch, smell, and sight meant more than they do today, in our print-dominated culture. We privilege the written word and the photographic print over the spoken word and the image on the retina, but "individuals in these [premodern] societies [were] 'performers' in the sense of being culturally fluent in speech, gesture, touch, smell, and taste." Thus the "touching test" in which a suspected witch might be forced to cure her victim and the power of the evil eye had the same sensory root. What people saw and felt had immense force as evidence in courts of law.[56]

A case from Salem demonstrated the widespread fear of the evil eye. John Willard, an impatient and often difficult man, stood accused of witchcraft in Salem in the middle of May 1692. Willard's grandfather-in-law, Bray Wilkins, deposed that he had been approached by Willard to join the accused man in prayer when the latter was first accused, but business had kept him from helping. Wilkins had a ready temper; it was he who had led the charge against the Reverend Bayley. In this case, Wilkins felt some guilt, but guilt changed to fear when Willard appeared at lunch and stared hard at Wilkins. The old man left the room for a moment and suddenly felt excruciating pain, "like a man on a rack." He could not urinate or move his bowels. He went to the Reverend Deodat Lawson, who was visiting in Salem, but found no aid, nor did a local woman's "means"—home remedies—help. She was a witch finder, however, and suggested to him that some "ewvil person" had done him harm. She is not named in the deposition—Wilkins protected her identity, for she was using a kind of white magic and might easily have been censured for employing "means" to help him. After three or four days of suffering, neighbors brought Mercy Lewis, one of the girls who had made themselves into witch finders in the village, and Lewis, a seventeen-year-old servant in Thomas Putnam's house, provided the anodyne to Wilkins' fears. According to Wilkins, she saw Willard sitting upon Wilkins' belly. The pain ended only when Willard was in prison, chained.[57]

Wilkins may have suffered from a urinary tract stone, whose symptoms include stoppage of urinary flow, great pain in the abdomen, and bowel spasms, or from something as mundane as an inflamed prostate, which spasmed when Wilkins feared Willard's evil eye. The symptoms returned when neighbors came to plead Willard's cause with Wilkins, after the defendant was convicted, but Wilkins replied that the jurors had not believed mere specters. No, indeed. Willard was found guilty because "the afflicted persons" testified against him, and by those who witnessed Wilkins' grandson Daniel's untimely and inexplicable death after he offended Willard. "About 1/4 hour after this [conversation, I] was taken in the sorest distress and misery my water being turned into real blood, or of a bloody color and the old pain returned excessively as before."[58]

Who were the victims of witches? In the main, they were people like Wilkins, men and women who had wronged the very people they would later accuse of witchcraft, for when the accusers fell ill or lost wealth, or suffered other reverses they could not explain, they remembered whom they had maltreated. And who in reality—not in fevered imagination or angry denunciation—were the accused? Very often they were men and women with long histories of fending off accusations—in effect "the usual suspects." Most often they lived literally and figuratively on the margins of communities. They were contentious and ungrateful for the charity they received. As English communities changed from medieval villages to outposts of European commerce, common land was enclosed, and farmers became day laborers or craftspeople controlled by the whims of foreign markets, accusations against witches grew. Witches, visibly "other" (hence caricatured as hags and routinely searched for "Devil's" marks) became dangerously other. In New England, a similar pattern soon emerged; relatively powerless women were progressively marginalized and simultaneously labeled as suspicious characters.[59]

Another group of potential suspects comprised providers of charms and folk remedies. When such remedies went bad, and when face-to-face dispute resolution failed, the customers who paid for the cures or the potions might conclude that the purveyor was at fault. Thus premodern malpractice became witchcraft. There is some evidence that the practice of countermagic in England and New England was increasing in the seventeenth century, and learned authorities recognized the phenomenon—indeed, one can see an uncanny similarity between the conjuring tricks of the village practitioner and the verbal gymnastics of the wise men of Cambridge and Oxford Universities who wrote learned treatises on the supernatural.[60]

The intimate relations between victims and accused were revealed when cases actually went to court, as neighbors came forward with tales that derived from generations of dealings with the suspect. The pattern in these was repeated enough to make them antitypes of cultural interactions. The accuser may have been guilty about mistreating the accused or worried that the person he or she turned away at the door would seek retribution through magic. As times became harder in England, for example, during the harsh winters of the late 1590s and early 1600s and the civil war era of the 1640s, the breakdown of traditional means of charity led to more guilt and fear, resulting in more suspicious ailments, destruction of property and livestock, and finally, accusations and prosecutions of witchcraft in courts of law.[61] The fact remains that relatively few people ever took their suspicions to court.

72

In part ordinary people did not bring accusations of witchcraft to court in anywhere near the numbers of suspected bewitchings because the laws that criminalized witchcraft did not match folk understandings of the offense. Family and friends wanted justice for harms done, but when the first English statutes were passed, the key issue for the authorities was the suspect's dealings with the Devil. *Maleficium,* or harmful magic, was made a felony by statute in Tudor England in 1542. A more comprehensive act in 1563 required that real harm accompany the act of using magic. In the statute of 1563, using witchcraft to search for lost treasure (treasure trove), or hurting and intending to hurt people or destroy property, was punishable by one year in prison. Dispensing love potions received a similar sentence. Conjuring evil spirits or causing the death of another became capital offenses. Scotland's James VI, personally convinced that witchcraft had been used against him and his wife, wanted stiffer penalties, and a year after he ascended the throne of England as James I in 1603, Parliament obliged. Treasure trove and casting spells intending to cause harm would earn life sentences, and all other witchcraft was punishable by hanging.[62] All of these statutes stressed the criminality of making or seeking to make a pact with the Devil, but actual harm was alleged in all cases that grand juries passed on to trial juries. What grand juries did on a case-by-case basis at the local level John Gaule, who wrote a popular account of witchcraft in 1646, begged the authorities to do as a rule. No court, he wrote, should seek the death penalty unless both the pact with the Devil and real harm could be established.[63]

Grand juries and John Gaule to the contrary notwithstanding, for church and state the *maleficium* was not so important as the pact with the Devil. The pact remained an essential ingredient in the criminalization of witchcraft, for the pact attacked the fundamental tie between the state and its established church. By contracting with the Devil, the witch undermined the state as well as the tenets of Christianity. Supporters of the archbishop of Canterbury in the last years of Elizabeth I's reign accused Puritan healers of secretly reintroducing exorcism, and the victim of demons became the object of religious politics. Puritans replied that the conforming ministers were not taking the Devil seriously enough. Again misogyny became a matter of politics, for the official literature far more than the folk belief indulged in the fantasy that the witch sought an amorous relationship with the Devil. Satan conjured and seduced the lustful widow and the lascivious maiden, just as the church of Rome had tried to seduce the good people of the realm before the Reformation was secure.[64]

Per capita rates of prosecution of witchcraft in England peaked at the end of the sixteenth century, although witchcraft scares periodically erupted in the first half of the seventeenth century. In England, for reasons that cannot be precisely determined, witchcraft became less important to authorities at the end of the seventeenth century. Judges, scientists, and philosophers began to doubt the efficacy of witchcraft. More concerned about science, technology, and manipulating the visible world than the demons and angels of the invisible one, learned elites at the bar and on the pulpit required more probative proofs of causation.[65] The number of accusations remained the same, for the common people clung to the fear of witches, but the number of indictments, convictions, and executions plummeted and then ceased.[66]

In New England, however, witchcraft continued to plague both elite and commoner. The signs of such witchery persisted in written sources and in oral, vernacular ways of looking at the world, and both traditional textual (mostly biblical) and folk beliefs were featured in the popular books of the supernatural. To New Englanders, the witch's intimacy with nature's secrets grew logically from the witch's connections with the animal world. Whether this represented a powerful residue of nature worship in the colonies and the home country, as some English scholars have argued,[67] or was simply a facet of living in a world filled with wild animals, the fact remained that every strange cat, menacing dog, eerie crow, and sinister snake cast the shadow of the witch in the New England imagination.

Take the case of John Godfrey. Godfrey was a herdsman and day laborer who wandered over much of Essex County, Massachusetts, in search of jobs and left behind him an unbroken trail of suspicion, lawsuits, and accusations of witchcraft. On March 13, 1665, Mary and Job Tyler and their two boys swore in court that Godfrey came to the back door of their house with "a thing like a bird . . . the bigness of a blackbird or rather bigger." The very same bird later swooped down upon John Remington Jr. while he was riding and caused his horse to bolt. The bird changed its size and its shape as it attacked the fifteen-year-old boy and his horse and bit his dog. When the boy told the story to Godfrey, the latter laughed and said a cocky boy would always be unhorsed. Godfrey, typically, was in the middle of a quarrel with Remington's father about back pay for herding the latter's cows, a job the father had given to the son. Neighbors were convinced that the black bird was Godfrey's familiar, an imp sent by the Devil to do Godfrey's mischief, or perhaps the Great Demon himself. Godfrey could also change himself into animals, they suspected. Most frightening of his spectral personae was a huge black snake, with great eyes and a gaping maw. Many swore they had seen it. Black snakes can grow as long as six or seven feet, and they are common in fields and barnyards in New England, but this was no ordinary snake, for it had the power to disappear and appear at will.[68]

Godfrey supposedly appeared in spectral form four years after he fought off the accusations of the Remingtons. On April 22, 1669, Elizabeth Button swore before Simon Bradstreet, "About twelve or one o'clock there was a great noise about the house which this deponent took to be the cattle but when she was awake she saw a shape of a man and sit in a great chair and being a great fire near the bed and near the chair within a yard and a half I saw Godfrey sitting and I would fain a struck him but could not put forth my hand." Godfrey came and went as he pleased that night, while Goodwife Button, whose husband had the usual run of dealings with Godfrey, quivered in fright.[69] As Godfrey traveled the length and breadth of the county, stories of his spectral powers followed. He was in and out of Salem, and its residents must have spoken of him often. Though he died a natural death in 1674, his supernatural legacy continued, blended with other stories of apparitions in published collections such as Increase and Cotton Mather's, and had indelibly printed itself upon the folklore of Essex a generation after his death.

In New England, everyone accepted the existence of witches and the efficacy of magic. For some, magic was an underground alternative to religion.[70] A group of quasi-professional fortunetellers and diviners exploited this belief, matching it with their own confidence in their powers. The confessions of the witches at Salem captured a part of this underculture, resisting the dominion of the ministers and rejecting the covenant with God.[71] The healer was vulnerable, of course, when the potion killed instead of cured. Ann Burt of Lynn, Massachusetts, was a cunning woman who gathered herbs and plants from nearby swamps and dispensed remedies. Known to some as the "old witch" of Lynn, she accepted clients from near and far, but when she was unsuccessful, patients and their relatives, as well as a competing physician, testified that she was a witch.[72] Cunning women could resent their being supplanted by others, and patients feared that this malignity of heart might turn the healer into the afflicter. The widow Katherine Harrison helped the ailing Jacob Johnson of Wethersfield, Connecticut, with "diet drink and plasters," a service she performed for others in the town, but when the Johnsons replaced her with Captain Atwood, Harrison appeared to the couple in spectral form and caused her former patient's nose to bleed "in an extraordinary manner" to his dying day.[73]

As in England, unexplained illnesses, particularly of children; the sickness of livestock, always a tremendous concern to New Englanders; and other misfortunes brought on suspicions of witchcraft. The more isolated the community, the more insecure its people, the more ominous such misfortunes loomed. It was inevitable that folk healers who tried to assist the child would be themselves vulnerable for rendering the help. The line was crossed—the helper became a suspect—when dissension and confrontation replaced friendly succor. It was conflict, mischief become malice, argument become feud, dispute become grievance, which led to accusations against someone whose art or cunning had heretofore been trusted.[74]

Such folk beliefs were plastic, subject to manipulation by the malign or the mischievous against the credulous. So George Burroughs of Salem and Casco Bay, Maine, touted his own almost supernatural strength and his ability to hear conversations when he was not present. Neighbors noticed and credited him with special powers.[75] Caleb Powell of Newbury on the coast of Massachusetts told his neighbors that he could find a witch "by his learning," advertising thereby his services.[76] The exploitation of folk beliefs might be more malicious: a believer might be tormented by a neighbor or a relative who was clever enough to conceal himself and his knavery. The victim would be assaulted by day with stones thrown by an assailant in hiding and by night with strange noises, lights, and the rattle of pebbles on a roof. The victim might conclude that he or she was bewitched and, fearing that, become ill or distraught.[77]

The most famous of these inversions of folk credulity by a predator was the haunting of William and Elizabeth Morse, of Newbury, Massachusetts. Grandparents who had grown up in the town and were honored for their virtues, they undertook to rear a grandson, John Stiles. Stiles was evidently a difficult child and may have waged a campaign against his grandparents by tossing pots and pans about the house when they were not looking. Caleb Powell recognized what the child was doing and offered to intercede. Once the lad was taken out of the house, its haunting ended. Unsatisfied, William Morse decided that Powell himself must have magical powers, and he accused Powell of bewitching the child, perhaps fearing that the sailor had alienated the child's affections, taking from the old couple an object of affection (and an aid in their later years). Meanwhile the neighbors, themselves frightened by the entire episode, began to voice suspicions about Elizabeth. Evidently she had a long history of causing harm, or at least being close by when harm occurred. The result was a series of trials, the conviction and for a time the incarceration of Elizabeth, despite William's passionate defense of her innocence. Throughout the episode, witnesses deposed that young Stiles had a mean temper, used foul language, and predicted that he would go to the Devil.[78]

Powell saw the boy playing tricks. The cure was simple: take the boy aside and make him stop. When Mary Warren, a servant in Salem, began to see specters of witches, her master, John Proctor, assayed the same solution as Powell's. As he told Samuel Sibley, a neighbor, at the height of the Salem crisis, Proctor "would his fetch his jade home and thresh the devil out of her." It worked until Warren went off to be with her friends, Mary Walcott, Mercy Lewis, and Elizabeth Hubbard.[79] Children rebelling against a strict religious regimen might concoct among themselves a plot to misbehave and get away with it—if some supernatural agent could be blamed for their misfortunes. Thus the Reverend Joshua Moody, of the First Church of Boston, reported to Increase

Mather the strange behavior of four of Boston stonemason John Good-win's children. They would cry out of sudden pains passing through various portions of their bodies and carry on in chorus. "[But] when the pain is over they eat, drink, walk, play, laugh as at other times [and] they are generally well at night." Moody continued that "physic" did not seem to help.[80] Moody told Mather because he knew that Mather was collecting information on unusual occurrences to continue his essay on illustrious providences. Little did Moody realize that Increase's son Cotton would intervene, examine the children, and conclude that witchcraft was afoot. As a "critical eye-witness" he took Martha Goodwin into his own home and later interviewed in jail the convicted witch, an old Irish washerwoman named Mary Glover.[81] Cotton Mather had none of his father's or Moody's hesitation—the younger Mather was a believer, and the Goodwin children had him fooled even if they were trapped by the success of their enterprise.

Cotton Mather's intervention was for him a viable alternative to folk usages. Divining and curing with spells was not acceptable to the fellowship of ordained ministers. It smacked of using the Devil's tools to catch the Devil. Increase Mather, the dean of Boston's ministerial association, warned against using herbs, fumes, music, blood, urine, and even horseshoes and especially against consulting "white witches," for by employing the Devil's cures, the innocent might be harmed and the victims would not be helped. Brought to the scene, conjured, in this way, the Devil might even take on the appearance of an innocent person and in that person's image torment others.[82] Mather merely repeated the conventional wisdom of the ministry: stay away from "white witches," conjurers, and all who held out cures or countermagic, for such magic could "raise up the Devil" by calling to him. Parris was not told at the time that into his house his servants and his neighbors had brought the pungent odor of folk beliefs. When he learned about the witchcake, he cried out in the church that they had gone to the Devil for help against the Devil, an affront to nature, good order, and God. But at the Lord's Supper on March 27, he forgave Mary Sibley, whose piety excused her ignorance.[83]

Ministers like Parris, Cotton Mather, and his father Increase might inveigh at lecture time against folk beliefs and propose that they, not unlettered cunning folk, act as witch finders, but in fact they were as credulous as their parishioners. The stories of ghosts which made the rounds of porches and parlors—the oral culture   resembled uncannily the stories of ghosts which the Mathers published in popular books of remarkable occurrences. Even the leaders of the fellowship of ministers like the Mathers collected fabulous tales, for they were just as portentous omens of God's plans as outbreaks of smallpox, Indian war, and shipwrecks.[84] The ministers participated in the campaign against witches because the men of God saw the threat that witches posed to the church in terms not accessible to less learned parishioners. The clergy feared the witch who made a pact with the Devil precisely because such a pact undermined the learned ministry. Thus John Davenport of New Haven warned against witches from his pulpit long before Cotton Mather was to make these warnings the centerpiece of his preaching, and minister George Moxon of Springfield accused witches of attacking his children nearly a half century before Samuel Parris came to the same conclusion.[85]

78

The law in Massachusetts favored such popular opinions, for unlike the Witchcraft Statute of James I, the Body of Liberties of 1641, followed by *The Book of General Lawes and Liberties* of 1648, simply stated, "If any man or woman be a witch (that is hath or consulted with a familiar spirit) they shall be put to death."[86] The Massachusetts Court of Assistants that heard these cases may or may not have recognized the limitations of the statute of James I, for Massachusetts cases (until the demise of the first charter in 1684) were heard under the evidentiary regime of the commonwealth's own code: the suspect need only consort with or have a familiar spirit to be culpable. This could be nothing more than an animal of some kind whose behavior could not be explained and whose presence was suspicious. The colonial law thus echoed the Elizabethan and Stuart statutes: the greatest danger of witchcraft was the threat it posed to an established church.

And as in England, local authorities modulated the church/state thrust of the statute by requiring proof of causation and actual harm. New England magistrates refused the code's invitation to hunt for witches or to credit popular mistrust of nasty neighbors. Cases were relatively few in number and isolated in space. Those that did occur were rooted in long-term suspicions against the accused. Each had an history of social dysfunction and frustration, but none led to a witch hunt like the European mass persecutions of the sixteenth century or the Essex County English cases of the 1640s.[87] More often than not, the victims were women and the suspects were women, raising the possibility that witchery and accusations of witchery were the way in which the powerless coped with their situation. Limiting the scope of accusations was the fact that by midcentury, magistrates were taking seriously English admonitions against credulity. They demanded proofs, not presumptions. Accused witches were more often than not acquitted but also warned, for where there was suspicion, there was disorder, and Puritans did not want disorder. The accused witch had caused grief and was to mend her ways. Still, the connection between witchcraft and deviltry which was the essence of the renewal of official persecution of suspected witches in Reformation England retained its force in Puritan New England. Suspected witchcraft was associated with irreligion, and irreligion would not be tolerated. When a suspected witch renounced God, her fate was sealed.[88]

The very marrow of Puritan polity and worship was a covenant with God. Just as had Abraham and his seed, the Puritans saw themselves as entering into a personal contract—a compact—with the Lord. Witchcraft inverted this covenant, for the witch supposedly entered into a compact with Satan. Many of the stories that the confessing witches in Salem trials would tell used the language of covenant or its more mundane cousin, contract.[89] Satan or his agents had approached them. "By way of a friendly conference [witches] are said to bargain with an evil spirit to do what they desire of him." The would-be witch was offered the riches of the world, or, more likely, a suit of fine clothing and other material goods. In return—the essence of contract, a bargained-for exchange—they were to sign the Devil's book. The Devil or his agent insisted on the signing—it made the contract secure against the new witch's backsliding. The Devil gained possession—in law "seisin"—of the signer's soul.[90]

Contract or no contract, the signing of the Devil's book mocked the holy covenant, as the Devil's mass supposedly attended by witches old and new parodied the sacraments. At such malign, inverted gatherings the Devil presided, a combination of popish priest and Antichrist, burlesquing the rite of communion and leading the revelry of his acolytes. Some of the confessions in the Salem trials included descriptions of masses held in fields and meadows throughout the region, attended by witches from all over New England, their numbers exceeding two hundred at times.[91] No one ever saw or heard these assemblies, near riotous affairs if one believes the confessors, except self-admitted witches, making this testimony questionable. None of the confessors volunteered how the participants concealed their activities from prying eyes; indeed, the black sabbaths and other revelry were loud, spirited, and public—a deliberate mockery of both the rituals and the solemnity of the meeting house.

For the magistrates and ministers who collected this evidence, the ridicule of the covenant by the witches and their mentor overturned trusted and safe conventions of life which made worship possible and meaningful. In Europe, common people might mock religious conventions at festivals, but these rituals of inversion were contained by the rules of the festivals during which they occurred. Witches' sabbaths and other demonic inversions were not tolerated on the Continent, in England, or in its colonies.[92]

Here as elsewhere in the witchcraft panic, the book culture of the ministry and the popular or folk culture made common cause, although formulators of the two cultures read the signs of Satan's work differently. The rumors of apparitions and strange animals which circulated with increased frequency during witchcraft scares brought together older men and women and pulled together pieces of experience to create entire narratives of attempted possession or affliction. Ministers recoiled and congregants nodded knowingly in shared apprehension. Such vivid recollections—fantastical or mundane—are common today, the product of "source memory defects." In these events, people mistakenly join memories and dreams, often stored in different parts of the brain, into wholes. Older men and women and younger children are most susceptible to source memory defects, misassembling pieces of information which should have been kept apart. The sources of the images are forgotten, and the new story becomes real to the individual. This physiological process explains how witch stories woven from miscoded memories were readily accepted as true stories of immediate experience.[93] Men remembered awakening at night with witches upon their chests or at their windows.[94] Sleep, a time for recuperation, became the witching hours. Even the "poppet" that the witch supposedly manipulated to cause harm was in other contexts a child's toy—a doll. Witchcraft changed an innocent plaything into a tool to cripple and kill. The inversion was even more painful, for the vileness of the poppet was often directed at children.[95]

The ministers were the colonies' first line of defense against witches in large measure because inversion of the rites of the church challenged the foundations of ministerial authority. Parris, for example, immediately condemned the participants in the witchcake episode for practicing the Devil's craft, but in so doing, he ironically transformed a bit of folklore into a proof that the Devil was at work. The language the young accusers would use, at first rooted in guilt and fear, became the proof that witches were abroad because of the intervention of ministers like John Hale, from neighboring Beverly, and Deodat Lawson, Parris's predecessor in Salem.[96] Unwittingly, ministers, magistrates, and neighbors were becoming the Devil's disciples, close students of his works. Inadvertently, like the bee who spreads pollen in the search for nectar, the leading men became the disseminators of the folk fears of witchery.

And Betty—whose ailment was the beginning of the storm? She grew more ill, and her symptoms grew better defined. So well defined were they that others began to share them. They took on a morphology that was familiar because her adult watchers were the interpreters of her illness. They took the incomprehensible and made sense of it. The witchcake was a crude diagnostic device, meant to determine an external cause, and it failed, but Griggs' despairing conclusion stood. Unintentionally, at least from her perspective, Betty's symptoms would become epidemic among her people.

betty's people

TO WHOM in her affliction could Betty turn? Who were her people? Tituba comforted Betty, later testifying that she "loved Betty,"[1] but her tales and her ways were different, and in times of trouble differences lead to suspicion and accusation. Like the African girls who went to mission schools early in this century, Tituba had learned to bake, to sew, and to pray like the English, but like the mission girls, she remained African.[2] Black slaves in Puritan households had to live in a twilight world, neither theirs nor their masters'.[3] Her language was English, not Bajan Creole, and she wore the dress of a servant, but like so many other slaves in New England, she apparently retained a sense of being different and a distinct identity. She was evidently not a Christian—at least not a full member of the church, despite being part of Parris's household for more than a decade. Unlike slaves in more southern climes, she could not retire to the slave quarters and be safe among her kind.

There was a middle ground, of course, for daily contact required negotiation and accommodation. Tituba's participation in the English folk remedy occurred on that middle ground. To the Puritans who participated, the cake had a familiar look and texture; to Tituba, its purpose was not so evident, but she indulged the white folk to save Betty from some force outside nature. All participated in a ritual to which they assigned different meanings.[4] There were other slaves in Salem, Mary Black and Candy, for example, and their otherness would make them targets of accusations later in the crisis. For now, Tituba had become the center of attention; she had become "the other."

Ironically and ultimately sadly for her, by participating in the episode, Tituba became more Indian in her masters' eyes, for the Puritans associated Native Americans with magic. From England, Richard Baxter reported with complete confidence that the Indians were worshipers of the Devil, and the "tawny" Indian became the icon of the Devil in times of conflict between Native American and European.[5] When her New Haven neighbors suspected the widow Elizabeth Godman of witchcraft, they mocked that her husband was "Hobbammock," the manitou or spirit respected by the Algonkin of southern New England.[6] Indian shamans were suspected of using sorcery to silence the farmers' watchdogs during King Philip's War.[7] In his treatise on wondrous prodigies and ominous events, Cotton Mather credulously reported cases of Native American magicians transforming themselves into animals. Mercy Short, of Salem, just released from Indian captivity, reported to Mather the Devil was "of a tawney, or an Indian color."[8] Tituba was transforming herself in the imaginations of her neighbors—becoming an Indian magician, and when that magic summoned the Devil, a witch.[9]

Betty's father cared for her in her illness, but fathers and daughters had complex emotional relationships. Girls Betty's age begin to gravitate toward the father to loosen the smothering maternal bond. The mother is not supplanted as the primary caretaker, but she gains a rival.[10] Samuel may not have seen this coming—his attention was otherwise engaged, and he was not the most sensitive person in any case—but in subtle ways Betty may have found her way to his side as little mother. If Samuel Parris resembled other Puritan divines whose diaries and sermons on child rearing have survived, he was concerned yet demanding. Parris's predecessor in the Salem Village pulpit, Deodat Lawson, warned his readers against overfamiliarity between parents and children.[11] Such fathers doled out love as a reward for obedience, dictated lifestyles to their children, and warned of parental and divine displeasure for those who disobeyed.[12]

Parris no doubt prayed with his girls, taught them to read and write, worried about their prospects, and in turn received deference from them.[13] They rose when he entered and sought his blessing, waited until he was done eating before eating themselves, uncovered their heads in his presence, and, hardest of all, tried to live up to his expectations for them. But what could these be? He could not ask his daughter to follow him into the world of commerce or into the ministry. Though a clergyman by calling, Parris was also a farmer. The village committee had deeded him land, and he must have spent part of his time working it. His son helped him in the fields, and daughters had farm chores of their own, closer to the house. If Parris resembled other Essex County farmers, his sense of patriarchal authority and paternal obligation was strong.[14] He kept the children close at hand to utilize their labor fully, because his "capital" was more human than material. They were the most valuable things he had in the world, but daughters were valuable in different ways than sons.

Parris anticipated that Betty would become a wife and mother, for which polite manuals decreed the virtues of modesty, compliance, and deference—in all, inoffensive invisibility.[15] Law joined literary prescription to confine women. Married, they were "covered" by their husband's authority.[16] Single or widowed they might act with more freedom, and young women found ways to exercise their autonomy within the limited sphere of a woman's place.[17] The ideal of the Puritan mother and wife still loomed above Salem's girls, however. Even in the terrors of the witchcraft trials, older defendants like Mary Bradbury depended upon their reputations as loving and faithful helpmeets to their spouses and diligent and industrious child rearers, whose prudence and cheerfulness persisted despite old age and weakness.[18] As far as Samuel Parris was concerned, Betty's life was laid out for her.

All the more reason why Betty's illness strained the father-daughter bond. Sick children, particularly children who do not respond to the ministrations of doctors, cause parents to doubt themselves. They begin to wonder if there was something they could have done to prevent the illness: if only they had acted sooner, or not come to that place and exposed the children to the contagion. They also sense a loss of authority which goes with the helplessness. Samuel and Elizabeth Parris had not surrendered to their doubts or their exhaustion, but they teetered at their wits' end, and such a precarious state of mind allows fearsome specters to enter unbidden. The fear of witchcraft was one.[19]

With her mother, Betty had a far stronger and more complex relationship than with her father. The mother-daughter bond constrains and liberates, chafes and nurtures. Girls talk, work, fight, and cry with

84

their mothers. With some exceptions (like witches, who were always assumed to be bad mothers), Puritan mothers loved their children and lamented bitterly their passing:

> No sooner come, but gone, and fal'n asleep,
> Acquaintance short, yet parting caus'd us weep.
>
> . . . .
>
> He will return, and make up all our losses,
> And smile again, after our bitter crosses.
> Go pretty babe, go rest with Sisters twain
> Among the blest in endless joyes remain.[20]

Mothers cared for children through illness and health, and for their girls, a mother's caring was the best tutor.[21]

In her effort to befriend Betty in her illness, Elizabeth Parris Sr. was not alone. Although a newcomer to the village, she was soon surrounded by a literal and figurative circle of other women who visited, comforted, helped, and shared information. The boundaries of the woman's world rarely extended beyond home and garden, but visiting stretched the bounds. Pathways through meadows to friends' houses and the cart track to the village center were never empty, for social courtesy was more than a pastime; it was an occupation. Women gathered in parlors and on porches to exchange information, gossip, or simply sit with one another. Even when one of their number was confined in jail on the eve of doom, neighbors arrived to provide moral support.[22]

When a woman went into labor, or "travail" as it was called, other women rallied to reassure the mother during delivery, and examine the infant after it was safely born, all the while offering remedies, assessments, and predictions.[23] On these occasions the authority of women over women's lives asserted itself, for although ministers and doctors as well as male members of the family shuffled about nearby, women dominated the scene. The midwife, invariably a woman, for doctors were not yet the captains of the delivery room, plied her craft, easing the delivery and dispensing medicines. Some midwives' fame spread for miles around, and their practices covered many towns and villages. Midwives had to swear on oath that they would use no magic, charm, sorcery, or invocation, but some plainly did. There were few accusations against these women for witchcraft, however, for without them, the circle of women would be incomplete.[24]

Whether she was at home or visiting, the New England mother kept busy, and daughters learned weaving, soap making, and livestock care.[25] Home industries were never quite self-sufficient, however, and it was not until the 1670s that textile production became at all significant.[26] For women as well as men, thus, Salem town became a magnet. The shops and stores along Main Street promised glittering relief from the drudgery of farm chores. In economic terms, the town served as a marketplace, the precursor of a true market system.[27] From their mothers and older sisters young Puritan girls learned consumer behavior, their preferences leading local merchants to stock goods from England, Europe, and the West Indies.[28] Such consumerism might, as a general phenomenon, only gradually have matured into a modern market system, but in individual cases it caused immediate friction and envy among those who could not afford to buy what others had. One of Satan's most powerful inducements, according to those who confessed to making a pact with him, was the offer of brightly colored clothing and pocket money to those who had neither.[29]

At home, many of the good wife's tasks revolved around food preparation.[30] One essential measure of neighborliness in women was the sharing of food. Even during travail, the mother of the childbearer was expected to provide refreshments for the attendants and the midwife.[31] A homemaker who would not furnish a passing neighbor with a drink of buttermilk showed bad manners, even if the passerby was a suspected witch. Goodwife Ball of New Haven denied the widow Godman a drink, recognizing the breach of courtesy. When the Balls' pigs and cow fell ill, Goodman Ball reasoned that Godman had taken revenge for his wife's action.[32]

Of course, not every insult resulted in such dire consequences, but sharing was a rule, and tools, clothing, and food made the rounds of every village's farmhouses.[33] To deny a neighbor a place in these exchanges was an palpable social offense. Girls in the household watching their mother discharge, or on occasion intentionally refuse to fulfill, social duties could hardly miss the message. The good wife was a good neighbor, and if she excluded suspected witches from the circle of exchange, she did so conceding that the witch had grounds for retaliation.[34]

When the poor of the village came to the door, the duty of succor went beyond neighborliness. Christian charity was a living ideal in these villages, and the poor depended upon it.[35] Although the number of "strolling poor" rose at the end of the century, and even though Puritanism did not celebrate poverty, leading Puritans nevertheless committed themselves to help those not able to help themselves.[36] The giving of charity was reciprocal, not unilateral, for the poorest in the community would sit with children when they were ill and parents had commitments. Poverty might also be part of the life course of neighbors, a period of hard times through which they were passing, and charity given might one day be returned the next. Widows like Elizabeth Godman might move in and out of this group. Sarah Good of Salem Village was an inveterate beggar, but she violated the rules of mendicancy when, denied the full measure of her requests, she went away muttering curses.[37]

Girls also learned proper (and sometimes improper) sexual conduct from their mothers. The Puritans did not frown upon sexual intercourse within marriage and allowed unmarried men and women who engaged in sex to remedy their misconduct with marriage vows. Indeed, fornication was, next to drunkenness, the most common offense that came before the county court. In September 1680, for example, John Ring and Martha Lampson of Salisbury stood in court for having a child out of wedlock, or so testified the midwife, Sarah Rowill. If they agreed to be wed "before noon" that day, however, their fine would be reduced and the usual corporal punishment set aside.[38]

Husbands could demand sexual union with their wives, but modesty muted those demands. Public kissing was permitted. No one expected privacy, and a household filled with boarders, kin, and servants exposed the older girls in it to unwanted caresses, lascivious looks, and persistent importunities to "uncleanness." Men imposed upon women, who sometimes but not always needed the protection of other men. The ultimate resort was to the justices of the peace and the courts, but long before that women talked among themselves, and rumor, with its attendant effect upon a man's reputation, might be enough to deter him from pleading his case too hard, although men got away with a good deal.[39]

The woman who wished to press her attentions upon a man was no less common but violated even more basic understandings of society. She invited obloquy that the promiscuous male could evade.[40] Accusations against some suspected witches had sexual structure, if not explicit sexual content. For example, many of the middle-aged male deponents in Bridget Bishop's case recalled that years earlier she had appeared to them while they slept, and stood or lay on them in their beds. She was thirty-eight years old when accused and must have been in her middle twenties when she made her appearance in their rooms. Both William Stacy and John Louder testified that they had met Bishop, and when they rebuffed her, she tormented them in the nighttime by sitting on their chests.[41]

From her mother and her mother's circle Betty had begun to learn what was expected of her, but only nine years old, Betty had before her a long passage from the openness of childhood to the subtleties of adulthood. At nine or ten, girls gained their own identity in the records of court and town—a name of their own, and responsibilities as well. Nevertheless, the gap between childhood and adulthood yawned perilously deep. For girls, its traverse absorbed all their energies, for they had to learn to hold up a face to the world which matched what they were expected to be, while concealing their own feelings. For some girls, the passage was fraught with betrayal and uncertainty, causing them emotional and physical pain.[42]

In times of psychic crisis like these, Puritans urged self-confession on one another, for they believed that the unregenerate soul punished itself. Self-confession might reveal the springs of sinfulness and enable the confessor to return to the right path. Self-confession for the girls only increased the terrors of approaching adolescence, however, for to them role expectations, bodies, and feelings were all changing simultaneously. In effect, they had no sure, safe place to stand, no fixed identity, when they examined themselves for signs of sin. Relationships that were once crystal clear to them were becoming far more complex, and the stories they told about themselves and others were transformed accordingly.[43]

For teenagers, the social and psychological process was even more intense and problematic. Adolescence came later then than it does now, but moderns did not invent adolescence,[44] nor was it limited to sexual maturation. Rather, adolescence's onset then as now was the struggle to redefine relationships. The adolescent wants herself to be separate from parents yet accepted and loved by them. To this end, without fully comprehending the means of her redemption, she may suddenly take ill, or revel in bad temper and sullenness, or act out aggressive fantasies. She may "behave outrageously in order to get a sharp response—no matter that the response is a protest. . . . [The] battles for her mother's support and admiration are frequently too bizarre to reveal their aims."[45] Thus the older teenage girls who entered the ring of accusers later—Lewis, Elizabeth Hubbard, Susannah Shelton, Mary Walcott, Sarah Churchill, and Mary Warren—joined in the discovery of witches for different reasons than those motivating the younger girls.[46]

For all of the girls the maternal bond was crucial—the girls were changing, and something of their afflictions grew from their demand that their mothers recognize those changes. Betty and Ann Putnam Jr. involved their mothers directly, for it was the parents who finally took action, bringing charges to the magistrates of the town against those suspected of witchcraft. Ann Putnam Sr. was attacked by the same witches as her daughter.[47] Other girls, notably Abigail Williams, Mercy Lewis, Mary Warren, and Elizabeth Hubbard, like Elizabeth Knapp a generation before, did not have mothers close at hand. They reached out to surrogates but had, in the end, other reasons for accusing witches of attacking. Nevertheless, without the parents—the Putnams, Walcotts, and others—the girls' behavior would not have resulted in any legal action. The parents' sudden intervention suggests that they feared losing their children. Ironically, the accusations bonded children to parents and parents to children—the closer tie that some of the girls may have sought.

Betty had people closer to her own age than Tituba or her father and mother, however, and the friendship among these youngsters provided the critical context for Betty's illness and her later accusations. Betty played with Abigail Williams, her cousin, who shared the house, and the girls practiced some fortunetelling. Alone, neither might have sought the aid of the cunning arts, but together they looked into a cup filled with milk and egg to find out who they might marry (the most important subject in their lives) and there, the story goes, saw a coffin that terrified them.[48] Soon after, both Betty and Abigail fell ill. The coffin symbolized death, but Abigail had seen coffins, and so had Betty. Death was very near all these girls. King William's War had made Salem a haven for refugees from French and Indian raids. Such a raid had carried off the parents and siblings of other girls their age. Epidemic diseases such as smallpox and typhoid regularly slaughtered the young. The Puritans had learned to prepare their children for death; indeed, they harped on the nearness of it.[49] To the girls, it was not the coffin itself that affrighted but the realization that they had violated Parris's rules for the godly. For the unregenerate, hideous death waited, and the coffin suddenly turned a game into the sternest of admonitions. They had played with the Devil's tools, and Parris had told them that the Devil was always waiting to trap the unwary and the unregenerate. The pinches they felt thereafter anticipated both the appearance of a demon hungry for their souls and an adult angry at their transgressions. Corporal punishment of the child in Puritan households was common, and often the punishment for girls was pinching.[50] This, coupled with the admonitions against misconduct, the parental admonition that witches would get them if they misbehaved, and their knowledge that they were using a form of witchcraft, led them to believe that they were bewitched. Again, there is no surprise here. One modern psychotherapist recently admitted, "At the age of thirteen I awoke from the long dream of childhood and was certain that I was a witch," for suddenly she could understand what had been mysterious to her before.[51]

Betty and Abigail played with other girls in the neighborhood, and these playmates must have been curious about the two little girls' sudden illness. Down the road a mile lived Sergeant Thomas and Ann Putnam, with little, bright Ann Jr. and Mercy Lewis, their servant. Nearer still were Elizabeth Hubbard, the niece of Dr. Griggs, who was also his maid; Mary Walcott, the daughter of Parris's neighbor and brother-in-law Jonathan; and John Proctor's servant Mary Warren.[52] The illness soon fashioned a crude ring around the girls in unintended parody of the domestic circle their mothers and aunts formed.

The number of afflicted would grow, but these seven remained the core. They knew one another, and their relations were framed in part by their social status, although the social hierarchy was truncated at the top. Betty and Ann Putnam occupied the highest rank, but they were the youngest of the group, and, even more important, neither a minister's child nor a well-to-do farmer's daughter could be sure that she would remain above other children in status. Abigail Williams and Mercy Lewis were servants in the Parris and Putnam households respectively, but domestic service was often part of the life course—the natural cycle of life—of a Puritan girl, and she might make a good marriage withal.[53] The friendships were fairly new (Betty and Abigail had moved into the neighborhood only a few years before) and made somewhat uneasy by the difference in circumstances of the girls, but as with the entire white, free population of the village, there was not much social distance within the young circle of friends.[54]

The record shows that none of the girls could sign her name. It is likely (but not certain, for some could read who could not write) that they were not avid readers.[55] None of the girls attended a common or dame school regularly, either, although colonial law mandated town schools and children were supposed to attend. Religious instruction presupposed the ability to read the catechism.[56] Salem Village did not have a school (the school was in Salem town), but Parris's duties included religious instruction of the children. For children at home, instruction was left to parents, and these parents were busy. Servant girls did not get such instruction, except, with all the other church members, through the teachings of the minister. Thus the girls' interactions were dominated by conversations in which stories must have been shared, embroidered, tested, and expanded as individual girls used anecdote and yarn to establish their places. Such friendships involve fantasy, secret sharing, and periodic overt tests of loyalty.

The girls felt uneasy when speaking to parents and ministers, but among themselves they could speak freely and, even more important, let their imaginations, and their storytelling skills, range freely. Tales of witchery and omens, danger and heroism came down from the forests and the frontier and titillated the girls that winter of 1691–92; the group performances these girls later put on during the examinations of Martha Cory, Rebecca Nurse, and others merely expanded upon the secret sharing they had perfected weeks and months earlier. The stories they told the adults lack the freshness and innocence of the fantasies they conjured up for one another—a shame that we have only the dry legal record of the pale public imitation of what must have been vividly hued private tête-à-tête.

There is a more disturbing possibility about the initial causes of the girls' distress which cannot be proven conclusively but should be considered. The abuse of children by adults in their household is too well documented now to be ignored, particularly when the victims begin to act out aggressive fantasies or show other common symptoms such as "excessive blaming and humiliation, frightening accusations, and name-calling."[57] Abuse of children and servants was common, if not epidemic, in the Massachusetts colony, as was sexual activity among servants and masters. Few cases of sexual abuse were heard by courts, but depositions in those cases suggest that the offense was far more common than anyone admitted in public. Often, servants or dependents only sought the protection of the magistrates after repeated incidents of abuse. What is more, the cases that were prosecuted came to the attention of authorities by chance, a bystander or friend informing the court that the abuse had occurred.[58] The anxiety, compulsiveness, and dissociative quality of the girls' testimony at times resemble the testimony in modern child abuse cases. Often, these involve a pattern of abuse which extends over time and includes a number of children.

What makes truth and fantasy in all these cases difficult to access for professional and lay people in the community is that the same investigatory process that reveals the hidden crime may induce false accusations. In child abuse cases, anxious parents, or if the parents themselves are accused, school, church, and civil authorities, may so prompt and otherwise give cues to the putative victims that the accusations become a product of the inquisitor's coaching. Single incidents of no real import may be altered in the child's mind, either through confabulation or through the desire to please questioners, into detailed accounts of abuse.[59] When unofficial interrogators have a clear conception of a crime in their own minds, they will very often press a child past denials and mumbled or nodded agreement to positive confirmations of the offense. The stronger the interrogator's belief, the more he or she will demand attestation from the child, and the more likely the child, especially a suggestible one, will be to provide that testimony.[60]

Were words put in the girls' mouths? That is the problem of evidence in modern child abuse cases, and it is very similar—despite the whole panoply of procedural safeguards and professional experts we have today—to the problem the parents and ministers faced in Salem. Recently a gifted British case worker summarized the stories she was told by abused children: "These children have touched me deeply and my life is richer for it. The metaphor is their metaphor, the imagery is their imagery, and the power of the individual human experience, albeit once removed *never fails* [italics added], I find, to create an impact. In a search for meaning and understanding we have tended to create a structure top-heavy, laden with theoretical constraints, some of questionable relevance. Procedures and guidelines for agencies involved in child protection work are clearly essential, but if framed in a general context of denial the risk must surely be that they prove ineffective and inoperable."[61] The problem with this moving account is that one does not hear the child's voice; one hears the voice of the interrogator, and it sorts and orders what might be other forms of mental anguish into evidence of the consequences of child abuse.

It is irresponsible to compare dedicated child welfare professionals working with abused children to a Matthew Hopkins, the infamous Essex, England, witch hunter of the 1640s, yet magistrates and jurors believed his reconstruction of the evidence of victimization and witchery.[62] Modern authorities are not immune to the same mistake. In a series of recent cases, grown women under a therapist's care have "recovered" memories of their molestation by other family members. Jurors and judges cannot decide how to evaluate these retrieved memories of past abuse.[63]

Some recovered memories have led to criminal prosecutions. In 1988, Richard Ofshe, a social psychology professor from the University of California at Berkeley, was called to the scene of a case of suspected satanic abuse of children in Olympia, Washington. He interviewed the girls whose accusations against their father had spiraled into a felony prosecution and concluded that the older girl was a "habitual liar" and her younger sister had followed "her lead." Ofshe doubted whether the girls had ever desired that their charges become public, but when they had, "the sisters pasted over the inconsistencies in their original accusations with ever more fanciful claims. The whole misadventure [which included charges of murder of infants in witchcraft rites] was a kind of mass folly—something that would be suitable mainly for folklorists [or students of the Salem cases] if it were not that innocent people's lives were being crushed. . . . When Ofshe left Olympia, he was convinced that a new Salem was in the making. The witch trials, he believed, were about to begin."[64]

Ofshe may have been right in his case, but in others trained observers have concluded that abuse was present, and it may be that the root cause of some of the older serving girls' discomfiture was sexual molestation. The language with which some male masters verbally abused their female servants in Salem bristles with sexual asymmetry. John Proctor, for example, publicly derogated his servant, Mary Warren, as "his Jade," a slang insult roughly interchangeable with "hussy."[65] In contemporary cases of premarital sexual advances and pregnancies, parents sometimes offered to forgive the sin if the young man offered to marry the daughter, but what was the psychological effect of unwanted sexual advances on the young servant girl who had no kin to protect her?

There is no incontrovertible evidence anywhere in the Salem witchcraft records to substantiate a charge of sexual abuse, but there are hints in the testimony of one of the accusers—indeed, the most vigorous of them—that she feared what appeared to her to be sexual advances. Mercy Lewis lost her parents in an Indian raid on Falmouth on Casco Bay, Maine, in 1689, and was taken into the household of the Reverend George Burroughs.[66] Shortly thereafter, she came to live with the Sergeant Thomas Putnams, the family whose patriarch had led the fight not to pay Burroughs his back salary in a contested court battle and lost.[67] Burroughs harbored no grudge, never dunning the town for the missing funds, but the Putnams evidently planned to add infamy to injury. Putnam clan leaders Thomas Putnam and Jonathan Walcott brought complaint against Burroughs on April 30, 1692, for witchcraft. Mercy Lewis was one of his supposed victims, and she joined her name to the list of complainants.[68]

On May 7, 1692, Lewis later told a grand jury, Burroughs' apparition appeared and sorely tempted her. Unlike others, who testified to Burroughs' uncanny strength and conjuring tricks and his supposed involvement in his two previous wives' deaths, Lewis struck a personal note. Burroughs, she swore, had tried to trick her into signing the Devil's book, calling it a "fashion book." Had he tried to tempt her with a gown, something her parents' death denied her? Deponents in this case and other cases described the book as the Devil's ledger, but not Lewis. He persisted, she demurred. "I have often been in his study but I never saw that book there," she told the magistrates. She then recalled what had happened two days later: "[Burroughs] carried me up to an exceeding high mountain and shewed me all the kingdoms of the earth and tould me that he would give them all to me if I would writ in his book and if I would not he would thro me down and brake my neck."[69]

The imagery is again compelling and distinct from the common charges. Other deponents testified that the Devil or the black man had promised them powers or trinkets or that another witch had carried them into the air, but never to the top of a mountain and never to ecstasy. The resemblance to Matt. 4:8 cannot be ignored; Lewis adapted the basic story line: the Devil carried Jesus to the mountaintop and offered Him the riches of the world should He but consent to pay homage to the Evil One. Begone, Satan, Jesus replied, and so said Mercy Lewis. But why did she borrow this imagery? Surely she had heard it at sermon time, but unlike other passages in Scripture, it resonated for her because it helped her organize her memories. At first blush, one might regard this as another case of "miscoded memory," for Burroughs had not carried her to the top of a mountain. Yet Burroughs, twice widowed, might have made some kind of sexual advance to fourteen-year-old Mercy, which she recalled, suddenly, or perhaps she had finally decided to say aloud what had troubled her for years. The language is allegorical, Mercy merging what she remembered with her own dark fears, but the structure of promise and threat is common and well documented in sexual abuse cases. The threat includes punishment for revealing the advances as well as resisting them. Mercy recalled that she replied to him, "I would not writ if he had throwed me down on 100 pitchforks."[70] Again the language is hers and reflects her fear of a man whose physical prowess amazed many. Lewis had a wonderfully vivid imagination and perhaps a growing attachment to Scripture, but the sexual connotation of the pitchforks cannot be dismissed out of hand. In her equally compelling denunciation of George Jacobs Sr., another older man with a randy reputation, she recalled him beating her with sticks to make her sign his copy of the Devil's book.[71]

Had Burroughs made unwanted sexual advances to Mercy Lewis? His wife had died, but he had remarried and had children. In documented—that is, explicitly identified—cases of "uncleanness," men did offer clothing and jewelry as compensation or inducement.[72] In shops in Salem town, toys and combs, laces and ribbons, were prominently displayed.[73] How attractive they must have been to servant girls living in rustic abstinence. Girls talked about boys and toys constantly. Lewis did not accuse Burroughs of lascivious conduct, however. One may infer it from the distinctive language she used to describe his attempt at demonic seduction, although the biblical reference may be no more than that.

It is incontrovertibly clear that Lewis was angry, and sometimes spite motivates accusations of sexual abuse. On May 9, 1994, a group of nine-year-old girls in a Chicago public school, angry at a substitute teacher, agreed to accuse him of fondling them. The ringleader promised to pay each of the accusers one dollar. What struck authorities as frightening was the ability of the girls to pull together their stories and link their accusations to the conventional evidentiary standard for adult sexual abuse of minors. In fact, all public schools tell children to report unwanted touching, in effect simultaneously teaching a child how to protect herself against abuse and tutoring an angry or frustrated child how to make a false accusation. In similar fashion, the common knowledge about witches and witchcraft available to the girls in Salem which might have provided cues on how to structure accusations could also have fooled observers. In the Chicago case, police were able to find inconsistencies in the children's stories, which led them to suspect a plot. When confronted with the suspicions of the adults, several children confessed to the lie, just as Ann Putnam Jr. did, in 1706.[74]

Even after they accused their neighbors by name of the terrible crime of witchcraft, the girls might not have realized the severity of their conduct. Angry neighbors often accused one another of being Satan's toads or wished that someone would go to the Devil, and nothing official happened to the accuser or the accused. There had been no trials for witchcraft in their neighborhood in their lifetimes. In Boston, four years earlier, Mary Glover went to the gallows for bewitching the children of John Goodwin, and adults in Salem knew the story well, but Salem was far from Boston, and the girls could not have grasped how well they mimicked Goodwin's young ones. The girls understood that witchcraft was a horrid crime whose punishment was death, but they had never seen a hanging for it. So was false accusation a dreadful crime, as their ministers and parents reminded them. It too was punishable by death under the old charter, but this dire fate did not deter them. They spun out fantasy, and fantasy so enveloped them that consequences were lost in the fog.

Nor did their minister press them to recant. When a parishioner was suspected of lying, ministers were supposed to inquire, counsel, and arrange for public apology.[75] Such lying had a devastating effect on those it injured and on those who told the lie. John Hale, Parris's counterpart in Beverly, recalled one case that should have taught everyone a lesson (though he recalled it five years too late): when a Watertown, Massachusetts, nurse told a lie that resulted in another woman being accused of witchcraft, God punished the liar. Jailed for her own adultery, the nurse delivered her baseborn child, but it died before she could suckle it. In Beverly, Hale himself cross-examined one of the witnesses against George Burroughs, demanding that the witness recant if anything she said was untrue, for bearing false witness was an unpardonable sin. The witness avowed that she had indeed seen Burroughs presiding over a Devil's sabbath in the village.[76] Parris had an affirmative duty to warn the girls that they must not lie. Still, they persisted and he did not curb them. Indeed, he abetted them once they had gone public.[77] The dynamics of their later accusations, with the almost choreographed displays of bite marks, pin pricks, and body movements, suggest that for some of them, panic was slowly being replaced by another emotion, a sense of exhilaration at the control they had gained over all the adults whose authority, until then, had been unquestionable.

What had begun in playful terror, the same sort of simulated horror which modern teenagers experience—indeed, seek to experience—at amusement parks and in movie theaters, became something else. Nineteenth-century historians such as Charles Upham thought that the girls were shamming or using tricks. Upham based his diagnosis upon nine-teenth-century ideas of rationality—there were no devils or witches, so the girls could not see what they said they saw.[78] The girls' parents could have reached the same conclusion, if they wanted to repudiate the sto-ries of their own children. Seventeenth-century English books and pam-phlets documented occasions when children, to excuse themselves from some malfeasance, claimed that witches were the cause.[79] Exposing the feigning witch had become an important alternative to exorcism in Eng-land; even King James tried his hand at it. By the end of the seventeenth century, assize court judges such as Francis North and John Holt tried to force accusers to admit that they had fabricated their stories of woe.[80] Puritan literature warned of the signs of such feigning in children: lying, profanity, truancy, and playing games; but the same literature saw the virtue of children who awakened from their vices to seek grace. Thus the unruly child was potentially the vessel of God's message to all.[81]

If the girls began as mischievous innocents, they soon had turned themselves from a circle of friends into what modern observers might equate with a gang of juvenile delinquents.[82] The subject of delinquency remains intractable to its students, but researchers agree that child abuse and delinquency are strongly linked, as are missing parents and delin-quency.[83] Such groups were not unknown in Puritan Massachusetts, but only bits and pieces of their function and structure come to light in the court records. Such gangs attract young people who are disaffected from the mores of their elders, and in the 1680s ministers and magistrates moaned that their children lacked the piety and purpose that marked the founders' generation. Young people mocked the values and virtues of their parents, wore their hair too long, walked unescorted at night, danced in public places, and mingled indiscriminately with servants, Indians, and members of the opposite sex. The Puritans had discovered juvenile delinquency in their midst and were appalled.[84]

Perhaps the Salem girls had no leader, or rather, leadership shifted from one to another of the girls. "Diffuse" packs of adolescents and near adolescents are more common than structured gangs. "Such groups have a regular nucleus, but rarely possess a leader or exert control over mem-bership." The line separating the diffuse pack from the general popula-tion is almost invisible in real life. One may liken it to a membrane through which individuals may pass at will. Those in the pack share romance, fantasy, and excitement—indeed, they may pose for one another tests just like those the girls created when they took turns describing the witches' spectral flights.[85]

There are still a number of missing pieces in this already puzzling picture. Even assuming the aptness of the gang metaphor—and it is no more than a metaphor—gangs flourish in gang-friendly environments. New gangs form from fragments of older gangs or by copying existing gangs. There is little evidence of widespread gang activity in Salem. To be sure, cliques of girls can be found everywhere. Such cliques were common in American public schools in the 1950s and 1960s, for example, and their activities included malicious mischief of all sorts, including false accusations of other girls. Female auxiliaries are common in modern American urban gangs. The essence of these groups is the heterosexual nature of the setting—the attraction of young men and women for each other.[86] In late-seventeenth-century New England, young men and women, often servants or apprentices, congregated together and sometimes committed misdemeanors that grew out of sexual attraction. They drank wine and beer and showed off or teased each other. Among the young people could be found offspring of some of the best families, as well as representatives of the lower classes.[87] The biggest missing piece in the gang story is thus the absence of any evidence of such heterosexual behavior among the girls. They seem to have kept to themselves.

Once constituted, the Salem girls developed their own ranking system. Packs and gangs have hierarchies that are internal as well as external, and often the two do not match.[88] Nine-year-old Betty and eleven-year-old Abigail and Ann could not lead the older girls. Mary Warren was old enough to lead, but she was an unwilling participant in the activities of the accusers and later attempted to recant her testimony. In the process, she intimated that she feared the other girls, an unlikely admission for a leader. Hubbard, Walcott, and Sheldon were in their late teens, but they were not the leaders, for if one examines their testimony in the pretrial hearings, one finds it imitative and uninventive. If the stories the girls told in public grew out of the tales they told one another, the three teenagers could not have been leaders. They followed what others said, confirming it. What is more, Sheldon and Hubbard were not always part of the indictments, unlike Putnam and Williams and one other girl—Mercy Lewis.

Lewis was old enough to influence the others; indeed, she may have brought Putnam into the circle. A servant, she had to be out and about more than the younger girls. More important, unlike the other girls, she was traveled, and her travels were painful ones, for she ran from the memory of dying parents, burning houses, and screaming infants. Such experiences can alienate a child, leaving a sense of anger and betrayal in their wake. Such feelings may have reinforced Lewis's lack of belonging in the community where she labored. Finally, there was her testimony. Of all the girls, she was far and away the most forceful, imaginative, and compelling in her accusations.

To continue in existence, an important motive for all pack and gang members, the girls had to find ways to conform their activities to the mores of the community. No gang or pack can survive without at least passive acquiescence from those in authority. The girls' witchcraft accusations gave many in Salem a chance to affirm that something was wrong with their lives and someone or something was to blame. In more complex ways, the entire process of seeking out witches enabled the community to restate its moral boundaries.[89] The ferreting out of suspected deviants not only kept the Devil at bay but also brought people together in cathartic rituals of self-scourging, at least so long as villagers believed what the girls said.[90] Not just to gain attention for themselves, not anymore, but to keep their group in being, they named witches and acted out the afflictions of the bewitched.

When they denounced witches, they were generally careful to name men and women who were not near neighbors. They did not find witches in the village center, among those who lived closest to the parsonage. Rather, at first, they saw the specters of Sarah Good, whose home was wherever someone would house her, her laborer husband, her infant, and her four-year-old daughter. The girls also named Sarah Osborn (or Osborne), whose house was almost two miles away, north of the Wolf Pits Meadow; Sarah Cloyse, who resided to the north and east of Osborn, on the Frost Fish Creek; John and Elizabeth Proctor, who dwelt two miles south of the training fields, at the foot of Felton's Hill; Giles and Martha Cory, whose home was two miles to the southwest, at the end of Proctor's Brook; and Bridget Bishop, whose ill fame had spread from Salem town when she married Edward Bishop in 1685 and moved to a house two and a half miles up the Ipswich road from the village center. She testified at her hearing that she had never been to the village center, a fact no one contested. The only two witches who lived in the girls' immediate vicinity were Tituba, who as a slave had no legal standing in the community, and Rebecca Nurse, whose family was engaged in a long-standing quarrel with the Putnams.[91]

When the girls had canvassed the likely suspects in Salem, they had to disband the group or seek out new fields to conquer. In April, they looked to Topsfield, where they found Abigail and Deliverance Hobbs, Sarah Wildes, and Elizabeth Howe, the last, like Cloyse, Nurse, and their sister Mary Esty (all née Townes), kin to Topsfield's anti-Putnam faction.[92] In May they found Andover's Martha Carrier, who, they must have heard, few in Andover liked. A month later, the request of An-dover's Joseph Ballard, son of one of the town founders, brought Ann Jr. and Mary Walcott to the town of Andover, where, blindfolded, they were touched by a parade of men and women suspected of bewitching Ballard's dying wife. Four they named as witches, all the while relishing the role of wandering witch finders. When the girls were finished in An-dover, Andover's citizens started accusing one another—resulting in a grand total of forty-one accused from the town.[93]

The girls had become good listeners, and adults around them inad-vertently provided cues to the identity of men and women long suspected of deviant ways or unpopular beliefs. Among these were the Quakers of Essex County, long persecuted and in 1692 uneasily tolerated. The girls found these men and women ready targets, for was not "quaking" akin to possession? In 1660, when Quakers faced death for persisting in their heresy, Massachusetts judges had told the defendants that their crime was, "like witchcraft," a rebellion against God and the colony.[94] Thus the girls not only saved their communities from the hidden evil of the Devil, but they also weeded out the ever dangerous Quakers. As it hap-pened, among the Salem accused, Elizabeth Proctor's family had Quaker connections, and Francis and Rebecca Nurse had adopted a Quaker son. A number of the Andover suspects also had Quaker affiliations. Quak-ers were not the only religious deviants upon whom the girls' denunci-ations fell. George Burroughs, though far removed from his old pulpit, was reputed to be a Baptist. He too was made vulnerable to accusation by religious apostasy.[95]

When the ranks of the commoners were depleted, the girls turned their attention to the elite of Salem and the colony. Even the crown pros-ecutor was impressed with how high they reached, later writing that "the afflicted spare[d] no person of what quality soever, neither conceale[d] their crimes tho never so hainous."[96] They began with their masters

Mary Warren naming John and Elizabeth Proctor, Sarah Churchill following with an indictment of George Jacobs Sr.[97] By May the girls were accusing Philip and Mary English, a rich French-born (he changed his name from L'Anglois) merchant and his wife, and even John Alden, one of Boston's sea captains turned merchant, who had to be pointed out to them.[98] Both men were quite comfortable in court: English was a veteran litigator to judge from the quarterly court records, and Alden feared no one—not even the governor—but both fled until the crisis was over.[99] Later rumor had the girls accusing the wife of the governor, but that rumor circulated when the crisis had passed.

Where had it all begun? As Luis Rodriguez, a prizewinning poet and journalist who grew up in the Los Angeles barrio, wrote, "Gangs are not alien power. They begin as unstructured groupings, our children, who desire the same as any young person. Respect. A sense of belonging."[100] For a time, scourging the witches of Salem may have brought this sense of belonging. In the end, of course, belonging can only come from a more positive contribution to life. Ann Putnam Jr. would marry and have children of her own, but as Thomas Hutchinson, then chief justice of the Massachusetts colony, wrote in 1768, "Some [of the accusers] proved profligate persons, abandoned to all vice, others passed their days in obscurity or contempt."[101] False accusation leaves a hole in the heart which no surgeon can repair. But if the accusers ended as a gang, they did not begin as one. It was the process of accusation and confession in a Puritan setting which raised the stakes of both and turned Betty's people into something far more potent and ominous than parents and friends.

accusations and confessions

SOMETIME between February 25, when Tituba fed the witchcake to an unsuspecting dog, and February 29, when the first arrest warrant was issued, Betty and Abigail named their afflicters: Tituba, Sarah Good, and Sarah Osborn. Betty told her parents that the girls had been approached by a man in black and promised cities of gold and baubles to hold.[1] When they rejected the Devil's offer, his witches began their assault. So Betty confessed to the men and women who gathered around her, women waiting to one side, comforting but worried, while men listened, probed, and finally acted on her accusation.

Betty, the first to complain of symptoms, in the end proved the least aggressive of the girls. Adults translated for her and prodded her, but then her parents delayed, advised to be patient by respected intercessors like John Hale. Parris may have hesitated because he believed that children were born in original sin; their nature was evil. Instruction, loving care, and wise counsel led them toward the light, but perhaps, even after all he had seen and his inclination to believe in witchcraft, the girls were lying.[2] One final motive may have stayed his hand: he was still the outsider in Salem and he knew it.[3] It was Ann Putnam's father, Sergeant

Thomas, his brother-in-law Joseph Hutchinson, and brother Edward Putnam who went to Salem to file an information with the magistrates.[4]

Both girls named Tituba, Sarah Good, and Sarah Osborn as their tormentors. There was no disagreement, and concert suggests more than mere compliance with the wishes of adults. Indeed, the almost verbatim similarity of the girls' testimony, the sequence of charges, the overlapping details, show prior consultation among the accusers—either that or the three women really did visit them in spectral form.[5] Betty and Abigail accused Tituba, but so, shortly, did Ann Jr. and Mercy Lewis. The girls in the two households must have talked among themselves; they planned and acted together. They did not merely enact their parents' fears or become the instruments of their parents' animosities. As Betty's parents gently but firmly pushed her off center stage, little Ann, prodded by her father and mother, assumed the starring role. Over time, different girls would share that role, but initially the local eminence of Ann's family gave urgency to the proceedings.

When the girls spoke, adults listened, in part because they believed in witches and the girls seemed genuinely troubled, in part because Betty was the minister's daughter and Ann's kin nearly monopolized local office. Sergeant Thomas could not let his daughter's travail go unattended. When the interrogations began, it was the Putnam clan that sat by their girls, took notes alongside the clerk and the justices of the peace, and put their weight behind the prosecutions. The Putnam elders signed depositions that they had witnessed the girls' suffering. The other accusers were related to the Putnams: Ann Jr. a daughter, Ann Sr. the wife of Thomas, Mary Walcott a niece, Mercy Lewis a servant in their home, Elizabeth Hubbard the servant and grandniece of supporter and client William Griggs, and Mary Walcott the daughter of brother-in-law Jonathan Walcott. There were others—girls like Susannah Sheldon and Sarah Churchill, who lived and worked in the village but were not part of the Putnam clan, and some adults, like the notoriously bad-tempered midwife Sarah Bibber, and later the confessors themselves—but the support of the senior Putnams was vital to the first accusations and remained so throughout the crisis.[6]

When the first round of investigations ended, Parris sent his daughter to live in Salem town at the house of Stephen Sewall, away, he hoped, from the terror engulfing Salem Village, ironically putting her in the center of the maelstrom, for Sewall would become the clerk of the court that heard the accusations and dealt out the sentences of death, and the court-house was but a short way down the main street and a quick turn of the corner from the clerk's house. Local lore had Betty suffering from return visits of the man in black until Mrs. Sewall convinced the girl that the Devil was a liar and "bid her tell him so if he came back to her again." He did; she did; and he never darkened her doorstep again.[7] Parris did not recuse himself, however, but putting aside the cautions urged on him by Hale and others, lent the meeting house for the examinations when the Ingersoll tavern proved too small and took notes when the magistrates could find no other to help them. He even allowed himself to be deposed in a number of cases, actively joining the witch hunt.[8] At the very least, by so doing he repaid the Putnams' loyalty to him.

These first accusations were themselves confessions; they had to be elicited from the girls. If one adds the women who later confessed to being witches to the accusers who confessed to being bewitched, one can find a clue to the psychodynamics of these first confessions. Girls and women confessed to men in public, for men were the ministers, magistrates, and jurors. Carol Karlsen has probed this relationship and concluded that sexual fantasies both open (as in carnal knowledge of the Devil) and covert were drawn by men from those who confessed,[9] although there was little that was explicitly or even implicitly sexual in the girls' accounts.[10] More important, what the girls told the adult male authority figures might not have been what they told others—at least initially. Privately these girls must have revealed something of their dilemma, if not their guilt, to older women.

Public confession was largely shaped by male expectations, but there also had to be conversation among the women. It was private, not recorded, but undergirded everything that went on the record. Confession is a form of "self conviction,"[11] and in conversation with other women the confessors probably admitted that they felt guilty about something in their lives—the inner conviction that they had failed to come up to the mark. Ordinary sins of greed and covetousness, of wantonness and anger, surely had invited the Devil to sojourn in the village long before he struck the first pact with the witches. Confession of sin was part of the ritual of purging oneself of sin and seeking God's forgiveness.[12]

The girls thought about naming Tituba because she had already become the focus of suspicion; that is undeniable. No doubt they had heard Parris blame Tituba, for later Tituba was reported to have accused Parris of beating her into a confession.[13] But Tituba was their friend; why accuse a friend? Tituba may have taught them some form of fortunetelling and practiced countermagic, but so did many women in the village. Why not point to Mary Sibley, the busybody neighbor, or those who made Parris's tenure so uneasy—the Porter women and their allies? Later accusations, principally those of little Ann Putnam, her mother, Ann Sr., and their servant, Mercy Lewis, leveled against Rebecca Nurse and her sisters, would take this form, but the first denunciations of Tituba and Sarah Good did not fit the model of witchcraft as a deadly surrogate for local feud.

Perhaps the girls believed that Tituba must pay because she had betrayed Betty and Abigail. They had always been her charges, and according to her later testimony she had loved and comforted them. Now, however, they had come to an age at which they were expected to perform part of the family work, to sew and carry, cook and clean.[14] Tituba, once a nursemaid, had become more distant and less caring. Why not name their mother, then?[15] Dorcas (or Dorothy) Good, Sarah Good's young child, did that, but only under severe duress, when Abigail named Dorcas a witch, and it is possible that Sarah was an abusive mother, for she abused all her neighbors.[16] Sarah Bibber was accused by her neighbors of cursing her own children—that was grounds, later in the crisis, to bind over Bibber for trial.[17] Elizabeth Parris had no such reputation.

Once named, Tituba had little defense. A slave, she was visibly, socially, and legally an outsider. Who could speak for her? Her master might, but he was already looking in her direction with suspicion in his eyes. She may have indulged the girls' fantasies, told them stories, passed the time of day with them. Later historians have suggested that she had a kind of second sight or that she actually entered trances.[18] Good was a disreputable beggar, and Osborn was old—Joseph Putnam sympathetically called her "gamar" in his notes, a common form of address for older women and one connoting the close, if ambivalent, tie between nurturing and witchcraft in New England.[19] Both were suspected of practicing witchcraft for a long time before 1692, and both had lost husbands to suspicious causes.

When the Putnams brought their suspicions to county magistrates Jonathan Corwin and John Hathorne, local suspicion turned into an official inquiry. The two justices of the peace issued warrants for the women named by the girls and arranged for an inquest. Hathorne and

Corwin were not village men, but they well knew the village and its denizens.[20] Both men were merchants, Corwin the son of one of Salem's first great merchants, Hathorne, whose family was equally venerable in the story of the town, the son of a successful farmer. They were also veteran politicians, among whose duties was the office of justice of the peace and county judge. In the courthouse in Salem, Corwin and Hathorne had heard civil suits, appointed administrators of estates, and punished those presented for misdemeanors in the village. They knew all the men and women who would appear before them as witnesses, accusers, and defendants in the witchcraft cases.[21] Corwin had opposed the Dominion of New England and Andros; Hathorne briefly joined its political councils. Both men had served long as selectmen of the town and were familiar with the village's troubles. Both had opposed severing the village from the town, pitting them against the Putnams. Hathorne was related by marriage to the Porters, but the relation had deprived him of land (his father, William Hathorne, had given it to the Porter girls as dower).[22]

The surviving legal record of these examinations preserves conversations: exchanges of words, signs, signals, and gestures. As in all such conversations, the speakers situated themselves in relation to one another, recalling talk that occurred in years past. For the speakers, conversation in these hearings was not easy talk—chatter—passing the time of day. For the girls, if they were truly afflicted, from whatever source, exposure to putative witches brought on new fits, hardly a pleasant experience. If they were shamming, they had to get it right, for exposure meant ridicule, punishment for lying, and perhaps suspicion that they were witches themselves. For the magistrates, the conversations were tests of their mettle as witch finders. They had to ferret out a deadly conspiracy before it struck at them or their children. Their target was not the witch only but the Great Adversary, hardly a being to be trifled with. They had to harden their hearts against instincts of mercy and sharpen their wits against fraud. They had to trap a wily foe.[23]

For the suspects, even more was at stake in this bartering of words. Some, particularly those against whom no prior accusation had been lodged, expressed bewilderment. They tried to persuade the girls to drop their accusations and the magistrates to lay aside their suspicions. Others, accustomed to such denunciation, retreated into hostility and cynicism. They professed their innocence with a hard-edged disregard for the whole proceeding. All of the suspects tried to talk their way out of the accusation, but none of the women and few of the men were practiced at public speech, and the record shows that they frequently misunderstood or could not keep up with the questions.

For witnesses, testifying literally hurt. It forced them to recall moments of terror when they came face to face with an apparition or a strange and horrifying animal, when they could not breathe or were paralyzed with fear. The memory was painful, and they trembled that its recital might arouse the dormant enmity of a witch. Witches were known to take revenge upon those who testified against witches. In general, the witnesses were not political figures, that is, their testimony was not a calculated ploy in some intravillage contest for power. Of course the Putnam clan hovered nearby, and although they did not speak much, they watched and listened. Everyone at the hearings had to run a gauntlet of Putnams. Other witnesses were friends, loved ones, and relatives of the suspects. Throughout the inquiry, they formed a quiet chorus, giving aid by their mere presence. On occasion, they offered character testimonials.

The examinations of the suspects began on the ground floor of Ingersoll's tavern house, but so many came to see the hearings that they were moved to the meeting house down the road. Thus what was to have been a civil event became a quasi-religious one.[24] Where might the two magistrates have sat, to distance themselves from the throng and yet control it? They could not stand at the pulpit; that would have violated custom and embarrassed Parris. They could not sit in the pews, surrounded by the multitude. The only answer is that they sat on one side of the communion table, with their backs to the wall of the meeting house. Witnesses and accused milled about on the other side.[25] The communion table had great significance in its meeting house setting. In Salem Village's meeting house, as in many other New England churches, communion was the most important sacrament and defined Puritan piety. Entry to this sacrament was limited to those who could confess to the congregation their state of regeneracy, so confession in this physical setting gained greater force, raising the stakes, as it were, of the girls' accusations. Testifying before the communion table, the girls had a credibility they might not have had if they stood next to the dirty, knife-gouged tables in Ingersoll's tavern.

In the meeting house the two magistrates confronted for the first time the girls' physical convulsions. In one sense, these contortions were conventional, that is, they fit into an established niche. The Goodwin children had fits. Elizabeth Knapp had fits. Other women and men possessed or attacked by evil sprites had fits. In their physical and auditory manifestations these were chronicled with care and credulity by Increase and Cotton Mather, and as John Hale noted, the accounts were widely read. The girls were bitten and pinched by invisible agents. In visible and audible agony, the victims twisted their arms and backs and contorted their faces. Sometimes they could not speak; other times they could not stop speaking. Those who watched were filled with compassion and fully convinced that the girls were truly afflicted.

But were they afflicted by witches? And were those witches the ones they named? The reason that John Hale and others counseled Parris to wait and pray was that such identifications might be mistaken. Parris was convinced for a time, but the Putnams were not. All their anger at events in the village spurred their impatience. They did not see the witchcraft accusations as a way to get at their betters—not yet, for Good and Tituba were not related to their rivals in the village. Later suspects, possibly Osborn, and particularly the Nurse-Cloyse family, would match this profile, but the Putnams could not predict that turn of events, though they may have welcomed or even encouraged the girls to shift their attention to Rebecca Nurse and her sister Sarah Cloyse. At first, however, impatience motivated the Putnams. They wanted action, not reflection, punishment, not healing.[26]

In front of the magistrates, the girls' afflictions had passed into a second, also conventional, stage—but one from which there was no healing, no returning, no chance for regret short of the formal processes of law. Mere suffering whose origin was idiopathic changed into legally cognizable evidence. If the conventionality of the girls' fits allowed parents and other caretakers to reconfigure otherwise novel and frightening events as familiar ones, and so cope with them, the girls' tormented accusations turned illness into proof of wrongdoing. As Hale and Lawson averred in their first-hand accounts, and as the magistrates must have come to believe, the girls could not have been faking when they first accused Good, Osborn, and Tituba.

The magistrates heard the accusations under their commissions as justices of the peace. Their authority was written, based on textual models taken from English books of forms, but the informality of the hearing, the close physical proximity and intimate social relationships among all

hanced the credibility of the older witnesses. Before the magistrates
these older men now came, for men predominated among the latter
group as women predominated among the afflicted. They recalled wooing that failed, bad butter, oddly shaped animals, and unnatural events.
The men ignored the danger of libel actions because they understood
that they did not speak for themselves. Rather, when these men came to
court, they were discharging a function the community expected them
to discharge, for Salem Village, though literate, needed its elders to recall the past. They did not come out of malice, because the affliction was
fresh in their minds, or because the damage was still unrepaired but
because it was their job to recount the common history of the people.
Like the Native American communities nearby, older men were oral recordkeepers. Again folk customs dominated legal proceedings.[40]

The examinations began on the first of March and continued for
three days. The accused had no legal counsel, but the form of the examination was not technically inquisitorial, for the suspects confronted
their accusers and could summon their own witnesses.[41] Nevertheless,
without formal legal advisors or patrons in the community, devoid of
experience with the courts in matters of such moment, the first suspects
must have found the examination inquisitorial whatever slender procedural rights they might have had. Good and Osborn stood firm—they
were not witches. Good was bitter and mistrusted the magistrates. In
counterpoint to her whining denials, the children, Betty, Abigail, Elizabeth Hubbard, and Ann Putnam Jr., screamed and writhed as if on cue.
Hathorne may have been convinced of Good's guilt (for he knew her
reputation), for he was harsh with her and she gave back venom. He
belittled her and she became confused. Finally, she named Sarah Osborn as the tormentor of the children.[42]
Hathorne, the primary questioner, had pressed Good despite her repeated denials, from which fact historians have concluded that Hathorne believed that Good was guilty.[43] No doubt he did, but his persistent style of interrogation, repeating the same question over and over,
is not uncommon or surprising. It had the imprimatur of John Winthrop, whose tenure as governor of Massachusetts spanned the colony's
first three decades. Convinced of the charges upon evidence, Winthrop
ordered that a magistrate was to press a suspect, examining "strictly."
The suspect was not to be allowed to stand mute but had to respond.[44]
In previous years, both Hathorne and his father had gained reputations

the participants, and the vividness of the girls' testimony gave substance
to the accusations more than did any books of forms.

Imagine a theater-in-the-round wherein everyone—actors, writers,
director, audience—could perform spontaneously, the plot merely sketched
out, the actors improvising lines and gestures as they went along. And
these were performances, as the girls soon realized. If they were not
trained actors working from a script, they could and did borrow the language of countless tales of specters and spells. The absence of supporting physical evidence, particularly the invisibility of the spectral forms
to all but the girls, did not diminish the impact of their performance.
Recall Macbeth's soliloquy at King Duncan's door: "is this a dagger I see
before me?" No one in the audience sees the dagger, but everyone believes
it is there because they see it through Macbeth's eyes. So the girls convinced onlookers that specters of witches flew through the room. The
girls used visible props as well. Pins, normally worn to keep dresses and
bonnets together, became instruments of torture, as the girls accused
defendants of pricking them. Mary Black, a slave of Nathaniel Putnam,
accused by Ann Putnam and others, was made at her examination on
April 22, 1692, to repin her neck cloth in front of the girls. They then
complained of being pricked. Mary Walcott was able to show Hathorne
and Corwin where blood came from a prick mark on her arm.[27] One
can speculate that Mary Black was not the only one who brought pins
to the examination. Witnesses for the defendants saw the act with pins.
Sarah Nurse caught Sarah Bibber, one of the older women who had
joined the accusers, pulling pins out of her clothing, hiding them in her
hands, pricking herself, and then crying out against Rebecca Nurse.[28]
Bruises were produced and bite marks displayed. Hathorne, like a director, could turn to the girls without warning and ask if the suspect afflicted
them, and they, without missing a beat, would be struck dumb or fall
into convulsions.[29]

Despite their familiarity with legal forms, neither Hathorne nor Corwin was a lawyer. Indeed, there was no lawyer present at these first hearings. Instead, they were gatherings of neighbors in which the conventions of ordinary social intercourse dominated the conversation. So it
was in the first session when Sarah Good's husband blurted that she was
"an enemy to all good."[30] William Good's public complaint about his
wife illustrated the way in which informal, oral, vernacular usages penetrated the examinations and changed their course. In the middle of a

formal legal proceeding in which words had (supposedly) precise and compelling, that is, categorical, meaning, he called his wife a witch. Did he mean that he knew she had committed the cognizable offense of witchcraft? No, he merely meant that she had not shown him the respect he thought he merited. Six months later, elderly Mary Bradbury of Salisbury and Andover stood before the magistrates, accused of witchcraft, and one of her accusers was a sailor, Samuel Endicott. He swore that eleven years earlier Bradbury had come down to the port to sell to his captain two tubs of butter. At sea the crew discovered that one of the tubs had gone rancid, "which made the men very much disturbed about it, and would often say that they heard that Mrs. Bradbury was a witch." If the butter had been sweet, would she have been as her neighbors later described her in a petition to the same magistrates—a loving and helpful model of Christian charity?[31] In such ways the vernacular culture— the nastiness of a bad marriage between ordinary New Englanders and a spoiled firkin of butter—intruded into the world of statutory definitions of crime, the learned world of law texts.

Before the Salem cases, neighbors had to be careful about what they said in such proceedings. Men and women who abused one another with assaultive speech were prosecuted in public forums and had to apologize. Such public confessions of error were an important ritual holding communities together.[32] In the heat of argument, Essex men and women did tell one another to go to the Devil, as Martha Cory shouted at a neighbor during a dispute over milk cows. Between 1672 and 1692, the Essex County courts heard forty abusive charges and countercharges of devilment. How many more there must have been which did not end in litigation is anyone's guess.[33] When neighbors did not mean to cast aspersions, they took pains to say so. During the inquiry into the cases of Hugh and Mary Parsons, Jonathan Taylor deposed that he called Goody Merick "a witch" because she was able to open a beer keg tap that he, with all his might, could not budge, but he hastened to add, "[B]ut I would not have you think it was by witchery."[34] Taylor was well aware that the usage of ordinary people could be taken quite differently when given in evidence in a criminal trial.

In quieter times, when war did not threaten the frontiers and companies of accused did not occupy the courts, women charged with witchcraft might respond with a countersuit for defamation or slander. Uncorrected by him, Taylor's words might have led to such a suit. Mary Parsons had been sued by the widow Marshfield for saying that after the widow

came to Springfield, there were unexplained lights night and, worse, that perhaps the widow had "witch that Parsons was supposed to bring to a neighbor's filed defamation suits on behalf of their wives. For Erasmus James brought suit for his wife against Pe had gone about telling his friends that Goodwife Jam ton in a boat and once safely at sea turned herself in ers believed him, at least to the extent of passing th ers. James won fifty shillings from Peter upon the j not collect from Peter's circle of friends.[36] In similar dicts survive, Massachusetts plaintiffs won fourtee prevailed but three times. Defamers then had to p also be ordered to confess error before their congre

Before Salem's travail, the courts also found wa tions based on confessions. They simply treated the romancer or witch as a liar and fined him or her tember 1652, John Broadstreet of Rowley was prese for having familiarity with the Devil, but the justi for lying repeatedly about his prowess. Broadstree court was clever—he had tried to trick the Devil, reading a book of magic when he heard a voice a did. Fearing that he was being addressed by th smartly: go make a bridge of sand over the ocean, up to heaven, and finally, ascend the ladder, "g back no more. Thus the Devil would stand befo achusetts would be safe. The court was not am Such dismissals of accusations and confessions o pattern well established in some parts of Europe Spain, and by 1692 in New Spain as well.[39]

The threat of defamation suits did not ward Salem, and that fact leads to a surmise about adult accusers. By early April, the girls were join who remembered strange episodes from past yea thirty years earlier, and who did not fear defam were not writers but talkers, and what they said in what was supposed to be a formal situation had weight because oral popular culture hon told. Thus the fabulousness itself of the witch as stern inquisitors, and their conduct was not different from that of modern prosecuting attorneys.[45]

Hathorne assumed that Good knew enough to be more forthcoming than she had been, but his real purpose was to elicit a confession, without which, despite all the testimony of neighbors and the girls' contortions, no conviction was sure. Good's final, exhausted concession rewarded Hathorne's persistence. Asked who it was, if not she, who pinched the children, Good said, "It was Sarah Osborn." The children concurred.[46]

Sarah Osborn was older than her fifty calendar years and sick, housebound for much of the winter. Confronted with the girls' torment, she denied that she had harmed them. Perhaps the Devil had assumed her form. Asked by Hathorne if she knew Good, she said she did not, plainly meaning that Good was nothing more than a casual acquaintance. Hathorne, always looking for a conspiracy of witches, asked when Osborn had seen Good last—as if the two had flown together to the most recent witches' sabbath. Osborn, obviously too ill to fly anywhere, replied that she had seen Good years earlier, in town. Well then, Hathorne sprung at her, what did you call Good then? "Sarah," replied Osborn. She was plainly tired but capable of some spunk. Were she not accused of witchcraft, Hathorne ought to have been properly abashed, for Puritanism valued the old and godly,[47] but he had learned that she did not attend church for more than a year. Why had she avoided going to meeting? The answer must have been written on her wretched face: she had been sick. A quarrelsome woman by all accounts, she was at the end of her tether. A mirror of the casual cruelty of these examinations: although she was not likely to flee the jurisdiction, the magistrates, upon the girls' testimony, remanded her to prison, where she died on May 10, denied the comfort of her own room and bed.[48]

Osborn's case raised a new question that Hathorne was unwilling or unable to confront. Her first husband was Robert Prince, a Salem Village man, and her in-laws were Lieutenant Thomas Putnam and Captain John Putnam. When her first husband died, he made his Putnam kin the executors of his estate. Sarah Prince broke the connection to the Putnam clan when she married her indentured servant, Alexander Osborn, an Irish immigrant. When the elder son of the first marriage reached his majority, the Putnams sought to settle him in his inheritance, but the Osborns resisted, and the parties grew quarrelsome. She had been an outsider when she married Prince, and now she threatened to disinherit two Salem Village lads.[49] Seen in this context, the accusation became a dispute over land waged by other means, in the same way that war is the continuation of failed diplomacy.

At last Tituba was called, and she at first denied any complicity. Had she remained adamant, Good and Osborn might well have been admonished and the affair ended. Hale opined that it was Tituba's confession, in which she named others as witches, which "encouraged those in authority to examine others that were suspected."[50] Had she continued to deny the charges, what would have happened to her, however? She had already recognized that she was in peril. Between the time that she baked the cake and the magistrates, summoned by the Putnams, arrived, Tituba had been questioned by Hale and other ministers and had admitted that "her mistress in her own Country was witch, and had taught her some means to be used for the discovery of a witch and for the prevention of being bewitched, etc. But said that she herself was not a witch."[51] Historians have read Hale to mean that Tituba had learned some countermagic in Barbados, but what English plantation mistress would take aside a young slave and teach her magic, much more confess to the slave that a mistress could be a witch?

One cannot just accept Hale's recounting; there was more to Tituba's story. She knew that suspicion was already falling on her and that she could become a scapegoat for the girls' suffering. How to begin to fashion a story for the ears of others which would protect herself was Tituba's dilemma. She was not accustomed to speaking to white authorities or to revealing her thoughts in public. Questioned in private by the ministers, she had nevertheless a chance to position herself, to try out an alibi—her story of the mistress's witchcraft. She was not a witch, but how could she help herself if her mistress had taught her countermagic?

This was not—no good alibi is—pure fabrication. A confession must be believable; it must convince the inquisitor. In fact, Tituba had allowed a little of her former self to show through; she had added memory—genuine recollection—to a denial of complicity, for she apparently did know some countermagic. If she admitted that she had learned how to bake the cake from her neighbors in Salem, who knew and practiced plenty of folk magic, then she must inform on them, and this she was not ready to do, at least until it proved necessary. Instead, her "mistress in her own country" was the culprit. Hale and others may have misinterpreted what Tituba said when she mentioned "her own country."

Tituba was not a Barbadian. She was African, and the first mistress she had would not have been white at all but African. It is entirely possible that Tituba genuinely related her early apprenticeship in some Yoruba divining order or perhaps mixed Yoruba countermagic with the Creole countermagic of Barbados. To this she added the pidgin countermagic of the cake. Everyone believed that she had some entry into the supernatural world. Did she know more than she was willing to tell? Was she a clairvoyant in a time when vision into the other world must surely "raise the Devil"?[52] In Yoruba rituals, a woman may be possessed by a deity and go into trancelike states. At birth, divination will tell whether a girl has this power in her future. Such participation is not hysterical but part of Yoruba culture, and those with a disposition toward such intimacy with the gods are encouraged to develop it.[53] Even those without the gift may have episodes of such possession.

Her tentative defense against suspicion came crashing down when the magistrates arrived and simply refused to believe her denials. She could see quite clearly that continued disclaimers would not move them, and she suddenly admitted that she had been approached by a tall, strong man from Boston with white hair. He told her he was God, and she was afraid. Sometimes he wore dark coats. At other times he appeared as a dog or a hog. The magistrates assumed he was the Devil—Ezekiell Cheever (clerking for the magistrates) recorded Tituba as saying that, but Corwin's longer and more accurate verbatim account suggests that the questioner (Hathorne, probably) put the Devil into the story. Tituba confirmed that Good and Osborn were witches, described their familiars in terms the girls had already used—brightly colored birds, for example, likely to catch the fancy of the girls—and added that she and four witches flew on poles through the air. She conceded that she had pinched the girls but did it only in fear of her own life.[54]

Some historians have claimed that she was so frightened by the proceedings that she allowed the magistrates to prompt her.[55] That is certainly possible, but she seems to have managed better than a mere victim. She found a way to manipulate her accusers—the girls—and her masters.[56] By confessing, Tituba shifted the lines of force in the room. No longer invisible, she had made herself a central figure in the inquiry. She now had power.[57] Again, just as in the witchcake episode, she combined African and English witchcraft on a middle ground. The mysterious man could turn into an animal, a power that African witches shared with English witches.[58] The tall man was clearly white, though later accounts would make him tawny or black. When William Barker of Andover confessed to being a witch on August 29, he told the magistrates that "the devil first appeared to him lyke a black man."[59] Did the Evil One appear to be dark, sidling up to Tituba as if from nowhere? What black characteristics were being attributed to the Devil—mere color, or something else? One must bear in mind that for the English the color black had evil connotations, but why would Tituba accept these derogatory associations?[60] She did not—the man was white. Like all white men in her life, he had power over her. What was she to do? Tituba had, in effect, replaced the shadowy "mistress" of her first story with a second, to her inquisitors more believable, culprit.

She had implicated others in the crime, which was exactly what the two justices of the peace wanted and feared to hear, for Hathorne and Corwin assumed that witches were always conspiratorial. Two years earlier, a runaway slave named Robert had testified that he was off to join a French and Indian expedition against the colony and he expected other Indians and blacks to join him. There was no expedition or general uprising, but because his story fed the authorities' worst fears of conspiracy, it was for a time believed.[61] Corwin and Hathorne put aside any hesitation they might have had in a less charged situation about crediting the testimony of a woman of color,[62] precisely because her story stoked their innermost concerns.

Tituba swore that she had been coerced into cooperating with the man in black. Approached by him, she ran to Parris for advice, but the fearsome man blocked her path. Confused and afraid, she made her mark in the strange man's book, and he told her that it contained Osborn's and Good's names, along with seven others. At last, when the magistrates wanted more than she could fabricate, she claimed that her sight had failed. She had lost her powers, again controlling what they could do to her. Although she was examined the next day, the magistrates got little more from her.[63]

What had happened? Let us try to see Tituba's conduct from the inside out. Tituba had survived the horrors of the middle passage and the challenges of service in Barbados, endured another trek to the cold New England of her adulthood, and surrounded by white people, people whose difference from her was irrevocable, found a way to cope. She had fixed in place the persona, the public mask she showed the world. If her confession submitted that person to the unchecked power of the magistrates, the self remained secret, yearning for a time and place far away.

116

the participants, and the vividness of the girls' testimony gave substance to the accusations more than did any books of forms.

Imagine a theater-in-the-round wherein everyone—actors, writers, director, audience—could perform spontaneously, the plot merely sketched out, the actors improvising lines and gestures as they went along. And these were performances, as the girls soon realized. If they were not trained actors working from a script, they could and did borrow the language of countless tales of specters and spells. The absence of supporting physical evidence, particularly the invisibility of the spectral forms to all but the girls, did not diminish the impact of their performance. Recall Macbeth's soliloquy at King Duncan's door: "is this a dagger I see before me?" No one in the audience sees the dagger, but everyone believes it is there because they see it through Macbeth's eyes. So the girls convinced onlookers that specters of witches flew through the room. The girls used visible props as well. Pins, normally worn to keep dresses and bonnets together, became instruments of torture, as the girls accused defendants of pricking them. Mary Black, a slave of Nathaniel Putnam, accused by Ann Putnam and others, was made at her examination on April 22, 1692, to repin her neck cloth in front of the girls. They then complained of being pricked. Mary Walcott was able to show Hathorne and Corwin where blood came from a prick mark on her arm.[27] One can speculate that Mary Black was not the only one who brought pins to the examination. Witnesses for the defendants saw the act with pins. Sarah Nurse caught Sarah Bibber, one of the older women who had joined the accusers, pulling pins out of her clothing, hiding them in her hands, pricking herself, and then crying out against Rebecca Nurse.[28] Bruises were produced and bite marks displayed. Hathorne, like a director, could turn to the girls without warning and ask if the suspect afflicted them, and they, without missing a beat, would be struck dumb or fall into convulsions.[29]

Despite their familiarity with legal forms, neither Hathorne nor Corwin was a lawyer. Indeed, there was no lawyer present at these first hearings. Instead, they were gatherings of neighbors in which the conventions of ordinary social intercourse dominated the conversation. So it was in the first session when Sarah Good's husband blurted that she was "an enemy to all good."[30] William Good's public complaint about his wife illustrated the way in which informal, oral, vernacular usages penetrated the examinations and changed their course. In the middle of a formal legal proceeding in which words had (supposedly) precise and compelling, that is, categorical, meaning, he called his wife a witch. Did he mean that he knew she had committed the cognizable offense of witchcraft? No, he merely meant that she had not shown him the respect he thought he merited. Six months later, elderly Mary Bradbury of Salisbury and Andover stood before the magistrates, accused of witchcraft, and one of her accusers was a sailor, Samuel Endicott. He swore that eleven years earlier Bradbury had come down to the port to sell to his captain two tubs of butter. At sea the crew discovered that one of the tubs had gone rancid, "which made the men very much disturbed about it, and would often say that they heard that Mrs. Bradbury was a witch." If the butter had been sweet, would she have been as her neighbors later described her in a petition to the same magistrates—a loving and helpful model of Christian charity?[31] In such ways the vernacular culture—the nastiness of a bad marriage between ordinary New Englanders and a spoiled firkin of butter—intruded into the world of statutory definitions of crime, the learned world of law texts.

Before the Salem cases, neighbors had to be careful about what they said in such proceedings. Men and women who abused one another with assaultive speech were prosecuted in public forums and had to apologize. Such public confessions of error were an important ritual holding communities together.[32] In the heat of argument, Essex men and women did tell one another to go to the Devil, as Martha Cory shouted at a neighbor during a dispute over milk cows. Between 1672 and 1692, the Essex County courts heard forty abusive charges and countercharges of devilment. How many more there must have been which did not end in litigation is anyone's guess.[33] When neighbors did not mean to cast aspersions, they took pains to say so. During the inquiry into the cases of Hugh and Mary Parsons, Jonathan Taylor deposed that he called Goody Merick "a witch" because she was able to open a beer keg tap that he, with all his might, could not budge, but he hastened to add, "[B]ut I would not have you think it was by witchery."[34] Taylor was well aware that the usage of ordinary people could be taken quite differently when given in evidence in a criminal trial.

In quieter times, when war did not threaten the frontiers and companies of accused did not occupy the courts, women charged with witchcraft might respond with a countersuit for defamation or slander. Uncorrected by him, Taylor's words might have led to such a suit. Mary Parsons had been sued by the widow Marshfield for saying that after the widow came to Springfield, there were unexplained lights in the meadow at night and, worse, that perhaps the widow had "witched away" the wool that Parsons was supposed to bring to a neighbor's house.[35] Husbands filed defamation suits on behalf of their wives. For example, in 1650, Erasmus James brought suit for his wife against Peter Pitford. Pitford had gone about telling his friends that Goodwife James sailed off to Boston in a boat and once safely at sea turned herself into a cat. His listeners believed him, at least to the extent of passing the rumor on to others. James won fifty shillings from Peter upon the jury verdict but did not collect from Peter's circle of friends.[36] In similar cases for which verdicts survive, Massachusetts plaintiffs won fourteen times; defendants prevailed but three times. Defamers then had to pay a fine and might also be ordered to confess error before their congregation.[37]

Before Salem's travail, the courts also found ways to deflect accusations based on confessions. They simply treated the self-proclaimed necromancer or witch as a liar and fined him or her accordingly. In September 1652, John Broadstreet of Rowley was presented by a grand jury for having familiarity with the Devil, but the justices fined him instead for lying repeatedly about his prowess. Broadstreet's explanation to the court was clever—he had tried to trick the Devil, not obey him. He was reading a book of magic when he heard a voice ask him what work he did. Fearing that he was being addressed by the Devil, he answered smartly: go make a bridge of sand over the ocean, then a ladder of sand up to heaven, and finally, ascend the ladder, "goe to God" and come back no more. Thus the Devil would stand before his judge and Massachusetts would be safe. The court was not amused and fined him.[38] Such dismissals of accusations and confessions of witchcraft followed a pattern well established in some parts of Europe, particularly Italy and Spain, and by 1692 in New Spain as well.[39]

The threat of defamation suits did not ward off the accusations in Salem, and that fact leads to a surmise about the critical role of the adult accusers. By early April, the girls were joined by a variety of adults who remembered strange episodes from past years, sometimes twenty or thirty years earlier, and who did not fear defamation suits. Such elders were not writers but talkers, and what they said, even when they spoke in what was supposed to be a formal situation like the pretrial hearing, had weight because oral popular culture honors the good story, well told. Thus the fabulousness itself of the witchcraft stories actually en-hanced the credibility of the older witnesses. Before the magistrates these older men now came, for men predominated among the latter group as women predominated among the afflicted. They recalled wooing that failed, bad butter, oddly shaped animals, and unnatural events. The men ignored the danger of libel actions because they understood that they did not speak for themselves. Rather, when these men came to court, they were discharging a function the community expected them to discharge, for Salem Village, though literate, needed its elders to recall the past. They did not come out of malice, because the affliction was fresh in their minds, or because the damage was still unrepaired but because it was their job to recount the common history of the people. Like the Native American communities nearby, older men were oral recordkeepers. Again folk customs dominated legal proceedings.[40]

The examinations began on the first of March and continued for three days. The accused had no legal counsel, but the form of the examination was not technically inquisitorial, for the suspects confronted their accusers and could summon their own witnesses.[41] Nevertheless, without formal legal advisors or patrons in the community, devoid of experience with the courts in matters of such moment, the first suspects must have found the examination inquisitorial whatever slender procedural rights they might have had. Good and Osborn stood firm—they were not witches. Good was bitter and mistrusted the magistrates. In counterpoint to her whining denials, the children, Betty, Abigail, Elizabeth Hubbard, and Ann Putnam Jr., screamed and writhed as if on cue. Hathorne may have been convinced of Good's guilt (for he knew her reputation), for he was harsh with her and she gave back venom. He belittled her and she became confused. Finally, she named Sarah Osborn as the tormentor of the children.[42]

Hathorne, the primary questioner, had pressed Good despite her repeated denials, from which fact historians have concluded that Hathorne believed that Good was guilty.[43] No doubt he did, but his persistent style of interrogation, repeating the same question over and over, was not uncommon or surprising. It had the imprimatur of John Winthrop, whose tenure as governor of Massachusetts spanned the colony's first three decades. Convinced of the charges upon evidence, Winthrop ordered that a magistrate was to press a suspect, examining "strictly." The suspect was not to be allowed to stand mute but had to respond.[44] In previous years, both Hathorne and his father had gained reputations as stern inquisitors, and their conduct was not different from that of modern prosecuting attorneys.[45]

Hathorne assumed that Good knew enough to be more forthcoming than she had been, but his real purpose was to elicit a confession, without which, despite all the testimony of neighbors and the girls' contortions, no conviction was sure. Good's final, exhausted concession rewarded Hathorne's persistence. Asked who it was, if not she, who pinched the children, Good said, "It was Sarah Osborn." The children concurred.[46]

Sarah Osborn was older than her fifty calendar years and sick, housebound for much of the winter. Confronted with the girls' torment, she denied that she had harmed them. Perhaps the Devil had assumed her form. Asked by Hathorne if she knew Good, she said she did not, plainly meaning that Good was nothing more than a casual acquaintance. Hathorne, always looking for a conspiracy of witches, asked when Osborn had seen Good last—as if the two had flown together to the most recent witches' sabbath. Osborn, obviously too ill to fly anywhere, replied that she had seen Good years earlier, in town. Well then, Hathorne sprung at her, what did you call Good then? "Sarah," replied Osborn. She was plainly tired but capable of some spunk. Were she not accused of witchcraft, Hathorne ought to have been properly abashed, for Puritanism valued the old and godly,[47] but he had learned that she did not attend church for more than a year. Why had she avoided going to meeting? The answer must have been written on her wretched face: she had been sick. A quarrelsome woman by all accounts, she was at the end of her tether. A mirror of the casual cruelty of these examinations: although she was not likely to flee the jurisdiction, the magistrates, upon the girls' testimony, remanded her to prison, where she died on May 10, denied the comfort of her own room and bed.[48]

Osborn's case raised a new question that Hathorne was unwilling or unable to confront. Her first husband was Robert Prince, a Salem Village man, and her in-laws were Lieutenant Thomas Putnam and Captain John Putnam. When her first husband died, he made his Putnam kin the executors of his estate. Sarah Prince broke the connection to the Putnam clan when she married her indentured servant, Alexander Osborn, an Irish immigrant. When the elder son of the first marriage reached his majority, the Putnams sought to settle him in his inheritance, but the Osborns resisted, and the parties grew quarrelsome. She had been an outsider when she married Prince, and now she threatened to disinherit two Salem Village lads.[49] Seen in this context, the accusation became a dispute over land waged by other means, in the same way that war is the continuation of failed diplomacy.

At last Tituba was called, and she at first denied any complicity. Had she remained adamant, Good and Osborn might well have been admonished and the affair ended. Hale opined that it was Tituba's confession, in which she named others as witches, which "encouraged those in authority to examine others that were suspected."[50] Had she continued to deny the charges, what would have happened to her, however? She had already recognized that she was in peril. Between the time that she baked the cake and the magistrates, summoned by the Putnams, arrived, Tituba had been questioned by Hale and other ministers and had admitted that "her mistress in her own Country was witch, and had taught her some means to be used for the discovery of a witch and for the prevention of being bewitched, etc. But said that she herself was not a witch."[51] Historians have read Hale to mean that Tituba had learned some countermagic in Barbados, but what English plantation mistress would take aside a young slave and teach her magic, much more confess to the slave that a mistress could be a witch?

One cannot just accept Hale's recounting; there was more to Tituba's story. She knew that suspicion was already falling on her and that she could become a scapegoat for the girls' suffering. How to begin to fashion a story for the ears of others which would protect herself was Tituba's dilemma. She was not accustomed to speaking to white authorities or to revealing her thoughts in public. Questioned in private by the ministers, she had nevertheless a chance to position herself, to try out an alibi—her story of the mistress's witchcraft. She was not a witch, but how could she help herself if her mistress had taught her countermagic?

This was not—no good alibi is—pure fabrication. A confession must be believable; it must convince the inquisitor. In fact, Tituba had allowed a little of her former self to show through; she had added memory—genuine recollection—to a denial of complicity, for she apparently did know some countermagic. If she admitted that she had learned how to bake the cake from her neighbors in Salem, who knew and practiced plenty of folk magic, then she must inform on them, and this she was not ready to do, at least until it proved necessary. Instead, her "mistress in her own country" was the culprit. Hale and others may have misinterpreted what Tituba said when she mentioned "her own country."

Tituba was not a Barbadian. She was African, and the first mistress she had would not have been white at all but African. It is entirely possible that Tituba genuinely related her early apprenticeship in some Yoruba divining order or perhaps mixed Yoruba countermagic with the Creole countermagic of Barbados. To this she added the pidgin countermagic of the cake. Everyone believed that she had some entry into the supernatural world. Did she know more than she was willing to tell? Was she a clairvoyant in a time when vision into the other world must surely "raise the Devil"?[52] In Yoruba rituals, a woman may be possessed by a deity and go into trancelike states. At birth, divination will tell whether a girl has this power in her future. Such participation is not hysterical but part of Yoruba culture, and those with a disposition toward such intimacy with the gods are encouraged to develop it.[53] Even those without the gift may have episodes of such possession.

Her tentative defense against suspicion came crashing down when the magistrates arrived and simply refused to believe her denials. She could see quite clearly that continued disclaimers would not move them, and she suddenly admitted that she had been approached by a tall, strong man from Boston with white hair. He told her he was God, and she was afraid. Sometimes he wore dark coats. At other times he appeared as a dog or a hog. The magistrates assumed he was the Devil—Ezekiell Cheever (clerking for the magistrates) recorded Tituba as saying that, but Corwin's longer and more accurate verbatim account suggests that the questioner (Hathorne, probably) put the Devil into the story. Tituba confirmed that Good and Osborn were witches, described their familiars in terms the girls had already used—brightly colored birds, for example, likely to catch the fancy of the girls—and added that she and four witches flew on poles through the air. She conceded that she had pinched the girls but did it only in fear of her own life.[54]

Some historians have claimed that she was so frightened by the proceedings that she allowed the magistrates to prompt her.[55] That is certainly possible, but she seems to have managed better than a mere victim. She found a way to manipulate her accusers—the girls—and her masters.[56] By confessing, Tituba shifted the lines of force in the room. No longer invisible, she had made herself a central figure in the inquiry. She now had power.[57] Again, just as in the witchcake episode, she combined African and English witchcraft on a middle ground. The mysterious man could turn into an animal, a power that African witches shared with English witches.[58] The tall man was clearly white, though later accounts would make him tawny or black. When William Barker of Andover confessed to being a witch on August 29, he told the magistrates that "the devil first appeared to him lyke a black man."[59] Did the Evil One appear to be dark, sidling up to Tituba as if from nowhere? What black characteristics were being attributed to the Devil—mere color, or something else? One must bear in mind that for the English the color black had evil connotations, but why would Tituba accept these derogatory associations?[60] She did not—the man was white. Like all white men in her life, he had power over her. What was she to do? Tituba had, in effect, replaced the shadowy "mistress" of her first story with a second, to her inquisitors more believable, culprit.

She had implicated others in the crime, which was exactly what the two justices of the peace wanted and feared to hear, for Hathorne and Corwin assumed that witches were always conspiratorial. Two years earlier, a runaway slave named Robert had testified that he was off to join a French and Indian expedition against the colony and he expected other Indians and blacks to join him. There was no expedition or general uprising, but because his story fed the authorities' worst fears of conspiracy, it was for a time believed.[61] Corwin and Hathorne put aside any hesitation they might have had in a less charged situation about crediting the testimony of a woman of color,[62] precisely because her story stoked their innermost concerns.

Tituba swore that she had been coerced into cooperating with the man in black. Approached by him, she ran to Parris for advice, but the fearsome man blocked her path. Confused and afraid, she made her mark in the strange man's book, and he told her that it contained Osborn's and Good's names, along with seven others. At last, when the magistrates wanted more than she could fabricate, she claimed that her sight had failed. She had lost her powers, again controlling what they could do to her. Although she was examined the next day, the magistrates got little more from her.[63]

What had happened? Let us try to see Tituba's conduct from the inside out. Tituba had survived the horrors of the middle passage and the challenges of service in Barbados, endured another trek to the cold New England of her adulthood, and surrounded by white people, people whose difference from her was irrevocable, found a way to cope. She had fixed in place the persona, the public mask she showed the world. If her confession submitted that person to the unchecked power of the magistrates, the self remained secret, yearning for a time and place far away.

When the magistrates began to press her for more information—hoping to make her the center of their inquiry—they compressed the mental space between the public persona and the hidden self, finally fusing the two. She declined to continue, averring that her sight had failed. She could no longer see the visions: no more specters; no more imps; no more confessions. She stopped. Believing that her life was all but forfeit, summoning up a world of experience which would daunt the most modern mind, she confessed and then informed them she would say no more. Yoruba witches are expected, near death, to confess everything they have done or thought they had done.[64] They save the confession for the end, for local punishment of witches was savage in Yorubaland. When they confessed, they lost their powers; they literally could no longer "see." In saying that she had lost her sight, Tituba recapitulated the Yoruba customs in the very moment of her trials. She defied the magistrates not only by refusing to answer further but by calling upon a Yoruba custom to frame that refusal. The self now spoke, and if the magistrates did not register the change in voice, Tituba heard. Her countrymen and women had thrown themselves from the slavers' ships into shark-infested waters so that their spirits might journey home. Quietly and with dignity, for none of the accounts suggests that she was hysterical in the meeting house, she did what so many captives had done before her. With one foot on the ladder to the scaffold, she had come home.

For the time being, the magistrates were done, but Salem was not quiet. How could it be, when there were still witches (by Tituba's reckoning) unaccounted for? On March 11, Ann Putnam was afflicted by a new cadre of witches. Three days later, Abigail Williams was attacked by the same spectral forms. Soon the same accusers of Good, Osborn, and Tituba fastened upon Martha Cory and Rebecca Nurse, older women in the village who, unlike their predecessors, were members in good standing of churches and apparently led upright lives. Both Cory and Nurse, warned by their neighbors, regarded the girls' antics as the prattling of malice, but the men who went from house to house seeking evidence for the accusations, watching the faces and gestures of the new suspects, either did not see or would not credit the older women's view of the new accusations. Cory's sarcastic dismissal and Nurse's earnest bewilderment at the charges did not deter the activities of the growing number of unofficial witch finders in the village.

Deciding to put the girls in their place, Martha and Giles Cory challenged the investigation. Both had a reputation for being ornery.[65] Hearing through gossip that she was suspected, Martha told the constable that she had anticipated his arrival. He reported that comment to Hathorne, who took it as an evidence that she was a witch. At her examination, "a child" murmured to Cheever (and he dutifully recorded), "There is a man whispering in her ear." Alert to the presence of the Evil One, Hathorne increased the tempo of his questions, badgering the old woman. She denied all, but her denials became rote, no longer compelling Hathorne to take them or her seriously. He offered her "the out"—a technique that the police use to this day: "Why, confess" he suggested, and she would feel much better. She refused, maintaining her innocence. Then Abigail cried out, and as one the girls became distracted. Mercy Lewis saw Cory's specter swing an iron rod (a spectral one, presumably), and two of the other girls dodged it. When Cory laughed at their antics, they redoubled their efforts. Cory bit her lip; the girls produced bloody lips. She had an arthritis attack, clenching her hands, and they writhed, their hands twisted in a cruel but effective mockery of her pain. She was committed with her husband to Salem jail. Parris wrote the verbatim account. Cheever was busy with the girls.[66]

Parris and his fellow ministers could have interceded, but they had no doubt that the Devil was abroad. They had come and seen with their own eyes in the meeting house. When Deodat Lawson visited Salem Village and preached in the meeting house, on the afternoon of March 20, Abigail Williams sat with the other girls. Mercy Lewis was there, as was Mary Walcott, Ann Putnam Jr., and Elizabeth Hubbard. Elizabeth Parris sat near the front, with Abigail and Ann. At the morning sermon, Abigail had been contentious and spiteful, but in the afternoon she went further.[67] She cried out, "Look where Goodwife Cloyse sits on the Beam suckling her Yellow Bird between her fingers." Ann Putnam boldly added that the yellow bird had flown to Lawson's hat, but sensing that she had gone too far, those sitting nearby hushed her. Williams and Putnam basked in the attention of the bewildered congregation. They had turned the auditory—the place where the congregation was to hear the minister—into a theater of accusations where the villagers had to listen to the two girls.[68] Cloyse was soon isolated. When the magistrates came to examine her at the end of the month, the girls had fits in front of them and accused Cloyse of being a witch. She was arraigned and imprisoned.[69]

After hearkening to the girls' wailing and watching them point fingers of accusation, Lawson preached an ambiguous sermon to the Salem congregation. Lawson's notes have not survived, and his printed sermon, some fifty pages long, was published (and clearly altered) in 1693, a year after he delivered it and the crisis had abated. Nevertheless, in it one can find the ambivalence that marked the ministers' deliberations. The message was simple: pray, pray, pray, and it neatly fit both the Jeremiad—the call to return to the older, purer faith of the founders of New England—and the way in which Puritans, from late in the sixteenth century, set out to combat the Devil's works. Even after he emended the sermon to conform to the posttrial ministerial position—that the Devil could take the form of the innocent—Lawson maintained that the Evil One had come to Salem. Yes, they were in the Lion's jaws. To the Devil and those who had chosen to follow him, the righteous must give no quarter. The people of Salem had to awaken to their sins; search their hearts; reform; eschew hatred, envy, and malice. Lawson rejected countermagic. There was to be no "horse-shoe nailed on the threshold." At the same time, he beseeched the magistrates to exert every effort to "check and rebuke Satan." Christ had defeated the Devil, and so would the true in spirit.[70]

What he said and what his audience made of it, however, were quite different. He was confident of final victory over the Devil through prayer and righteous living, but some in the pews came away shaken. Ann Putnam Sr. was particularly disturbed, and she adopted Lawson's language to bring her own accusation before the magistrates. A week before Lawson preached, Putnam, exhausted from her daughter's travails and her maid's complaints, lay down for a nap and, vulnerable, was beset by the specter of witches. She recognized them as they pressed upon her chest. One was Martha Cory, the other Rebecca Nurse. Their supposed assault on Ann Sr. abated on the Sabbath but returned in full fury when the day of worship was done. This time, Nurse did more than pummel Putnam; she insisted that Christ had no power to save the anguished mother. The threat of witchcraft had taken on theological dimensions. Putnam swore to the magistrates that only God had delivered her "out of the paws of those roaring lions"—the very words that Lawson had used in the meeting house.[71]

The elder Putnam was susceptible to suggestion. She had lost a six-week-old child, little Sarah, who would have been Ann Jr.'s younger sister, and evidently still grieved. Sometime between the beginning of March and the middle of May 1692, she was visited in her bed by the ghosts of Samuel Fuller and Lidia Willard. They ordered her to go to Hathorne and tell him that they were murdered by John Willard, a neighbor who had lost his wife, Lidia, and infant child not long before. John Willard, she now learned, was the witch who had caused the death of her little Sarah. This she swore was true, and if she did not so testify, she warned, the ghosts would come before the magistrates and speak on their own behalf. It was a terrifying prospect, to others as well as to her.[72]

The potency of Lawson's language gave religious sanction to the continuing process of accusation. Following her mistress, Mercy Lewis revised her account of the girls' travails. It now had a Christological structure, anticipating her denunciation of Burroughs. On April 1, Lewis had a fit in which she saw spread before her the table of a black mass, in which the witches ate red bread "like a man's flesh." She refused to join them, crying out, "'[T]hat is not the bread of life,'" according to Lawson, who heard her confession. He reported that she saw in her fit "a white man and was with him in a glorious place, which had no candles nor sun, yet was full of light and brightness; where there was a great multitude in white glittering robes."[73]

Lewis exhibited the very essence of Puritan yearning to be close to Christ. In her fit she had seen Him and taken comfort from Him, for as she related, He warned her how long it would be between fits, and He gave her peace. It would be easy to say that she gave her audience what she knew it wanted, that Lawson and Parris and the other ministers had cued her. Yet might she not also have longed for peace, for reassurance in the midst of the public crisis she knew she and the other girls had brought on? She would not have been the first teenager, in the midst of personal and public crisis, to seek comfort in the bosom of Jesus.[74]

The girls' targets were not just older women. On March 23, Samuel Brabrook, the town marshal's deputy, arrested four-year-old Dorcas Good on the order of Hathorne and Corwin. Lewis, Walcott, and Ann Putnam Jr. all testified that the specter of the child had bitten and pinched them. Little Dorcas was jailed in Salem, where on the 26th, Hathorne, Corwin, and John Higginson visited her. Hathorne and Corwin were there to catch a tiny witch. Higginson was there to save a soul. Together, they heard her confession. Tearfully, she held out a forefinger and told them where her "familiar," a little snake (for a little girl), used to suck, "where they observed a deep red spot, about the bigness of a flea bite," which it probably was. Kept in jail for the next eight months, she watched her suckling infant sister die, her mother led away to the gallows, cried her heart out, and went insane.[75]

Summoned by the extemporaneous conversation between ministers on the pulpit and the girls in the pews which led to new accusations, the magistrates reappeared and resumed the interrogation of suspects. This time they were troubled, for the accused were not outsiders or marginal members of the community like Osborn, Good, and Tituba but fully integrated participants in village and church life. The girls, however, by now had the chance to polish their performance. In all, the stakes were higher, but the girls had found a corporate identity and new status in the community by bringing accusations and became the center of attention by acting them out. They rehearsed when Martha Cory was examined. One would call out that she saw the specter of Cory attacking another of the accusers, and the latter would cry out in pain. Their accusations played to packed houses. The cathartic effect was real, just as it was in Greek tragedy. The girls were never alone, never separated from one another, never examined in camera. Thus they could engage in ensemble acting.

Introduced with Cory, the melodrama could be reprised in the crucial case of Rebecca Nurse. Her husband, Francis, had been a constable and a juryman. Both had fine reputations in the town. If the girls could pull her down, their power to debase would be unstoppable. On March 24, after Lawson had preached, Goodwife Nurse was brought to the Ingersoll tavern, held for a time, and then transported up the steps to the meeting house. She had traveled this route so many times, in other circumstances, that she must have felt the irony of her new role. Did it also frighten her? Not from the evidence of her replies to the magistrates' questions. At first, they were gentle, for the magistrates presiding over the interrogations did not want to believe all they heard. Hathorne turned to the girls and asked if they recognized Nurse, which they did. She was the afflicter. Putnam and Williams cried out, and a plainly bewildered but composed Nurse denied that she was the cause of their pain. "God will clear my innocency," she maintained. Hathorne for a moment might have wished it so, for he answered, "[T]here is never a one in the Assembly but desires it [more than I]"; yet if she were guilty, he was convinced that God would "discover" her.

Hathorne here revealed that he believed in the medieval idea of ordeals, in which God demonstrated who was innocent and who was guilty. He needed a sign, and Ann Putnam Sr. rushed to the aid of her daughter by accusing Nurse. She said, "Did you not bring the Black man with you, did you not bid me tempt God, and dye?" Goodwife Putnam verged on hysteria—she was not playacting—and her passion gave credibility to the girls' testimony. Her references to suicide must be taken seriously, for her daughter had exhibited the fits for almost two months, and the mother was beside herself with worry.[76] Williams and Ann Putnam Jr. began wailing, and Mary Walcott and Elizabeth Hubbard, hitherto quiet, added their voices to the clamor.[77]

Nurse was struck dumb by it all, and Hathorne, changing his tone, baited her: how could she have dry eyes when so much suffering poured out around her? What did Nurse say to the "grown persons" who joined the accusers? Hathorne again showed a little of his hand: he did not wholly credit the girls' accusations, but when their elders spoke—particularly Ann's mother—their words had to be weighed with care. Again, he offered Nurse an out: "Possibly you may apprehend you are no witch, but have you not been led aside by temptations that way[?]" She had not, she replied. Here was another refusal to help him, just like Cory's, but again he hesitated, moved perhaps by Nurse's friends, who had begun lamenting as well. Hathorne now tried a different tack, one he would repeat in later hearings: could the suspect help him explain the fits? "Do you think these suffer voluntarily or involuntarily?" he asked. Was it a trap? "I cannot tell," Nurse replied. He persisted, "That is strange[,] everyone can judge," and they had, but Nurse was at the end of her tether. "I cannot tell," she repeated. A good Puritan, she would not judge another. To have accused the girls of feigning was to charge them with perjury. To understand how the Devil worked was beyond her powers. Pressured, she finally guessed that the girls were not naturally afflicted but bewitched. Impressed by Nurse's calm, Hathorne gave her a last chance. Tituba loved Betty but affirmed that her specter, out of her control, must have afflicted the girl. Might not Nurse's apparition have done the same? Nurse was having none of it, however. "[Why do you] have me bely [belie] myself," she retorted, but she did allow that the Devil might have taken her shape.

Exhausted, sick, and overcome, Nurse had nevertheless produced the one argument that was irrefutable in defense. Osborn had already assayed it. No one could stop the Devil from assuming the shape of a good person and using his powers to hurt others. Even Increase Mather had conceded as much, and he was a believer in the malign powers of witches.[78] Neither her defense nor her frailty deterred Hathorne from committing Nurse to jail, no doubt to chain her there (for chains, every-one knew, prevented the witch's specter from escaping her body), but the argument would continue to trouble everyone in authority.

The girls were not done, not just yet, however. As she was taken away, visibly fatigued, Nurse held her head to one side. Elizabeth Hubbard, closely observing the detainee, immediately bent her neck to the same side and Abigail Williams cried out, "[S]et up Goody Nurse's head. . . . [T]he maid's [Hubbard's] neck will be broke," and when Nurse's neck was forcibly straightened, Hubbard's head was magically restored to its normal posture.[79]

Parris might have doubted the testimony of a few servant girls and his own frail daughter, but he could not—for political reasons if for no other—ignore the sworn oath of Ann Putnam Sr. in his own meeting house. A few days later, on March 27, with the second batch of sus-pected witches in custody, Parris went even further than had Lawson. Although the girls had extended their accusations to Rebecca Nurse, whose status and reputation in the village was impeccable, he refused to stem the tide or even divert it. There were demons and he wanted to exorcise them. It would have taken a special kind of courage for him to try to stop the momentum of accusation, and he had never shown such courage. Instead, he took refuge in another Jeremiad. He no longer doubted that witchcraft had come to Salem Village, and he preached, "There are devils as well as saints in Christ's church," sinners and wicked people hiding in the covenant of the church. God knew how many these were and had given His true believers the means to discover the Devil's mischief. Beset himself, Parris cast his terrible anxieties among his con-gregants like seeds in planting time.[80]

The effectiveness of Lawson's and Parris's preaching rested not on the Scriptures to which they alluded but on the moral and emotional force of their discourse. Bent as they were by the cries of the afflicted, so their congregations were inclined. The book culture in which the Puritan ministers were trained merged into a vernacular mode of signing just as surely as the magistrates' formal proceedings were altered by the flood of oral testimony. People calling out in services, rumors flying all over, butting into the gliding specters of the witches in the rafters of the meet-ing house, made it nearly impossible for the two ministers to maintain church discipline. Whether or not they could have contained the con-tagion—bound down the Devil and his works—within the meeting house is a matter of conjecture. The fact is, they were not the men to try.

The examinations now convened on a regular basis, the episodic quality of the first month's revelations giving way to a continuous feature of Salem life. Seen for the first time, the hearings might have appeared to be disorderly affairs. In fact, they had a clear, discursive structure. In some, for example that of Good, and later Bridget Bishop, the examiners, notably Hathorne, directed the girls' performance, prompting them into their fits by asking them to identify the suspects, cuing the girls to interject their own voices and act out in chorus their afflictions. When Elizabeth Cary was summoned for her hearing, the girls did not recognize her by sight, but then she was identified, and there was no way she could save herself. Her husband, Nathaniel, observed the proceedings and later reported them with a mixture of horror and bewilderment. There was no longer any room for innocence. The accused faced the magistrates—to do otherwise would imperil the accusers, who might be struck dumb at a glance from the suspect. When the magistrates asked the girls to speak, they told of spectral evil. Particular girls were brought to the suspects, whose touch cured the fits, for a time at least. Touching was a regular part of many premodern English public rituals, as when the sovereign touched a sword to the shoulders of a new knight, barons kissed their vassals on their cheeks, and magistrates boxed the ears of youthful offenders in court. There was always a minister present, sometimes Hale, often Nicholas Noyes, always Parris. They were willing to ask the girls to reconsider, but most often failed to gain the least concession. Cary concluded that the hearing could have but one end, and the trials the same. He arranged for his wife's escape from custody.[81] As the web of accusations spun out beyond Cory and Nurse, to Sarah Cloyse and Mary Esty, Nurse's sisters, John and Elizabeth Proctor, to Elizabeth Cary and others in good standing in the church and the town, the magistrates no longer hesitated. The girls added new names to the list, and the magistrates brought all the accused to confront their accusers.

So dramatic and so portentous were these events that the deputy governor, Thomas Danforth, and four of the former Assistants—the governing council of the colony under the old charter—traveled to Salem to witness the spectacle on April 11. They were not disappointed. The meeting house was packed. Elizabeth Parris was gone, sent by her father to safety with Stephen Sewall, one of the four who came to hear and see the agony of the village girls. Abigail was there, joined by Indian John, who had started to have fits of his own (no doubt to avoid the fate of his consort), Mary Walcott, Mercy Lewis, and Ann Putnam Jr. They had found a new way to avoid bearing false witness. When asked who it was that afflicted them, they were struck dumb. Lewis's mouth was stopped; Putnam could not utter a word; Williams's fist was "thrust in her own mouth." Their silence became the accusation. Parris took notes as Cloyse and Elizabeth and John Proctor, his own parishioners, stood accused.[82]

Until this day, the Salem investigation had been a local affair; after all, these were neighbors and Salem was still one town. The boundaries of the inquiry expanded when Danforth, senior magistrate present, decided to take charge. At first he frightened the girls, telling them that lying would be punished in another, higher court. Awed by his manner and his office, Elizabeth Hubbard backed away from her earlier testimony that Cloyse and Elizabeth Proctor had come as specters and hurt her. In the middle of the examination, with Indian John showing his bruises and Ann Jr. and Abigail bawling, Proctor turned to the girls and admonished them gently but firmly, as she would her own children, that there was another, higher judgment, but Williams brazened out her earlier charges. In 1671, Elizabeth Knapp had made a similar accusation against an older church member in Groton, but minister Samuel Willard had interceded, brought the supposed witch to pray with Knapp, and Knapp recanted. The Devil had deceived her, the girl concluded, according to Willard.[83]

Danforth might have seen through the maze of contradictions and asserted his authority to quiet the crisis, but he faltered. Unsure whether to believe the girls but certain that the Devil was abroad and that witches were his agents, Danforth left the matter where it was. Another opportunity had been lost, but in fairness Danforth was not looking for such opportunities. He, more than the villagers, knew that the entire colony was in peril from the French and Indians to the north and west and the politicians in Westminster. The men returned to Boston. By the end of the summer, almost 150 women and men stood accused, and magistrates and victims were rushing all over Essex County taking depositions with the aid of the victims—for the girls had become witch finders, able to see into the recesses of suspects' hearts and the dark woods where the accused made their assignations with the Evil One.

Over time, the girls' performance approached professional quality; there were no slips, no muffed lines, as when Sarah Buckley was brought before Corwin and Hathorne on May 18. Abigail said, "[T]his is the woman that hath bit me with her scragged teeth a great many times."

Walcott and Putnam, standing nearby, had their mouths stopped by some supernatural force. Mercy Lewis swore she had seen Buckley the night before, in her spectral form. Elizabeth Hubbard agreed. The clerk, Samuel Parris again, in what had become his second career, continued, "Susan Sheldon [a late but eager addition to the girls' chorus] the like. Mary Warren, the like." No need to repeat repetitions. Buckley protested her innocence, to which Sheldon piped up, "[T]here is the black man [the Devil] whispering in her ear.[84]

By the beginning of the summer, the girls had only to fill in the blanks of the witch's name and make their own mark at the end of the deposition to secure an arrest. Thus Hubbard, Walcott, and Putnam all testified that they were beset by a woman who called herself Mistress Bradbury and that, when Mary Bradbury was brought before them, they recognized her. In every case, the specter of Bradbury then tortured the girl. There was no variation—Bradbury evidently lacking imagination as well as grace.[85]

The speed of the process crippled the ability of neighbors and family to resist accusations against their friends and loved ones. The oral networks that had tied neighbors together now were frayed by suspicion and accusation. Adults' animosities and fears were loosed by the flood of accusations and flowed into the hearings. Husbands turned against wives and wives against husbands. Frightened, disoriented (and perhaps abused) children informed on parents.[86] The accusations radiated out from Salem. In custody were women from Lynn—such as Sarah Basset, the sister of Elizabeth Proctor, from Topsfield, Abigail and Deliverance Hobbs, Sarah Wildes, and Elizabeth Howe, another of the Topsfield enemies of the Putnams—and a fair portion of Andover's adult population. Common fame had already labeled some as witches, such as Rachel Clinton of Ipswich and Susannah Martin of Amesbury. Husbands and fathers were held for questioning as well; indeed, whole families like the Barkers and Carriers of Andover were made to stand in fear.[87]

The tidal wave of accusations overwhelmed the institutions of criminal justice which had, until now, served the colony adequately. From a functional point of view, the purpose of a criminal justice system is to process those accused of crime. The key elements of colonial criminal justice—speed, inexpensiveness, social control—were adequately served in Massachusetts. But function did not dictate form. Rather, culture—the culture of a community of saints—shaped the laws and the institutions of criminal justice. The culture demanded that those whose conduct was hardly saintly conform to the norms laid down by the saints. The result was much contention but a remarkable degree of order.[88] The essence of Massachusetts criminal procedure, except in notorious cases, had been to force the accused to accept guilt and then to arrange for some punishment that permitted the accused to reinstate him- or herself in the social web.[89] Thus most accusations of witchcraft had failed to lead to conviction, even when neighbors complained over many years. Instead, some admonition or threat by the magistrates forced the suspect to conform more closely to the expectations of neighborliness and quieted, for a time at least, the community's fears. In this way, witchcraft accusations served to "protect group life."[90] Salem's trials did not, however, perform this function. Something went wrong.

Hunted in their homes, the faces of their neighbors turned against them, confined to jail in conditions that were degrading and unhealthy, more of the suspects began to confess.[91] The first had been Tituba. The next was Abigail Hobbs, on April 19. "I will speak the truth," she told the magistrates. "I have seen many sights and been scared. I have been very wicked. I hope I shall be better, if God will help me." Hobbs did not have the opportunity, like Tituba, deliberately to misunderstand and then reconfigure the magistrates' questions. She admitted she had seen the Devil. She reported their conversations. She described her familiars. She confessed to pinching Putnam and Lewis at the Devil's command, that she might have fine things. The next day, she identified Sarah Good as another witch and described how she had eaten the red bread and wine at the witches' sabbath in Parris's pasture.[92]

It was nonsense, and she knew it, but she had become an informer and could not stop. Her safety, for the executions began on June 10 with Bridget Bishop, depended upon the verisimilitude and the appropriateness of her testimony. When the magistrates wanted confirmation that George Burroughs, then living in Maine, was the leader of the witches' coven (no woman would do for that role), Hobbs obliged. From the Salem jail, on May 12, she deposed that Burroughs had brought the poppets to the other witches and showed them how to stick pins in the dolls.[93] She testified against John Proctor as well, on June 29.[94] She, more than Tituba, gave the magistrates what they wanted—evidence of a conspiracy of witches which threatened the colony.

Now Mary Warren, Proctor's servant, was brought before the magistrates. At first she blurted out that the girls had dissembled, and they responded by falling into fits. She turned informer on the accusers, and the gang reacted by denouncing her. Accused of witchcraft, without aid—there were no parents or ministers or legal counsel to help her—she swooned. Coming to, she spoke wildly and then was taken outside for fresh air. She could not continue, but summoned privately before the two justices of the peace, she recognized that salvation in this world required confession and contrition, and she admitted that she had seen the Devil. More gently now, Hathorne and Corwin led Warren through her story. For two more days she provided the confirmation that they needed and sought of the conspiracy of witches. Later, like Hobbs, she would be brought periodically from jail to accuse some new suspect.[95]

The danger that Warren posed to the other young accusers went beyond breaking ranks with the gang. Bearing false witness, perjury in a felony case, was itself a felony, and children were early taught the evils of such acts. Indeed, was not the Devil the "father of lies"?[96] If Warren were believed, then the other girls had perjured themselves in a felony prosecution that could end in the execution of the accused. All their own necks would be exposed to the gallows. Did the girls know this? One assumes that they knew lying was a sin and that lying under oath was a crime. Warren recanted just in time for everyone on the prosecution side to breathe easier, and none more than the other girls.[97]

The magistrates did not warn Warren that her recantation could lead to her prosecution for lying or false witness. Rather, they were looking for evidence confirming their suspicion, verging now on certainty, that a conspiracy of witches threatened the colony. Tituba had told them that there were other witches, and sure enough, more witches appeared. Even the girls had to fear that others might name them—in effect, their accusations, like Warren's, alone kept them safe from others' accusations. All of this fed the magistrates' fears, for by this time they had committed themselves to the search for witches and sought all confirming evidence.

The more they heard which confirmed the work of the Devil, the more skeptical of contradictory evidence the magistrates became. It is a classic example of the avoidance of cognitive dissonance. Dissonant evidence was discarded or attacked; consonant evidence was believed and integrated into the story. When Sarah Churchill confessed on June 1 to signing the Devil's book brought her by Ann Pudeator and then sticking pins into dolls to hurt Mercy Lewis and the other girls, she was believed. She had already implicated her master, George Jacobs Sr., and Bridget Bishop, to whom she now added Pudeator.[98] What the magistrates expected was what fit into their increasingly detailed cognitive scheme of the conspiracy. Suspects could offer contrition—copious tears, signs of repentance, admissions of guilt—and would be believed and welcomed, but angry countercharges, repeated denials, and tearful insistence on innocence could not be credited without cognitive dissonance.

The magistrates' dogged resistance to inconsistency and recantation rested upon more than their aversion to dissonance. They shared the larger psychology of Puritanism, a state of mental tension and unease. Election—salvation—lay wholly in the hands of God. People could not save themselves, though they might search penitently for signs of grace and order their steps upon the straight and narrow.[99] In the gap between justification through God's unhindered grace and the orderly life every good Puritan was expected to lead lay days of worry and nights of yearning for signs that he or she was truly regenerate. The magistrates were not immune to agonies of uncertainty about their own souls' state, and the stakes were raised by the witchcraft accusations. These were no ordinary crimes of violence. The Devil was about, and to be uncertain about his intentions was to lay open all of God's commonwealth to the Great Deceiver's evil plan. Their own religious convictions thrust upon Hathorne and Corwin the need to be sure, certain, unwavering, and right.

Churchill immediately told Sarah Ingersoll, the tavern keeper's wife, that Churchill feared for her soul, for she had undone herself through false accusation. When Ingersoll replied that she believed Churchill's confession, Churchill cried and explained that the magistrates had threatened her with incarceration in the same cell as George Burroughs (who Churchill was sure was a witch). Even those who knew they had perjured themselves and falsely accused others also believed that some of the accused were witches. Why had Churchill not recanted? She had been told that if she confessed, she would be trusted, but if she denied she was a witch, no one would believe her.[100] Thus even those accounts that defied common experience, like witches holding midnight sabbaths in open fields to which they flew on poles, were credited, for the alternative was to discredit an entire structure of belief and testimony. There was no way to limit credulity. Of course, witchcraft itself defied common experience, and some of the most popular learned writers of treatises on witchcraft admitted that the Devil might empower women to assume the shapes of animals or go from house to house in spectral form. The greater the stress on them to find the truth, the more the magistrates clung to what they had been told.[101]

130   Confession was good, for confession above all other things confirmed the case for the accusers.[102] What was more, confession fed confession, for each confession elicited more accusations. That was why the confessors themselves were kept safe for the time being at least. Some of them, notably the Barker family from Andover, confessing on August 29, when the trials were nearly over (though no one could yet predict it), told the examining magistrates that there were in excess of three hundred witches in the county, that they all flew to mass meetings in Salem, and that the Devil, a black man with a club foot, led services for them there.[103]

On May 14, help arrived, not from above—not God answering their prayers—but in the person of Governor William Phips, returned from England with a new charter and the power to do something about the crisis. As Cotton Mather, one of Phips' great admirers, later wrote, with characteristic hyperbole, "Sir William Phips, at last being dropt, as it were, from the Machine of Heaven, was an instrument for easing the distresses of the land."[104] Hardly the deus ex machina described by the younger Mather, Phips was a professional sailor, merchant, courtier, and warrior, a rude man who had risen from life on the Maine frontier to a place at the side of kings. He was not learned and had other problems on his mind. A politician, he was beset by those in the antiroyal party who did not want his mission to England to succeed. The witchcraft scandal made him look bad.[105] The new charter he brought was itself untested, and the control over the government of the colony it gave to the king was disquieting to many Puritans. Meanwhile, the jails were filling, and the colony teetered on the brink of chaos. Phips had to do something, but what?

the diviners

ON MARCH 1, Tituba had testified that the tall man with the white hair came from Boston. To her, Boston was not some exotic far-off place; she had lived there with her master and remembered the noisy, dangerous, fire-ridden, crowded, smoky, smelly, and cold streets. Yet when she reported that the tall man had come from Boston, she might have exhibited some of the second sight later attributed to her, for from Boston there soon arrived distinguished men to judge the suspected witches. With the judges came others, wizened, clothed in black, some of whom had white hair.[1] Were they witches too, these judges and ministers, their pious ways a sham? Puritans feared secret unregeneracy and prayed that they had not fooled themselves about their desire for grace, for God could not be fooled.

Tituba had found a chink in the Puritans' armor, and at least one of the pastoral fellowship felt her barb. Cotton Mather did not suspect that he was a witch, but he felt the hot, angry breath of Satan brush over his sleeve. He had already warned his compatriots, "An Army of Devils is horribly broke in upon the place which is our center," and vowed to stride forth against the foe armed with the shield of righteousness and the sword of good works.[2] In 1688, he had sniffed the sulfuric approach of the Evil One in the suffering of bewitched children. These were the

Goodwin boys and girls, whose travails Mather had revealed to the world beyond Boston in 1689.[3] By 1692, Mather detected that the Devil had turned his attention even closer to home: "And I myself expect not few or small buffetings from Evil Spirits."[4] In Cotton Mather the elite and the vernacular, the religious and the legal came together. He was, in some literal sense, the archetypical Puritan divine, and he faced the witchcraft crisis with great hopes and many fears.

Law and religion kept company in Puritan Massachusetts—although by the 1690s the companionship had grown quarrelsome. Religion depended upon faith, which for Puritans was all encompassing and everywhere, but religion was established in the colony not by faith but by law. With the demise of the original charter in 1684 through a legal process in the king's courts, the law that mandated Puritan belief was rescinded. Loosed on the colony by the Toleration Act of 1689 in England, the Anglicans, Quakers, and other disrupters of Puritan hegemony could no longer be contained.[5]

Yet even as it threatened to topple the reign of the saints, law could never make itself independent of religion in Massachusetts. Even in the years without a charter, the law in practice (as opposed to the law on the books in England) rested upon the religious ideal of a covenanted community. This law was God's law, embodied in codes of governance Massachusetts settlers had written for themselves, and the strictures of moral order persisted in people's minds. The criminal codes fashioned in 1641 and 1648 made such biblical offenses as blasphemy and disobedience to parents into capital crimes. It is not clear whether anyone was ever executed for these offenses, but they remained an exhortation to the sinner and the saint to stay within of the boundaries of good conduct. Whether English or biblical in origin, criminal law drew lines on the ground which men and women crossed at their peril.[6]

By the late spring of 1692, when the Puritan authorities had most need of the old certainties, the tried and true ways of ferreting out the Devil and his witches, the document upon which these truths rested, the first charter, was long gone, and the uncertain basis of Massachusetts criminal law and courts increased the danger and the visibility of witchcraft. There had been no trial of witches since 1688. Was the Devil using the ouster of Andros and the delay in obtaining a new charter as an opportunity to overthrow God's commonwealth? Political uncertainty made the acting government in Boston as nervous about witchcraft in general as the Indian raids in the north had made the people of Salem, Andover, and Beverly fear the malice of particular witches.[7]

The new charter told Phips and his councilors to conform to English law, but English law had not developed sure rules of evidence. Formal rules of evidence in criminal trials had not yet evolved and would not for many years after the 1690s.[8] The modern standard of "beyond a reasonable doubt" was not fully deployed in courts until the end of the eighteenth century and its meaning remains controversial to this day.[9] The foundational concept of empirical measurement of truth by a reasonable observer was emerging in English jurisprudence and philosophy by the end of the seventeenth century, but in any particular case the jury still had before it a mass of circumstantial and contested evidence.[10] Although Massachusetts law under the first charter had standards for legal proof, these were vague to the point of uselessness. Proof was to be convincing and sufficient, but the rules as written did not distinguish between conviction as a psychological state and conviction as a matter of moral certainty.[11] On what proof might conviction for witchcraft then rest? Sufficient evidence, of course, but witchcraft was a hidden crime. Who but another witch might know that the suspect had struck a pact with the Devil, or spot that the strange animal in the lane or the loft was a witch's "familiar"?

The best evidence of crime is probative: it proves to the jury that the facts are as alleged. Probative evidence may be direct, that is, eyewitness testimony, or indirect, re-created through a convincing sequence of circumstantial inferences. The worst evidence is mere prejudice, which induces a jury to reach a verdict on an improper basis. Witchcraft cases threw these precepts into confusion, for only perpetrators' or confederates' confessions could establish that a pact with the Devil existed (no one else saw him), and indirect evidence—the causal chain—rested upon spectral evidence that only victims could see. Such testimony might easily prejudice a jury, and defendants could not refute accusers' assertions because no one else could observe what the accusers swore they saw.

Judges bore the burden of deciding what evidence the jury was permitted to hear. In earlier English history, the trial jury determined the verdict based upon its own knowledge. In effect, the jury generated the evidence. By the 1690s, this had been displaced by the notion that the jury was to hear and see the evidence presented at trial and, weighing that alone, putting aside their own preexisting conceptions, reach a finding of fact.[12] The jury was allowed to hear the reading of depositions of witnesses and victims even though these people were available to testify in person. Today the best evidence is always the person himself or herself, although a deposition taken earlier may be used to impeach the veracity of the witness's testimony at trial. Hearsay, which cannot be admitted in a modern criminal proceeding, save when an accessory, with corroboration, testifies to a conspiracy, was perfectly fair game in these trials (as it was in England, to be sure, although there it was highly suspect by the end of the seventeenth century).[13] On the civil side of the docket of Massachusetts courts, particularly in cases involving land ownership, hearsay was a staple. Those proceedings took the form of neighbors and kin coming to court and deposing that they remembered that someone told them that someone else recalled a third person running the survey line of the disputed parcel past the old oak tree by the edge of the meadow. In general, judges allowed into evidence a wide array of assertions, tales, surmises, and gossip.

Judges could instruct juries on how they were to weigh any piece of evidence, but judges could not tell juries what they were to believe. A juror's "conviction" depended not on a judge's ruling but on the cognitive structures of that juror's mind. Judges instructed seventeenth-century jurors to look to their conscience, but conscience was not only a moral faculty, it was a way of sifting truth from falsehood. "A safe conscience" meant a discerning intelligence, and witchcraft presented special problems for even the most informed conscience.[14] Jurors needed help that went beyond legal rulings—they needed to know what was real and what was imagined, what they could trust and what they ought to disregard in the evidence. The jurors required a diviner.

When witchcraft disrupted a West African village, the victimized family consulted a diviner. The diviner sought to find the origin of the forces that had disrupted the family's well-being. Victims and suspects then joined in the rituals of cleansing, paying reparations if necessary or sacrificing to the gods.[15] To the Puritans such a rite would have seemed primitive and unwholesome, but that is the essence of what the jurors—indeed, what the victims and their families as well—wanted the authorities to do: find the cause of their illness, cleanse and make them whole. The magistrates in Salem turned to the governor of the colony, newly arrived in Boston. He repaired to his council and created a special court. The court turned to the ministers. Not only were the latter the keepers of the conscience of the churches, they were well-trained intellectuals, versed in the signs and dissimulations of witchery. They would know what to look for and how to see it. Just as Tituba had envisioned, men in black robes were bringing their books to Salem.

Together, the judges and ministers were diviners, spokesmen for God's will, His regents, who could penetrate and expose the Devil's plot. Massachusetts law revered ministers and respected judges.[16] Yet every diviner has to earn his way. Only those who correctly foretold the future would be credited in the future. Witches and wizards held themselves out as diviners, and "the country people" were easily deceived by such false conjurers and tricksters. The "illiterate" masses needed a guide, and such guide had to be "learned, very learned." The people were to shun the cunning man and the wizard, for they were witches themselves. The private witch finder, like Caleb Powell in Newbury and Matthew Hopkins in England, who would "defame ten that [were] innocent before he discover[ed] one that [was] guilty," was almost as dangerous as the witch. Instead, divining witchcraft's malignity was to be left "to the power of the magistracy and the ministry."[17]

The court that heard the first witchcraft cases in 1692 was specially convened—a court of oyer and terminer—literally, in the old "law French" that was the second tongue of English law, to "hear and determine" a case. Such courts were common in the colonies.[18] As in any of the other royal colonies such as Virginia or New York, in Massachusetts the governor had the discretion to commission courts specially. True, Phips did not have explicit authority from the new charter or the home government to create such a court, and he could—perhaps should— have waited until the new General Court (the colonial assembly) met in early June or later in October.[19] The fact is that he did not wait, for waiting, he judged, would only lead to more accusations, more incarcerations, and perhaps the spread of cases from Essex County all over the colony. Far away in England, John Evelyn pierced to the heart of the matter, noting in his diary: "unheard of stories of the universal increase of witches in New England; men, women, and children devoting themselves to the Devil so as to threaten the subversion of government."[20] Phips could not have put it better.

The commission he issued revealed these concerns. Promulgated on May 27, "in council," that is, figuratively in front of the councilors named in the new charter to aid Phips in governing the colony, the commission demonstrated that Phips was worried about public order, not justice. He began, "[T]here are many criminal offenders now in custody" (presumably guilty, else they were not offenders), and against them the commissioners were to hear and determine "all manner of crimes and offenses." The judges were to act "according to the law and custom of England and of this their Majesties' Province," a command dictated by the charter and somewhat disingenuously (or perhaps just negligently, for Phips was no lawyer) ignoring the difference between the law of the two jurisdictions. Phips delegated authority to a number of his councilors, doubling as the commissioners, to resolve the matter expeditiously. He was a military man and wanted action, having little use by temperament or training for delicate compromise, much less deliberation, and none for niceties of legal procedure. No, the real problem was that there were "many inconveniences attending the thronging of the jails [by suspects] at this hot season of the year." The prisoners might die of disease or, worse, might break out en masse. Either way his reputation and good order in the colony were at stake. He knew that the contagion, literal and figurative, had expanded far beyond Salem Village, for the commission conceded that the court would hear all cases "within the counties of Suffolk, Essex, Middlesex, and each of them."[21]

Of the councilor-judges he named, William Stoughton, John Richards, Wait Winthrop, and Samuel Sewall had been judges of the Court of Assistants that met under the old charter. It was natural for Phips to turn to those who had superior court credentials and were already in office, although he could not have overlooked the fact that a few days earlier he and the council had reestablished the courts.[22] In effect, the lawmakers doubled as the judges, just as they had been under the old charter. There was no bar to holding more than one office in the American colonies. Indeed, Stoughton, the chief judge of the hastily assembled court, was the lieutenant governor of the colony and, as a councilor, a member of the upper chamber of the legislature.

Trained for the ministry at Harvard, Stoughton sought in vain evidence of his own conversion. Without a visitation of grace, he wavered in his choice of career. In his youthful sermons he railed against the hypocrisy and degeneracy of his own generation, then embraced its vices by exchanging the pulpit for politics. By middle age an unattractive character but an astute manager of his own affairs, with experience as a land speculator and defrauder of the Native Americans, he had the highest political ambitions, and his skills in political infighting were superbly honed. During the old charter, he had gone to England to lobby for the colony against revocation of its charter, then changed sides to serve his political ally Joseph Dudley during the brief period of councilor government in 1686 after the charter was revoked. He remained a judge under Governor Andros, while managing to convince most of his countrymen that he still favored their interests over the Crown's, and then landed on his feet "like a cat" when Andros was jailed and his government overturned in 1689. When Phips was recalled in 1694, Stoughton succeeded him. Years later Stoughton remained convinced that he had done right by God and country in his conduct of the trials.[23] A portrait of him done late in life shows a dour, long-faced man, his features doughy and slack.[24]

Returning to Salem from Boston with Stoughton was Bartholomew Gedney, a Salem physician and merchant (one of the new breed who had wanted a second church in the town and closer ties to England) and an old cohort of the chief judge. They had sat together on Dudley's short-lived council, along with Hathorne. Unpopular for a time in Salem, Gedney and Hathorne nevertheless sniffed the wind and joined in the rebellion against Andros in time to be reinstated in power under the new charter.[25] Corwin would sit on the bench after the June 2 trials, but he was the last judge from Salem. The others were not Salem men.[26]

Stoughton brought with him to the special court's bench a crew of time servers and pole climbers such as Connecticut-born and -bred Wait Winthrop, grandson of John Winthrop, a man who lacked the moderation of his father and the statesmanship of his grandfather. The youngest Winthrop spent most of his time feuding with his in-laws over the division of his father's real estate, dabbling in commercial ventures, and seeking political office, which he managed to hold under the old charter, the Dominion, and after the ouster of Andros, the interim government. His real skills lay largely in the area of self-promotion and sycophancy, a politic combination.[27] Expressing his confidence in Winthrop, Cotton Mather had dedicated *Memorable Providences* to him: "Your knowledge has qualified you to make those reflections on the following relations, which few can think, and this not fit that all should see." Stoughton had watched with near paternal pride (for the lieutenant governor was a bachelor) the progress of young Mather.[28] Judge John Richards was a merchant from Boston, a leader of the mercantile party there, and a supporter of Phips. Richards had joined Stoughton in Dudley's government. Like Stoughton and Winthrop, he was a close personal friend of Cotton

Mather and a member of his church. Ironically, Winthrop, with Richards and Stoughton, sat on the Court of Assistants that would have heard the Salem cases had it not ceased to exist after March 1692.[29]

138

The other members of the court were less closely associated with the Mathers but had long experience with the courts in the colony. Nathaniel Saltonstall was a farmer-soldier from Haverhill whose fairness, leniency, and repute had made him a perennial choice for the Assistants and later the council. He served as a justice of the peace for the county and sat on the quarterly courts in Salem on occasion.[30] After the first trial of suspected witches, he left the court and had no more to do with the trials.[31] Samuel Sewall, a Boston merchant whose diary shows profound sensibility and good sense, was also troubled by the trials. He had gone to Harvard with George Burroughs and counted him a friend, but Sewall was also a man of traditional beliefs. He had no doubt that witchcraft was abroad and sat through the summer without recording in his diary or letters any overt dismay with the conduct of the trials. He participated in all of them but five years later made a public confession of his error.[32]

When Phips sent a court to Salem to hear and determine the witchcraft cases, the question of proof became paramount. The judges had to divine whether the girls' claims of spectral visitations were creditable, that is, whether they might properly go to the jury. This was the threshold question, and the judges had no sure guides to its answer. They turned to the prosecutor. The first crown prosecutor that Phips appointed, Thomas Newton, had experience as a prosecutor in a highly charged political case not three years earlier. Newton presented the crown case against Jacob Leisler, who had accomplished in New York what a number of the judges sitting in Salem had done in Massachusetts—overthrow a royal government—but Leisler would not relinquish power to King William's appointees. Leisler was hanged. At thirty-two, Newton expected that a long and prosperous career lay ahead for the man who swiftly drove the Devil out of Salem, but nothing in his political aspirations told him whether spectral evidence ought to be admissible.[33] Newton was replaced on July 27 by Anthony Checkley, the newly appointed attorney general of the colony. He was an experienced Salem lawyer (he represented Corwin among others in court) but no jurist.[34]

Newton and later Checkley and the judges had before them conflicting and controverted English opinion. Sewall and Winthrop had recently returned from England and could only have reported that witchcraft cases were disappearing from the courts.[35] Learned opinion was divided, although leaning strongly against the possibility that witches could do what was attributed to them. To instruct the jurors, the judges needed to know themselves what was plausible, in the words of Increase Mather, "without offering violence to reason and common sense."[36] But Increase Mather was a "tactician," and he preferred to remain in the background rather than advise the court.[37]

Not so his son. No divine had more to do with the forthcoming trials than Cotton Mather. His story is inextricably interwoven with the cases, for he was more than an elite spokesman for a book-bound priesthood.[38] Mather was a believer in the invisible world, the world of amazing events that gave a window into God's purposes.[39] With a mixture of arrogant carelessness and true belief Mather aspired to bridge the gap between the popular and the elite across a span of miraculous prodigies. He continued his father's efforts to collect accounts of supernatural events and placed himself at the center of such inquiries when they occurred locally. Mather's account of the only Boston witchcraft case to come to trial after 1655, the supposed bewitching of the Goodwin children in 1688, made him appear to be a source of wisdom on witches. In 1692, he was poised to speak for the elite to the people and for the people to the elite. Only lacking was the occasion.

The close tie between ministerial roles and magisterial roles in New England made the judges' recourse to the ministers a natural step. Church courts were an alternative to criminal courts for many misdemeanors, and many crimes were religious in origin. The ministry was also highly politicized, as it had been since the founding of the colony, making the clergy into an informal network of political advisors. Ministers did not sit as judges, but they had already played a hand in the struggles that surrounded the dismantling of the Dominion and the ouster of Andros. This connection may seem untoward to us, with our well-mortised wall of separation between church and state, but then the ministers were more than preachers and pastors. They were adepts, in a time when moral judgment and natural truths were not severed from each other by a belief in the efficacy of science. They expected to be consulted in the crisis.

With Increase Mather away in England trying to negotiate a new charter for the colony, Cotton aspired to the first place among these political divines. He had preached openly against the Dominion and was on the list of proscribed ministers when the Dominion fell—indeed, a warrant for his arrest had been issued, and he was sought at the very moment that Andros's government was crashing down. Long an advocate of reform of the General Court, Cotton Mather had tried to marshal public opinion, in the form of a great revival of piety, in the service of political faction as well as God.[40] Mather may have confused the two, for at the opening of the year, he searched the heavens and the earth for a "miraculous thing" to report to his diary. He was ready to fight the Devil himself in any arena of the latter's choosing.[41]

Had Mather been less defensive and more reflective, he might have conceded that until 1692 his life had been a series of unrealized promises made and unredeemed in his father's shadow. One of these bore directly on the coming furor. Increase had published the first fruits of his effort to collect omens and prodigies; Cotton continued the task. Tales of witchcraft were central to this anthology of omens and prodigies.[42] If the scrutiny of unusual events and their meaning was long a part of Puritan self-examination, it took on new and heightened importance in the 1690s. Matters of religious doctrine, once the prime battleground for Puritans, were no longer so important, and after the Toleration Act there was no going back to the persecution of Baptists, Anglicans, and Quakers which had sated the fighting instincts of earlier generations of Puritan divines. Instead, Mather correctly reckoned, the crucial ministerial issues for his generation were moral and social, part of the goal of recovering the founders' community spirit and the purity of worship. Against this, he judged, the threat of witchcraft was primarily directed, for witchcraft did not raise doctrinal problems so much as social ones.

Asked by Judge Richards to come to the first session of the court of oyer and terminer in June, Mather demurred. His health would not permit travel; his constitution was broken by toil. He had offered to take some of the girls into his own home, as with the Goodwin children. This might have been a mark of his skepticism about their fits. An astute observer of nature (he regularly sent his horticultural experiments to the Royal Society in England), he needed to see for himself before he decided.[43] At the same time, the offer evidenced a self-centeredness, an exaggerated belief in his own centrality to these events, which could bend his judgment out of shape. He wrote a letter to Richards on May 31, and in it Mather rearranged the arguments of previous generations of English clerics and jurists on the issue of proof of witchcraft. In treatises and tracts, charges to grand juries and philosophical lectures, these Englishmen had debated "Cases of Conscience" wherein men and women stood accused of witchcraft. Mather, a bibliophile, had read them all, and the result he passed on to Richards.

The outlines of the debate itself were clear by 1692, for the argument was coming to its close in England. English Puritans always had an important stake in the question. Witchcraft, conceptualized by the Elizabethan statutes and later the Jacobean statute of 1604, as a religious crime as well as a crime against persons, attracted Puritans' attention because a number of nonconforming preachers had set themselves up as diviners. With the Roman Church and its rituals of exorcism banished in Reformation England, there was no defense against possession save prayer and soul-searching, at which the Puritans excelled. Puritan laypersons went about the countryside curing the afflicted of possession, and Puritan divines supported these efforts.

The nondissenting churchmen suspected and found, in some cases, that the possessed and the demon chasers both were fraudulent, but under the prodding of King James I, cases under the statutes still went to the courts, and judges told juries how to weigh the testimony and physical evidence of witchcraft. With the ordeals of burning the hand and sinking the body of suspected witches gone, other means had to be found to identify witches, but how were juries to determine that a defendant had actually made a pact with the Devil when the Devil was careful to keep himself concealed? The European witch hunt gathered its evidence through intimidation and torture, but English courts, with some exceptions, eschewed these methods. Instead, a jury had to be convinced. In 1584, Reginald Scot, who professed to believe in witches and the Devil, nevertheless dismissed most of the claims made by witch hunters and the confessions made by witches as pure nonsense—old women deluded themselves and gullible men listened:

> The common people have beene so assotted and bewitched, with whatsoever poets have feigned of witchcraft, either in earnest, in jest, or else in derision, and with whatsoever lowd liers and cozeners for their pleasures heerein have invented, and with whatsoever tales they have heard from old doting women, or from their mother's maids, and with whatsoever the grandfoole their ghostlie father, or anie other morrow masse preest had informed them; and finallie with whatsoever they have swalled up through tract of time, or through their owne timerous

nature or ignorant conceipt, concerning these matters of hagges and witches [that they are credulous to a fault].[44]

In reply, William Perkins, a Puritan divine wholly trusted and openly admired a century later by Cotton Mather, believed that the Devil was a more potent enemy than Scot would concede and that witchcraft was "rife" in England in the 1590s—the same conclusion Cotton Mather reached about Massachusetts a century later.[45] Perkins offered a compendium of old and new techniques of proof to the justices of the peace, who were the gatherers of evidence in cases of serious crime.[46] They examined witnesses and suspects, bound over the latter for trial, and insured that the evidence and the defendant were put before the grand jury and the trial jury at the semiannual holdings of the assize courts. Perkins solemnly reminded these magistrates that they were not to act on slight causes or through malice. They were to weigh "presumptions" of witchcraft, signals that the accusation was to be taken seriously but not quite proofs that the accusation was true. Perkins, no lawyer, used words such as "probably," "conjecturally," and "presumption" as though they were synonyms. Common fame, a notorious reputation, was the first of these presumptions, but common fame might be no more than slander. The confession of fellow witches had to be taken seriously, but it was not sufficient, for it too might be motivated by malice. Curses followed by the illness of the person cursed were important signs, as were quarrels that seemed to precede a mysterious illness. If the suspect was a relative of a known witch, the matter was to be noted. The magistrate might look for the Devil's mark, but such a mark was not proof of concourse with the Devil. If the suspect contradicted herself, she might have a guilty conscience, and that was a serious matter as well. The presumptions singly and together did not amount to proof but prompted further inquiry. Perkins missed the irony here, or he did not wish to credit it: the presumptions were the very same acts and omissions, muttering, illnesses, bad fortune, and animus, which led to the accusation in the first place. Calling suspicion presumption did not calibrate it or confine its virulence, for in real life presumption easily turned into certitude.

Perkins offered his readers more strenuous "proofs," including a "free and voluntary confession" taken after due examination upon pregnant circumstances. If two established witches testified that they saw the defendant make a pact with the Devil and also witnessed the defendant performing acts of witchcraft, that was enough. Perkins was aware that such proofs could be faked or result from duress, and he had his readers consider carefully: without proof, there could be no death sentence: "[F]or though presumption be never so strong, yet they [presumptions] are not proofs sufficient for conviction, but only for examination." Jurors were not to have on their consciences "innocent blood." Perkins wrote as a minister, and his desire was not to punish all the guilty—that was already arranged by God—but to prevent injustice from damning the accuser and the trier of fact.[47]

Perkins was cautious, but those who popularized him were bolder. Typically, Michael Dalton, whose much read and respected *The Country Justice* (1619) became a manual for justices of the peace in Massachusetts as it was in England, warned that magistrates could expect no "direct evidence," for the witches' works were "the works of darkness." He told his readers to look for what the witch had hidden: familiars and poppets, threats and curses, and the appearance of the witch's "apparition to the sick party in his fits." Common fame, denunciation by other suspects, a corpse bleeding when touched by the supposed witch, the confession of children of the suspect, and "when the victim [saw] visibly some apparition" were sure proofs. Dalton, a compiler, compiled everything without exercising any critical judgment, and he welcomed spectral evidence.[48]

With Dalton in hand, magistrates freely bound over witches for trial, but other Puritan writers recognized that Perkins meant to dampen the ardor of witch hunters, not fan it. Richard Bernard, a Puritan divine who modestly described himself as a "plain country minister" but was widely read, tried to counter prosecutorial credulity in a *Guide to Grand Jury Men* (1630). Bernard claimed to have seen many cases of supposed witchcraft, and he counseled grand jurors to be careful. God allowed the Devil to do evil, and the Devil knew that irreligious people were the first to blame witches for their own faults. There were wholly natural (if uncommon) illnesses that presented themselves as possession or bewitchery. There were even those who counterfeited symptoms for gain or revenge, to gull others, and to make themselves the center of attention. Such playactors could be convincing. Bernard did not doubt that there were witches, and he condemned the actions of "good" witches and bad ones, for even cunning folk depended for their prowess upon dark forces. The remedy for witchcraft was prayer, not unsubstantiated accusation or "white" witchcraft. Maleficent witches had to be executed, but only with proof, and proof meant witnesses to the act.[49]

Bernard believed that witches were a genuine danger, and his cautions were matched by his zeal for punishment, but the next widely read pamphlet for grand jurymen went further than Bernard's position. Puritan John Gaule, appalled by Matthew Hopkins' short but brutal reign as witch finder of Essex in the mid-1640s, warned that confessions had to be freely made and accompanied by facts, for confessions by a deluded suspect had to be suspect themselves. Hopkins and his crew had tortured suspects to get admissions of guilt. The best answer to suspicion of the supernatural was prayer, thanksgiving, and a pure heart, not the witch hunt.[50]

In 1653, shortly before he died, Robert Filmer, a royalist squire and a great and vocal opponent of the Puritans, jumped into the controversy. Filmer, later known for his treatise on the biblical origins of rightful authority, *Patriarcha,* linked Puritan witch finders like Perkins to Jesuits like Martin Del Rio. "Neither Mr. Perkins nor the Jesuit" seemed to accept the inherent difficulty of proving guilt, for the witch was only an accessory; it was the Devil who was truly guilty. Filmer told magistrates to ignore Perkins entirely, for Perkins mistook indications for proofs and ignored how facilely innocent people confessed when put in fear or under duress. Filmer's purposes were as political (he derided the Puritans for their sanguinary credulity) as jurisprudential, but he was not alone. Philosopher Thomas Hobbes openly declared that witches could not take spectral form (much less fly through the night), and poet Samuel Butler lampooned the excesses of Hopkins and his witch hunters.[51]

One can imagine Cotton in his library with all the texts scattered about, opened to the relevant pages, trying to make sense of the debate, under terrific stress with so much at stake. Presumption was a matter of logical inference, and the science of logic was well established in Perkins' time, but the nature of empirical causation—that is, what kinds of causes a rational person ought to credit—was in a state of flux. Reading Perkins in his own time, one would find it easy to accept that a quarrel with a possible witch, followed by an illness, or denying a possible witch charity, followed by harm, could mean that the victim had been bewitched. Logic, in and of itself, was not proof against contemporary belief, for the first premises of any logical argument are those dictated not by logic but by culture.

To read Perkins in the 1680s with these same notions of empirical causation was another matter entirely. Concepts of probability, rationality, and causation had changed in the passing of a century, as some later English commentaries on Perkins' work demonstrated. Indeed, by the second half of the century, the argument over proofs of witchcraft had merged into a larger debate over probability, rationality, and empiricism. To be sure, the triumph of science over the supernatural was hardly complete in 1692. In fact, learned defenses of belief in witchcraft underwent a modest revival in the 1660s and 1670. In the absence of uncontested authority, Cotton Mather was free to prefer Joseph Glanvill's assertion that spectral evidence was valid to John Webster's attack on "gross, absurd, impious and popish opinions" that magnified "the powers of demons and witches."[52] After all, Glanvill was a major theologian; Webster was obscure. Mather believed that witches did make pacts with the Devil, even if other English authorities did not.[53]

In the end, Mather elected to read Perkins as though the later commentaries on Perkins and the process of criticism they represented were a gloss upon a contemporary text rather than the rethinking and refinement of a century. Mather was aware of Webster and other critics of the older view, and his letter to Richards seemed to straddle the controversy rather than resolving it, but in the end he made clear that he believed in spectral evidence. He wrote, "[Y]ou do not lay more stress upon specter testimony than it will bear. When you are satisfied or have good, plain, legal evidence that the demons which molest our poor neighbors do indeed represent such and such people to the sufferers, tho' this be a presumption, yet I suppose you will not reckon it a condition that the people so represented are witches to be immediately exterminated." Devils could chose the shapes of innocent people to do their mischief, just as Sarah Osborn and Rebecca Nurse had pleaded at their examinations, a little more than two months earlier. Yet those accused might be "malignant, envious, malicious" and thereby open their souls to the Devil's importunities. Still, if upon purely spectral evidence, that is, the victims' claiming to see a vision of the defendant in spectral form, the court found convincing proof of witchcraft, then a door would be opened, "for the Devils to obtain from the courts in the invisible world a license to proceed unto most hideous desolations upon the repute and repose of such as have yet been kept from the great transgression." In other words, no one would be safe from such accusations. At the same time, Mather was convinced that in Salem "a horrible witchcraft" had been uncovered and that many innocents suffered from the witches' activities. The effects were "dreadfully real," and the cause of them was "a capital crime." Mather fretted, "Our neighbors at Salem are blown up after a sort, with an infernal gunpowder, under the floor," an obvious reference to Guy Fawkes' Roman Catholic plot to blow up the houses of Parliament. Though the plot was nearly a century old and was uncovered before the conspirators could do any damage, it was still fresh in the Protestant imagination, for it connected religion, politics, and demonology. Mather, following Glanvill, Baxter, and others, was convinced that the Roman church encouraged demons and witches. Thus Puritans joined hands with Anglicans to celebrate the ouster of James II, a Romanist, and to welcome England's new Protestant king, Prince William of Orange. The Reformation was not secure for these men, and they publicly petitioned King William to scourge the land of papists at the same time as the ministers mounted a new campaign against devilish practices in the church.[54]

146

Mather could have chosen a different course. He might have rejected spectral evidence outright, aligning himself with the "moderns." The battle between the moderns and the ancients was a current topic for men and women of letters, important enough to be parodied by Jonathan Swift in his "Battle of the Books" only a few years later. For Swift, the "moderns" in this mock heroic contest among the books on the shelves of the St. James Library were a "confused multitude" of "rogues and ragamuffins," though they ultimately won their struggle against the classics.[55] In some matters Mather sided with the moderns. He considered himself a scientist, and his work in botany and other subjects commended him to the Royal Society and eventually gained him membership in it.[56] For Mather, perhaps, specters were not an exception to modernism, for contemporary scientific opinion could not rule out what today one might call out-of-body or extrasensory experiences. That is to say, although the witches might not be able to fly, they might be able to project their image into the psyches of impressionable subjects and harm those subjects. If intentional—that is, carried on by the witches themselves, rather than the Devil masking his appearance with that of an innocent person—such spectral visitations would be a form of battery. If the victim suffered serious harm, the battery would amount to a wounding. If the subject died, the battery became murder. Voodoo operates in this fashion on those individuals who are predisposed to belief in its efficacy.

Again the problem was one of evidence, and it is not an easy one, not then, not now. Here Mather could find no answers in his library. He had to step into the street and enter the world of ordinary people. No abstract theory or abstruse theology could dictate commonly accepted contemporary notions of testamentary credibility.[57] The parallel to children's evidence in child abuse cases is again striking and informative. Modern authorities, at least until quite recently, tended to believe what children said in cases of suspected sexual abuse because the authorities could not accept the possibility that children could make up such stories. In recent years, such a conclusion has been challenged. Children— even very young children—are so tutored in the danger signs of abuse that they know how to fashion a plausible accusation and have, just as girls in Salem knew enough about witchcraft to fake the symptoms. And Mather had seen the suffering of children—his own and others'. He knew how suddenly and senselessly death could come to the young.[58]

Despite Cotton Mather's inclination to believe the girls, an inclination based upon his own experience with the Goodwin children and contemporary standards shared by the entire community, he could not bring himself to rely entirely upon the popular or the profane. There had to be some formal legal authority upon which to base his "learned, very learned" opinion, and he found it: a printed account of Chief Justice Matthew Hale's trial of accused witches at Bury St. Edmunds, at the Lent Assizes in 1664.[59]

Mather's version of the cases, dated 1682, recounted the suffering of the two Durent children and others supposedly at the hands of Rose Cullender and Amy Duny. When the girls took sick, a doctor advised their mother to hang the children's blanket in the chimney corner all day and to shake it out at night. Plainly this was a form of countermagic, for the good doctor was convinced that the girls' fits could not have a natural cause. When the mother shook it out, a toad fell to the floor, which the girls' brother burned in the fire. Duny was in pain the next day. Soon the girls' fits worsened, however, and they saw specters of the witches. In court, they renewed their fits and pointed to the spectral forms of the defendants. They vomited pins and convulsed themselves, and only the execution of the sentence of death upon the accused ended the children's misery. Indeed, they recovered completely. Hale evidently instructed the jury that spectral evidence was acceptable. That Hale's view was disputed at the time—indeed, at the very same moment he was crediting spectral evidence, his fellow judges at the Somerset Assizes were dismissing it— might have dissuaded a trained jurist from citing Hale without corrective, but these considerations did not deter Mather.[60]

A confession was best, and Mather tended to believe confessions, as

Filmer and Webster did not. Had not some of the witches already confessed? In other countries, such confessions were regarded by inquisitors with derision or incredulity—the confessors had to be deranged or liars[61]—but in England and New England they had become an accepted proof of complicity, as Increase Mather reported in his *Illustrious Providences* (1684): "It is a vain thing, for the patrons of witches to think they can sham of this argument, by suggesting that these confessions did proceed from the deluded imaginations of mad and melancholy persons." Although some confessions were undoubtedly forced or foolish, others were not. That is how Increase read Perkins, at least.[62]

Moreover, Cotton Mather allowed that the suspected witches' words could be used against them even when the suspects denied being witches. He did not require that collaborators' testimony be corroborated in some way, but that was a technical point, and he did not trace out the technical points of law. Mather even hinted that the marks and ordeals that his predecessors explicitly ruled out might be brought back in, when the circumstances were pregnant, for Mather was certain in his heart that the Devil was behind the evil events in Salem.[63] Cotton Mather read Perkins' caution in the light of Salem's and Massachusetts's exigency—in particular, the political crisis of the colony and the terrors of war. War against the Devil and war against the popish French and their Indian allies were the same in his mind. Caution played into the hands of the enemies of Cotton Mather's brand of Puritanism, and he urged Richards to credit what he heard.

On June 2, he did. The first defendant brought to trial was Bridget Bishop. As in a state trial, which the prosecution cannot afford to lose, the most notorious offender is the first presented to the jury. Bishop fit that description. As early as 1679 neighbors suspected her of witchcraft. Wonn, a black slave, had seen her image in a barn, stealing eggs. When he approached, she vanished, to reappear, he later testified, as a mysterious black cat.[64] No one came forward then or later to argue for her. At her hearing in Salem in 1692, she was contrary and diffident by turns. Hathorne had tried to trap her in a lie and succeeded.[65] Accused of being a witch, she puffed, "I am innocent to a witch, I know not what a witch is." Hathorne pounced: "How do you know then that you are not a witch?" Bishop, who surely did know what a witch was, for she had been accused of it before, and everyone knew what witches were, fell back upon deafness: "I do not know what you say." When Hathorne pressed on that Bishop had been accused by confessed witches, she retorted, "I know nothing of it," and Hathorne again had caught her lying. The clerk read to her that "John Hutchinson and John Lewis in open court affirmed that they had told her." Hathorne crowed: "[W]hy look you, you are taken now in a flat lye." What could she say? She stood alone, naked to her enemies, and they were legion.[66]

As the trial date approached, the magistrates gathered an impressive array of affidavits to her malignity and misconduct. Confessed witches Deliverance Hobbs and Mary Warren deposed that Bishop was one of them. Samuel Grey and others swore that Bishop had visited them at night and tormented them. The Reverend Hale passed on hearsay from his parishioners (for Bishop lived on the border with the town of Beverly) that she was the cause of evil among them. A jury of matrons found unnatural "excrescence of flesh . . . not usual in women" on Bishop's body. The grand jury found four indictments against Bishop for exercising "certain detestable arts called witchcrafts and sorceries" on Lewis, Williams, Hubbard, and Ann Putnam Jr. The indictments did not cite the earlier acts of suspected witchcraft, however, but only the spectral visitation of Bishop upon the girls as they testified against her at the April 19 hearings. Thus spectral evidence was the crucial evidence.[67]

At trial, on June 2, Bishop pleaded not guilty, but again the girls testified that it was her specter that afflicted them. With this testimony admitted, the door was opened to all manner of spectral testimony, and Samuel Grey, John Cook, John Bly and his wife, Richard Coman, Samuel Shattuck, John Louder, William Stacy, and William Bly described in vivid detail to the jury how they came to believe that Bishop was behind the misfortunes that had befallen them over the years. The pattern was always the same: a quarrel with Bishop, followed by bad luck. Sometimes she appeared in spectral form to claim credit for her work. The *pièce de résistance*: "As this woman was under a Guard, passing by the great and spacious Meeting-house of Salem, she gave a look towards the house, and immediately a daemon invisibly entering the Meeting-house, torn down a part of it."[68] The jury was convinced, and some days later Stoughton signed the death warrant. Bishop was hanged in Salem on June 10.[69]

Appalled by the conduct of the trial and wishing no more to do with it, Saltonstall resigned. Corwin was named to replace him. Sewall kept his own counsel, but his minister in Boston, Samuel Willard, would not be muzzled and, with Saltonstall, may have contacted Phips. Phips had created the court and then gone off to fight the French and Indians in

Maine. He was dismayed at the news of dissent on the bench and formally asked the ministers to report their thoughts to him and his council. Some of the ministers, including John Hale and Willard, had witnessed what happened at the first sitting of the court, the writhing of the girls and the absurd performance of Indian John, the reappearance of medieval forms of proof like the touching test, the absence of due process—even the little due process given suspected felons—and they recoiled. Mather had not traveled to Salem and could not dispute their account, nor did he wish to demean the honesty of their feelings. At the same time, they had not seen his letter to Richards, condoning in advance the very techniques they found revolting when the session was done.

The Ministerial Association met at Willard's insistence and asked Mather to prepare for its members a "Return of Several Ministers." On June 15, it issued forth. The "Return" retreated from Mather's own views and insisted that the court reduce the noise and openness of the trials. More important, no spectral evidence was to be admitted, nor were the suspects to be forced to touch the afflicted. The letter stopped short of condemning the outcome of the trial, however, and more important, ended with a final paragraph that Mather had undoubtedly written on his own—that is, it was his contribution to the letter, and the other signatories had to accept it as his price for signing on. On behalf of all thirteen signatories he urged "the speedy and vigorous prosecution of such as ha[d] rendered themselves obnoxious."[70] All Cotton's life had led to this moment; all his aspirations and his achievements were now bound in the few pages that he sent on to Salem.

For the judges preparing for their second sitting, the issue was simpler than it was for the ministers. The latter had to reconcile science and theology, Bible and reason. The judges had only to decide whether spectral evidence still could be admitted in court. The "Return" of the ministers said to stop using spectral evidence, but Mather was using a backstairs entry to the judges' chambers, and he supported the use of spectral evidence.[71] The final paragraph of the "Return" was an amalgam of politics and presumptions, and this is what urged the judges to complete their work as they had begun it. Mather was an ally of Phips, an admirer of Judge Stoughton, and did not wish to injure or annoy them.[72] The two men would later reply in kind with support for his writings. No doubt at the time they signaled their approval of his views to him. Cotton was already defensive about the effect of his earlier advice to

150

Richards, a posture stiffened by the criticism he sensed from the other signers, who had seen that the final paragraph went where they did not want it to go. Willard might have said something, for his opposition to the trial had become vocal since he signed the letter, and he regularly met with Mather and other Boston ministers.[73] Meanwhile, the judges continued to admit the girls' visions as evidence at trial.

The conviction and execution of Bishop had led to the very situation that Phips had feared. The contagion spread. Andover, Beverly, Rowley, and Boston women and men had fallen under suspicion. There was no end in sight, and the judges were just getting started. Phips may have been worried, but Mather was jubilant, for as the numbers of cases increased, Andover defendants began to confess en masse to their supposed crimes.[74] Mather now came out in the open with what he had kept to himself: a belief that the entire colony was beset with witches.[75] The confessions had convinced Mather that he was right. "Our God is working of miracles," he wrote to another minister. "Five witches were lately executed, impudently demanding of God a miraculous vindication of their innocency. Immediately upon this, our God miraculously sent in five Andover witches, who made a most ample, surprising, amazing confession of all their villanies, and declared the five newly executed to have been of their company."[76] Throwing caution to the wind, on August 4, a day of fasting, he preached an apocalyptic sermon warning that the Last Judgment was near. The Devil must be worried, for he knew he would be judged as well.[77]

Although scholars have found a shifting in Mather's position in favor of the admission of spectral evidence, perhaps owing to the confessions at Andover, perhaps to the unsettled politics of the summer, the August sermon and the May letter to Richards are not much different. Mather merely emphasized in the former certain parts of the latter. The Devil was all around. The only difference was that by August the forces of evil were aiming their barbs at him. In the sermon Mather confronted the armies of Satan and heroically stood at the bridge to bar their way into the city of God. With him stood a brave governor, Phips, a learned lieutenant governor, Stoughton, and eminent councilors.[78] To John Foster, a member of Phips' council who did not sit in judgment of the witches, Mather reconfirmed his belief that the executions were warranted. Spectral evidence alone, he told Foster on August 17, should not prove guilt (Perkins' point) but should and had led the court to a close examination of other evidence. The Devil could take the form of the innocent and even cure victims when touched by a falsely accused person, but Mather trusted the judges to see through the invisible wiles of the Evil One.[79]

On August 19, Mather went to view the execution of the objects of his dire warnings and found that life did not exactly follow his art. George Burroughs, allowed to speak, said the Lord's Prayer perfectly, something folklore said a witch could not do, and greatly moved the crowd. Mather had to intercede, reminding the many that Burroughs was duly convicted.[80] But the minister was shaken, and more shocks were to come, for the confessors had begun to recant. The day before he was scheduled to die, Burroughs met with one of his accusers, Margaret Jacobs, at her request. She sought his pardon; he forgave her.[81] In a letter to the honorable judges, dated August 20, the day after the executions, Margaret Jacobs admitted that "through the magistrates threatenings, and [her] o[w]n vile and wretched heart," she had "confessed several things contrary to [her] conscience and knowledge, tho to the wounding of [her] own soul." Her confession had led to the execution of her grandfather and Burroughs; her father was under indictment; her mother was crazy with worry; and Margaret was repentant. At her examination, she recalled, she was frightened by the spectacle of the girls and since had regretted the false confession that fear had drawn from her. She had implicated Burroughs "to save [her] life and have [her] liberty." Now she wanted the court to know that she was not a witch and never had been.[82] Confessions had been to Mather the surest sign of the Devil's work. The recantations made him pause. He needed to be more cautious.

While Mather waffled, his Boston counterpart Samuel Willard steadfastly admonished his congregants to check their credulousness. Willard, like Mather, had seen children in agony of demonic possession but had acted differently and by so doing had prevented a crisis. In 1671, Willard, then a young minister in Groton, Massachusetts, kept a record of the unaccountable behavior of Elizabeth Knapp, a seventeen-year-old serving girl in his household. In the fall of the year, she had apparently been possessed by spirits, and her possession attracted colonywide attention. As Willard told the story (and remember, it is thus his story, not Knapp's), on October 30, Elizabeth began to act out in violent fashion. She shrieked, leaped about, and tried to harm herself. There would be moments of calm, followed by more fits. The seizures went on for three months, over the course of which Elizabeth would confess her sinfulness repeatedly and in piteous terms. Her behavior attracted attention. Willard sought help; doctors pronounced that they were stumped, and as she began performing for larger audiences, she began to intimate that she was bewitched. In the last phase of her seizures, she twice named an older woman as her assailant, but Willard defused the accusation. His intervention prevented a witchcraft incident. Willard kept a detailed record of the events, which he sent to Increase Mather, who then included it in his *Illustrious Providences*.[83]

Knapp went on to marriage, a houseful of children, and a normal life. Willard, who came from one of the best families of the colony, indeed, was one of its leading native sons, went on to the pastorship of the Third Church of Boston and there preached a more optimistic version of Calvinism than Cotton Mather would tolerate. Ministering to his congregation in that terrible summer of 1692, Willard must have recognized the difference between his technique and Mather's. He had urged Knapp not to blame others; Mather, in the earlier Goodwin case, sought the names of witches. More important, the difference in outcome of the cases troubled Willard. Throughout the season, he restated Perkins' and Bernard's cautions in strong and pointed terms. In June, he warned against defamation of neighbors, urging love and forgiveness instead. He told his parishioners, one of whom, Edward Bromfield, kept careful notes, that the Devil could fool anyone, by implication, even the magistrates, although Willard was careful not to impugn the wisdom of the judges directly.[84] Off the pulpit, he spread his doubts widely. The rush to judgment in the Salem trials ignored his pleas, replacing them with imaginary specters. Judges Peter Sergeant and Samuel Sewall were members in good standing of his church, but so was John Alden, who fled from the judgment of his fellow church members. Willard's warnings, for the time being, went unheard.

trials

FOR ALL the drama of the trials, they would not loom so large in our imaginations were it not for one fact: all eighteen of the women and men brought to trial between June 2 and September 19 were convicted. That insurmountable, stubborn detail appeared to prove Cotton Mather right and Samuel Willard wrong. No jurisdiction in the American colonies had such a high conviction rate for felonies—not in earlier witchcraft trials in Massachusetts, where the majority of defendants were exculpated;[1] not in other felony (that is, capital) offenses.[2] Even in treason trials, wherein the whole apparatus of government was bent to the prosecution of a crime, conviction was never so sure, certain, and deadly as it was that spring and summer in Salem. The outcome of the Bishop trial may be explained away, for she had managed to turn the world against her, but her fate was to be shared by women of valor like Nurse.[3] Something was happening at those trials, something very special.

Here, where we yearn for simple answers, our narrative becomes more complex and speculative. The cast of characters multiplies and familiar figures vanish. Tituba was gone, caged first in Salem, then in Boston, and finally cleared by an Ipswich grand jury on May 9 but still incarcerated, for even the innocent had to pay "costs." The outcome of her case differed from all that came before. She confessed—indeed, she continued to tell her story throughout the months of March and April—but was not even indicted. The bill of indictment brought against her charged her with making a contract with the Devil—sufficient for an indictment under the Stuart witchcraft statute—but not with harming anyone. Evidently the girls had refused to press their accusation that she had tried to cut their heads off. Perhaps the grand jury that rejected the bill of indictment had believed Tituba's confession but was not persuaded that the mere compact was enough. As we have seen, many English commentators required proof of both a pact with the Devil and evil acts. Yet if the jurors credited the confession, would they not conclude also that the contract was based on coercion? After all, Tituba swore that the man in black made her sign the book. Without her volition, no contract could be valid; that was the law. Or perhaps the jurors did not credit her confession, recognizing that it was riven with fear and threat.[4]

And what of the others? Betty was hidden away in Stephen Sewall's house, around the corner on Main Street from the two-story courthouse. Cotton Mather's spectral form hovered over the proceedings, but he was too ill to attend the trials until August. Samuel Parris, the Putnams, the Porters, and others from the village came as witnesses, but they had already said their most important lines. In their place appeared Stoughton and his retainers, Newton, and crowds of jurors, defendants, witnesses, and spectators. Only the girls, Hathorne, and later Corwin provided continuity.

The setting was new as well—no longer the farms and marshes, the rocky fenced fields and dirt roads of the village. Whole processions of villagers flowed to Salem down the Andover and Ipswich roads; down the hill through what is now the town of Peabody went the witnesses and the accused, reversing Parris's trek three years earlier. Thomas Putnam and his two Anns had to travel the farthest of any of the villagers, from the northwestern extremity of the settlement, five and a half miles as the crow flies, but the trip was far longer on the ground. The Putnams had to hitch the oxen to the wagon and traverse the late spring roads, muddy in the shade, dusty in the sun. Bridget Bishop, the first to be tried that early June, had once lived at the edge of the North River, just a few houses away from the courthouse. Many of the other suspects were already in jail in Boston or Salem, missing the end of the spring planting season in their fields to sit in the heat and dust of the second-floor courthouse. Bound and taken by the sheriffs or the constables, they had passed down the main street, past the corner of Summer Street, where Judge Corwin lived in well-furnished elegance, and Stephen Sewall's house, and then turned north up Prison Lane to the Salem jail. They had traveled this route before, to bring their goods to market or to buy from Salem storekeepers, even to worship in the Salem church, now under repair. This trip was different and full of dread.[5]

156

Were the story still played out by local characters, one might try to tell it the way historians have told its prologue, but the crisis was now colonial, not local, and the local focus becomes blurred. The whole colony watched, and so, if one believes Cotton Mather and William Phips, did the authorities in England. The witchcraft contagion had to be contained, or it would flow outward from Salem into other parts of New England. Connecticut was already experiencing a minor rash of witchcraft accusations. Ministers and legal authorities in New York, sheltering Alden, English, and others who had fled the commonwealth, warned Governor Phips about the trials.[6] These admonitions came to nought, but who could tell where Satan's writ ran? Yet if there was no conspiracy, no flights of hundreds of witches through the cold winter night air, then the issue had to be put to rest speedily, lest suspicions undo all that Increase Mather and Phips had accomplished in England.

More daunting still is the absence of any actual trial record. True, we can pencil in the outlines of procedure, for the trials were to be conducted in the English fashion, modified by Massachusetts practice. Defendants were given their "day" wherein they could speak for themselves, for this was all due process amounted to in criminal trials: an "altercation" in front of a judge and jury.[7] No one spoke for the defendant at trial, although she could call her own witnesses, cross-examine witnesses for the prosection, and produce physical evidence. Neither she nor her witnesses could testify on oath, although prosecution witnesses did. In a criminal justice system dependent upon the sacredness of oath taking and oath giving, the defendant was at a disadvantage.[8] The judges called the grand jury and submitted to them evidence regarding all those men and women in custody. A day was set aside for grand jury hearings. At the January 1693 trials, for which the records survive, two grand jurors from the nearby towns were chosen by either town constables or town meetings. Two trial jurors were selected in the same manner. Altogether, there were four panels of trial jurors, for a defendant had the right to object to jurors "for just and reasonable cause." The next day the court sat to hear trial on those true bills found by the grand jurors.

The trial was swift, rarely more than a few hours, sometimes less than an hour. The "petit" or trial jury was called, sworn, and seated. The defendant was brought forward and either accepted the jury or made her objections. Once the final panel was chosen, the indictments were recited. These were followed by written evidence read aloud, including depositions from the pretrial hearings. Oral examination and the defendant's case ensued. The jury then retired, discussed its verdict, returned, and gave it.[9] The verdict had to be unanimous. Perplexed, members of a jury might seek the aid of the bench by rendering a "special verdict" (allowing the judge to decide whether the jurors' finding of a particular set of facts amounted to a crime) or by giving a partial verdict (guilty of A but not of B). They might even seek the aid of those in the courtroom.[10]

Unfortunately, colonial courts did not prepare verbatim accounts of trials—there was no court stenographer then as there is today—but clerks did record the bare essentials: the names of witnesses and jurors; the orders of the court; the verdict of the fact finders. We know these records were prepared for the summer trials, because Stephen Sewall made them available to Cotton Mather to write the latter's semiofficial defense of the trials: the *Wonders of the Invisible World*.[11] The pretrial examinations and eyewitness accounts of the sessions of the court survive, along with bundles of depositions taken for use at trial, but no actual record remains of testimony, court rulings, pleas, or the give and take of trial from June through September, save in their altered form in *Wonders*.

Would that we could trust that tract, but its author was a partisan, and nothing could be farther apart than the accounts of the trials in Mather's *Wonders* and Robert Calef's later *More Wonders of the Invisible World*. Neither man was present at the trials he described. Neither was a lawyer. Both had axes to grind. Mather solicited and received the record that clerk Stephen Sewall kept, and Stoughton certified that Mather's account was accurate,[12] but Mather lionized the judges and approved everything they did, casting some doubt upon the validation process.

Calef thought the whole proceeding a deadly farce, mixing superstition and the evil determination of the ministers to use the trials to cement their power over the credulous. The ministers and the magistrates had "let loose the Devils of envy, hatred, pride, cruelty, and malice against each other; yet still disguised under the mask of zeal for God, and left them to the branding of each other with the odious name of witch . . . to accuse and prosecute . . . children their parents, pastors and teachers their immediate flock unto death, shepherds becoming wolves, wise men infatuated, people hauled to prisons, with a bloody noise pursuing to, and insulting over, the (true) sufferers at execution." The minsters were guilty of a "zeal governed by blindness and passion and led by a president [of the court, that is, Stoughton]" who knew no mercy. Although his account most closely accords with modern sensibilities, Calef wrote five years after the fact, with materials supplied him by opponents of the trials.[13]

The absence of the crucial documentary records and the bitter, persistent divergence of the contemporary readings of what we, at this distance, cannot see provide some of the fascination of these cases—an enduring open-endedness that will continue to attract scholars to the trials just as it brings tourists to the "witch house" in modern Salem (actually Corwin's home). Yet we are not without our powers of conjuration. The trials are an empty space, but all around them the canvas is filled. The characters are more or less delineated for us by their conduct before and after the trials. The empty space becomes smaller as we move the characters into it and then capture their motion as they emerge.

Absent the transcript that Sewall gave Mather, we can try to make sense of the outcomes of the trials by reconstructing the surviving bits and pieces of the documentary as we did the pretrial hearings. Instead of just reading the record, we listen in it for the voices of the participants. Although the court met only five times, each time for a brief span of days, and compared with the trials, the conversation at the hearings was almost leisurely, nevertheless, at each trial, the Salem courthouse buzzed with sound. Indeed, the noise in the courtroom, combined with its primitive acoustics, the jostling and rustling of spectators, and the loud anguish of the victims, dictated the way in which the evidence was heard. As clerk Stephen Sewall later reported to the Nurse family about her trial: "In this trial are twenty papers, besides this judgment, and there were in this trial, as well as other trials of the same nature, several evidences *viva voce* which were not written so I can give no copies of them, some for and some against the parties. Some of the confessions did also mention this and other persons in their several declarations. Which being premised and considered, the said 20 papers herewith filed is the whole trial."[14] If we do not have the full text of this conversation—a verbatim stenographic "concordance," much less an electronic record—we can fill in gaps with the pretrial and other legal documents, the accounts of eye-witnesses, and the later recollections of participants.

As at the hearings, conversation in the courthouse was relational, gaining full meaning from the relationships among the speakers and the audience. The social distance between the performers was as important as the real space in which they performed. Thus the judges (like the magistrates before them) were almost certainly more courteous to those who had high status, which explains why the higher-status suspects were not brought to trial immediately, whereas the nineteen defendants tried first had, with two exceptions, low status in the communities where they resided. Higher-status suspects thus had more room to maneuver, to argue for themselves, and even to escape from custody.

Conversation in these face-to-face confrontations was temporally contexted. The exchanges could stretch back in time over weeks, months, even years, as speakers "remembered" incidents aloud or couched their recollections in terms of longstanding alliances, rivalries, attachments, and enmities. Memory and cultural convention scripted the conversation, and rules and customs of criminal procedure allowed the judges to direct the courtroom drama. Still, there were improvisations and unexpected twists. Over and over, popular culture triumphed over elite precept, folklore trumped erudition, and rumor became probative. The power of rumor in the trials confirms the efficacy of noise—for the rumors were longstanding ones, which changed their shape and became death sentences.[15]

Listening once again to the conversation at the trials helps us to understand their outcome. What was said and how it was said determined the verdict in cases far more than the dictates of any book of rules. Who spoke? The most imposing voices, the ones that commanded the attention of other speakers, belonged to the judges. Their place—the bench—was raised and at the front of the courtroom, and everyone could hear what they said. Their voices were loud, literally and figuratively, for they had on occasion to shout over the noise of the assemblage.

There is no mention of the participation of the bench in most surviving early American criminal court records, but over every defendant fell the long shadow of the judges. Unlike modern trials in America, the judge played a leading role in the colonial criminal court. Judges questioned witnesses and pressured jurors, although they might not punish the latter for their verdict unless it was corrupted. Judicial discretion in

this area was framed by concepts of fairness on the one hand and political imperatives on the other. In England, during the "Popish Plot" and
the "Rye House Plot" of the 1680s, judges had demanded that juries find
the defendants guilty. On other occasions, judges were willing to let
juries find their own verdicts.[16]

160

Did Stoughton, presiding, speak for the entire bench, as Hathorne
had during the pretrial hearings? The record hints that Stoughton and
his brethren did much of the questioning and spoke more frequently
than anyone else, but unlike English judges, Stoughton was a politician,
not a jurist. In England, the preeminence of the judge's voice in criminal trials was a tribute to the learning and professional status of the
judges.[17] In Salem, the bench was experienced, but none of the judges
were lawyers. These may have been, as some scholars argue, a group of
able men in other walks of life, but no law was cited or debated in the
court. Instead, the judges relied upon hearsay, spectral evidence, and
folk witch-finding techniques like the touching test and examination for
witch marks.[18]

Would a learned bench have made a difference in the outcome of the
case? We must not ignore the force that legal formalism has upon those
who practice law for a living. Professional lawyers and judges have audiences of other professionals at the bench and bar whose opinion is an
important curb on discretion and misuse of power.[19] Such professional-
ism was doubly important in cases like these, in which questions of evidence were central, because the judges questioned witnesses and parties
to the case. A defendant might ask a question of the accusers, and the
accusers might add to their stories, but everything was initiated, generated, controlled, and limited by what the judges asked and where they
wanted to go with the answers.[20] Matthew Hale, the most respected
English jurist of the 1650s and 1660s, had credited spectral evidence, but
more recently leading English jurists had become skeptical of such testimony.[21] The judges at Salem seemed unaware of the latter development.

A learned bench might have tried to protect the rights of defendants,
although the concept of procedural guarantees in criminal proceedings,
while a vital part of the Glorious Revolution in England, did not always
seep down to the commoner slouching in the dock.[22] Mary Esty and
Sarah Cloyse asked the judges to intervene for them and "direct" them
wherein they stood "in neede."[23] They conceded that they had no right
to assistance from the bench but seemed to have known that judges

sometimes offered it to defendants, though only upon their own discretion, and only to remedy errors in law. In state trials, trials that were politically important to the authorities, judges rarely interceded for the defendants—quite the reverse was usually the case, as judges made the state's case plain to the jury.[24] There is no evidence that the Salem judges either helped or refused to help defendants when they faltered.

Could politics have combined with the relative lack of juridical sophistication to press the judges toward a sanguinary stance? The English high court judge, though he served at the pleasure of the Crown and was always aware of the Crown's displeasure, was not usually a politician. Stoughton and the others on the court of oyer and terminer were first and foremost partisans. It might have seemed to them that convictions in these cases would shore up the new government, but they were the same bench that presided over the conviction of old and addled Mary Glover three years before Phips and the new charter arrived. Where was the political motivation for conviction then?

The fact remains that the judges directed the course of these trials. The most striking example of judicial intervention—in part because it is the one best documented—occurred at the end of Rebecca Nurse's trial. The jury found her not guilty, a verdict that might have reached far beyond her own case, for she was, unlike those previously convicted, a woman of unblemished reputation and a church member in full communion. Her acquittal would have set a precedent that a good reputation could counter spectral evidence. The court intervened, in the person of Chief Judge Stoughton, according to the recollection of juryman Thomas Fisk, and directed the jury's attention to Nurse's words about Deliverance and Abigail Hobbs, two confessed witches who had turned informants. Nurse supposedly said, "'What, do these persons give in evidence against me now, they used to come among us.'" Stoughton told the jurors that such words could only mean Nurse admitted that she too was a witch. Some of the jurors asked the court's permission to retire to reconsider their verdict. When they retired, Fisk told his fellow jurors he was not certain what she meant, and he wanted her to have the chance to interpret her remarks for the jury. The jury returned and Nurse was asked what she meant, but old and hard of hearing, she missed the point. The jury then reversed itself and found her guilty. Informed of the change in her fortunes too late, she explained that she objected to being condemned by those who had admitted their miscarriages and weakness. Why should a jury believe such women and not her?[25]

The semiprosecutorial stance of some of the judges might have been offset by legal counsel for the defendants. But here, where we would expect to find the eloquence of criminal bar, there was only silence. The Crown had lawyers: Thomas Newton and Anthony Checkley, but they were prosecutors and could be expected to use every effort to get convictions. Perhaps, as Newton wrote before the first trial, he was awed by the testimony of the girls, perhaps not.[26] In a truly adversarial system defense counsel have tricks of their own, but no lawyers stepped forward for the defendants. Although the Massachusetts codes had implied that defendants had a right to counsel, the codes were gone. There were lawyers about, but Massachusetts did not permit lawyers to practice for fees until 1705. English precedent did not aid the defendants, for counsel was not permitted accused felons in England until 1836 (except in treason, and that in 1696). By the eighteenth century, first in the colonies and later in England, counsel for the defense did appear in a small portion of the total number of cases, but judges did not encourage defense lawyers. Their sharp words and quick wits, their colloquies with the judges, and their caustic, sometimes brutal, examination of witnesses undermined the authority of the bench. One irony of the absence of counsel in Salem was that during the crises of the 1680s in England, spokesmen for the Crown had argued strenuously against lawyers representing suspected opponents of James II. When the Whigs took power under William of Orange in 1689, defense lawyers began to appear in state cases. Stoughton and his brethren had thus made common cause with those whose political opinions all Puritans abhorred, against those whose successful coup the Puritans applauded. Even if absence of counsel was not unusual, its effect was particularly harsh in Salem, for counsel for the accused could have cross-examined witnesses, finding loopholes and contradictions in their stories or malice in their motives. Counsel might have informed the judges of the outcomes of contemporaneous English trials. Such counsel become part of a judge's audience, and judges are often influenced by them or seek their aid.[27]

Without the participation of trained lawyers, the defendant was thrown back upon her own counsel. Defendants' voices were raised at the trials, but we cannot be sure what they said. An otherwise articulate defendant such as John Alden or John English, who could read and write and carried on extensive businesses involving legal matters, may have consulted both lawyers and lawbooks, but they preferred flight to trial. For the commoners, there was another kind of counsel. Friends and neighbors were ready sources of legal advice, even if they did not know the book law. As "attorneys" neighbors often appeared in civil cases to speak for one another.[28] Among these people there was just as ready a supply of popular legal wisdom as there was of folk countermagic. A vernacular version of legal rights and duties was well established in the colony and governed the erection of fences and the treatment of servants far more effectively than any book law. The essence of this customary lore was that the courts were not distant gladiatorial arenas but "agent[s] of orderly social change and economic growth" bringing together members of the same community to air differences and resolve disputes.[29]

Almost all of the defendants in the witchcraft trials had been in court for one reason or another before 1692, some serving as jurors, others acting as witnesses, making complaints, or giving excuses for some alleged misconduct. They were used to standing before local notables like Hathorne and Corwin and dutifully paid fines, obeyed court orders, and accepted corporal punishment. On these occasions, neighbors, co-defendants or co-plaintiffs, shared among themselves prior experience with the courts and court clerks, creating a store of informal rules for getting along in the courthouse. At the core of these rules was submission to the authority of the bench. In turn, the courts might order pains and punishments but generally returned the parties to their place in the community, even in cases of suspected witchcraft. The Court of Assistants had performed this function in earlier witchcraft cases. For example, mere suspicion of consorting with the Devil was not enough to convict a suspect.[30]

The defendants in the Salem cases, and later, those from Andover, were thus unprepared for the special court of oyer and terminer, a court whose function was to not to make the community whole but to excise a few of its number to insulate the rest. The clerk, Stephen Sewall, was no help to the accused. Politely couched addresses to the bench did no good, in part because men like Stoughton and Richards were not from Salem. Nevertheless, the accused still relied upon the lore of law to save themselves. Nathaniel Cary sought a change of venue to protect his wife, Elizabeth, against the power of the girls. Esty and Cloyse asked the judges for help. Sarah Buckley's husband William sought and obtained testimonials of his wife's Christian carriage from their ministers, John Higginson and Samuel Cheever. Confessing to everything, William Barker Sr. swore that he had "not known or heard of one innocent person taken up and put in prison"; his wife, accused with him, confessed but assured the judges that she was totally in the power of Goody Johnson and Goody Falkner, who threatened to tear her to pieces should she oppose them.[31]

Withal, as in Nurse's case, the defendants did have the courage and intelligence to plot defenses for themselves. There are clues to these defense tactics in the defendants' petitions to the court during and after the trials. In most cases, the defendant made his or her mark at the end of the petition, meaning that it was dictated to another. One of these petitions is especially moving and reveals much about the conversation at trial. Its language is common, at times even coarse. Its sentiments mix the contrived and the resigned. Its force, however, is undeniable, even after three hundred years, and it proves that the condemned were not silent, passive, or acquiescent. Mary Esty was Rebecca Nurse's sister-in-law, a member of a Topsfield clan especially brutalized by the accusations and trials. To Phips and to the bench she addressed her appeal:

164

> That whereas your poor and humble Petition[er] being condemned to die Doe humbly begg of you to take it into your Judicious and pious considerations that your Poor and humble petitioner knowing her own Innocencye Blessd be the Lord for it and seeing plainly the wiles and subtility of my accusers by my Selfe can not but Judg charitably of others that are going the same way of my Selfe if the Lord stepps not mightily in[.] I was confined a whole month upon the same account that I am condemnd now for and then cleared by the afflicted persons as some of your honours know and in the two dayes time I was cryed out upon by them and have been confined and now am condemned to die[.] The Lord above knows my Innocencye then and Likewise does now as att the great day will be known to men and Angells—I Petitione to your honours not for my own life for I know I must die and my appointed time is sett but the Lord he knowes it is that if it be possible no more innocent blood may be shed which undoubtedly cannot be Avoydd in the way and course you goe in[.] I question not but your honours does to the uttmost of your Powers in the discovery and detecting of witchcraft and witches and would not be guilty of innocent blood for the world but by my own Innocencye I know you are in the way[.] [T]he Lord in his infinite mercy direct you in this great work if it be his blessed will that no more Innocent blood be shed I would humbly begg of you that your honors would be pleased to examine these afflicted persons strictly and keepe them apart some time and Likewise to try some of these confessing witchs[,] I being confident

there is severall of them has belyed themselves and others as will appeare if not in this world I am sure in the world to come wither I am
now going and I Question not but youle see an alteration of these
things they say[.] My selfe and others having made a League with the
Divel we cannot confesse I know and the Lord knowes as well shortly
appeare they belye me and so I question not but they doe others[.]
[T]he Lord above who is the Searcher of all hearts knowes that as I
shall answer it att the Tribunall seat that I know not the least theinge
of witchcraft therefore I cannot I dare not belye my own soule[.] I beg
your honers not to deny this my humble petition from a poor dying
Innocent person and I question not but the Lord will give a blessing to
yor endeavors.[32]

Mary Esty respected the bench but was hardly in awe of the judges.
She knew that some of her neighbors had spoken untruths, and she was
partly confounded by the scope of their false witness and partly out-
raged by it. The accusers must have appeared to her to be in concert, an
able perception, for the examining magistrates, rather than acting as
sifters of evidence, had become, as we have seen, builders of the prosecution case. In the process, they had not only given cues to prospective
witnesses and bullied recalcitrant confessors but allowed the accusers to
listen to one another's stories and prepare a coherent final version. Esty
urged the judges to give more weight to the inconsistencies in the accusers' stories, particularly when they were confessed witches themselves
(the same point that Nurse made about Hobbs). If these are the arguments that Esty made at trial, she represented her case well.

Esty's petition was more than a brief for the defense. She wanted the
judges to know that she had not lost her faith—not in them and, more
important, not in God. Her petition was a devotional, a confession not
of guilt but of trust in the justice of the Lord. By testifying to her obedience, she made herself into one of the martyrs so much beloved by all
sects in the seventeenth century. The Quakers had martyrs, as did the
Puritans, the Roman Catholics, and the Anabaptists. Ironically, the trials
had brought people like Esty and Nurse closer to the church and to God
than they had been before. Witchcraft accusations restored or reinvigo-
rated some defendants' godliness, surely the best proof of all that they
were not witches.[33]

Some defendants thought about impeaching the impartiality, or at
least the credulousness, of the bench. Consider the exchange between

John Alden and Bartholomew Gedney, friends and fellow merchants, the latter now turned Alden's inquisitor and judge in Salem. The account is Alden's: "Mr. Gidney bid Aldin confess, and give glory to God. Aldin said he hoped he should give glory to God, and hoped he should never gratify the Devil; but appealed to all who ever knew him, if they ever suspected him to be such a person. . . . Mr. Gidney said he had known Aldin many years, and had been at sea with him, and always look'd upon him to be an honest Man, but now he did see cause to alter his judgment: Aldin answered, he was sorry for that. . . . [T]hey bid Aldin look upon the Accusers, which he did, and then they fell down. Aldin asked Mr. Gidney, what Reason there could be given, why Aldin's looking upon *him* did not strike *him* down as well."[34] Alden broke jail and did not return until the trials were over. His case was later discharged by proclamation.[35] He was a tough old salt of seventy years; he did not fear the wrath of the authorities or trust their judgment but could see a storm and like a good sailor ran from it.

Defendants could also challenge physical evidence produced at trial. Juries of midwives examined the suspects for unusual marks, so-called witches' teats. Such examinations had a place in the lore of witchcraft and were used in English trials. In theory, a familiar needed a place at which to suckle. In the Salem cases, familiars were seen in both real and spectral form, but proof that one did not have such a teat did not alleviate suspicion. The result was a no-win situation for the defendant. Some, nevertheless, demanded a fair examination. For example, Rebecca Nurse asked for a different jury of midwives to examine her for "witchmarks," wanting only "most grand wise and skillfull" midwives for the task. She had already gone through two prior examinations with conflicting results.[36]

The defendants and their witnesses not only attacked the reliability of physical evidence and the motives of the accusers but impugned the motives of prosecution witnesses as well. One of Nurse's witnesses gave testimony that the identity of defendants was first suggested to the girls by their elders. John Tarbell testified that he was at the Putnam's house on March 28, and he then asked how Ann Putnam Jr. was able to identify Nurse. Subtly he nosed around and found out that Ann Jr. had not known who the "pale woman" was who afflicted her, and he discovered that the servant Mercy Lewis identified their neighbor as the culprit. "Thus they turned it upone one an other saying it was you and it was you that told her."[37] Lewis's role as a leader of the gang was already apparent.

The best defense for a suspect was not what she said, however, but what others said of her. Evidence of a good reputation might sway a jury, although character evidence could work both ways. Most often, evidence of a person's good reputation directly refuted the accusations of witnesses or victims. Contemporary English jurists such as Matthew Hale instructed juries that they were to found their verdicts upon their own beliefs, informed by, but not dictated by, what character witnesses testified. They could credit or discredit such testimony, even when given under oath.[38] Nevertheless, as William Lambard wrote in his much respected and much copied manual for justices of the peace, *Eirenarcha,* if the accused was a person of quality, jurors were to consider that in the defendant's favor; so too they were to take into account the defect of defendants' having evil parents, exhibiting an evil nature, keeping bad company, having no job, or being accused of a similar crime in the past. Two hundred years later, character remained a guide to New England juries.[39]

Some of the character testimony survives in petition form. The voices of friends and family did not speak to the legal issues; they spoke of duty and caring: this is a person who has lived among you for many generations in good repute. How can you take her to be a witch now?[40] At the behest of Goodman Francis Nurse, thirty-nine neighbors, including all of the Porters, as well as Benjamin and Sarah Putnam and of course Joseph Putnam, testified to their belief that Goodwife Nurse was a woman of unblemished character, and they brought these testimonials to court. Nathaniel Putnam Sr. added his qualified agreement.[41] The problem with character or reputation testimony in a witchcraft case was that, if the suspect were a witch, her misconduct would be so concealed that she might bear a good reputation in the daylight and carry on her mischief at night. Thus Rebecca Nurse could be a witch, despite her reputation, without the common ill fame that had doomed Sarah Osborn, Bridget Bishop, and Sarah Good.

The accusers spoke as well. Cotton Mather reported that the girls testified in person, sometimes while writhing in agony, reacting with such vigor to their spectral tormentors that the judge and jury were appalled and frightened. As at the pretrial hearings, the girls' performance convinced in part because the roles they performed were so familiar that the audience could already visualize what it could not see, and in part because the girls had so polished their lines and their pantomime that they conveyed, even to skeptics, the existence of the invisible world. The judges asked the defendants, "What say you?" to the girls' agony, and the defendants either had to admit that the girls were assaulted by unknown demons—that is, that the invisible world really existed—or that the girls were faking. The former concession fell into the prosecutors' trap, for if witches could take spectral form and in that form could harm corporeal bodies, then the girls' testimony must be credited. Why not then credit the girls' identification of the specter? Rebecca Nurse stumbled into this snare. To sneer at the girls and deny that there were witches, George Burroughs' defense, risked losing the sympathy of the jurors. As Hathorne told Nurse at her hearing—how could she look upon the girls' pain and not be moved by it?[42]

Even when the girls were silent, they could persuade. At the trials, they did not have the opportunity to coordinate their accusations as they had in the village or out of doors. They developed instead a signing code (again the parallel to a modern gang suggests itself). They used facial expressions and touching—an ironic inversion of the "touching test" that proved a suspect was a witch—to communicate. "They did in the Assembly mutually cure each other, even with a touch of their hand, when strangled, and otherwise tortured," Deodat Lawson reported of the victims. This mime was intermixed with verbal commands to one another, as Lawson recalled, "They did also foretel when anothers fit was a-coming, and would say, 'Look to her, she will have a fit presently,' which fell out accordingly, as many can bear witness, that heard and saw it."[43] The most impressive of all the silent moments involving the girls came, however, when the judges required that the defendants touch a girl to relieve her symptoms. This occurred periodically throughout the trials and made a strong impression upon the jurors. Increase Mather, joining Perkins and other authorities, had objected to "ordeals" such as placing a suspected witch in water to see if she would float, taking blood from the suspect, or burning her. Doctor Cotta thought the touching test a sham, for if the supposed victim was a fraud, he or she might use the test to repeat the fraud.[44] The court did not heed the good doctors of the soul or the body on this matter, however.

In the end, the defendant's life and limb depended upon convincing two sets of jurors that he or she was not guilty. The first of the two types of juries to hear the girls, the accused, the accusers, witnesses, and the magistrates, was the grand or presenting jury. This relic of much older

English criminal procedure once presented suspects to the king's justices upon the personal knowledge of the jurors. Grand juries still performed this function in New England, presenting fornicators, nonchurchgoers, and other minor miscreants based on the grand jurors' own information.[45] In felony cases, that is, serious crimes whose punishments might mean loss of life or limb, grand juries merely certified whether there seemed to be probable cause to hold the suspect for a trial. The suspect then might plea-bargain for a lesser charge, confessing to it whether he or she was guilty or not. That is in effect what some of the suspected witches tried to do, a far better explanation of their accounts of flying through the air and seeing men change into animals than hysteria or some other psychological or spiritual experience. Until 1692 such confessions availed little, but the accused had learned (again oral networks superseding book law) that confession would lead to a happier result on this occasion. In fact no one who confessed, and many did, was executed, unless he or she recanted the confession.

Reviewing the records of the investigations and comparing these with the "ignoramus" written on the back of the indictment proves that the grand juries were exercising a good deal of independent judgment as they talked among themselves. The professions and contortions of the girls could not convince a grand jury to indict a suspect, nor was spectral evidence persuasive, without confirmation from more conventional sources. Despite the convulsions of Indian John before Danforth and the other notables on April 11, Sarah Cloyse was not indicted by the grand jury.[46] When people other than the girls and Indian John came forward to testify to mysterious death, disease, or damage, then the grand jury acted. The grand jurors were not proof against the power of rumor, however, and panic rumors had driven the first prosecutions. It was only when these rumors died down—when the first panic had abated and the Devil had not shown his own face—that grand jurors started to doubt openly what they heard.

The independent-mindedness of the grand juries can be teased from the pattern of true bills. First, nearly half of the defendants were related to one another in some way, primarily by marriage, often by ties of parenthood, occasionally as siblings. This was common in England as well, for authorities and locals perceived that witchcraft was a family crime—or more accurately, a profession taught by mothers to daughters. Thus one would expect that entire families would be accused and examined, but Massachusetts grand juries did not unreflectingly indict everyone in a suspect family. More often than not, only one or two of the adult women would be indicted. Grand jurors simply refused to believe that witchcraft corrupted entire families. The grand jurors also resisted indictments based on unsupported assertions by the girls. One tentative, gendered conclusion suggests itself: the memories of men, whether respected men or lower-status men, were more imposing than the visions of the girls—that is, more influential with the men who sat on the grand juries. Men listened to and placed more faith in the observations of other men than in the testimony of women and girls.

170

The trial jury was supposed to sift through the words of the many parties and arrive at a verdict of fact, but instead of acting as a finder of fact, the trial juries in Salem put the community seal of approval upon the judges' decision to admit spectral evidence. They were thus more credulous than the grand jury. Of course, the grand jurors did not have to watch the girls at their demonic play; the trial jurors did. Unlike the grand jurors, who gathered themselves apart from the judges, the trial jurors had to see and hear the bench, and the judges could see the jurors' faces. To have opposed the bench when its members so obviously wanted to convict the accused would have taken an act of collective courage—but the trial jurors may have believed the accusers for the same reason as the judges and the ministers, at least at first. Everyone believed in witches, feared Satan, and was appalled and convinced by the girls' testimony—that is, so long as the girls were permitted to testify to the maleficium of apparitions. Once the central fact—that the girls were bewitched—was established beyond dispute, the jurors could lay aside their qualms about spectral evidence. The judges' decision to admit spectral evidence thus reified the jurors' preexisting belief rather than commanding the jurors to credit what had hitherto seemed improbable to them. At trial, the language that the jury heard, guided by the implicit, if not explicit, instructions of the judges—that is, the cues the judges gave by their questions, their visual language, and their willingness to admit all manner of hearsay—then reinforced popular belief. All this conceded, the trial jurors obviously did not require more or better proof than the grand jury, in effect inverting the function of the two juries.[47]

Were trial jurymen bound by the stern mien and unequivocal instructions of the judges to accept spectral evidence in any particular case? Today, such evidence might be ruled more prejudicial than probative, but we have rigid and expansive rules of evidence and the jury is only a finder of fact.[48] Could the jurymen of Salem have disregarded the bench and interposed themselves between their neighbors and the judges? Colonial juries could find law as well as determine facts, argue William Nelson and J. R. Pole.[49] Some modern anthropologists insist that in its local manifestations, law is always a matter of negotiation in which the power of the state is channeled and contained by local understandings. In such situations, juries can make law as well as find facts.[50] Juries had set themselves up as lawgivers in cases of prosecution of Quakers and other political trials in England.[51] Jury "nullification" in the face of book law in criminal cases may have been common in an earlier period, although by the end of the seventeenth century, it almost always occurred with the connivance of the judge. In felonies such as robbery and grand theft, juries were known to "mitigate" the offense, that is, fully recognizing that the defendant was guilty as charged, the jury nevertheless entered into a complex bargaining situation with the judge, and sometimes the victim, to reduce the severity of the offense by openly altering the fact situation before pronouncing its verdict.[52] Sometimes such verdicts were "special," that is, they actually laid out the terms of the bargain: reducing a grand theft (a felony) to a petty theft, for example. In effect, the jury was brokering a variation of the charge, not changing the law or making law but moving the defendant from one legal category to a lesser one.

In Massachusetts witchcraft trials, however, trial juries were not sources of leniency. They did not nullify or mitigate. They might find, as they did on a few occasions, that the defendant was not guilty of witchcraft "under the law," but in these cases the jurymen were only following the judges' instructions. Some of the defendants at Salem spoke directly to the trial jurors to influence their view of the law. At his trial, Burroughs passed them "a paper" purporting to prove that there were no witches. According to Cotton Mather, the jurors were not persuaded. More often, the judges reversed or held in abeyance a jury guilty verdict upon their own reluctance to convict given the evidence presented in court. We can be certain that judges in Salem did not signal juries that the bench would be amenable to jury mitigation in these cases.[53]

The selection of Bishop as the first defendant in this context was brilliant. No jury would be likely to believe her, and with that disbelief, the jurors committed themselves to join the judges in crediting spectral evidence. She was already disliked and mistrusted, and she added to it by her demeanor at her trial. Before the jury came many accusers who remembered that years earlier (sometimes nearly twenty years earlier) a sow had died under suspicious circumstances, or a child had sickened suddenly, after a vituperative visit from Bishop. Younger folk testified that they had seen apparitions of Bishop in their rooms in the still of the night, and she had practiced her mischief on them. True, none of these claims had formal weight at her trial, for Bishop was indicted only for assaulting the girls during the pretrial hearings, and the trial jury could only render a verdict on crimes for which the defendant was indicted, but the other assertions had a different kind of gravity. They demonstrated to the jury what many on it already knew, that Bishop had alienated and offended a large segment of the community—indeed, three generations of her neighbors were willing to come to court to make complaint against her. In finding a verdict of guilty, the jury had taken into account all the rumor, hearsay, and long-banked anger against her, matters of popular disrepute rather than legal culpability. In its verdict against her, the jury represented and spoke for community opinion.[54]

With the execution of Bishop, a door closed for the girls. Willing and witting lies that damaged others were punishable in Massachusetts under the old charter with a fine and, for a second offense, a double fine and whipping.[55] With Bishop dead, however, her accusers could be accused themselves of bearing "false witness" against a neighbor. Dalton's *Country Justice* had warned that perjury was a crime against God, the magistrates, the innocent, the commonwealth, and the perjurer's own soul, and commentators on English law continued throughout the century to castigate perjury as "of all crimes the most infamous."[56] The *Lawes and Liberties* of 1648 in the colony warned, "If any man rise up by false witness wittingly and of purpose to take away any man's life, he shall be put to death," citing for authority Deuteronomy, chapter 19.[57] Some of the convicts realized the force of these laws and from the edge of the grave reminded the judges in writing that the witnesses' perjury should be counted against them.[58] For their part, the girls knew that the capital laws punished false witness,[59] and now they had nowhere to go but on, continuing to find new witches, or they risked their own lives. Bishop's execution not only confirmed the judges in their course and co-opted the trial juries, but it prevented the girls from backsliding.

After the first session, juries condemned defendants in groups. The babble of voices had quieted. With each trial there was less furor. The number of defendants per session increased, and given the limitations on time, the trials proceeded more swiftly. On June 29 the court reassembled after receiving the "Return" of the ministers, and the juries took little more than three days to send Rebecca Nurse, Susannah Martin, Sarah Wildes, Sarah Good, and Elizabeth Howe to the gallows. They were hanged on July 19. A week later Checkley replaced Newton as prosecutor, but the turnover in personnel had no effect upon the defendants' chances. On August 2, the third session of the court convened, and within four days George Jacobs Sr., Martha Carrier, George Burroughs, John and Elizabeth Proctor, and John Willard were tried, convicted, and condemned. Elizabeth, pregnant, was reprieved. She was to be spared until after her child was delivered (and, in fact, was given a chance to rear her fatherless child by Governor Phips, who would later dismiss her case by proclamation). Jacobs, John Proctor, Willard, and Burroughs were executed on August 19. On September 19, six more were tried: Martha Cory, Mary Esty, Alice Parker, Ann Pudeator, Dorcas Hoar, and Mary Bradbury put themselves "on king and country" and were convicted. Bradbury broke jail with the aid of what seems to have been her entire neighborhood. Hoar confessed and was saved for a time—time enough for Phips to reconsider the conduct of the court and suspend its operation. A week and a day later, Margaret Scot, Wilmott Redd, Samuel Wardwell, Mary Parker, Abigail Faulkner, Rebecca Eames, Mary Lacy, Ann Foster, and Abigail Hobbs were brought to trial. The verdicts were all the same. On the 22d, Cory, Wardwell, Scot, Esty, Parker, Pudeator, Redd, and Parker were "turned off" at the gallows. Noyes and Cotton Mather publicly expressed their satisfaction—justice had been done. Parris preached an incendiary sermon against those who had made war with the lamb—with Christ—for Cory had been a member of his church and had violated it with her crime.[60]

The private conversation among the ministers on that occasion is lost to us, just as the conversations among the jurors are lost, but the conviction rate must have been uppermost in the ministers', jurors', and judges' minds. The judges could not have arranged for such unanimity without the consent of the jurors. Was it the juries themselves, then, who chose to believe what they could not see or hear because witchcraft was so insidious and threatened everyone, if not with harm, then with seduction of the soul? In cases like Bishop's and Martha Carrier's—bad neighbors, suspected thieves, complainers—the choice may have been easy, but the juries hesitated in some of the cases and had to be pushed.

Who pushed them? It was not just the judges, for New England juries could be mulish and a Salem jury might be awed the first time a Stoughton or a Winthrop came among them, but not the nineteenth time.

It was the voice of neighbors which pushed the jurors: the witnesses who swore under oath that they were certain that the defendant had harmed them; the farmers and merchants who discussed the cases out of doors—doors with horseshoes nailed over them. The jurors were not sequestered but went about their business between trials and listened to the panicky gossip and the fearful rumors. A few voices were raised in defense, and as time wore on, more joined. Enough was enough, they seemed to say, but only when the jails were filled with people whose lives were exemplary and the gallows had shaken with the tears of the repentant and the innocent; only then would the murmur of accusations turn to self-doubt and then recrimination.

By September the jails were overflowing with nearly two hundred persons accused of witchcraft and awaiting disposition of their cases.[61] Colonial jails were flimsy holding pens where suspects waited for trial or bail.[62] Sometimes the wood was so rotten that those incarcerated could knock down the walls and walk away. In 1680, "Josiah Gatchell testified that he knew Salem prison was not sufficient, for any man having no instrument except his own hands could come out as he pleased. . . . He saw one man pull up one of the boards overhead in the prison with his hand, going into the chamber of the prison, and others went out under the groundsill and some went out next to the watchhouse. . . . They found not one room there that was sufficient to keep in a man who had the dexterity of an ordinary man."[63] Gatchell should know: he spent much of the late 1670s and early 1680s in Salem jail on a variety of charges. Massachusetts law required jails in all towns, but not to house hosts of women and children. Most of the inmates were debtors who had either refused to pay what they owed or had not yet signed a statement that they had no resources to pay the debt. The incarcerated paid for their own firewood and food or had it delivered by friends and family. The poor in prison thus suffered most. Jailers—called keepers—were jobbers and often negligent. They allowed suspects to go home and receive visitors freely.

The prisoners talked to one another in their cells or in the yard. Most stayed, expecting justice, too tired to risk flight, or simply resigned to their fate. Osborn, shuffled back and forth between Boston and Salem, died, as did Roger Toothaker, Lydia Dustin, and Ann Foster. To the court they spoke through their families, whose courageous and persistent petitions to the very authorities who had incarcerated their spouses, children, and parents raised the spirits of the inmates. These addresses were respectful, the petitioners couching their appeals in the language of good subjects of a lawful sovereign.

Some prisoners, particularly in Boston, were allowed to roam more freely and used that freedom to arrange with friends to escape. Mary and Philip English broke jail, leaving behind their spacious house, its furnishings, its silver plate, and the mixed feeling of their neighbors. Daniel Andrew, scarcely less wealthy than English, and more closely allied to the Porter clan, had more friends and still fled. Edward and Sarah Bishop left as well, proving that not only the well-placed could flee. With them went Dudley and John Bradstreet, he a justice of the peace in Andover whose refusal to sign any more arrest warrants brought suspicion upon him; Elizabeth Cary, with the help of her husband Nathaniel; George Jacobs Jr., the most feared of all the incarcerated, to hear the girls tell it; and Hezekiah Usher and John Alden, of Boston, undoubtedly with the help of friends. They risked forfeiture of their property, which was considerable, but life was more precious, and they could see in their mind's eye the signature of the judges on the death warrants.[64]

Stretching our imagination, we may compare the massive program of detention of suspected witches to the arrest of loyalists in the revolutionary era, and perhaps even more appropriately, to the "relocation program" of Japanese Americans in 1942. It is clear that those "yellow Devils" were regarded as suspects even though there was no proof that any of them had done anything wrong. They were simply different looking and sounding: "People were rightly fearful of the Japanese," U.S. Supreme Court justice Hugo Black wrote in 1971, defending his role in maintaining the relocation centers; "they all look alike to a person not a jap"[65]—much the same stereotyping mechanism as in the "hag" image of the witch. Those we fear we find ugly.[66]

The sentence for witchcraft was death, and it was carried out fairly speedily after trial. Only Giles Cory, difficult and stubborn to the last, refused to be tried and was pressed to death. There were reprieves of women who were pregnant or who, having confessed, requested more time to prepare themselves for death. Dorcas Hoar, for example, due to be executed the next day, asked John Hale to intercede for her. She needed more time to prepare her soul for its journey. He did, for he knew that a clear conscience was a necessary first step in true repentance.[67] Their death warrants waited in Chief Judge Stoughton's writ bag.

Punishment for crimes among the Puritans was public. Public shaming, for example, or time in the stocks, and even lashes at the whipping post served to remind the convict that the crime was against the community. Such public scourging also taught the community that misconduct would be punished. If the offense was a misdemeanor, or a "clergyable" felony,[68] reintegration into the community followed punishment. Witchcraft was not clergyable.

Here again there was a conversation, for the script for the execution ritual was fully developed. Everyone knew his or her role, even the condemned. The public execution was the most severe of penalties. These were solemn occasions, in large measure because the role of public opinion was crucial to the effectiveness of the criminal justice system. There was no extensive police system—it was too expensive—and the general public had to keep order for itself. Neighbors watched and warned of crime. Posses of neighbors chased criminals. In Puritan Massachusetts, as in England, the accused rode to the gallows with a minister. The minister comforted the convict, showing the way in Christ's mercy for repentance, even in the shadow of the noose. The minister then read a sermon to the crowd, reminding them that they too would be judged. Ideally, the convict then confessed, discharging the guilt and allaying the fears of the multitude.

At her execution, Sarah Good refused to confess, however, and warned the ministers who berated her that they would suffer for their misdeeds. Rebecca Nurse too declined to confess, and her demeanor was so decent and pure that many began to doubt the verdict.[69] George Burroughs preached to the throng, and were it not for the loud and authoritative intervention of Cotton Mather, he might have been freed.[70] Mather was unhappy; the script was not being followed. But Nicholas Noyes of Salem was there for the last set of executions in September, and he found the sight invigorating, supposedly "turning him to the bodies [and] said, 'what a sad thing it is to see Eight Firebrands of hell hanging there.'"[71] John Higginson, well along in years, attended as well and was not as pleased as his Salem counterpart. In his introduction to John Hale's memoir, Higginson recalled that the events were tragic and left "in the minds of men a sad remembrance of that sorrowful time; and a doubt whether some innocent persons might not have suffered and some guilty persons escape," for, in truth, although the judges and juries acted "according to their best light," some of the rules the judges used were "insufficient and unsafe."[72]

The refusal of the convicts to confess cast a pall over the entire ritual, for confession on the scaffold was not only good for the soul of the accused, it was necessary for the peace of the community. The guilty and the innocent were linked together in their submission to the authority of God and the knowledge that all would have to be judged—those on the scaffold, and those below who watched. "The ritual of execution day required that condemned prisoners demonstrate publicly that they were penitent, and the execution sermons repeatedly pounded the chord of penitence."[73] Confession in the moment before death could not be recanted and meant that the process itself was validated—that the truth had come out. The suspicion grew that Nurse and Burroughs had been wrongly convicted. If so, the rituals of punishment which cleansed the crime, allowed the evildoer to repent, and made the community whole did not work.

In ironic fashion, the failure of the rituals of execution to purge the community of ill feeling kept those who confessed safe from death. If the people they accused were not guilty, then the confessors' own admissions of guilt were cast into doubt. Perhaps they had indeed been pressured, frightened, or deluded by the Devil, or by their accusers, or by the authorities. If so, then the entire process of weighing confessions so heavily was laid open to the criticisms raised by Reginald Scot, John Gaule, John Webster, and other English writers.[74] Rumors that those who had confessed were tortured into confession, if true a violation of longstanding customary restraints upon torture, had surfaced and diminished the value of such confessions in court. The *Lawes and Liberties* of 1648 permitted humane torture after conviction to gain the names of conspirators.[75] Surely the witchcraft crisis fit that model, for the magistrates from the outset of the accusations feared that a great conspiracy existed among the witches and their evil mentor. Nevertheless, men of education and science such as Harvard College's Thomas Brattle had decided that some of the defendants were "distracted, crazed women," whose confessions could not be admitted in a court of law.[76]

The doubts of the learned to one side, the confessions had flowed in such profusion and growing elaboration that grand juries would have been taxed and trial courts overburdened with sorting out all the stories. In the confessions the number of secret witches grew from tens to scores to hundreds. At trial, some of the confessions were retracted, as Samuel

Wardwell of Andover did his. Whatever the judges had intended to do at the outset of the crisis with those who confessed, there were by September far too many of them to try, convict, and execute the confessors. It was much better to wait, to allow time to intervene, before executions of the confessed witches and more of the accused were ordered.

178

What was equally important, the trials of witches had not quieted the colony, as Phips had hoped, but inflamed it further. Each new trial seem to bring in its train a battalion of new accusations. Phips' original plan to have a limited number of sittings of the special court had been undone by the number of cases, and what emerged was a standing witchcraft tribunal resembling, to some of its critics, the Inquisition. Accusations had driven some of the leading merchants in the colony to flee for their lives, and no one seemed proof against the wrath of the tormented girls.

pardon

8

THE BRAKES were applied to the careening trial court not by the outrage of kinfolk of the accused but by a segment of the educated elite of the colony. The two cultures—popular and learned—always so near each other in Puritan Massachusetts, had overlapped in the witchcraft crisis to a greater extent than ever before. The recollections of the many had for a time become potent guides to public policy, replacing the divinings of the ministers. Recognizing that this world turned upside down threatened the purity of the word they preached, and brought with it the specter not of witches but of social chaos, the ministers joined together to pull their congregations back from the brink of the abyss. But the ministers did not speak quickly, or as one, against the danger.

While Cotton was battling the Devil at arm's length, hurling sermons against the squadrons of specters which circled Salem, the Ministerial Association was in more or less continuous session. Unlike Cotton, many of its members had traveled to Salem to see the first trials as well as the executions. Their advice in the "Return" against the use of spectral evidence had been misunderstood (that was charitable) or ignored. Either way, they were not heard, and that rankled. To a man, they believed that the Devil was abroad, for his works were plain to see, and the trials must be his doing as well. Entire communities roiled in conflict. Congregations slashed themselves apart; good men and women languished in dungeons.[1]

Willard, frustrated by his fellow ministers' inaction, was already speaking against the trials, if not against the judges. Visiting his own parishioners in jail, he may even have aided some of them to flee. He wrote all his objections to the trials, beginning with his suspicions of the girls' veracity and ending with his thoughts on the power of the Devil to wreck a commonwealth, but was banned by Phips' gag proclamation from airing them in Boston. Secretly, he arranged for them to be printed there, but with the misdescription that they had in fact come from the Philadelphia press of William Bradford.[2]

Following Webster and Filmer, Willard insisted in *Some Miscellany Observations* that satisfactory proof of witchcraft was almost impossible to obtain. Cast in the style of a philosophical dialogue much like the first Puritan work on witchcraft, Henry Holland's *Treatise Against Witchcraft* (1590), Willard's message was simple: conviction by mere suspicion was "contrary to the mind of God." "[B]esides, reason tells us, that the more horrid the crime is, the more cautious we ought to be in making any guilty of it." But had not divines and lawyers given great weight to such presumptions? No, said Willard, Perkins and Bernard had warned against conviction upon presumption—a clear slap at Cotton Mather's reading of the two Puritan authorities.[3] Instead, the judges had to have before them a matter of fact "evidently done and clearly proved," that is, they needed to have proof of causation. This was precisely what the judges did not have unless they admitted spectral evidence. It was the specter that caused the pain, and only the victims could see, or professed to see, the specters. Even if the judges credited the girls' testimony, such specters could only be created by the Devil, and crediting spectral evidence thus made the Devil a creditable witness. In his own heart, Willard refused to believe the accusers, for if their evidence could not be checked, there would be "no security for innocence." Indeed, one of the girls, Abigail Williams, had even accused Willard of being a witch, but, ushered out of the courtroom, she was told that she was mistaken. She took the hint and recanted.[4] Willard concluded that history proved that innocent people could be sent to their deaths by such means, for they made the Devil an informer against himself—surely the very sort of distortion of the truth that the Devil enjoyed best.[5] Willard knew that in the human heart there was room for "concupiscence," an impulse to serve an evil master, and for grace, the ability to rise above temptation.[6]

Aware that Willard was busy with his own condemnation of trials, seven of his brethren met in the College Hall at Harvard on August 1 and asked Increase Mather for another statement on evidence.[7] He was the acknowledged leader of the Ministerial Association, and the judges and the governor would have to listen to him. Had he not helped Phips become governor, and had he not brought the colony its new charter— whatever opinion some had of the document?[8] He had stayed on the sidelines thus far, in part because he had gone on record in *Illustrious Providences* as favoring many of the assumptions the judges made, and in part because he strongly supported the current administration. Nevertheless, Increase was a masterful politician. He waited until the trials were suspended at the end of the summer and then presented his work, *Cases of Conscience,* to the association on October 3. Willard was delighted, said so in a long preface, and, with thirteen of the other ministers, signed. Cotton did not, because he saw clearly that he and his father profoundly disagreed. Silently, he rushed ahead with a compilation of his summer sermons, accounts of the trials, and extracts from the books in his library which he had used in preparing his letter to Judge Richards.[9]

A copy of *Cases* was rushed to Phips, who read and understood its implications immediately. Cotton Mather later judged that his father's tract was the reason Phips ordered the court to disregard spectral evidence.[10] Unlike his son, Increase was a fine and forceful writer. Phips disbanded the court of oyer and terminer, then in recess, and reprieved the five who were in jail awaiting execution. Within five months, he would discharge all others accused, empty the jails, and end the trials. When the newly established Superior Court of Judicature, a standing supreme court created by the legislature, came together in January to hear more witchcraft cases, Phips prevented Stoughton from admitting spectral evidence. The jurors then acquitted all but three of the remaining suspects.

The extent of Increase Mather's influence on Phips may be debated. Perhaps Phips had finally seen Stoughton's political ambitions and curbed the chief judge. Stoughton resigned from the court after Phips insulted him by quashing the death warrants. At the same time, we must recognize that Increase had written what amounts to the first American tract on evidence in powerful and thoughtful prose. It is simply one of the great works of American legal literature, ranking with Joseph Story's treatises, Oliver Wendell Holmes Jr.'s essays, and Louis Brandeis's judicial opinions.

Cases began with an address to the Christian reader which echoed Willard's injunction: the more execrable the crime, the more care accusations required. There was a Devil, and He reveled in the admiration of His witches, but Christian charity and legal caution demanded close attention to the rules of evidence in cases of witchcraft. Increase then offered in sequence a probable-cause and a beyond-a-reasonable-doubt test. "Charity is not to be foregone as long as it has the most preponderating on its side" was a theological version of the probable-cause test the grand jury used. Applying it to those suspected of witchcraft in Salem might have resulted in fewer indictments. Grand juries had not been particularly charitable in these cases, but they had found "no bills" on some occasions. Increase then turned to the standards for proof at trial. "[If the testimony and other evidence] do not infallibly prove the crime against the person accused, [the court] ought not to determine him guilty of it." This requirement exceeded Perkins' and Bernard's cautions and presaged the modern doctrine of beyond a reasonable doubt. Reasonable doubt is that which would stay a prudent person when confronted with the evidence. In the nineteenth century, Chief Justice Lemuel Shaw of Massachusetts used the phrase "moral certainty," which, in 1850, meant psychological certitude. That definition was carried into the twentieth century but has been modified by the United States Supreme Court, for the meaning of "moral" has shifted. Under the Court's decision in *Sandoval v. California* (1994), reasonable doubt does not depend on moral certainty, now "ambiguous in the abstract," but on an "abiding conviction" in the jurors' minds that the charge must be true. However criminal court judges charge the jury about the meaning of reasonable doubt, the jurors are to reach their conclusion through their reasoning powers, not their moral sense. Whatever standard our courts select, the requirement is close to that Increase Mather proposed, and far from that Cotton Mather adopted.[11]

Increase continued that reliance upon spectral evidence or the ordeal of forcing the suspect to touch a victim "would subvert this government, and disband, yea ruine, Humane Society." In support of his admonition, he warned that devils could impersonate innocent people, even those who were truly godly, and delighted in the commotion and mistrust such impersonations caused: precisely the defense Osborn and Nurse raised and Hathorne dismissed at the pretrial hearings. Bewitched persons might think that anyone touching them was the witch and so would be cured, for many supposed witchcrafts were natural distempers, and the power of the imagination was strong enough to restore these people to health, as it had rendered them ill in the first place. Only God could heal, and no witch's touch could cure a sick person—to think otherwise was blasphemous. Finally, just as in the crediting of spectral evidence, using the ordeal of touching to determine guilt was indulging in the Devil's own work. Why should the sudden recovery of the victim be more believable than the protestations of innocence of the defendant?[12]

Increase concluded that evidence of witchcraft must be as clear as evidence of any other felony. This was Willard's point, and Increase elaborated on it. After a swipe at the credulousness of Roman Catholic jurisdictions, Increase confronted the issue of confession. A free and voluntary confession was a proof, if the confessor had full possession of her faculties and was not coerced, but confessions that included impossible things suggested coercion or derangement. For this reason, the confession of one witch against another was not to be accepted on its face. The malice that one suspect might bear another could easily motivate such accusations. So, too, the testimony of two honest persons to the fact of witchcraft—seeing and hearing the suspect do her mischief—had to be credited, but none of these had appeared in the Salem trials, save as spectral evidence. In the end, "[i]t were better that ten suspected Witches should escape than one innocent person should be condemned."[13]

Throughout *Cases* Increase told stories, sometimes the same stories that Cotton told in his August 1692 sermon, but Increase told them differently, in aid of a different argument. For both men, story was a way of proving. The Bible was true story, but it had to be interpreted, and both men used examples of witchcraft from the Bible to support quite different propositions. On the blamelessness of the judges they agreed, but their common stance had, in the context of their larger arguments, a different meaning. Cotton believed that the judges were right. Increase felt they had honestly erred.

They had talked about the cases throughout the summer. Did Cotton listen respectfully, keeping his own counsel, as his father crafted *Cases?* That was not his way; he preferred to talk and must have interjected his views, for a rivalry was brewing between father and son.[14] Now an outsider, replaced, as it were, by his father in the councils of their brethren, Cotton had to concede pride of place or compete with his father. Cotton chose the latter course. They went about Boston together, saw the same events, and came to different conclusions. Unable to criticize the older man, deterred by genuine affection and respect, yet all but overwhelmed by the rivalry that had naturally arisen, Cotton responded in a creative and forceful manner. He went on with the project of his own treatise on the cases.[15] Later, in the preface to the published version, he would write that none "but the Father, who sees in secret," knew the troubles that beset Cotton Mather, which may have been an unconscious reference to his own father as well as a cliché about God.[16] When he did mention those who nibbled and caviled at his work, he described them as "fourteen worthy ministers" and did not mention his father. Yet Cotton now added the pinching and biting the witches' advocates laid on him with "sinful and raging asperity" to the wounds inflicted on him by the Devil.[17]

184

Although he finished writing after his father, with his father's text, or pieces of it, in front of him, Cotton rushed to publish his tract first. The August sermon became the first chapter of *Wonders of the Invisible World,* in which Cotton demonstrated that witches could become specters and specters could afflict people. The Devil, whether tawny or black, made witches "the owners of spectres," and these could give corporal blows to living people. They could steal money and infect the unwary with disease. Knowing that the ministers in Boston had asked his father to prepare a stronger statement against the acceptance of spectral evidence, Mather set out to prove that the convictions were justified. He asked for and received Phips' and Stoughton's support, other fathers, political ones, and pressed Stephen Sewall for a copy of the trial records.[18] Cotton rehashed Perkins and Bernard, ignoring their cautions; rehearsed the dangers to which the Devil had subjected New England, including Indian magic; and moaned, "But what will become of this poor New-England after all? Shall we sink, expire, perish, before the short time of the Devil shall be finished?" All America looked to New England for guidance, and New England looked to Cotton Mather.[19]

If specters had these powers, then the judges were right in their instructions to the jury. If Mather believed that specters had these powers, why was he averse to convicting the suspects upon spectral evidence? The answer is, he was not opposed to it. He admitted that the Devil himself could take the spectral shape of an innocent person and that additional evidence was needed, beyond spectral display, to convict "the Witch Gang."[20] The only safety was to renew the covenant with the Lord, walk humbly into His churches, and "give up" sin. Yet what of the apparently blameless, the sanctified members of the Lord's churches in Salem and Andover who were executed for witchcraft? They were not really saints at all. Burroughs acted through specters, as did Susannah Martin, Elizabeth Howe, and Martha Carrier. In Mather's retelling of their trials, there was no mitigating evidence. He regarded his version as objective and factual; his unwillingness to accept exculpating evidence was very close to the judges' own refusal to credit the defendants' denials. The concordance was no accident; Mather professed throughout *Wonders* his trust in and loyalty to the judges.

185

Knowing that *Wonders* was written in the shadow of his father's great tract, we can begin to give a different interpretation to the venom and the anxiety of some of its passages. They are the extension of the conversations the two men must have had, but transformed for the reading public into a different form. They are filled, we now see, with the same sort of narcissistic rage which John Demos has found in some of the witchcraft accusers.[21] The anger and rejection Cotton felt at the hands of his father's colleagues he transformed into the Devil's rage at New England. Cotton became the victim of the Devil and suffered agonies, in reality a blend of sadness and rage. Unlike some clinical patients whose narcissistic fury leads to fragmentation of the personality, Cotton did not fly apart at the seams, but he would not be silenced by his elders' volte-face. Increase, reading his son's work, sensed the pain and tried to ease it in a postscript to *Cases*, but the breach was palpable. *Cases of Conscience Concerning Evil Spirits Personating Men* is as wise and caring as *Wonders* is narrow and mean spirited. The two tracts have a tangled and complex relationship both as text and as familial discourse.[22]

Although his father still protected him, Cotton was not easy in his own conscience. Every attempt to mitigate the horror brought more evidence that he might have been wrong. In mid-October, as he was finishing *Wonders,* he visited confessed witches jailed in Boston to pray with them and discovered to his dismay that these women, like Martha Jacobs the previous August, were recanting their testimony. Eight of the confessors now disclosed to Cotton that they had foresworn themselves to please the judges, whom they feared, and to prolong their lives.[23] As the year drew to a close, he nevertheless persisted in his belief that "there seemed an execrable Witchcraft, in the Foundation of the wonderful Afflication, and many Persons, of diverse Characters, were accused, apprehended, prosecuted, upon the Visions of the Afflicted." He recognized that the recriminations had begun, that he was in the thick of them, and offered, "[F]or my own part, I was always afraid of proceeding to convict and condemn any Person, as a Confederate with afflicting Daemons, upon so feeble an Evidence, as a spectral Representation. Accordingly, I ever testified against it, both publickly and privately, and in my Letters to the Judges, I particularly, besought them, that they would by no means admit it; and when a considerable Assembly of Ministers gave in their Advice about that Matter, I not only concurred with their Advice, but it was I who drew it up."[24]

To friends and enemies he repeated the litany of his innocence, albeit in a huffy, wounded voice. He was a small, weak servant of the church of God who only meant to help those who summoned him in their battle against the temptations of the Evil One.[25] So history was rewritten before it was forgotten, Mather covering his tracks with words. But Mather, who faced down the Devil in Salem, could not stop fighting Him in Boston. Despite a shift in public opinion away from further trials,[26] Cotton continued to believe that armies of devils circled Massachusetts. Perhaps the judges made an error in relying on spectral evidence, but if God let the Devil take on Himself the image of innocent men and women, "it would scarce be possible ever to convict a witch."[27]

In *A Brand Pluck'd Out of the Burning* (1693), Mather further exploited the storytelling genre to bolster his case against the Devil. He recounted the horrors that young Mercy Short endured and linked them to the panic that Salem had experienced. Short had survived an Indian raid on Salmon Falls, New Hampshire, in early 1690. Her entire family was slain, but she was carried into Canada and ransomed by the Phips expedition. Removed to Boston, she was a servant when she went past Sarah Good's jail cell. The old woman asked her for tobacco; the young woman refused and almost immediately thereafter fell into fits. The convulsions supposedly caused by the witch led to bouts of delirium, in which Short had complete recall of the Indian raid. She saw the Devil, who was at first black but later became tawny—in other words, like Tituba he went from African to Indian.[28]

The Devil and his minions bewitched, then tortured, then starved Short. Those who prayed with her and kept vigil saw her pain and heard her shrieking. She carried on monologues with the Devil and plainly feared that she would suffer the same fate as the condemned witches, for she named some of them. Then, overcome with her own emotions, she would "frolick" about and make fun of the ministers who came to save her. In these manic states, she could see specters, proof to Mather that his views had been correct all along. Short also told Mather that she had a good specter who protected her against the evil ones. Mather believed it all and reported it all. We might hazard a guess that Short's personality was fragmenting into good and evil parts, but it would be unfair to demand Mather recognize modern ideas of multiple personality. Mather never finished his story. The manuscript broke off abruptly, though Mercy Short continued to have bouts of severe depression, accompanied by hallucinations.[29]

187

Mather was more successful later in the year with Margaret Rule, who suddenly fell down and cried out that eight specters attacked her, directed by a short black man. At the beginning of September 1693, Mather had gone back to Salem to gather material for his planned history of the church in America. Preparing three sermons for his visit, he lost his notes, decided that the Devil's agents had taken them, and was delighted to discover that he remembered most of what he intended to say. Thus "the Devil gott nothing." With these thoughts foremost in his mind, he returned to Boston and found one of his neighbors "horribly arrested by *evil spirits*."[30]

It was the late afternoon of September 10, 1693, the day after a woman in the neighborhood, long suspected of being a witch, had treated Margaret Rule badly. Fearing that another witch hunt would begin (Cotton wrote later), Cotton and Increase raced to the scene. If they could intervene in time, Rule might not make public what rumor had already spread abroad. They visited her regularly after that, pressing her not to believe the promises or fall to the tortures of the Evil One. Around her had gathered a crowd of young people, before whom the ministers, joined by other notables, performed their "service to humanity." Evidently, scoffers had also barged in, watching the ministers as well as the girl, looking for signs of fakery. Everyone remembered what had happened in Salem, but Cotton Mather had no doubt that Rule's possession was real.[31]

While the Mathers struggled between themselves and with their critics to make the story come out right, Phips tried his hand at damage control. His London masters had to be informed of the cessation of the trials, and Phips had to protect his position. In October, he reported that on his arrival in May the province had been aboil with accusations. To sift through the claims he appointed a special court, and he then left to defend the colony's northern frontier. When he returned, he found dissatisfaction brewing not only with the conduct of the trials but with his administration as well. Most vexing was this: "I found the Devil had taken upon him the name and shape of severall persons who were doubtless innocent and to my certain knowledge of good reputation for which cause I have now forbidden the committing [to jail] of any more that shall be accused without unavoydable necessity, and those that have been committed I would shelter from any Proceedings against them wherein there may be the least suspicion of any wrong to be done unto the Innocent." Phips wanted instructions, and in the meantime he had forbidden anyone to write or publish comments on the affair. Phips had heard the groaning of the innocent, but more important were the political implications of the affair. Too many important people had come under assault, giving a lever to the popular party—the party opposed to Phips.[32]

On February 21, 1693, Phips continued his report, now pleading that he had depended upon the special court "for a right method of proceeding" and it had acted against many people thought to be innocent. He applauded Increase Mather's essay and relied upon it to argue that the Devil had taken the shape of the innocent. Phips had also found a scapegoat—Stoughton. "The Lieutenant Governor upon this occasion [of Phips reprieving those in prison] was enraged and filled with passionate anger and refused to sit upon the bench in a Superior Court then held at Charles Towne and indeed hath from the beginning hurried on these matters with great precipitancy and by his warrant hath caused the estates, goods, and chattels of the executed to be seized and disposed without my knowledge or consent."[33] Robert Calef would later report that the governor had acted when the girls accused his wife of being a witch, but Calef was, as time would prove, a master of dramatic extrapolation.[34]

While Phips blustered and fumed, the newly animated General Court met again in the second week of October 1692. Ordered by Phips to restrict the scope of the trials, it listened to appeals from the families of the incarcerated. Their petitions were couched in humble, even piteous terms, for they trusted the reconstituted assembly to aid them. Before the charter was revoked, the General Court had been just that—a court; the deputies, the lower house, and the magistrates, or "assistants," the upper house, heard both civil and criminal law cases.[35] The General Court still had the power to grant relief through private bills and acts.

John Osgood and eight others approached the honored General Court in October. His wife and their loved ones remained in jail, no threat to anyone, without proper food or clothing or heat as the winter approached. Might they not be sent home "under bond"?[36]

A flood of petitions followed. At first, the petitioners' aim was to ease the suffering of those in jail. No one attacked the jurisdiction of the court, the motives of the judges, or the outcomes of the previous cases, although out of doors the criticism had grown loud. Aided by family, numbers of the prisoners themselves petitioned for redress of grievances. From the Ipswich jail, the widow Penny and nine others asked that they might return home on bail for the winter—"for we are not in this unwilling nor afrayed to abide the tryall before any Judicature apoynted in convenient season"—but winter in the jail would surely kill some of the older prisoners, and perhaps as well one of their number who was pregnant and another who was nursing a ten-week-old baby.[37] Francis Dane, pastor in Andover, wrote to the assembly as well. He had lived in the town for "above" forty years; he knew the Carriers, the Johnsons, and the Barkers, entire families from his church which languished in jail on the basis of confessions extorted through "flatteries" and "threats." He had heard and seen no evidence of witchcraft from them, particularly from his daughter, Elizabeth Johnson, or his granddaughter, also Elizabeth, who was but "simplish at best." Could they not be spared, he pleaded, adding, "and let the Lord doe with me, and mine, what seems good in his owne eyes."[38]

The General Court responded by passing a bill against witchcraft modeled upon the Jacobean statute. By so doing it fulfilled the first command of the new charter, that all laws be in conformity with those of England. It also locked the door on spectral evidence first shut by Phips. All the offenses punishable under the law required corroboration. Conjuration, entertaining any evil spirit, taking up the dead from the earth, using sorcery whereby any person was killed or lamed—these were to be punishable with death. Treasure finding and preparing love potions were punishable with one year in jail. Under the statute the Superior Court of Judicature for the colony sent warrants to the towns to choose grand and petty (trial) jurors for the next round of trials. On January 3, the court met, its bench consisting of Stoughton, Danforth, Richards, Wait Winthrop, and Samuel Sewall.[39] Stoughton ordered those women who had been reprieved "for the belly" prepared for execution, but Phips stayed the order until the Crown signified its pleasure.[40] When word reached Stoughton at the end of the month that Phips had quashed the orders, the judge stalked off the bench fuming that he was just about to "clear the land" of witches when Phips interfered.[41]

Without the aid of spectral evidence, the cases of all but three of the thirty-one accused in the dock in January ended in acquittal. Grand juries had indicted them, but now trial juries had doubts, and that was enough.[42] The juries had reversed their spring and summer roles, the trial juries proving harder to convince than the grand juries. There is no reason given in any of the brief records of the cases why the twenty-eight were discharged or the three convicted. The exclusion of spectral evidence need not have changed the jurors' thinking, for all of them had either seen the girls in action or heard about the specters. A judicial ruling banishing specters from the courtroom could not erase the jurors' memory. What the new rule did was prevent the girls from testifying so vividly, and that may have made all the difference. Calef reported one of these cases in a little detail. Sarah Duston (or Daston), a woman of about seventy or eighty years, was confronted with "a multitude of witnesses . . . but what testimony they gave in seemed wholly forreign [i.e., irrelevant], as of accidents, illness, and etc. befalling them, or theirs after some quarrel." Spectral evidence was barred, and the jury "soon brought her in not guilty."[43]

There were still a few convictions, however. Sarah Wardwell, who had confessed, was convicted, but there is nothing in her confession which differed from the other Andover confessions except her admission that she was baptized by the Devil. She was contrite and promised not to backslide.[44] Mary Post of Rowley was convicted, for some reason that is not clear. There is no record of the evidence against her.[45] Simple-minded Elizabeth Johnson Jr., Dane's granddaughter, was convicted as well.[46]

The Superior Court of Judicature met again in April, and juries found five more defendants not guilty. John Alden was discharged by proclamation, having previously fled and now returned. Mary Watkins was held over on a charge of slander, for accusing another woman of infanticide.[47] In May, Phips emptied the jails and sent the prisoners home. They and their relatives soon approached the General Court seeking reparations. This round of petitions dragged on for another two decades, the General Court reversing the attainder of individuals and finally voting a repudiation of the trials and paying off the claims of the kin of those who were executed. Even Cotton Mather supported these petitions, admitting in 1710, "[T]here have been errors committed."[48] The children of George Burroughs were still filing papers with the legislature in 1750.[49] Some of those who fled did not regain lost property, because they had committed another crime—jail breaking.[50]

In Boston, a small chorus of criticism of the judges and the court arose. Late in 1693, Thomas Brattle, whose professed respect for authority was so strong that he would have "sooner [bitten his] finger's ends than willingly cast dirt on authority, or any way offer reproach to it," nevertheless wrote on October 8 a letter to a friend for private circulation which asserted, "I never thought judges infallible; but reckoned that they, as well as private men, might err." When such errors were "fundamental" and perverted justice, they undermined genuine authority and had to be exposed. Brattle would do so. Because a "poor child" had a fit and accused men or women of parts, judges who had known the suspects for years and thought them honorable and pious now changed their opinions and sentenced them to death. Brattle, a man of science, condemned the credulity of the judges, believing as they did that the touch of a suspected witch might cure a possessed girl of her affliction. Meanwhile, midwives' juries were allowed to conduct physical examinations of the bodies of the accused, looking for witch marks, a "very general and inclusive term." Who did not have some mark on their body which might fit this description? This "Salem philosophy" was false, and even if it had some basis in the supernatural, it could easily be manipulated by the Devil himself. The admission of "spectre evidence" made the accused guilty without the power to prove their innocence. Halfway through the letter, Brattle paused to express his admiration for those who had, covertly and overtly, resisted the witch hunt. Boston justices of the peace had allowed men and women accused of witchcraft to leave the province, sometimes by breaking jail, and did not pursue them to their sanctuaries. Men of parts such as former governor Simon Bradstreet, Danforth, Increase Mather, and Samuel Willard finally spoke out against the conduct of the trials. Even in Salem, there were many who quietly opposed the whole affair.[51]

Brattle passed on much of the information he gathered to another merchant in Boston, Robert Calef.[52] Calef, never a believer in the Devil's work, read what Brattle wrote, and decided to see for himself. On September 13 and 19, 1693, he visited Margaret Rule's room to watch Cotton and Increase pray with the girl. Amused and appalled at the same time, he tried to begin a conversation with Cotton, sending letters through intermediaries, trying to arrange meetings, and, as provocation surely, passed around a manuscript of his own account of Rule's "possession." After four years of chasing Cotton around Boston, fighting off a lawsuit for libel, and deluging Cotton's fellow ministers with letters, Calef decided to compile the whole, along with "An Impartial Account" of what happened at Salem (implying that others' accounts were biased), into a book—*More Wonders of the Invisible World.*

Calef's work was a jumble of genres, part pamphlet polemic, part epistolary collection, part narrative. Portions of it resembled the popular "martyrologies" of Quakers and opponents of arbitrary royal power which circulated in the seventeenth century.[53] The overarching structure, however, was a dialogue between Calef and the absent Mather. Dialogues were conversations between allegorical speakers, a form of essay well known to every literate English speaker and already employed by Willard, whose work Calef had read.[54] Calef's style wedded the common wisdom of ordinary people—he portrayed himself as the voice of everyman—to the barbed wit of a Daniel Defoe or Jonathan Swift, but Calef owned no special pride of authorship. Unlike Mather, whose most self-effacing pieces still exhibited a defensive, stuffy arrogance, Calef called himself a collector, whose only guidelines were truth and reason.[55]

Of course, such modesty was a literary pose itself, but Calef was not a modest, impartial observer. He was angry with Mather. Mather had pointedly snubbed Calef, terming him a mere weaver who styled himself a merchant—mocking him as an unlearned man, a blockhead, to whom Mather, at one point, generously offered access to his library.[56] In return, Calef pilloried Mather, who for all his books believed that devils walked the streets, clanking chains, stinking of brimstone. How appropriate that Mather made the Devil into a bookman, who went about enrolling the "proud, froward, ignorant, envious, and malitious" in his ledger. Who could credit Mather's fear that witches dropped everything to rush off in spectral form to meetings and thence to bedrooms and dark roads where they pinched, scratched, and bit their victims? Such nonsense "gave the brand of infamy" to all New England.[57]

According to Calef, only a man as self-absorbed and egotistical as Cotton Mather could fail to see how the Salem episode had debased the colony. The same self-regard led Mather to ignore Calef's offer to sit down and talk. Thus, though he was aware that by 1697, when he finally circulated his miscellany of letters, eyewitness accounts, and tracts (they

192

were not published until 1700, and then only in London), some would accuse him of "raking in the coals" of a dying fire, Calef retorted, "[W]e cannot recall those to life again that have suffered." Only the Devil and Cotton's friends would be pleased by allowing injustice and imposture to go unexposed. What was more, another witch hunt had erupted in Scotland—might not some lives there be saved by the timely exposure of Salem's tragedy? Calef admitted a more sordid motive as well: he had been hailed into court by Cotton's friends to answer a charge of slander. With the record in print, anyone might see he was without guilt.[58]

What he brought to the public—for he held a conversation directly with his reader as well as indirectly with the specter of Cotton Mather—was his common sense. No "necessary learning," no extensive, expensive "libraries" full of superstitious nonsense in vellum bindings were necessary to expose the learned inanity of Mather's writings. With a stroke Calef inverted the superiority claimed by the ministers and elevated the natural skepticism of ordinary men of affairs. He conveniently ignored the fact that popular clamor and popular fears had led to the crisis in the first place, for he believed that the crisis was the work of a conspiracy of ministers and magistrates seeking to retain control of the government for themselves.[59]

Yet once more there was an ironic twist to the Salem story, for Calef could not have punctured Cotton's claims without Cotton's active help, because the younger Mather still believed in demons and witches and went about trying to help those afflicted by spectral agents. When Mather ostentatiously rushed to Margaret Rule's bedside, according to Calef, Mather did not find the Devil but an imposture. Unwittingly he fed the girl her lines, just as the inquisitors of Betty Parris had, in February, a year earlier, and Rule played Mather for a fool. When the ministers were gone, Calef recalled, Rule bid the other women leave and asked the young men to stay. Their company was not offensive. Her former "Sweet-heart" she pulled back to his seat, saying, "[H]e should not go tonight." When Calef returned, on the 19th, Rule was attended by eight people, who ministered to her every whim, bore her screams with tender concern, and worried about her safety. Suddenly, she turned merry and was full of laughter. "She said she wondered any people would be so wicked as to think she dissembled," a crude swipe at Calef, whom Rule regarded as a "spy."[60]

Indeed he was, but not on her, for it was Cotton Mather's conduct that Calef condemned. When Calef circulated his own account of the events that day, they were critical of Cotton Mather for believing what was so obviously faked and for touching the girl's chest. Mather, who had written but not published an account of Rule's travails, lent it to Calef, and Calef used it not to emend his own manuscript but to preface the latter in the book. So Cotton's protestations that he was a mere "servant of mankind" and had always opposed "the excessive credit of spectral accusations" stood in dramatic equipoise as a hollow and forced prelude to Calef's own more measured and sensible comments.[61] Thus Calef created a literary fiction that he and Mather were talking to each other: let the reader decide who made the most sense. Mather refused to reply after January 1694, but Calef continued to supply both voices, expanding the dialogue to address Brattle, Willard, Dutch ministers, and even an unnamed Scot who had inquired of Mather about witchcraft.

Calef's narrative of the events in Salem lacked the drama and the originality of his contrived dialogue with Mather. It was based upon secondhand accounts, a selection of the original documents, and interviews with those men and women most likely to find fault with the treatment of the suspects. Calef's skills as a controversialist did not carry well into the project of a narrative. There was some humor, however, as Calef related the efforts of judges to attack invisible specters with their swords and sticks. "One justice broke his cane at this exercise."[62] No rumor that reflected badly on the Mathers or the judges was omitted, Calef unable to distinguish narrative from polemic. But then, who could?

Meanwhile, in Salem Village an uneasy truce had prevailed throughout the trials. Tentative efforts to repair the damage to families now seem pathetic: when the Essex County Quarterly Court met on September 27, 1692, the selectmen and grand jurors of Ipswich reminded the judges that they must provide for the care of John Willard's fatherless children, some of whom were quite young. Corwin and Hathorne ordered they be placed "into good and honest families."[63] The agony of the village and its neighbors made little lasting impression upon the local courts. The families of the accused did not sue the accusers for false witness or defamation. In the local courts, Corwin and Hathorne presided over business as usual—typically: *Perkins v. Boardman,* replevin, for four oxen, three cows, and four yearlings.[64] The Putnams and their allies continued to dominate the lists of trial and grand jurors in the quarterly courts and later, in 1694, the new courts of common pleas and general sessions of the peace.

Pardon

Early in 1693, when the trials were winding to their close and the detainees were returning home, the villagers attempted a reconciliation of sorts, but the effort was short lived for the same reason that the original crisis had erupted. People could not talk to one another without becoming embroiled in old animosities; conversation became argument and argument exploded into accusation.

At first, Parris himself tried to preach conciliation, but his words failed to soothe, for he remained convinced that some of the more stiff-necked congregants still mocked him and the church by refusing to come to the Lord's Supper. He disclaimed any blame for what might have been miscarriages of justice.[65] Parris's supporters could pay his salary privately, but for the next year and a half, they could not gain control of the village meeting or of the committee it elected. The meeting house needed repairs, but none were assayed. Petitions flew back and forth between the village and the General Court. The dissenting villagers, as Parris dismissively called them, were led by Nurse and Cloyse, but underwritten by the Porters, in their struggle for control of the pulpit. The issue had become clear. Parris had to assume some responsibility for his too-ready belief in the guilt of his own neighbors and for his lack of charity toward those who opposed him. Under far lighter fire, his predecessors had resigned, but Parris hung on, grimly, resisting attempts to call a convocation of ministers to hear the dissenters' grievances, labeling the protests "libels" in the church record that he kept, and managing to prevent the meeting for more than a year after the General Court had ordered it be held.[66]

Parris was capable of guile as well as gall. When he finally met with the whole town on November 26, 1694, he turned the tables on his opponents and admitted to having a sore conscience. He had spoken too soon and with too much acerbity in those days and had believed where he should have doubted. His "Meditations for Peace" as he styled them sought a reconciliation. Forgiveness, under the "mantle of love," would repair what had been rent. They were still his "beloved flock." Had the calamity not broken first upon him, in his family, perhaps he could have used better judgment. Even so, he took it as a judgment upon him that he was so afflicted. God had spat in his face, by bringing down both illness and reproach upon him. He owned his error, though he meant only to do justice, and apologized to those who had been harmed. Above all, he was deluded by Satan, as others were.

There was more self-pity and shifting of blame in his meditation than real contrition, something the Nurse and Cloyse families must have recognized, for they had suffered far more. For them, Parris's apology came a little late and was a little forced. Unmoved, they asked for a copy. He refused, unless they gave him a copy of their grievances. It was replay of the January 1692 confrontation and ended the same way: both sides retiring, still enemies, to tend their wounds and plan for the next battle. The council of local ministers which met in April 1695 to mediate the quarrel forcibly suggested that Parris go but refused to condemn him. Instead, its members, led by Increase and Cotton Mather, condemned the village for its factiousness.[67] After a year's additional recrimination, Parris finally left, still unbowed, perhaps unaware of the damage he had done, his pride—the pride of the master class, a planter's pride—hurt but intact. He found another pulpit, briefly, then returned to a merchant's life, remarried, and had sons, one of whom he named Noyes in honor of the minister who stood by him to the end.

Behind him the rawness remained, but not for long. True, the village was now more than ever before split between two factions looking in different directions. On the Ipswich road, the Porters and Joseph Putnam had firmly cast their lot with the commercialization of the town. The villagers who supported Parris, often the poorer farmers led by the Putnams, had lost the fight for control of the church, but not for control of the future. There would always be a place for farmers in New England. The reintegration of village life began, like the healing of a long-suppurating wound, its scarred edges still visible. Ann and Thomas Putnam resumed their life, but neither was healthy. Thomas began selling off his patrimony, including parcels to the Townes family of Topsfield, whose sisters Nurse, Cloyse, and Esty Ann Putnam Jr. and Sr. had condemned in the trials. Thomas passed away in 1696, a worn-out man in his forty-sixth year. His brother Edward was joined by his half-brother Joseph, the Putnam who had married into the Porter clan, to administer the estate.[68] A new, young minister, Joseph Green, came to the village fresh from Harvard in 1697, avoided quarrels, held out the right hand of fellowship, invited the dissenters to return, and brought the villagers together again.[69]

Nearby, John Hale, the minister in Beverly, who had watched the crisis unfold from its inception, grew uneasy in his conscience. Writing about it was harder for him than for Brattle or Calef, because it involved his own actions. He had been an accuser himself. Giving evidence against Sarah Wildes, who was executed on July 19, 1692 (no doubt in part because of the weight of evidence like Hale's—from an unimpeachable source—with a jury of sober men), he recalled that some fifteen or sixteen years earlier in Beverly, Goodwife Reddington of Topsfield had come to him to complain that she was bewitched by Wildes. He told the magistrates then, and no doubt the judges at the trial, that Reddington was visited by Wildes' son, who confessed that his mother was a witch.[70] Hale felt no compunctions (nor was his conduct unusual) in passing on stale rumor, hearsay, and unsubstantiated accusation. He was no less a part of the vernacular culture—the network of oral storytelling and information sharing—which sustained the bulk of social intercourse in northern New England then. As a minister, he was situated at a node in the network, a place where many lines of communication came together and then branched out again.

Gradually, over time, he had seen the error of his ways. In 1697 he composed his own judgment of the affair and left it in the hands of fellow minister John Higginson of Salem, who, when Hale died, published the account with an introduction. Hale had supported the prosecutions but came to believe that he acted in error. He confessed, "I have been from my youth trained up in the knowledge and belief of most of those principles I here question as unsafe to be used." It was hard to disavow these principles, but the events at Salem had led him to question, and by questioning, to discard error. His conscience was now "tender," and with grief in his heart he acknowledged that the innocent had suffered. Hale began his apology with the same tales that the Mathers had used, reexamined in the light of what later occurred. Hale disclosed that false witness and natural causes were responsible for some of the prosecutions, mingled with malice and ignorance among the accusers. For his own part, he begged that some effort be made to repair the reputations and restore the estates of those wrongly convicted and punished.[71]

One more act of contrition marked this year of healing. At the beginning of 1697, the General Court ordered a day of fasting and soul-searching for the tragedy at Salem, the day that many had wanted the General Court to proclaim in October 1692. Deeply moved, and fearing that his own guilt had led to illness and death in his family, Samuel Sewall reconsidered his role on the court. To his minister, Samuel Willard, Sewall gave a copy of a confession of sin.[72] Willard read it aloud at the fast day, as Sewall stood in silence in his pew, and it was posted: "Samuel Sewall, sensible of the reiterated stroke of God upon himself and family; and being sensible, that as to the Guilt contracted, upon the opening of the late Commission of Oyer and Terminer at Salem (to which the order for this day [of fasting, passed by the General Court] relates) he is, upon many accounts, more concerned than any that he knows of, Desires to take the Blame and Shame of it, Asking pardon of men . . ."[73] Sewall was a pious man and a conventional one. He believed in witches and feared the Devil. He was also a man of exceeding good sense, a practical man, and he realized, if belatedly, that somehow God's people had become the Devil's disciples.

198

conclusion

WHERE to end? At the close of every good story there is a moral.[1] Salem's travail is replete with them. When our sense of loss and our anger ebb, Salem's agony reminds us of the contingency of historical events. Chance brought Tituba and Samuel Parris together, compounded by Betty's illness and Cotton Mather's need to be needed, a hard winter and a harder war, without which there would have been no trials and no executions. I am not advocating a "people of standing" approach to great events; there is no need to rehash the old "kings and battles" school of historical interpretation.[2] Rather, my point is the opposite, that people of all kinds of consequence in the social hierarchy can be the makers of their own histories, be those histories triumphant or tragic. Such contingency does not deny the efficacy of human choices or the agency of human will. Again, the reverse is true—human beings do make their world, although with imperfect vision and impaired feeling.

As the gathering of these particular players was accidental, the stage on which they performed was set by another, larger contingency. In 1692, Salem was contested ground, not just by the Putnam and Porter clans, but by whole cultures. Forest and glade reached to the northwestern edge of the village, almost touching the busy coastal lands that joined the village on the east. The village was the "edge" of the two worlds, where a vast Atlantic commercial system, throughout whose reaches people and consumer durables were in constant motion, met a wilderness, whose natives, long put upon by a foreign force, still struggled to protect their ways and their land. There witchcraft beliefs and warfare fed each other, creating the stresses and shaping the images of the crisis.

To Salem had also come the burden of war. In its physical manifestation, King William's War brought devastation, panic, and death. In moments when the guns were still, the war was fought with words. Salvos of Puritan sermons condemning Roman Catholic France cratered the ground on which accusers and accused trod. In eastern New England the last battles of the Reformation raged. Cotton Mather and Samuel Parris agreed with Richard Baxter, whose works the New Englanders eagerly read, that Satan and his minions had joined forces with the French and their Indian allies. The advance scouts of the enemy column were the witches of Salem.

A last contingency, perhaps more ironic than the others: in retrospect, Salem witchcraft was a temporal anomaly. The tragedy there did not bring witch hunting in New England to an end, for that era was almost over and done. The events in Salem came too late to affect the decline of witchcraft prosecutions in England. Salem's troubles were more provincial, and the abrupt end to the trials was more evidence of the impact of English modernism on New England, filtered through the hesitant cautions of men like Increase Mather and Thomas Brattle and the liberal theology of men like Samuel Willard. Henceforth, elite minds would reject witchcraft accusations when popular clamor threatened to revive them. If the Salem cases heralded a new world, it was a world marked by the now familiar division of elite and vernacular cultures in law and in religion. New Englanders remained wedded to folk religion, but those customs no longer dictated judges' readings of book law. Witchcraft accusations periodically surfaced, even in Salem, where one "Old Granny Ober" supposedly bewitched cows, but the Salem trials had become a reason to withhold judgment. In Littleton, Massachusetts, early in the 1700s, three young sisters began to suffer in ways reminiscent of Betty Parris. Questioned, they accused an older neighbor of bewitching them, but authorities did not bite. Years later, one of the sisters confessed to her minister that the girls had fabricated the story because they wanted the attention. He knew as much already. New rules of evidence emerged which discounted hearsay and rumor.[3] New England Puritanism accommodated itself to empirical science, and Cotton Mather, still searching for his own, authentic voice, joined in the chorus. Cotton Mather continued to believe in the Devil and witches, but by the early 1720s he concluded that the witches at Salem did not make a pact with the Devil—the very offense that had so frightened the early Puritans into denunciations of witchcraft. His shift away from omens was omen itself that the worlds of wonder were no longer supernatural.[4]

There is nothing of "Whig" history—the inevitable history of progress—in my tale, however, for Salem's agony was not the last time that local rumor, deep-seated fears and guilt, and official confusion would spur a "witch hunt" in colonial America. In the bitter winter of 1741, New York City faced conditions similar to those that whipped panic in Salem. The West Indies trade was faltering, the persistent cold had reduced fuel and food supplies to critical levels, and fears of invasion from the sea and Canada kept the garrison awake and the free white population frightened. There were others as well—increasing numbers of slaves, some fresh from Africa, others seasoned in the West Indies—for whom bitterness and anger had become a way of life. One among the latter, Caesar, became the center of an informal network of free blacks, slaves, and unemployed white laborers. They met at a tavern and boasted of what they might do—violent fantasies that led to a wave of thefts and arson. Thus was born the infamous "Slave Conspiracy of 1741."

As the authorities probed the apparent crime wave, suspects were interrogated and perhaps fed stories that came back to the authorities as a full-blown conspiracy to massacre the whites. Paramilitary organizations were now seen in the silhouettes of blacks' street gatherings, although none of the supposed principals in the conspiracy exhibited any martial ardor. Through the spring and summer, 160 Africans and African Americans and 21 Europeans were arrested. Mass trials followed, based upon forced confessions, and public executions were planned to warn other slaves and free sympathizers of what awaited them if they harbored thoughts of resistance. Four whites were hanged, as were seventeen blacks, Caesar among them; thirteen blacks were burned at the stake, a punishment not used in the Salem cases. Seventy additional slaves were transported to the West Indies—primarily Barbados—a sentence close enough to death given the demography of that island.

On what evidence? The confession of three young people who feared for their own lives and one soldier, confused but eager for the notoriety. The judges fed the key witnesses, particularly young Mary Burton, the lines, and she gave them the answers they wanted. There was indeed a conspiracy, she swore, and each suspect they paraded before her she duly identified as a participant in the plot. The trials only ended when Burton began to recall that some among the conspirators were not rabble or slaves but the better sort. Then the judges brought the affair to a hasty end.[5] Yet even after the executions and banishments were completed, interrogators fed lines to children and children repeated what they thought authorities wanted to hear.[6] The parallel to the events in Salem is striking, though the conclusion was more grisly because no one stepped forward to denounce the rumors and the ensuing panic as unfounded.

Over the 250-plus years since 1741, riots and violence in our cities, vigilantism and lynching in our towns and countryside, have been fueled by the same kind of rumor, panic, fearfulness, cultural dysfunction, and official incapacity as brought on the Salem trials. What is more, today there exists a professional class of demon hunters not far removed from the witch finders of the seventeenth century. The modern diviners go from place to place, holding press conferences and giving interviews in their effort to ferret out and punish those who worship Satan.[7] The world of Tituba, Betty, and Cotton Mather had changed after Salem, in part as a result of the tragedy of it, but their sacrifice has not saved us from our worst suspicions of one another.

Then again, perhaps we have learned something. On another occasion for assembly of the community, May 30, 1994, Memorial Day, hazy sun and dusty wind blow down Maple Street in Danvers, which includes old Salem Village. Danvers is still poor compared with Salem; there are no resort hotels, restored waterfronts, or Chestnut Street mansions in Danvers as grace the port city. Today the town has come out in its multitude—mothers in shorts and halter tops, fathers in tee shirts and tractor caps, children of all sizes—to watch the parade. Down Elm Street, across Maple, creep the fire engines and Humvees, followed by troops of Boy Scouts and packs of Cub Scouts, all in uniform. The crowd cheers, and little ones rush out to walk beside their older siblings. Hard faces, for Danvers is an industrial town and feels the force of post-industrial layoffs and blight, break into smiles. Neighbors enjoy their neighborhood; veterans and those who did not serve in the armed forces together celebrate the fact that they live and work in Danvers. The old exclusiveness of ethnicity is forgotten, borne over by waves of Irish and German, Eastern European and Asian, African and South American immigration. Shoulder to shoulder, equal in law and increasingly equal in buying power, the many peoples of the world, now denizens of Danvers, watch the trucks and marchers pass.

Down Hobart Street, in quiet, leafy lanes, the last few houses that survive from the 1690s sit, marked by tablets that proclaim their antiquity and their first owner. Only the foundations of Parris's parsonage remain, and the meadow where the witches supposedly cavorted is overgrown with brush. The Ingersoll Tavern has survived, but no traveler frequents it. It is quiet now, dowdy, in need of another coat of paint. A half mile down Pine Street, surrounded by meadow, much as it had been three hundred years earlier, the Nurse farmstead dominates a small grassy knoll. This day it hosts a theatrical troupe, filming an epic on the witchcraft episode for the Discovery Channel, to be aired on Halloween. The actors and crew lounge outside the restored meeting house, catching a smoke or shooting the breeze alongside the equipment truck. Bob Osborne, who lives in the Nurse house, chats with the one visitor who has driven up the long, dirt road to see the honorable militia, in period 1776 costume, practice in the meadow below the farm. In the heat of the early afternoon they march back and forth firing ragged volleys of black powder.

In the silences between the volleys, one can hear the distant shouts of children, and in those cries of delight and determination is the lesson of this Memorial Day. It is the weekend of the Danvers Soccer Invitational Tournament. Behind the memorial to the men and women executed for witchcraft which stands, its granite wings spread, across the road from the original site of the meeting house, there are two soccer fields. On them, at one o'clock in the afternoon, four teams of twelve-year-old girls play. Watched by adoring parents and monitored by gentle referees— men in black who are no kin to the black-robed ministers of 1692—the girls romp in the field. Dressed in shorts and uniform shirts, the players are uninhibited, frolicsome, and fiercely determined to kick the ball into the net.

Three hundred years ago, the Puritans of Salem Village would have been shocked, for such play was not allowed in their fields and commons, particularly not on the Sabbath. Nor were girls to go about dressed in such fashion. The men in black on Sundays, days of thanksgiving, and fast days were not referees of games. Today the Bettys and Abigails have a new outlet for the pressures and fears of oncoming womanhood. The parents have other ways to encourage and teach their children. The authorities still watch for crime, and Danvers has its share, but the children fantasize about winning trophy cups, not about witches.

True, there are witches in Salem today, much more visible now than in 1692. The "official witch of Salem," Laurie Cabot, is a media figure.[8] In 1992 and 1993, during the two-year-long tricentennial of the trials, the city celebrated with "haunted happenings"—more than eighty Halloween-related events scheduled for tourists between October 23 and October 31. How different these observers are than the ministers and magistrates who came to Salem to watch the trials in 1692. The First Church, now Unitarian, readmitted the supposed witches excommunicated there a hundred years earlier. Cable news stations ran programs on the local coven. Its leaders explained that they were not malevolent but a group of women who believed in the importance of nature and the power of folk healing in a woman-centered world.[9] In the window of one of the many occult shops near the Essex Street Mall in the restored section of Salem, the Artes Magicae Bookstore, a placard advertised the "Women's Power Drum Group," which met from six to eight in the evening. So numerous were its members that "reservations [were] requested." All this on Lynde Street, less than a block from the jail where so many languished and little Dorcas Good, bound in chains so her specter could not torment older girls, lost her reason for living.[10]

What's in a Name?
Tituba's Origins

TITUBA DID not belong in New England; on that all historians agree. Whence came she then?[1] The trial records show that she was described as "Titiba, an Indian Woman" when she gave oral testimony before the magistrates on March 1, 1692, and later as "Titibe" (both spellings the work of magistrates John Hathorne's and Jonathan Corwin's clerk, Ezekiell Cheever), as "the Indyen woman" by Joseph Putnam when he kept his own records of her testimony that day, and as "Titiba an Indian Woman" in the mittimus by which she was transferred from Salem to the Boston jail, probably the work of Ezekiell Cheever again. Robert Calef, in *More Wonders,* calls her "the said Indian woman, named Tituba." John Hale, a minister who had been involved with many suspected witches before and during the Salem trials, describes in his *Modest Inquiry* (1697) "an indian man servant [Indian John] and his wife, . . . the indian woman named tituba."[2] On March 2, 1692, a day after she had denied charges of being a witch, Sarah Good reportedly told one of her warders that she faced "but one evidence, and that an indian [for Tituba had in her confession named Good as a witch], and therefore she fear[ed] not."[3]

Throughout the colonial period, English-speaking authorities faced the task of categorizing the many ethnicities that populated their American empire. Unlike the Spanish, who had names, and with them legal categories of some complexity, for mixtures of races—"mestizo" (Indian and Spanish descent), "sambo" (Indian and African descent), "mulatto" (African and Spanish descent)—the English insisted upon loose, single categories of human origins, willingly or unwittingly losing the mixedness of so many people who lived or passed through the Caribbean. Thus Tituba's ethnicity was narrowed and frozen; she must be one thing or another—not the many that she might have been. By calling her an Indian the magistrates also reduced her to a single, manageable object of Puritan public policy—a policy that had, by 1692, changed from uneasy coexistence punctuated by angry confrontations into hardened animosity and prejudice. She was diminished by a name.[4]

If Indian, of what provenance? Tituba might have been a northeastern Algonkin, for some of them were enslaved by order of Massachusetts's government in the wake of Metacom's war for Indian independence—King Philip's War—others were "illegally kidnapped" by private entrepreneurs, and a few of the latter were even carried into the West Indies. In general, these were men, not children. A few girls were enslaved and sold locally.[5] If she was one of these unfortunates, Tituba had returned to her home through a singular stroke of good fortune, but if New England was her home, she might well have simply walked away from her servitude, like the many who left the "praying villages" the Puritans established and rejoined their Algonkin cousins to the north and west.[6]

More important, if she were Algonkin in origin, her name would not have been changed, unless it was changed to an English name, for of the thirty-two children sold out to servitude after King Philip's War, only one, a boy named Sawoonawuk, kept his Algonkin name. All the others gained an English forename, John or Anne, or another like it.[7] But Tituba is not an English name, nor is it an Algonkin name. Algonkin women's names usually ended with the *skw* sound, meaning woman (or as now rendered, "squaw"). A vowel ending was impossible. Nor does the spelling conform to the way that New England civil authorities rendered Massachusett and other Algonkin names in written form. In the next century, a name like Tituba might have resulted from a marriage of an African and an Indian, but then Tituba would have been preceded by an English or biblical forename.[8]

Some scholars argue that Tituba was Carib or Arawak, from the West Indies.[9] Charles Upham followed this usage in his 1867 book, after ignoring her in his 1831 lectures, probably because he had read Drake's 1866 volumes, which included Calef's writings. Whatever his inspiration, Upham makes Tituba an immigrant to Barbados from some unnamed "former residence in the neighborhood of the Spanish Main."[10] It was true that many Indians were enslaved in the West Indies and on the coast of Latin America, but there is no evidence whatsoever that Spanish slaves were carried into Barbados. Perhaps with this fact in mind (a fact that Hansen ignores, because he has no interest in the Caribbean part of the story), by the end of the nineteenth century George Bancroft and John Gorham Palfrey, followed in the early 1900s by John Fiske and George Lincoln Burr, and finally by Samuel Eliot Morison, made Tituba into a "half breed," a term that managed to libel both Native Americans and Africans.[11] Starkey turned Tituba mean, lazy, and southern but kept her "half savage."[12] Hansen admitted that he was perplexed over this transformation from Carib to half Carib and even more troubled by the final stage of Tituba's resurrection as an African, for by the 1950s, in the hands of Arthur Miller, Tituba became African and practiced voodoo instead of Indian magic.[13] John Demos accepted this identification in his earlier work on New England witchcraft.[14] Tituba was omitted from *Entertaining Satan*.

There are problems with the identification of Tituba as Carib or half Carib. Barbados was deserted, its Carib inhabitants dead and gone, when the English arrived. Throughout the seventeenth century, a small number of Carib Indians either came of their own accord or were transported by force to the island. The survivors of these original Indian imports sued for their freedom and won, although as late as the 1670s, even Quakers held Indian slaves. Governor Willoughby's raid on Dominica may have increased the number of Caribs as late as 1668, but these were men captured in war, and most were sold to planters in Jamaica. Shortly thereafter the English concluded a treaty of amity with the island Caribs, and from 1668 to 1678, "Indian slaves were not imported" into Barbados. The peace ended in 1674–75, but renewed hostilities did not lead to increased importation of Caribs. In 1676, the Barbadian legislature forbade the importation of Caribs as slaves, in large measure because they were liable to resist slavery, and did so with some success. By 1684, there were an estimated 72 Caribs on the island.[15]

Throughout the Caribbean islands, there were Carib-African unions that produced children of mixed parenthood, but these children were not likely to land in Barbados, in part because the authorities there were busy fending off Caribs when not demanding that they return runaway African slaves.[16] The relations of the English on Barbados with the Caribs on islands other than Barbados were never peaceful, and in the years when Parris purchased Tituba, the governor of Barbados was plotting a "final solution" to the Carib problem.[17]

Tituba is unlikely to have been Carib. Might she have been Arawak? Long before the Spanish decimated the Caribs, the Caribs had performed the same barbarity on the Arawaks, driving them to the margins of the Caribbean. In Surinam and elsewhere Arawaks still lived, and some of these were taken, against colonial policy, back to Barbados. Could Tituba have been one of the two or three young girls brought to the island in 1673 and 1674 in illegal raids by filibusterers? These raids did capture girls, and despite official efforts to return the captured Arawaks to their homes in the Orinoco basin, some evidently were sold to planters. Once on the island to stay, these Amerindians were incorporated into the life of the sugar plantations, alongside the larger number of African slaves. Some young girls of Arawak parentage were evidently cared for by African families. The former were listed, however, as Indian, on plantation inventories.[18]

Was Tituba then an Arawak name? Arawak men and women kept their names secret, often addressing one another only by kin designations—brother, sister—and certainly did not tell European enslavers or masters their real names. They might have identified themselves by tribal names, however, and one Arawak tribe from the interior of the Guiana was the Tetebetana (in English, the "nightjar bird"). A female Tetebetana would have been a Tetebetado. Was Tituba an English corruption of Tetebetado? Planters recorded their Indian slaves—when they were recorded—as "Indian," or by their place of origin, Surinam for example. In addition, Indians who were identified as such usually were given an English or biblical first name, much as Algonkin slaves received.[19] Consider Tituba's consort—"Indian John" (or John Indian)—brought by Samuel Parris with her to Boston and then Salem: his forename was English, followed by a designator. If Tituba revealed to her captors or her purchasers that she was a Tetebetado, would they have rendered it as Tattuba, as one planter did for a young female slave, or Tituba? In general, when such names are shortened by those who do not understand them or speak the language, it is the beginning of the name that is retained—hence, Susan for Susannah. But consider Beth, Betty, or Betsy for Elizabeth. Thus Tetebetado might become Tituba or something similar, or it might not.

The one fact that shines out in all this surmise is that Tituba is a familiar name in another language, a language spoken by a great many young people brought to Barbados. What's in a name? As in Tetebetado, an entire world of culture. Naming is magic, for naming captures a piece of reality. Tituba had an African name; even advocates of her Caribbean origins concede as much,[20] and that is the starting point of an alternative line of inquiry into her origins.

Let us assume that Tituba was brought from Barbados to New England by Samuel Parris, her master during the witchcraft crisis. Why was Tituba called Tituba? The answer is disarmingly simple: often, first-generation—that is, immigrant—Africans kept African names. Not always—sometimes planters gave Christian names to their slaves, as a form of social control. These might be baptismal names, or phonemes for African names, although Barbados planters resisted baptizing their slaves.[21] More often than not, the planters simply called their bondsmen and -women by the closest approximation to their own African names. "The names listed in plantation records were those by which the estate chose to call the slaves; but it is unlikely that bookkeepers forced slaves to reject their own names as long as they were relatively easy to pronounce, or to accept alternatives."[22]

Tituba is a Yoruba name. Planters did not make up African names for their slaves. Rather, the slaves maintained an African culture and used naming—gave names, remembered names, kept names—in order to make that culture work. Creole cultures retained original language, including naming, the most important part of language, to build community that accommodated the realities of slavery while keeping African ways alive. I believe that Tituba was African and stayed African.[23]

But I cannot be sure, for there is Candy's case to contemplate. Candy was the servant woman (for which read "slave") of Margaret Hawkes, of Salem town. The merchants and artisans of the peninsula of the town had more slaves than the village, being more wealthy, and Candy labored among them. On July 4, 1692, she stood before magistrates Bartholomew Gedney and John Hathorne, fresh from their service on the special court of oyer and terminer that tried, convicted, and sentenced Bridget Bishop to death for witchcraft. Candy was accused of the same crime. "Candy no witch in her country," she told them; "Candy's mother no witch.

Candy no witch [in] Barbados."[24] Candy confessed that she had been urged to become a witch by her mistress in Salem but had resisted. The grand jury believed her innocent of wrongdoing, despite the accusations of Mary Walcott and Ann Putnam Jr., two of the girls whose afflictions were the basis of many other indictments.

Candy was almost certainly an African. Her name is a common English transliteration of a female Akan day name.[25] She may have been the child of an African or brought to the island of Barbados as a child herself from what was then called the "Gold Coast" and is now more or less the shore of Ghana. What is more, she told the magistrates that she came to Salem town from Barbados. What is troubling for my identification of Tituba is that the clerk identified Candy as "a negro woman" in both the record of the examination and the formal indictments.[26] If Candy's African origins made her "negro" (a word the English borrowed from the Spanish meaning "black" and used by the Spanish authorities to denote African origins), why was Tituba "indian"? I have no answer to that, unless, of course, Tituba became Indian because her husband was Indian John. His identity became hers, just as women took their husbands' names and their husbands took married women's property. There were a number of such intermarriages in the eighteenth century, in which racial identity shifted from African to Indian.[27] Could Tituba's Indian identification be explained this easily?

Notes

Preface

In a prefatory note to his play *The Crucible,* entitled "On the Historical Accuracy of This Play," Arthur Miller confided, "As for the characters of the persons, little is known about most of them excepting what may be surmised from a few letters, the trial record, certain broadsides written at the time, and references to their conduct in sources of varying reliability. They may therefore be taken as creations of my own, drawn to the best of my ability in conformity with their known behavior, except as indicated in the commentary I have written for this text." Miller made Abigail a little older, invented dialogue, and took some dramatic liberties with the roles of his characters, but his caveat about the extent of his, and our, knowledge of their personalities remains remarkably true. To the best of my knowledge, I have not invented anything, and where I have speculated, I have tried to warn the reader of the imprecision of my arguments.

1. Paul Boyer and Stephen Nissenbaum, eds., *The Salem Witchcraft Papers: Verbatim Transcripts of the Legal Documents of the Salem Witchcraft Outbreak of 1692* (New York, 1977), 3:994 (hereafter cited as *SWP*). All dates in the text and the notes have been modernized.

2. Charles W. Upham, *Salem Witchcraft* (Boston, 1867), 2:509–10. Ann stood quietly in her place while her minister, Samuel Parris's successor,

Joseph Green, read her confession. Such confessions were a prerequisite to full membership in the village church and other Puritan churches in New England. A photographic copy of Putnam's handwritten statement of 1706 concludes the "Days of Judgment" exhibit in the Essex Institute first-floor gallery, in Salem, Massachusetts.

3. Samuel Parris, "Meditations for Peace," November 1694, in *Salem-Village Witchcraft: A Documentary Record of Local Conflict in Colonial New England*, rev. ed., ed. Paul Boyer and Stephen Nissenbaum (Boston, 1993), 299 (hereafter cited as *SVW*).

4. Thomas Fisk and eleven others, "Confession of Error in the Salem Trials," in *More Wonders of the Invisible World* [1700], by Robert Calef, in *The Witchcraft Delusion in New England* [1866], ed. Samuel G. Drake (New York, 1970), 3:134–35.

5. David Hackett Fischer, *Albion's Seed: Four British Folkways in America* (New York, 1989), 127.

6. Samuel Willard, *Rules for the Discerning of the Present Times, Recommended to the People of God in New England* (Boston, 1693), 8.

7. Cotton Mather, *The Wonders of the Invisible World* [1692], and Calef, *More Wonders,* both of which are excerpted in Drake, *Witchcraft Delusion,* and George Lincoln Burr, ed., *Narratives of the Witchcraft Cases, 1648–1706* (New York, 1914).

8. The "[w]icked perjury and wilful malice" school was led by Charles W. Upham, *Lectures on Witchcraft, Comprising a History of the Delusion in Salem in 1692* (Boston, 1831), 51, expanded, possibly after Upham read Drake's *Witchcraft Delusion,* to the two-volume *Salem Witchcraft,* followed by Brooks Adams, *The Emancipation of Massachusetts* (New York, 1887): "Mr. Parris behaved like a madman" and put evidence in the mouths of the girls (224); Caroline E. Upham, *Salem Witchcraft, in Outline, The Story Without the Tedious Detail, Illustrated* (Salem, 1895), and William P. Upham, *House of John Proctor, Witchcraft Martyr* (Peabody, Mass., 1901), the descendants of Charles Upham making a family industry out of the cases; and George Lincoln Burr, *New England's Place in the History of Witchcraft* (Worcester, Mass., 1911): "I cannot acquit our ancestors on the ground that their belief in witchcraft was universal or was not discreditable or more logical than disbelief" (33). There were those who saw witchcraft in the air, however, including Barrett Wendell, "Were the Salem Witches Guiltless?" *Essex Institute Historical Collections* 29 (1892): 129–47 (hereafter cited as *EIHC*), and George L. Kittredge, *Witchcraft in Old and New England* (Cambridge, Mass., 1929), finding precedent in England divided on the validity of spectral evidence.

9. The instant "witch hunt" is mentioned, Salem comes to mind, and

with it, the power of superstition, unwarranted and unjust harassment, and unfair trials and punishments. The apologies to the dead began soon after the executions ended and go on to this day. From the popular press: e.g., Ellen Hopkins, "Abusing the Rights of Parents," My Turn, *Newsweek,* October 18, 1993, 26. In the legal literature: Vincent Blasi, "The Pathological Perspective and the First Amendment," *Columbia Law Review* 85 (April 1985): 451 (the Salem trials were an example of pathological conduct); Margaret A. Berger, "The Deconstitutionalization of the Confrontation Clause," *Minnesota Law Review* 76 (February 1992): 564 (Salem a notorious example of overzealous prosecution); Douglas O. Linder, "Journeying through the Valley of Evil," *North Carolina Law Review* 71 (April 1993): 1116 (Salem trials rank with Nazi crimes against Jews); and Martha M. Young, "The Salem Witch Trials Three Hundred Years Later," *Tulane Law Review* 64 (November 1989): 235 (modern rules of evidence a great reform). And even in Congress: Hon. Nicholas Mavroules of Massachusetts, *Congressional Record,* 100th Cong., 2d sess., Wednesday, March 23, 1988, 134, E 790, admitting that Salem's history was shaped in part by the "witchcraft hysteria."

10. John N. Mangieri, "A University's Rush to Judgment," *Chronicle of Higher Education,* July 13, 1994, B2.

11. "The Drumhead," an episode of *Star Trek: The Next Generation* aired the week of April 29, 1991, featured a trial based on the presumption of guilt which rang "with echoes . . . of the Salem witch-hunts." Larry Nemecek, *The Star Trek, the Next Generation Companion* (New York, 1992), 163.

12. Michael E. Ruane, "A Nasty Winter Storm Blows in Hot Air," *Philadelphia Inquirer,* January 28, 1994, A1.

13. See Don Corrigan, "Rumor Mill Runs Wild in Child Killings," *St. Louis Journalism Review* 23, no. 162 (winter 1993–94). David Konig kindly sent me the clipping. On the "panic rumor" syndrome in cases of supposed satanic worship and ritual sacrifice, see Jeffrey S. Victor, *Satanic Panic: The Creation of a Contemporary Legend* (Chicago, 1993), 40–69.

14. *Daily Kansan,* October 31, 1994, 7A.

15. Boyer and Nissenbaum, *SVW*; Boyer and Nissenbaum, *SWP*; David D. Hall, ed., *Witch-Hunting in Seventeenth Century New England: A Documentary History, 1638–1692* (Boston, 1991); Richard B. Trask, ed., *"The Devil Hath Been Raised": A Documentary History of the Salem Village Witchcraft Outbreak of March 1692* (West Kennebunk, Maine., 1992).

16. Paul Boyer and Stephen Nissenbaum, *Salem Possessed* (Cambridge, Mass., 1974); Marion Starkey, *The Devil in Massachusetts* (New York, 1949); Chadwick Hansen, *Witchcraft at Salem* (New York, 1969); Larry Gragg, *The Salem Witch Crisis* (New York, 1992); Wendel Dean Craker, "Cotton

Mather's Wrangle with the Devil" (Ph.D. diss., University of Georgia, 1990); Bernard Rosenthal, *Salem Story: Reading the Witch Trials of 1692* (Cambridge, England, 1993).

17. Carol F. Karlsen, *The Devil in the Shape of a Woman: Witchcraft in Colonial New England* (New York, 1987); John Putnam Demos, "Underlying Themes in the Witchcraft of Seventeenth-Century New England," *American Historical Review* 75 (1970): 1311–26, and Demos, *Entertaining Satan: Witchcraft and the Culture of Early New England* (New York, 1982); Richard Godbeer, *The Devil's Dominion: Magic and Religion in Early New England* (Cambridge, England, 1992); David D. Hall, *Worlds of Wonder, Days of Judgment: Popular Religious Belief in Early New England* (Cambridge, Mass., 1990); David Thomas Konig, *Law and Society in Puritan Massachusetts: Essex County, 1629–1692* (Chapel Hill, 1979); Richard Weisman, *Witchcraft, Magic, and Religion in Seventeenth-Century Massachusetts* (Amherst, Mass. 1984).

18. David C. Brown, whose dissertation on the trials is forthcoming from Yale University, has been writing on the Salem events for many years, including his *Guide to the Salem Witchcraft Hysteria of 1692* (Worcester, Mass., 1984), as well as "The Case of Giles Corey," *EIHC* 121 (1985): 282–300; "The Salem Witchcraft Trials: Samuel Willard's *Some Miscellany Observations*," *EIHC* 122 (1986): 207–36; "The Forfeitures at Salem," *William and Mary Quarterly*, 3d. ser., 50 (1993): 85–111 (hereafter cited as *WMQ*). Enders A. Robinson, a descendant of Sarah Wardwell, one of the condemned witches reprieved by Chief Judge William Stoughton and pardoned by Governor William Phips, recently used family papers to compose *The Devil Discovered: Salem Witchcraft, 1692* (New York, 1991). At a conference entitled "Perspectives on Witchcraft: Rethinking the Seventeenth-Century New England Experience" held at Salem on June 18–20, 1992, a gathering of scholars added their insights to the record. Talks by Elaine G. Breslaw, Alfred A. Cave, Barbara Ritter Dailey, Richard P. Gildrie, Jane Kamensky, Louis J. Kern, Mary Rhinelander McCarl, Daniel G. Payne, Mark A. Peterson, and Elizabeth Reis were published in *EIHC* 128 (October 1992) and 129 (January 1993). My ten-year-old son Louis, spurred by his father's obsession with the case, recently bought Stephen Krensky, *Witch Hunt—It Happened in Salem Village* (New York, 1989), a Random House "Step into Reading" book. Alas, there are no footnotes, but the account is able and highly readable. It joins many other fictionalized accounts, including the venerable Esther Forbes, *A Mirror for Witches* (New York, 1928), the more recent Ann Rinaldi, *A Break with Charity: A Story about the Salem Witch Trials* (San

Diego, 1992), and my old favorite, Ann Petry, *Tituba of Salem Village* (New York, 1964).

19. The list is from Weisman, *Witchcraft, Magic, and Religion*, 192–203, and covers only Massachusetts. Godbeer, *Devil's Dominion*, 235–37, tallies trials in New England (59), and Demos, *Entertaining Satan*, 401–9, includes all legal proceedings in the region (131).

20. C. L'Estrange Ewen, *Witch Hunting and Witch Trials* (London, 1929), 262–65; Keith Thomas, *Religion and the Decline of Magic: Studies in Popular Beliefs in Sixteenth and Seventeenth Century England* (London, 1971), 570–83.

21. Brian P. Levack, *The Witch-hunt in Early Modern Europe* (London, 1987), 212 ff.

22. Clifford Geertz, "'From the Native's Point of View': On the Nature of Anthropological Understanding," in *Culture Theory: Essays on Mind, Self, and Emotion*, ed. Richard A. Shweder and Robert A. LeVine (Cambridge, England, 1984), 125.

23. John Demos, *The Unredeemed Captive: A Family Story from Early America* (New York, 1994), xii.

24. James H. Merrell, *The Indians' New World: Catawbas and Their Neighbors from European Contact through the Era of Removal* (Chapel Hill, 1989), 62.

25. Denis Donoghue, *Ferocious Alphabets* (Boston, 1981), 101, 146–47.

26. Charles Lloyd Cohen, *God's Caress: The Psychology of Puritan Religious Experience* (New York, 1986), 164.

27. Erving Goffman, *Forms of Talk* (Philadelphia, 1981), 3.

28. John M. Conley and William M. O'Barr, *Rules versus Relationships: The Ethnography of Legal Discourses* (Chicago, 1990), 9.

29. Ronald Takaki, "Teaching American History through a Different Mirror," *Perspectives: The American Historical Association Newsletter* 32 (October 1994): 9.

Prologue: Tituba

1. Such a simple name, and so many variants of its spelling. In a single document, Justice of the Peace Jonathan Corwin's notes on her examination, March 1–2, 1692, we have "Titiba," "brought before us by Constable Joseph Herrick of Salem," which becomes "Tittuba" on the heading of the testimony and changes to "Tittubee" in the text of the verbatim testimony on March 1. Corwin's clerk, Ezekiell Cheevers (or Chevers; every name in these records had variant spellings), preferred "Titiba" in his version of the March 1 examination (there were two versions of the verbatim testimony),

which became "Tittapa" on the indictment, written May 9, 1692. *SWP,* 3:746–53.

2. The debate on Tituba's origins goes back to the nineteenth century. See Appendix: What's in a Name?

3. It seems indisputable to me that the target of witchcraft prosecutions was women and that this was so in part because men fashioned the offense to persecute women. On the continent of Europe, during the height of the witch hunting, "those who advocated witch trials saw nothing remarkable in this sexual imbalance [of suspects]. It conformed perfectly with the dominant notions of female inferiority, while it confirmed the legitimacy of woman-hatred with each new case." Joseph Klaits, *Servants of Satan: The Age of the Witch Hunts* (Bloomington, Ind., 1985), 52. The atmosphere of misogyny which pervaded Germany and the other European countries during the Reformation was somewhat dissipated in Massachusetts by English Puritans' ideal of women as a "necessary good" rather than a necessary evil, but there remained an undercurrent of suspicion of women. Karlsen, *Devil in the Shape of a Woman,* 173. This suspicion could be mobilized to victimize women who did not fit in, or who had property that was desired by others, or who struck out at neighbors in their community. To say, however, that witchcraft should be primarily viewed as "persecution by gender" or that the suspected witch "might have felt like a hunted animal" (Ann Llewellyn Barstow, *Witchcraze: A New History of the European Witch Hunts* [San Francisco, 1994], 11, 149) may be going too far. More often than not in New England, women were the accusers as well as the accused. What is more, although Barstow concedes that the prosecutions were more modest at the "margins" of the European heartland and does discuss women's roles in them, her overarching theme is the vulnerability of women and the power of men. By making the female suspect a victim without recourse to her own abilities, skills, or intelligence, Barstow effectively denies the agency of women. I think it better to compare these women to the men and women who resisted the dehumanization of labor in the mills and mines of England and France and India in the early years of the industrial revolution. They would not be reduced to cogs in the machines they tended. Louise A. Tilly, "Connections," *American Historical Review* 99 (1994): 20.

4. *A Dictionary of the Yoruba Language* (Ibadan, Nigeria, 1979), 224; Ihechukwu Madubuike, *A Handbook of African Names,* 2d ed., rev. (Colorado Springs, Colo., 1994), 82–83. A guide to Yoruba naming is M. Odupe Oduyoye, *Yoruba Names: Their Structure and Their Meanings* (Ibadan, Nigeria, 1972); see, e.g., 13: Títí l'ola = "endless is our honor."

5. Chinua Achebe, *Things Fall Apart* (London, 1958), 54. The cultural

meaning of naming is discussed in Margaret Thompson Drewal, *Yoruba Ritual: Performers, Play, Agency* (Bloomington, Ind., 1992), 56–88, and William Bascom, *Sixteen Cowries: Yoruba Divination from Africa to the New World* (Bloomington, Ind., 1980), 34–36.

I am grateful to Sandy Barnes, of the University of Pennsylvania, and to Joseph Olusola Faludon, of the University of Ile-Ife, Nigeria, and Lincoln University, Philadelphia, for helping me discover additional possibilities in Tituba's name.

6. When we only have the name, there is only a great deal of speculation and the danger of unwarranted invention. Consider the possibilities: Alex Haley claimed that he discovered an ancestor, one Kunta Kinté, who had a Mandinka name, and was thereby able to trace the village from which the young man had been stolen. Subsequent research into his notes suggests there was no such ancestor; the story, like the research supposedly producing it, was fabricated. Alex Haley, *Roots* (New York, 1974), 572 ff.; Philip Nobile, "Alex Haley's Hoax," *Village Voice,* February 23, 1993, 31–38.

7. See Timothy A. Awoniyi, "The Word Yoruba," *Nigeria* 134–35 (1981): 104–7; Renate Wente-Lukas, *Handbook of Ethnic Units in Nigeria* (Stuttgart, 1985), 350–53; S. O. Biobaku, ed., *Sources of Yoruba History* (Oxford, 1973), 1–8. So where did the word *Yoruba* come from? It was probably the term that Europeans heard when Hausa and others described the inhabitants of the former Oyo lands: Yarawaba. Now, however, Yoruba proudly use this term.

8. Peter Morton-Williams, "The Oyo Yoruba and the Atlantic Trade, 1670–1830," *Journal of the Historical Society of Nigeria* 3 (1964): 25–46; Robin Law, *The Oyo Empire, c. 1600–c. 1836: A West African Imperialism in the Era of the Atlantic Slave Trade* (Oxford, 1977), 202–35 (the economics of empire required a slave trade internally, and war provided the commodities of the trade); Paul Lovejoy, *Transformations in Slavery: A History of Slavery in Africa* (Cambridge, England, 1983), 154–55 (an explosion of the trade out of the Bight of Biafra during the late seventeenth century caused by the Oyo wars); Robert Smith, *Kingdoms of the Yoruba,* 2d ed. (Madison, Wisc., 1988), 29–40 (Oyo military aggression provides grist for mill of slavery).

9. John Thornton, *Africa and Africans in the Making of the Atlantic World, 1400–1680* (Cambridge, England, 1992), 72–97.

10. Ibid., 98–125; Nigel Tattersfield, *The Forgotten Trade: Comprising the Log of the "Daniel and Henry" of 1700* (London, 1991), 75–80.

11. Ernst Van Den Boogart, "The Trade between Western Africa and the Atlantic World, 1600–1690: Estimates of Trends in Composition and Value," *Journal of African History* 33 (1992): 384.

12. Joseph Miller, *Way of Death: Merchant Capitalism and the Angolan Slave Trade, 1730–1830* (Madison, Wisc., 1988), 52; *Barbot on Guinea: The Writings of Jean Barbot on West Africa,* ed. P.E.H. Hair et al. (London, 1992), 2:549.

13. Patrick Manning, "The Slave Trade in the Bight of Biafra, 1640–1890," in *The Uncommon Market: Essays in the Economic History of the Atlantic Slave Trade,* ed. Henry A. Gemery and Jan S. Hogendorn (New York, 1979), 115.

14. Michael Craton, *Sinews of Empire: A Short History of British Slavery* (Garden City, N.Y., 1974), 60–61.

15. David Galenson, *Traders, Planters, and Slaves: Market Behavior in Early English America* (Cambridge, England, 1986), 30, 39. A.W. Lawrence, *Fortified Trade-post: The English in West Africa* (London, 1969), 54–56.

16. Manning, "Slave Trade," 117; Tattersfield, *Forgotten Trade,* 144.

17. Olaudah Equiano, *The Interesting Narrative of the Life of Olaudah Equiano or Gustavus Vassa the African,* ed. Paul Edwards (New York, 1967), 12, 3, 5, 7, 13.

18. Ibid., 8, 12.

19. Ibid., 30, 32.

20. The arguments for market forces and changes in sensibilities are laid out in Thomas Bender, ed., *The Antislavery Debate: Capitalism and Abolitionism as a Problem in Historical Interpretation* (Berkeley, Calif., 1992).

21. "Samuel Ajayi Crowther to Commander Bird Allen, 1841," ed. J.F. Ade Ajayi, in *Africa Remembered: Narratives by West Africans from the Era of the Slave Trade,* ed. Philip D. Curtin (Madison, Wisc., 1967), 303, 304, 308.

22. The name is not Akan, my informant Peter Wilmot tells me. Nor is it Bantu, according to my colleague David Schoenbrun. I do not find anything like it in the Bantu names in Winifred Kellersberger Vass, *The Bantu Speaking Heritage of the United States* (Los Angeles, 1979), or in John Thornton, "Central African Names and African-American Naming Patterns," *WMQ,* 3d ser., 50 (1993): 727–42. Krio speakers from Sierra Leone recognize the name, however, possibly because Krio is a hybrid language, derived mainly from pidgin English and Yoruba. Krio (from Creole) is itself a language, however, and its speakers immediately knew that *Tituba* was a female name. I am grateful to Josephine Beoku-Betts for my introduction to Krio. Tituba could not have had a Krio name (or, thereby have been from west of Yorubaland), however, because Krio is a nineteenth-century language.

23. Planters shared the slave traders' belief that diversity among the slaves prevented revolt. Richard Dunn, *Sugar and Slaves: The Rise of the Planter Class in the English West Indies, 1624–1713* (New York, 1972), 257. Dunn be-

lieves that this strategy may have worked—there was no rebellion on Barbados until 1675.

24. Maureen Warner Lewis, "The African Impact on Language and Literature in the English Speaking Caribbean: Continued Existence of African Languages: A Case Study of Yoruba in Trinidad," in *Africa and the Caribbean: The Legacies of a Link,* ed. Margaret E. Crahan and Franklin W. Knight (Baltimore, 1979), 104. To one Western ear—mine—Yoruba sounds mellifluous and musical, like Welsh or Lakota. I can see why its speakers would want to preserve it.

25. Mervyn C. Alleyn, "A Linguistic Perspective on the Caribbean," in *Caribbean Contours,* ed. Sidney W. Mintz and Sally Price (Baltimore, 1985), 155–75.

26. Galenson, *Traders, Planters, and Slaves,* 56.

27. Elaine Breslaw, "The Salem Witch from Barbados: In Search of Tituba's Roots," *EIHC* 128 (1992): 225. Breslaw notes, quite accurately, that *Tituba* was a type of "African-Caribbean name that was commonplace in Barbados" (225) but then concludes that the names "were probably invented by a planter after enslavement and given to the slave to signify her new status." But why would her master invent and give her an African name? There is no evidence that masters ever gave a slave a name that was not English. On the preference for the young, see Galenson, *Traders, Planters, and Slaves,* 112–13. On naming, see Appendix: "What's in a Name?"

28. Michael Craton, *Searching for the Invisible Man: Slaves and Plantation Life in Jamaica* (Cambridge, Mass., 1978), 56–57; Gordon K. Lewis, *Main Currents in Caribbean Thought: The Historical Evolution of Caribbean Society in Its Ideological Aspects, 1492–1900* (Baltimore, 1983), 78; Harry Bennett, *Bondsmen and Bishops: Slavery and Apprenticeship on the Codrington Plantations of Barbados* (Berkeley, Calif., 1958), 85.

29. Dunn, *Sugar and Slaves,* 225–62; Richard B. Sheridan, *Sugar and Slavery: An Economic History of the British West Indies, 1623–1775* (Barbados, 1974), 124–47.

30. See Thornton, *Africa and Africans,* 240–41. Like the rest of Afro-Caribbean culture, these ways became creolized. To the European, they seemed impenetrable. See, for example, H. H. J. Bell, *Obeah: Witchcraft in the East Indies* [1889] (Westport, Conn., 1978), 14ff. To the recent arrivals from Africa, however, witches were quite real and quite dangerous. See, for example, Richard Price, *Alabi's World* (Baltimore, 1990), 19.

31. On witches in Yorubaland, See Bascom, *Sixteen Cowries,* 21–22; Judith Hoch-Smith, "Radical Yoruba Female Sexuality: The Prostitute and the Witch," in *Women in Ritual and Symbolic Roles,* ed. Judith Hoch-Smith and

Anita Spring (New York, 1978), 245–67 ("In the beginning, God gave the world to the witches": Yoruba Gelede dancer [245]); J. Omosade Awolalu, *Yoruba Beliefs and Sacrificial Rites* (London, 1979), 79–90 (witchcraft is real to the Yoruba—secret, feared, and associated with women, but in deeper ways an explanation of failure, illness, misfortune, and communal enmi-
220   ties); B. Hallen and J. O. Sodipo, *Knowledge, Belief, and Witchcraft: Analytic Experiments in African Philosophy* (London, 1986), 100–118 (*witch* is a label, and a labeling mechanism moves the acceptable use of supernatural powers into the category of witch, or *àjé*). These modern anthropologically ori-ented categories are applicable to late-seventeenth-century Yorubaland. The oral sources—the traditions—and the written sources of contemporary ob-servers seem to confirm the similarities, if not the details. See, for example, Ade Fioye Oyesakin, "The Image of Women in Ifa Literary Corpus," *Nige-ria* 141 (1982): 19–20.

32. Barbara Bush, *Slave Women in Caribbean Society, 1650–1838* (Bloom-ington, Ind., 1990), 69–70.

33. "In classical African terms, planters would have been viewed as witches and sorcerers, who had the capacity to cause harm and promote their own interest, either directly or indirectly, by harnessing the power of one of the spirits." Gary Puckrein, *Little England: Plantation Society and Anglo-Barba-dian Politics, 1627–1700* (New York, 1984), 77.

34. Dunn, *Sugar and Slaves,* 302–11; Craton, *Searching for the Invisible Man,* 57.

35. Miller, *Way of Death,* 47.

36. Of course this is a composite picture, but Yoruba practices were not much different from the overall depiction here. See Igor Kopytoff and Su-zanne Miers, "African Slavery as an Institution of Marginality," in *Slavery in Africa: Historical and Anthropological Perspectives,* ed. Igor Kopytoff and Suzanne Miers (Madison, Wisc., 1977), 3–80, and Victor C. Uchendu, "Slaves and Slavery in Igboland, Nigeria," in Kopytoff and Miers, *Slavery in Africa,* 121–31.

37. See, for example, Alan Watson, *Slave Law in the Americas* (Athens, Ga., 1989), 67–68.

38. [John Nicholson,] comp., *An Abridgment of the Laws in Force and Use in Her Majesty's Plantations* (London, 1704), 238–43; Bradley J. Nichol-son, "Legal Borrowing and the Origins of Slave Law in the British Colonies," *American Journal of Legal History* 38 (1994): 46, 49–51.

39. James Stephen, *The Slavery of the British West India Colonies Delin-eated, As it Exists, Both in Law and Practice* (London, 1824), 33 ff.

40. Eugene Genovese, *Roll, Jordan, Roll: The World the Slaves Made* (New York, 1974), 515–19.

41. Act of 1653, Will Bentley, comp., *Acts and Statutes of Barbados* (London, 1654), 146.

42. Dunn, *Sugar and Slaves*, 238–42; Puckrein, *Little England*, 79.

43. Compare V. S. Naipul, *The Middle Passage* (London, 1962), 26–27.

44. Carl Bridenbaugh and Roberta Bridenbaugh, *No Peace beyond the Line: The English in the Caribbean, 1624–1690* (New York, 1972), 250–67; Hilary McD. Beckles, *A History of Barbados: From Amerindian Settlement to Nation-State* (Cambridge, England, 1990), 27–33; Winthrop Jordan, *White over Black: American Attitudes toward the Negro, 1550–1812* (Chapel Hill, 1968); 40–43, 63–66, 91–98; David Eltis, "Europeans and the Rise and Fall of African Slavery in the Americas: An Interpretation," *American Historical Review* 98 (1993): 1399–1423.

45. [Nicholson], *Abridgment of the Laws*, 238, 239.

46. Orlando Patterson, *Slavery and Social Death: A Comparative Study* (Cambridge, Mass., 1982), 268–69.

47. Bennett, *Bondsmen and Bishops*, 18.

48. Eric Hobsbawm and George Rudé, *Captain Swing: A Social History of the Great English Agricultural Uprising of 1830* (New York, 1968), 97.

49. Joan Wallach Scott, *Gender and the Politics of History* (New York, 1988), 42, 44; Richard Dunn, "Sugar Production and Slave Women in Jamaica," in *Cultivation and Culture: Labor and the Shaping of Slave Life in the Americas,* ed. Ira Berlin and Philip D. Morgan (Charlottesville, Va., 1993), 60.

50. Michael Craton, *Testing the Chains: Resistance to Slavery in the British West Indies* (Ithaca, N.Y., 1982), 105–11; Hilary McD. Beckles, *White Servitude and Black Slavery in Barbados, 1627–1715* (Knoxville, Tenn., 1989), 98–114.

51. Dunn, *Sugar and Slaves*, 256–58.

52. Jerome S. Handler and Robert S. Corruccini, "Weaning among West Indian Slaves: Historical and Bioanthropological Evidence from Barbados," *WMQ,* 3d ser., 43 (1986): 111–17; Bush, *Slave Women in Caribbean Society,* 6–9, 14–15, 20–29, 36, 37, 46, 73–77, 86–87, 91–142; Marietta Morrissey, *Slave Women in the New World: Gender Stratification in the Caribbean* (Lawrence, Kans., 1989), 29–31.

53. See the Appendix on naming customs.

54. Morrissey, *Slave Women*, 145–51.

55. Dunn, *Sugar and Slaves*, 252–55.

221

56. Roger D. Abrahams, ed., *African Folktales: Traditional Stories of the Black World* (New York, 1983), 25–26.

57. Godfrey Lienhardt, "Self: Public Private: Some African Representations," in *The Category of the Person: Anthropology, Philosophy, History,* ed. Michael Carrithers et al. (Cambridge, England, 1985), 143.

Chapter One: Samuel Parris

1. Marilynne K. Roach, "'That Child, Betty Parris': Elizabeth (Parris) Barron and the People in Her Life," *EIHC* 124 (1988): 1–27; Larry Gragg, *A Quest for Security: The Life of Samuel Parris, 1653–1720* (Westport, Conn., 1990), 177–89. My oldest, Williamjames, tells me that after all our family's moves in search of jobs, education, and research funding, he never felt he could make friends or trust people fully.

2. Warren Alleyn, *Historic Bridgetown* (Bridgetown, Barbados, 1978), 13, 21.

3. Gragg, *Quest for Security,* 10–13.

4. Dunn, *Sugar and Slaves,* 84–87.

5. Gragg, "A Puritan in the West Indies: The Career of Samuel Winthrop," *WMQ,* 3d ser., 50 (1993): 769.

6. Bridenbaugh and Bridenbaugh, *No Peace,* 220–21; Dunn, *Sugar and Slaves,* 96, 111.

7. The cured or salted herring and cod from the New England fisheries which could not be sold in Europe because it had spoiled could be repacked in the holds of the merchant ships and sold in the West Indies. Daniel Vickers, *Farmers and Fishermen: Two Centuries of Work in Essex County, Massachusetts, 1630–1850* (Chapel Hill, 1994), 99.

8. Gragg, *Quest for Security,* 12–16.

9. Rachel Wilder, ed., *Barbados* (Boston, 1993), 17–35; Alleyn, *Historic Bridgetown,* 6.

10. William Pierson, *Black Yankees: The Development of an Afro-American Subculture in Eighteenth-Century New England* (Amherst, Mass., 1988), 26. Starkey, *Devil in Massachusetts,* 29, calls Tituba ageless, but if Breslaw's research is correct, Tituba would have been in her teens when Parris bought her around 1680.

11. Bernard Bailyn, *The New England Merchants in the Seventeenth Century* (Cambridge, Mass., 1955), 87, 111.

12. G. B. Warden, *Boston, 1689–1776* (Boston, 1970), 15–33.

13. Ibid., 49.

14. Ibid., 51; Bailyn, *New England Merchants,* 168–92.

15. Roach, "'That Child'" 3–4; Helena S. Wall, *Fierce Communion: Fam-*

ily and Community in Early America (Cambridge, Mass., 1990), 97–105. We do not know why Abigail lived with her uncle rather than her parents. Common reasons for taking in a child were the inability of the parents to take care of the child, orphanhood, or some financial arrangement between the two households.

16. The portrait is reproduced in Trask, *"Devil Hath Been Raised,"* viii. The sons to whom the portrait descended, by name Noyes and Samuel, must have been born to his second wife, after he left Salem in 1696.

17. Gragg, *Quest for Security,* 30–32.

18. John Bunyan, *The Pilgrim's Progress* [1678], rev. ed. (New York, 1964), 30.

19. Gragg, *Quest for Security,* 31–35.

20. Stephen Foster, *Their Solitary Way: The Puritan Social Ethic in the First Century of Settlement in New England* (New Haven, 1971), 99–126; Bernard Bailyn, ed., *The Apologia of Robert Keayne* (New York, 1964), xi.

21. Norman Pettit, *The Heart Prepared: Grace and Conversion in Puritan Spiritual Life* (New Haven, 1966), 203–7.

22. Cohen, *God's Caress,* 162, 164.

23. Parris, Deposition [1697?], in *SVW*, 184.

24. Higginson, despite his years and his reputation, faced a schism in the church and calumny outside it. Christine Alice Young, *From "Good Order" to Glorious Revolution: Salem, Massachusetts, 1628–1689* (Ann Arbor, 1981), 129; *Guppy v. Higginson,* June 1674, in which Ruben Guppy was to be whipped and made to apologize for publishing a "reproachful scandalous report" of Higginson. George Francis Dow et al., eds., *Records and Files of the Quarterly Courts of Essex County, Massachusetts* (Salem, 1911–73), 5:355 (hereafter cited as *Essex County Court Records.*

25. Gragg, *Quest for Security,* 46–49.

26. Ibid., 92.

27. *Essex County Court Records,* 5:429.

28. David Lovejoy, *The Glorious Revolution in America* (New York, 1972), 239–45.

29. Laurel Thatcher Ulrich, *Good Wives: Image and Reality in the Lives of Women in Northern New England, 1650–1750* (New York, 1980), 106–25.

30. Quoted in Gragg, *Quest for Security,* 84.

31. Parris, Sermon, January 3, 1692, in *The Sermon Notebook of Samuel Parris, 1689–1694,* ed. James F. Cooper Jr. and Kenneth P. Minkema (Boston, 1993), 184.

32. C. John Sommerville, *The Discovery of Childhood in Puritan England* (Athens, Ga., 1992), 25 ff.

33. Cooper and Minkema, *Sermon Notebook*, 183.

34. Terri Apter, *Altered Loves: Mothers and Daughters during Adolescence* (New York, 1990), 57–109. Apter's insight, based on twentieth-century studies, holds true for Puritan mothers and daughters three hundred years earlier because her insights seem to fit the historical evidence.

35. Martine Sonnet, "A Daughter to Educate," trans. Arthur Goldhammer, in *A History of Women in the West*, vol. 3, *Renaissance and Enlightenment Paradoxes*, ed. Natalie Zemon Davis and Arlette Farge (Cambridge, Mass., 1993), 111. I have more to say in chapter 5.

36. See, for example, Laurel Thatcher Ulrich, *A Midwife's Tale: The Life of Martha Ballard Based on her Diary, 1785–1812* (New York, 1990), 12–13; *Diary of Anna Green Winslow: A Boston School Girl of 1771*, ed. Alice Morse Earle (reprint, Boston, 1985), 20–21.

37. *Essex County Court Records*, 7:141, 410, 411, 425; *SWP*, 1:179–81.

38. Boyer and Nissenbaum, *Salem Possessed*, 56.

39. Vickers, *Farmers and Fishermen*, 145–48.

40. George Francis Dow, *Everyday Life in the Massachusetts Bay Colony* (Boston, 1935), 143–65; Howard S. Russell, *A Long Deep Furrow: Three Centuries of Farming in New England*, rev. ed. (Hanover, N.H., 1982), 57–65.

41. Richard P. Gildrie, *Salem, Massachusetts, 1626–1683: A Covenanted Community* (Charlottesville, Va., 1986), 166 ff.; Young, *"Good Order,"* 133, 139, and passim; Robinson, *Devil Discovered,* 321–23. I found Main Street on the James Duncan Phillips 1933 map of "Salem in 1700" hanging in the Phillips Library of the Essex Institute in Salem. The shape and style of houses are described in Harriet Silvester Tapley, *Chronicles of Danvers* (Danvers, Mass., 1923), 7.

42. Salem streets from Phillips, map of "Salem in 1700," and Marilynne K. Roach, *A Time Traveler's Maps of the Salem Witchcraft Trials* (Watertown, Mass., 1991). The importance of salt- and freshwater marsh hay is documented in Russell, *Long Deep Furrow,* 31.

43. Boyer and Nissenbaum, *Salem Possessed*, 85; *SVW*, 394, 400–401.

44. *SVW*, 229–34.

45. Russell, *Long Deep Furrow,* 103–5.

46. A. P. Putnam, "Historical Sketch of Danvers," in *Danvers, Massachusetts* (Danvers, Mass., 1899), 3–4.

47. John R. Stilgoe, *Common Landscape of America, 1580 to 1845* (New Haven, 1982), 190; Susan Allport, *Sermons in Stone: The Stone Walls of New England and New York* (New York, 1990), 111.

48. See, for example, Boyer and Nissenbaum, *Salem Possessed*, 124–26; Konig, *Law and Society,* 68.

49. William Cronon, *Changes in the Land: Indians, Colonists, and the Ecology of New England* (New York, 1983), 52.

50. Dow, *Everyday Life*, 96–97, Russell, *Long Deep Furrow*, 89.

51. Cohen, *God's Caress*, 162.

52. Boyer and Nissenbaum, *Salem Possessed*, 80–81, estimate 215 persons over the age of twenty-one. Given standard age compositions of eastern Massachusetts towns in the 1690s, this would give a total of inhabitants between 450 and 500 people. See Susan L. Norton, "Population Growth in Colonial America: A Study of Ipswich, Massachusetts," *Population Studies* 25 (1971): 440–41. Nearby Andover, on the northern boundary of Salem, had a population explosion in the 1680s and 1690s, in which many more children survived to adulthood than had in the two decades previously. Philip J. Greven, *Four Generations: Population, Land, and Family in Colonial Andover, Massachusetts* (Ithaca, N.Y., 1970), 103–13. If Salem shared this phenomenal growth rate, the number of children in the town would be even larger than standard distributions estimate. 225

53. Robinson, *Devil Discovered*, 72–73.

54. The Ingersoll Ordinary still stands in Danvers, at the convergence of Hobart and Holten Streets. Information on it courtesy of the Danvers Historical Society. Shuffleboard is described in Dow, *Everyday Life*, 110–11. The accusations against Bishop are reported in *SWP*, 1:95.

55. For example, see *Essex County Court Records*, 5:39 (horse racing at taverns); 35 (fighting at the "King's Arms"). Richard P. Gildrie, "Taverns and Popular Culture in Essex County, Massachusetts, 1678–1686," *EIHC* 124 (July, 1988): 158–85.

56. Ibid., 5:361.

57. *Essex County Court Records* for the years 1680–83 averaged more than fifteen presentments per year of individuals for public drunkenness, excessive drinking, or drinking-related abuses, such as giving "strong water" to the Indians. The list of alcoholic beverages involved in these incidents included ale, beer, brandy, cider "liquor," rum, sack, samp, strong water, and wine (8:290, 346, 481–82). There were additional presentments for failure to renew licenses to sell alcohol, keeping disorderly houses, and similar offenses.

58. Ibid., 5:233.

59. Gragg, *Quest for Security*, 49.

60. Danvers Historical Society archaeological dig, 67 Center Street, Danvers; Brown, *Guide*, 98.

61. On Puritan improvement of time, see Fischer, *Albion's Seed*, 158–66.

62. Salem-Village Book of Record, entry for Oct. 28, 1690, in *SVW*, 351.

63. Robert J. Dinkin, "Seating the Meetinghouse in Early Massachusetts," in *Material Life in America, 1600–1860,* ed. Robert Blair St. George (Boston, 1988), 408, 409, 410, 412.

64. Salem Village Meeting House reconstruction, Pine Street, Danvers. I am grateful to Bob Osborne, who occupies the Nurse farmstead on which the reconstruction stands, for discussing its form and function with me. See also Putnam, "Historical Sketch," 4, and Ola Elizabeth Winslow, *Meeting House Hill, 1630–1783* (New York, 1952), 50–65. Abbott L. Cummings, "Meeting and Dwelling House: Interrelationships in Early New England," in *New England Meeting House and Church, 1630–1850,* ed. Peter Benes (Boston, 1980), 4–17, suggested the parallel between meeting house and dwelling house, and an examination of the Osborn and Holten farmhouses, built on the Salem road at the same time as the meeting house, made clear that the villagers had merely borrowed the plan of the large farmhouse as their model. The colors of the meeting house are discussed in Peter Benes, "Sky Colors and Scattered Clouds: The Decorative and Architectural Painting of New England Meeting Houses, 1738–1834," in Benes, *Meeting House and Church,* 51–52. The importance of the Lord's Supper is explored in Philip D. Zimmerman, "The Lord's Supper in Early New England: The Setting and the Service," in Benes, *Meeting House and Church,* 124–34. Parris's view of the Supper is mentioned in Cooper and Minkema, *Sermon Notebook,* 10–11.

65. Cohen, *God's Caress,* 163.

66. Parris, November 19, 1689, Ordination Sermon, in Cooper and Minkema, *Sermon Notebook,* 38. Phillips' age is given as sixty-seven in his 1692 testimony in favor of accused witch Elizabeth Howe, of Rowley. *SWP,* 2:442.

67. Charles E. Hambrick-Stowe, *The Practice of Piety: Puritan Devotional Disciplines in Seventeenth-Century New England* (Chapel Hill, 1982), 116–23, 126–29.

68. See, for example, Owen Fiss, "Objectivity and Interpretation," *Stanford Law Review* 34 (1982): 744.

69. Cooper and Minkema, *Sermon Notebook,* 38.

70. *SVW,* 268–69.

71. Cooper and Minkema, *Sermon Notebook,* 38–39; Patrick M. Malone, *The Skulking Way of War: Technology and Tactics among the New England Indians* (Baltimore, 1993), 119–25.

72. See, for example, Theodore Dwight Bozeman, *To Live Ancient Lives: The Primitivist Dimension in Puritanism* (Chapel Hill, 1988), 14–16, 154; Alan Heimert, *Religion and the American Mind: From the Great Awakening to the Revolution* (Cambridge, Mass., 1966), 67, 105–6.

73. Cooper and Minkema, *Sermon Notebook,* 50–51.

74. Cohen, *God's Caress,* 168–70.

Chapter Two: Salem Village

1. Michael Zuckerman, *Peaceable Kingdoms: New England Towns in the Eighteenth Century* (New York, 1970), 123–53.

2. Or perhaps such "community " never really existed, except, after the fact, as a memory of a "sunny little dream." Darrett Rutman, *Small Worlds, Large Questions: Explorations in Early American Social History* (Charlottesville, Va., 1994), 299.

3. Young, *"Good Order,"* 132 ff.; Konig, *Law and Society,* 98 ff.; *Essex County Court Records* 5:378, 427. New Haven—an ark of Puritan conformity—vainly tried to cope with the same problem as Salem's. Wall, *Fierce Communion,* 7, 9.

4. Young, *"Good Order,"* 131, 137, 141.

5. Vickers, *Farmers and Fishermen,* 22, 51, 60.

6. Edward M. Cook Jr., *The Fathers of the Towns: Leadership and Community Structure in Eighteenth-Century New England* (Baltimore, 1976), 19, 115–18.

7. Allan Kulikoff, *Tobacco and Slaves: The Development of Southern Cultures in the Chesapeake, 1680–1800* (Chapel Hill, 1986), 205–7 ff., suggests this process changed the human geography of the Tidewater; I borrow the notion for the Salem region.

8. Robinson, *Devil Discovered,* 74–77.

9. Maps in *SVW,* 408, 406; the genealogy and wills are on 202–12.

10. Boyer and Nissenbaum, *Salem Possessed,* 128–29. On the Putnams' wont to litigate, see, for example, *Essex County Court Records,* 6:7–8; Boyer and Nissenbaum, *Salem Possessed,* 124–26.

11. Boyer and Nissenbaum, *Salem Possessed,* 113, 119–21.

12. See, for example, *Essex County Court Records,* 5:428 (Jacobs pays for driving others' horses into the river and threatening to drown them); 5:430 (Francis Nurse takes in child of Elizabeth Clungey, servant, who left it behind).

13. *SWP,* 2:375 (Good, turned away without getting lodging, mutters curses).

14. Boyer and Nissenbaum, *Salem Possessed,* 115.

15. Gildrie, *Salem,* 128–29.

16. *SVW,* 237, 238, 239.

17. Boyer and Nissenbaum, *Salem Possessed,* 86–87.

18. Gildrie, *Salem,* 128–29, 167.

19. George Lee Haskins, *Law and Authority in Early Massachusetts: A Study in Tradition and Design* (New York, 1960), 68–79.

20. Konig, *Law and Society,* 55–57.

21. See, for example, *Allen v. (Nathaniel) Putnam,* June 1681, *Essex County Court Records,* 8:116–21.

22. Ibid., 8:395.

23. Konig, *Law and Society,* 108.

24. Peter Charles Hoffer, *Law and People in Colonial America* (Baltimore, 1992), 54–55.

25. At the close of his account of litigation in seventeenth-century Essex County, including a chapter reviewing the events in Salem, David Thomas Konig writes that "residents of Essex faced the eighteenth century confident in the ability of their system of local justice to help them regulate their social affairs and impose order." *Law and Society,* 187. The willingness of the Putnams to go to law supports this conclusion, but the litigation did not reassure them.

26. *SVW,* 235–37.

27. Essex County Quarterly Court dockets and file papers, Essex Institute, [hereafter ECCR (ms)] 47:42-1, 2, 4; 55-1.

28. Robinson, *Devil Discovered,* 61–62. Robinson has laid out the genealogical fault lines in Salem Village.

29. *SVW,* 240–42.

30. Ibid., 242–55.

31. Ibid., 171–75.

32. Ibid., 173–79; *Essex County Court Records,* 9:30–32, 47–48.

33. Ordination could only come through a congregation and sometimes took years or did not happen at all. Konig, *Law and Society,* 99.

34. ECCR (MS), 46: 72-1, 2.

35. Boyer and Nissenbaum, *Salem Possessed,* 57–58.

36. *SVW,* 270.

37. Boyer and Nissenbaum, *Salem Possessed,* 62, 83–84.

38. Ibid., 57, 58, 65, 66, 82–84; *SVW,* 356, 357.

39. Lovejoy, *Glorious Revolution,* 340–53. The argument that the courts played a vital integrative function belongs to Konig, *Law and Society,* 115, 154–57 ff.

40. Hambrick-Stowe, *Practice of Piety,* 117; W. C. Ford, ed., *Diary of Cotton Mather* (New York, 1911), 1:180 (Mather, "tho' it would be a considerable diminution of [his] auditory" to encourage a number of his parishioners to form their own church, tells them to do so).

41. Christopher M. Jedry, *The World of John Cleaveland: Family and*

Community in Eighteenth-Century New England (New York, 1979), xiii. Cleaveland, a minister in Ipswich, near Salem, in the second half of the eighteenth century, faced some of the same problems that Parris did, but Cleaveland married into the landed elite of the town and, though not from Essex County (he was Connecticut-born and -bred), knew the rules of the game.

229

42. Cooper and Minkema, *Sermon Notebook,* 170, 171, 180.

43. Ibid., 182.

44. One would thus expect Parris to lean to the Porters' point of view, but he did not. Personal attachment and political loyalty outweighed a more abstract "commercial outlook."

45. Perry Miller, *The New England Mind from Colony to Province* (Cambridge, Mass., 1953), 27–40.

46. Gragg, *Quest for Security,* 89–90.

47. Here as elsewhere throughout the sermons and in his teaching, Parris proved himself a member of the conservative wing of American Puritan ministry—no compromises with modernity for him.

48. Cooper and Minkema, *Sermon Notebook,* 10–11, 19.

49. Young, *"Good Order,"* 137.

50. Stephen Foster, *The Long Argument: English Puritanism and the Shaping of New England Culture, 1570–1700* (Chapel Hill, 1991), 236–39.

51. Hall, *Worlds of Wonder,* 140, 142–43, 156.

52. A year later, his assailants were still at it. *SVW,* 256–57, 281–82.

53. Cooper and Minkema, *Sermon Notebook,* 186, 187, 190.

54. See, for example, Thomas Shepard, *The Sincere Convert* [preached late 1620s, first published ca. 1640], reprinted in *The Works of Thomas Shepard* (Boston, 1853) 1:61.

55. Konig, *Law and Society,* 101. Concord, Massachusetts, 1766: belying its name, the town seethed in discord. There was the same division between town and village; the same drive for secession by the extremities; the same battle over a new, young, proud minister's conduct; the same contention among leading families; and soon a gathering of neighboring ministers to mediate, as in Salem—but no accusation of witchcraft. Robert Gross, *The Minutemen and Their World* (New York, 1976), 16–29.

56. Terror was not just an emotion; it was a tactic both sides had mastered. John E. Ferling, *A Wilderness of Miseries: War and Warriors in Early America* (Westport, Conn., 1980), 34–35, 45.

57. James E. Kences, "Some Unexplored Relationships of Essex County Witchcraft to the Indian Wars of 1675 and 1689," *EIHC* 120 (1984): 179–212.

58. James Duncan Phillips, *Salem in the Seventeenth Century* (Boston,

1933), 230–32; Russell Bourne, *The Red King's Rebellion: Racial Politics in New England, 1675–1678* (New York, 1990), 142–43.

59. Yasuhide Kawashima, *Puritan Justice and the Indian: White Man's Law in Massachusetts, 1630–1763* (Middletown, Conn., 1986), 149–79; *Essex County Court Records,* 7:135.

230

60. Demos, *Unredeemed Captive,* 23.

61. Mary Rowlandson recalled that she had once slept without fear; after her captivity she could not; but she had learned to be in the same room with the dead and the dying. Rowlandson, *A True History of the Captivity and Restoration of Mary Rowlandson* (London, 1682), 5; Hall, *Worlds of Wonder,* 136.

62. Ulrich, *Good Wives,* 166–83; Kathryn Z. Derounian, "The Publication, Promotion, and Distribution of Mary Rowlandson's Indian Captivity Narrative in the Seventeenth Century," *Early American Literature* 23 (1988): 240.

63. Bozeman, *To Live Ancient Lives,* 39–40.

64. Ulrich, *Good Wives,* 184–87.

65. Victor, *Satanic Panic,* 28–42.

66. A conspiracy had been detected, but like the witches, when the authorities undertook to counter it, it became spectral. Konig, *Law and Society,* 167.

67. Greven, *Four Generations,* 123–24.

68. Cooper and Minkema, *Sermon Notebook,* 185; Winslow, *Meeting House Hill,* 57.

Chapter Three: Witchcakes

1. John Hale, *A Modest Inquiry into the Nature of Witchcraft* [1697], in Burr, *Narratives,* 413; Calef, *More Wonders,* in Burr, *Narratives,* 342; Cotton Mather, *Magnalia Christi Americana, Books I and II* [1702], ed. Kenneth B. Murdock (Cambridge, Mass., 1977), 327.

2. Hale, who ministered to the flock in neighboring Beverly and joined Parris in his vigil over the children, later opined that everyone knew about Mather's account. Hale, *Modest Inquiry,* in Burr, *Narratives,* 414.

3. *SVW,* 256–57, 281–82.

4. Cooper and Minkema, *Sermon Notebook,* 17.

5. Such eavesdropping had already led to court suits and provided testimony in criminal cases in seventeenth-century Essex County towns. Dow, *Everyday Life,* 44.

6. Cotton Mather, *Utilitia* (Boston, 1716), 276–77.

7. Edmund S. Morgan, *The Puritan Family: Religion and Domestic Rela-*

tions in Seventeenth-Century New England, rev. ed. (New York, 1966), 97, 102.

8. Hale, *Modest Inquiry,* in Burr, *Narratives,* 414.

9. Samuel Willard, *Small Offers toward the Service of the Tabernacle in this Wilderness* (Boston, 1689), 18.

10. Sewall's infant, Henry, became ill a week after his birth and died four days later. M. Halsey Thomas, ed., *The Diary of Samuel Sewall, 1674–1729* (New York, 1973), 1:87–90; Hambrick-Stowe, *Practice of Piety,* 9–12. The Puritans believed that death was always ready to strike. See David Stannard, *The Puritan Way of Death: A Study in Religion, Culture, and Social Change* (New York, 1977), and Fischer, *Albion's Seed,* 111–16.

11. Hambrick-Stowe, *Practice of Piety,* 145.

12. As when Sarah Bridgman's infant died in Northampton. The mother feared witchcraft, but neighbors who spent time with her and her poor infant reported that he died of persistent looseness, that is, diarrhea. Hall, *Witch-Hunting,* 104–6.

13. Carol Gilligan, "Women's Psychological Development: Implications for Psychotherapy," in *Women, Girls, and Psychotherapy: Reframing Resistance,* ed. Carol Gilligan et al. (New York, 1991), 17.

14. Carolyn Heilbrun, *Reinventing Womanhood* (New York, 1979), 105. Such rage was, of course, guilt producing and could lead to any number of disorders.

15. John Cotta, *The Triall of Witchcraft* (London, 1616), 101, 15, 115.

16. See, for example, John Brinley, *A Discovery of the Impostures of Witches and Astrologers* (London, 1680), preface.

17. As contemporary accounts, particularly those of Deodat Lawson and John Hale, evidence, the doctors of psychic and spirit were as terrified of the symptoms, the inexplicable contortions and pains, as were the patients. See G. S. Rousseau, "A Strange Pathology: Hysteria in the Early Modern World, 1500–1800," in *Hysteria before Freud,* ed. Sander L. Gilman et al. (Berkeley, Calif., 1993), 92.

18. Ernest Caulfield, "Pediatric Aspects of the Salem Witchcraft Tragedy," in *Witches and Historians: Interpretations of Salem,* ed. Marc Mappen (Huntington, N.Y., 1980), 50–63.

19. Rousseau, "Strange Pathology," 100.

20. It would be hard to improve on Demos's now classic exposition of the victims' "fits." See *Entertaining Satan,* 153–210, but is rage exhibited differently by young men and young women?

21. Hinkley's case quoted in Emil Oberholzer, *Delinquent Saints: Disci-*

plinary Action in the Early Congregational Churches of Massachusetts (New York, 1956), 122.

22. Donald F. Tapley et al., eds., *The Columbia University College of Physicians and Surgeons Complete Home Medical Guide* (New York, 1985), 461–64.

23. Mather, *Magnalia,* 327.

24. The problem of diagnosis at this distance is almost intractable, but see Oswei Temkin, *The Falling Sickness: A History of Epilepsy from the Greeks to the Beginnings of Modern Neurology,* 2d ed., rev. (Baltimore, 1994), 137–46.

25. *The Book of General Lawes and Liberties Concerning the Inhabitants of the Massachusets* [Cambridge, Mass., 1648], ed. Thomas G. Barnes (San Marino, Calif., 1975), 6 (hereafter cited as *Lawes and Liberties*); Douglas Besharov, *Recognizing Child Abuse: A Guide for the Concerned* (New York, 1990), 117; Jean Goodwin, "Recognizing Dissociative Symptoms in Abused Children," in *Sexual Abuse: Incest Victims and Their Families,* 2d ed., ed. Jean Goodwin (Chicago, 1989), 175–76.

26. *Lawes and Liberties,* 6.

27. N. E. H. Hull suggested in a personal communication to the author that Betty's illness may have begun as a conscious or even subconscious attempt to gain her mother's attention. Betty's younger sister, Susannah, was a rival for that attention, particularly if, as her early death implies, she was a sickly child.

28. Not unusual, with the Devil abroad. See D. P. Walker, *Unclean Spirits: Possession and Exorcism in England and France in the Late Sixteenth and Early Seventeenth Centuries* (Philadelphia, 1981), 44–83. Possession could be the work of the Devil himself; it need not entail charges of witchcraft. John Bernard, *Guide to Grand Jury Men* (London, 1630), 4, 11–18.

29. Karlsen, *Devil in the Shape of a Woman,* 231–32, 226–28.

30. See Michael MacDonald, ed., *Witchcraft and Hysteria in Elizabethan London: Edward Jorden and the Mary Glover Case* (London, 1991), xiv. Sanford J. Fox, *Science and Justice: The Massachusetts Witchcraft Trials* (Baltimore, 1968), 51–52. But other medical authorities such as Cotta still insisted that all natural causes had to be ruled out before the doctors called for the judges. Thomas, *Religion and the Decline of Magic,* 278.

31. Samuel P. Fowler, *An Account of the Life, Character, etc. of the Rev. Samuel Parris* (Salem, 1857), 6.

32. *SWP,* 1:125.

33. John Gaule, *Select Cases of Conscience Touching Witches and Witchcraft* (London, 1646), 60.

34. Parson's case documents, and Hale's comments, are reprinted in Hall, *Witch-Hunting*, 31.

35. Ewen, *Witch Hunting*, SWP, 1:94. The illnesses of children were perplexing and common; it was easy to ascribe them to the maleficence of a witch. According to Weisman's figures, 63 percent of the victims of "bewitchment" in seventeenth-century Massachusetts were females under the age of nineteen. Weisman, *Witchcraft, Magic, and Religion*, 51.

36. William Perkins, *A Discourse on the Damned Art of Witchcraft* (Cambridge, England, 1610), 222; Bernard, *Guide*, 8–9; Gaule, *Select Cases*, 136, 151; Increase Mather, *An Essay for the Recording of Illustrious Providences* [1684], ed. James A. Levernier (New York, 1977), 268–69; Hale, *Modest Inquiry*, in Burr, *Narratives*, 414.

37. Wall, *Fierce Communion*, 94–95.

38. Trask, *"Devil Hath Been Raised,"* 130–31.

39. The story is told in Deodat Lawson's first-hand account of the events, *A Brief and True Narrative of Some Remarkable Passages . . .* [1692], in Burr, *Narratives*, 162–63. Lawson talked to everyone, in part because he knew just about everyone, as Parris's predecessor and still on good terms with many in the village. More important, he had witnessed the girls' transformation from private players to a public troupe during his sermon at the end of March.

40. Godbeer, *Devil's Dominion*, 42–45.

41. I have searched the "practicum" literature on West African witchcraft and can find nothing equivalent to the baking of a witchcake with the urine of the victims. The urine of those afflicted was a part of some divining practices, but it was never baked with meal. Indeed, baking was not common in West Africa until missionaries introduced it in the nineteenth century, except for *moi-boi,* bean cakes wrapped in leaves, but these were really steamed rather than baked. I am grateful to my colleague Josephine Beoku-Betts for information about cooking customs. Witches were accused of "eating" the body of their victims, especially while night walking in their spectral bodies. See, for example, Barbara E. Ward, "Some Observations on Religious Cults in Ashanti," *Africa* 26 (1956): 55. There is no single manual for West African healing or divination, in part because Western observers were not fully aware of the uses and origins of the roots and other ingredients in various preparations and native experts did not willingly offer their secrets. The most intriguing look into the magical-medicinal pharmacopeia is Paul Stoller and Cheryl Olkes, *In Sorcery's Shadow: A Memoir of Apprenticeship among the Songhay of Niger* (Chicago, 1987). I have to conclude that

the witchcake was not African but English, and in Tituba's participation we have here a true case of pidgin countermagic.

42. The pudding episode is traced in Hall, *Witch-Hunting,* 32–33, 51–53.

43. Ibid., 162.

44. Nor were Puritans alone in this. Consider the sudden epidemic of malaria in the region of the Tiber north of Rome, A.D. 450. The men and women who lived in this region were Christians, but faced with the unexpected and inexplicable death of so many neonates and young children from wasting fevers, the parents reverted to the old magic. In the graves of the infants archaeologists have found decapitated puppies, ravens' talons, and other signs of magical rites. John Noble Wilford, "Malaria at Decline of Rome Signaled in Child Cemetery," *New York Times,* July 26, 1994, C1.

45. Endecott's prescription quoted in Dow, *Everyday Life,* 183–84.

46. Hallen and Sodipo, *Knowledge, Belief, and Witchcraft,* 111. Countermagic could also be bought over the counter, as it were. See, for example, Hans W. Debrunner, *Witchcraft in Ghana: A Study on the Belief in Destructive Witches and Its Effect on the Akan Tribes* (Accra, Ghana, 1961), 87–102.

47. Alan MacFarlane, *Witchcraft in Tudor and Stuart England* (New York, 1970), 147–206; Thomas, *Religion and the Decline of Magic,* 502–69.

48. David Cressy, *Coming Over: Migration and Communication between England and New England in the Seventeenth Century* (Cambridge, England, 1987), 162. Of course, the fear of witchcraft already waited in America, for the Native Americans had their healers and their witches and suspected that the Europeans brought more witchery with them. See Richard White, *The Middle Ground: Indians, Empires, and Republics in the Great Lakes Region, 1650–1815* (Cambridge, England, 1991), 14–15; Amanda Porterfield, "Witchcraft and the Colonization of Algonquian and Iroquois Cultures," *Religion and American Culture* 2 (1992): 103–24.

49. This was a sign of witchcraft according to Bernard, *Guide,* 163, 165. Bernard cited cases famous in his day, and there's a wealth of marvelous detail in these cases. Among those Bernard mentioned, one can start with G. B. Harrison's edition of *The Trial of the Lancaster Witches* (London, 1929), on the witches of Pendle (1612), in Lancaster, and Michael MacDonald's *Witchcraft and Hysteria,* on the Mary Glover Case in London (1602). Barbara Rosen has collected broadsides in *Witchcraft in England, 1558–1618* (Amherst, Mass., 1991), as has Joseph H. Marshburn in *Murder and Witchcraft in England, 1550–1640* (Norman, Okla., 1971). These precedents are relevant to Salem because they show how common fame and mysterious illness among previously healthy children led to accusations of bewitching.

50. J. S. Cockburn, *A History of the English Assizes, 1558–1714* (Cambridge, England, 1972), 98.

51. For example, the case of the Pendle witches, retold in Thomas Potts, *The Wonderful Discoverie of Witches in the Countie of Lancaster . . . 1612* (London, 1613), is replete with these formulas. Each trial account exhibits outrage and prurient curiosity merged into a credulous, misogynistic narrative of horrors.

52. Gaule, *Select Cases*, 4–5, 53, 54.

53. Richard Baxter, *The Certainty of the Worlds of Spirits* (London, 1691), preface, n.p.

54. Gaule, *Select Cases*, 128–29; Perkins, *Discourse*, 128, 149, 174.

55. *SWP*, 1:208.

56. See, for example, ibid., 1:75, 328; Bernard J. Hibbitts, "'Coming to Our Senses': Communication and Legal Expression in Performance Cultures," *Emory Law Journal* 41 (1992): 883.

57. *SWP*, 3:847–48.

58. Ibid., 3:848.

59. Thomas, *Religion and the Decline of Magic*, 505–69; MacFarlane, *Witchcraft*, 147–77; Demos, *Entertaining Satan*, 85; Lyle Koehler, *A Search for Power: The "Weaker" Sex in Seventeenth-Century New England* (Urbana, Ill., 1980), 281–83.

60. Thomas, *Religion and the Decline of Magic*, 227; Godbeer, *Devil's Dominion*.

61. Thomas, *Religion and the Decline of Magic*, 552–53; MacFarlane, *Witchcraft*, 171–75.

62. MacFarlane covers the subject concisely in *Witchcraft*, 14–22. He even tabulates penalties under the various statutes.

63. Gaule, *Select Cases*, 183.

64. Louis J. Kern, "Eros, the Devil, and the Cunning Woman: Sexuality and the Supernatural in European Antecedents and in the Seventeenth-Century Salem Witchcraft Cases," *EIHC* 129 (1993): 3–38.

65. Thomas, *Religion and the Decline of Magic*, 576–83; Barbara J. Shapiro, *"Beyond Reasonable Doubt" and "Probable Cause": Historical Perspectives on the Anglo-American Law of Evidence* (Berkeley, Calif., 1991), 42–98.

66. Wallace Notestein, *A History of Witchcraft in England, from 1558 to 1718* (New York, 1911), 271–73; Ewen, *Witch Hunting*, table at 101.

67. See, for example, Katharine M. Briggs, *Pale Hecate's Team* (New York, 1962).

68. Hall, *Witch-Hunting*, 124, 126, 117–18. John Godfrey's difficulties with his neighbors are recounted in Demos, *Entertaining Satan*, 36–56.

235

69. Hall, *Witch-Hunting,* 130–31; Demos, *Entertaining Satan,* 51.

70. Godbeer, *Devil's Dominion,* 30–31 ff.

71. Hall, *Worlds of Wonder,* 98, 146.

72. Hall, *Witch-Hunting,* 185–88.

73. Ibid., 180–81.

74. As documented with pellucid clarity in Demos, *Entertaining Satan,* 86 ff.

75. *SWP,* 1:161, 163.

76. Hall, *Witch-Hunting,* 235; Mather, *Illustrious Providences,* 142–56; Essex County Court Records, 7:355–59.

77. As in the tormenting of Nicholas Disborough. Hall, *Witch-Hunting,* 189–91; Mather, *Illustrious Providences,* 159–60.

78. The depositions can be found in Hall, *Witch-Hunting,* 231–59. The story is retold in Demos, *Entertaining Satan,* 132–52.

79. *SWP,* 2:683.

80. Moody to Increase Mather, October 4, 1688, in Hall, *Witch-Hunting,* 266–67.

81. Cotton Mather, *Memorable Providences, Relating to Witchcrafts and Possessions* [1689], in Burr, *Narratives,* 110; Kenneth Silverman, *The Life and Times of Cotton Mather* (New York, 1984), 83–86.

82. Mather, *Illustrious Providences,* 252, 244, 264, 265, 268, 269.

83. Parris to his congregation, in church, March 27, 1692, in *SVW,* 278. The choice of the day was significant. Parris regarded the monthly offering of bread and wine at the Lord's Supper as a special time to resanctify the covenant between those in communion and God. Cooper and Minkema, *Sermon Notebook,* 12.

84. Hall, *Worlds of Wonder,* 7, 84–86, 98–102, 112–15, 144–46, 162–63, 189–92, 242–43, 272.

85. Hall, *Witch-Hunting,* 37, 62.

86. *Lawes and Liberties,* 5.

87. The literature on the European persecutions is vast. A good summary is Levack, *Witch-hunt in Early Modern Europe.* Even swifter summary is Klaits, *Servants of Satan.* More recent is Barstow, *Witchcraze.* The Essex County cases of the 1640s are the subject of MacFarlane, *Witchcraft,* 135–43.

88. Godbeer, *Devil's Dominion,* 235–37; Weisman, *Witchcraft, Magic, and Religion,* 192–203; Demos, *Entertaining Satan,* 401–9.

89. Elizabeth Reis, "Witches, Sinners, and the Underside of Covenant Theology," *EIHC* 129 (1993): 103–18; Ian Bostridge, "Debates about Witchcraft in England, 1650–1736" (Ph.D. diss., Oxford University, 1990), 27–31.

90. William Hawkins, *A Treatise of Pleas of the Crown* (London, 1716),

1:5; Richard Bovet, *Pandaemonium, Or, the Devil's Cloyster* (London, 1684), 48.

91. For example, *SWP,* 1:74–75, 135, 139–40, 245; 2:647–48.

92. Stuart Clark, "Inversion, Misrule, and the Meaning of Witchcraft," *Past and Present* 87 (1980): 102.

93. "Miscoding Is Seen as the Root of False Memories," *New York Times,* 237 May 31, 1994, C1, C8, citing the work of Dr. Daniel Schacter, of Harvard University, and Dr. Morris Moscovitch, of the University of Toronto. When children miscode memory, they "confabulate" fantasy with memory and mismatch memories. Lucy S. McGough, *Child Witnesses: Fragile Voices in the American Legal System* (New Haven, 1994), 42.

94. See, for example, *SWP,* 1:104. Richard P. Gildrie, "The Salem Witchcraft Trials as a Crisis of Popular Imagination," *EIHC* 128 (1992): 276–77, argues that these hallucinations were actually experienced but, like all such epiphenomena, were culturally structured. Thus the haglike visage of the nighttime afflicter became clearer in the minds of potential accusers as the names and faces of the supposed witches were identified by others in the hearings.

95. *SWP,* 1:101; Calef, *More Wonders,* in Drake, *Witchcraft Delusion,* 3:88.

96. Karlsen, *Devil in the Shape of a Woman,* 34–42.

Chapter Four: Betty's People

1. *SWP,* 3:753.

2. I am grateful to Barbara Moss for this analogy. Her study of the mission girls in Zimbabwe is forthcoming.

3. Pierson, *Black Yankees,* 14; the black population of New England comprised fewer than one thousand souls, and many of these assimilated, but only as much as their masters permitted (29).

4. White, *Middle Ground,* 50–93.

5. Baxter, *Certainty of the Worlds of Spirits,* 107.

6. Hall, *Witch-Hunting,* 62, 68 n. 3.

7. Alfred A. Cave, "Indian Shamans and English Witches in Seventeenth-Century New England," *EIHC* 128 (1992): 249.

8. Mather, *Memorable Providences,* in Burr, *Narratives,* 99; Cotton Mather, *A Brand Pluck'd Out of the Burning* [1693], in Burr, *Narratives,* 261.

9. The links between Tituba's actions and Indian magic, albeit the magic of Arawak Indians from the Orinoco River basin rather than Algonkin Indians of New England, are traced in Elaine G. Breslaw, "Tituba's Confession: Fueling the Fantasies of Her Accusers," paper read to the American Historical Association Convention, San Francisco, January 8, 1994.

10. Nancy Chodorow, *The Reproduction of Mothering: Psychoanalysis and the Sociology of Gender* (Berkeley, Calif., 1978), 129, 140.

11. Morgan, *Puritan Family*, 77.

12. Lawrence Stone, *The Family, Sex, and Marriage in England, 1500–1800* (New York, 1979), 464–65; Philip Greven, *The Protestant Temperament: Patterns of Child-Rearing, Religious Experience, and the Self in Early America* (New York, 1977), 32–43.

13. Hambrick-Stowe, *Practice of Piety*, 145; Gragg, *Quest for Security*, 112.

14. Vickers, *Farmers and Fishermen*, 76.

15. Life was always fragile for children, and parents had too many to allow the self-fulfilling (or self-indulgent) style of parenting. See Ulrich, *Good Wives*, 156–58; Sommerville, *Discovery of Childhood*, 80–81.

16. Coverture is explained in Marylynn Salmon, *Women and the Law of Property in Early America* (Chapel Hill, 1986), but see Cornelia Hughes Dayton, "Women before the Bar: Gender, Law, and Society in Connecticut, 1710–1790" (Ph.D. diss., Princeton University, 1986), on the broad scope of Connecticut women's legal activities.

17. See, for example, Ilana Krausman Ben-Amos, *Adolescence and Youth in Early Modern England* (New Haven, 1994), 135.

18. *SWP*, 1:117–20; Hansen, *Witchcraft at Salem*, 150.

19. See Myra Bluebond-Langner, *The Private Worlds of Dying Children* (Princeton, 1978), 214–17.

20. Anne Bradstreet, "On my dear Grand-child Simon Bradstreet Who dyed on 16. November 1669 being but a month and one day old," in *Seventeenth-Century American Poetry*, ed. Harrison T. Meserole (New York, 1968), 34.

21. Ulrich, *Good Wives*, 154–62.

22. Hall, *Witch-Hunting*, 82–85.

23. Ulrich, *Good Wives*, 126–31.

24. Thomas, *Religion and the Decline of Magic*, 259; Demos, *Entertaining Satan*, 80; Ulrich, *Midwife's Tale*, 374; but see Karlsen, *Devil in the Shape of a Woman*, 144, and Thomas R. Forbes, *The Midwife and the Witch* (New Haven, 1966), 127, 146, arguing that midwifery did make women vulnerable to such accusations.

25. Dow, *Everyday Life*, 91–100.

26. Gloria L. Main, "Gender, Work, and Wages in Colonial New England," *WMQ*, 3d. ser., 51 (1994): 53.

27. Cook, *Fathers of the Towns*, 79; Winifred Barr Rothenberg, *From Market-Places to a Market Economy: The Transformation of Rural Massachu-*

setts, 1750–1850 (Chicago, 1992), 80 ff. Rothenberg considers the years after 1750, but much of her analysis applies to the post-1680 period in Salem.

28. Stephen Innes, "Fulfilling John Smith's Vision: Work and Labor in Early America," in *Work and Labor in Early America,* ed. Stephen Innes (Chapel Hill, 1988), 36; Allan Kulikoff, "The Transition to Capitalism in Rural America," *WMQ,* 3d. ser., 46 (1989): 120–44.

29. For example, Sarah Wardwell confessed that she was snared by the Devil's promise of good clothing. *SWP,* 3:791. Karlsen, *Devil in the Shape of a Woman,* 77–116, links economic animus directly to witchcraft accusations.

30. Ulrich, *Good Wives,* 13–14, 15, 20–21.

31. Ibid., 127.

32. Hall, *Witch-Hunting,* 71.

33. Ulrich, *Good Wives,* 51, 59.

34. Demos, *Entertaining Satan,* 295–96.

35. Ulrich, *Good Wives,* 62–63.

36. Foster, *Their Solitary Way,* 147, 150.

37. *SWP,* 2:375.

38. *Essex County Court Records,* 8:15.

39. Ulrich, *Good Wives,* 89–106; Roger Thompson, *Sex in Middlesex: Popular Mores in a Massachusetts County, 1649–1699* (Amherst, Mass., 1986), 128–40.

40. Thompson, *Sex in Middlesex,* 141–54; Karlsen, *Devil in the Shape of a Woman,* 168.

41. *SWP,* 1:92–95.

42. Gilligan, "Women's Psychological Development," 8, 22–23.

43. Lyn Mikel Brown, "Telling a Girl's Life: Self Authorization as a Form of Resistance," in Gilligan et al., *Women, Girls, and Psychotherapy,* 84.

44. See, for example, Barbara A. Hanawalt, *Growing Up in Medieval London: The Experience of Childhood in History* (New York, 1994), 110–14, 118–20, and Joseph E. Illick, "Childrearing in Seventeenth-Century England and America," in *The History of Childhood,* ed. Lloyd DeMause (New York, 1974), 303–50, for some comparisons. The Puritans, Sommerville argues, were especially sensitive to the dangers and differences of adolescence. *Discovery of Childhood,* 34.

45. Apter, *Altered Loves,* 75. Boyer and Nissenbaum, *Salem Possessed,* 145–46, have the girls projecting their aggressions against real oppressors (of their families) onto surrogates, in this case, Elizabeth Porter, who married Joseph Putnam and so betrayed the Putnam clan to their archenemies. The projection of anger onto surrogates, whether the Hansel and Gretel evil-stepmother motif used here or the more general psychodynamic described in

239

Demos, "Underlying Themes," in 1970, is based on a conception of daughter-mother relationship which is questioned by modern feminist analysts. See, for example, Chodorow, *Reproduction of Mothering,* 120–29.

46. There is a real difference between a young child's ability to remember and to reason from memory and the corresponding powers of an older child. Today, the cutoff seems to be at about age eleven or twelve. McGough, *Child Witnesses,* 67.

47. *SWP,* 2:603–5.

48. Hansen, *Witchcraft at Salem,* 30.

49. Fischer, *Albion's Seed,* 111–16; Stannard, *Puritan Way of Death,* 57.

50. Stone, *Family, Sex, and Marriage,* 167.

51. Annie G. Rogers, "A Feminist Poetics of Psychotherapy," in Gilligan et al., *Women, Girls, and Psychotherapy,* 34.

52. Robinson, *Devil Discovered,* 57.

53. Ben-Amos, *Adolescence and Youth,* 154–55.

54. It simply was not a sharply differentiated social structure. Vickers, *Farmers and Fishermen,* 61. Vickers is describing the social relationships of working men, not women, but even though social status of women was derived from male relations, the argument is tenable.

55. Kenneth Lockridge, *Literacy in Colonial New England: An Enquiry into the Social Context of Literacy in the Early Modern West* (New York, 1974), 38–42 (arguing that New England law and practice discriminated against girls).

56. Morgan, *Puritan Family,* 100–101; Lawrence Cremin, *American Education: The Colonial Experience, 1607–1783* (New York, 1970), 124–25, 180–82, 187.

57. Goodwin, "Recognizing Dissociative Symptoms," 174.

58. Thompson, *Sex in Middlesex,* 17–110. I am grateful to Mary Beth Norton for sharing with me her findings on cases of abuse from the colonial New Hampshire court records. These will appear in Norton, *Gendered Power and the Forming of American Society* (New York, 1996), chap. 2. David H. Flaherty, "Law and the Enforcement of Morals in Early America," *Perspectives in American History* 5 (1971): 228, and Konig, *Law and Society,* 129, argue that the effort to use law to control morality failed, but this may be so for the reasons Norton has advanced: victims would or could not bring their troubles to court.

59. Hollida Wakefield and Ralph Underwager, *Accusations of Child Sexual Abuse* (Springfield, Ill., 1988), xviii (summarizing the Jordan, Minnesota, cases of 1984, in which a prosecutor pressed the cases even after contradictory evidence began to accumulate).

60. Ibid., 31.

61. Madge Bray, *Poppies on the Rubbage Heap: Sexual Abuse: The Child's Voice* (Edinburgh, 1991), 48.

62. MacFarlane, *Witchcraft*, 137.

63. Mark Hansen, "More False Memory Suits Likely," *American Bar Association Journal* (August 1994): 36–37.

64. "Recovered memory may be faulty in the same way, initiated by malice, then expanded by authorities eager to find the causes of larger social malaise." Lawrence Wright, *Remembering Satan: A Case of Recovered Memory and the Shattering of an American Family* (New York, 1994), 110–45, 146.

65. *SWP*, 2:683; *Shorter Oxford Unabridged Dictionary* (Oxford, 1968), 1057, offers *jade* as a derogatory word for women, synonymous with *hussy*, first used in the 1590s.

66. Robinson, *Devil Discovered*, 72; Karlsen, *Devil in the Shape of a Woman*, 227–28.

67. *Essex County Court Records*, 9:47–48.

68. *SWP*, 1:151.

69. Ibid., 1:168–69.

70. Ibid. The image of the pitchfork is obviously suggestive, but in a farming community it had connotations other than sexual ones. Lewis may have suffered from delayed traumatic confabulation of memories, the trauma of the original episode first clouding, then confusing the actual events in her mind. McGough, *Child Witnesses*, 48–49.

71. *SWP*, 2:483.

72. See, for example, Thompson, *Sex in Middlesex*, 77.

73. Dow, *Everyday Life*, 153.

74. *Philadelphia Inquirer*, May 18, 1994, A4.

75. Oberholzer, *Delinquent Saints*, 184.

76. Hale, *Modest Inquiry*, in Burr, *Narratives*, 409–10, 421.

77. Parris Sermon, March 27, 1692, in Cooper and Minkema, *Sermon Notebook*, 194.

78. Upham, *Salem Witchcraft*, 2:289 ff.

79. Thomas, *Religion and the Decline of Magic*, 541.

80. Ibid., 459–60.

81. In 1671, James Janeway wrote *A Token for Children: Being an Exact Account of the Conversion, Holy and Exemplary Lives and Joyful Deaths of several Young Children*—a best-seller for Puritan parents who wondered what lay in store for their tearaways. Sommerville, *Discovery of Childhood*, 55–57.

82. My inspiration is Upham, *Salem Witchcraft*, 2:90–97. Juvenile delinquents commit acts of delinquency because their friends are juvenile delin-

quents, not because they do not like or respect their parents, or because they are unable to assimilate the norms of the larger culture. They imitate. Travis Hirshi, *Causes of Delinquency* (Berkeley, Calif., 1969), 135–61.

83. See, for example, James Garbarino, "A Researcher's View," in *The Child Abuse-Delinquency Connection,* ed. David N. Sandberg (Lexington, Mass., 1989), 68; Carl M. Rosenquist and Edwin I. Megargee, *Delinquency in Three Cultures* (Austin, Tex., 1969), 435; Carson Markley, "The Female Juvenile Delinquent and Her Behavior," in *Problems of Adolescents: Social and Psychological Approaches,* ed. Richard E. Hardy and John G. Cull (Springfield, Ill., 1974), 28, 29–30.

84. Thompson, *Sex in Middlesex,* 90; Foster, *Long Argument,* 182.

85. David M. Downes, *The Delinquent Solution: A Study in Subcultural Theory* (New York, 1966), 117, 199, 132.

86. Kitty Hanson, *Rebels in the Streets: The Story of New York's Girl Gangs* (Englewood Cliffs, N.J., 1964), 11, 15.

87. Thompson, *Sex in Middlesex,* 84–90, 103.

88. On the social dynamics of gang formation and activity, see Martin Sanchez Jankowski, *Islands in the Street: Gangs and American Urban Society* (Berkeley, Calif., 1991), 24–38 ff.

89. Kai T. Erikson, *Wayward Puritans: A Study in the Sociology of Deviance* (New York, 1966), 10–11.

90. Demos, *Entertaining Satan,* 309.

91. Households and distances from the Roach Map of Salem, 1990, courtesy of the Danvers Historical Society. See also Boyer and Nissenbaum, *Salem Possessed,* 192–94. Plainly my reconstruction of the geographical pattern of accusers and defendants is at odds with that in *Salem Possessed,* 83–86, which aligns those two groups along a west-east axis. The brilliance of its reconstruction of the topography of accusations notwithstanding, it seems to me merely to recapitulate the crucial role of the Putnams and their supporters in the accusatory process. The defendants not only lived along the Ipswich road on the eastern border of the village but dwelt on the edge of Topsfield in the west as well.

92. Robinson, *Devil Discovered,* 292–95, 301–4. Francis Nurse's chief antagonist in the courts was not a Putnam, however, but an enemy of the Putnams, Zerubbabel Endecott, whose family holdings the Putnams also coveted. ECCR (MS) 49: 3-1 to 21-4 (*Endecott v. Nurse*); 49: 22-2 (*Endecott v. Jonathan Putnam*).

93. Sarah Loring Bailey, *Historical Sketches of Andover* (Boston, 1880), 201–8; Claude M. Fuess, *Andover: Symbol of New England, the Evolution of a Town* (Andover, Mass., 1959), 84–90.

94. Edwin Powers, *Crime and Punishment in Early Massachusetts, 1620–1692* (Boston, 1966), 346; Cotton Mather, *Decennium Luctuosum* (Boston, 1699), 182.

95. Christine Leigh Heyrman, "Specters of Subversion, Societies of Friends: Dissent and the Devil in Provincial Essex County, Massachusetts," in *Saints and Revolutionaries: Essays in Early American History,* ed. David D. Hall, John Murrin, and Thad Tate (New York, 1984), 48–52. In the decade before 1692, agitation against the Quakers in the county had quieted, but evidently the quiet masked a lingering animus. Gildrie, *Salem,* 134–37. On Burroughs, see Rosenthal, *Salem Story,* 129–50.

96. *SWP,* 3:867.

97. Ibid., 2:684–85, 480.

98. Ibid., 1:51–55, 313–21; Bryan F. LeBeau, "Philip English and the Witchcraft Hysteria," *Historical Journal of Massachusetts* 15 (1987): 1–20.

99. See, for example, ECCR (MS), 50: 7-1 (Alden defies governor's orders); Inferior Court of Common Pleas, Essex, Docket Book 1686–1718/19, Essex Institute, Salem Sessions June 25, 1695 (English resumes his litigious ways).

100. Luis J. Rodriguez, *Always Running: La Vida Loca, Gang Days in L.A.* (New York, 1993), 250.

101. Thomas Hutchinson, *The History of the Colony and Province of Massachusets Bay* [2d ed., 1768], ed. L. S. Mayo (Cambridge, Mass., 1936), 2:47.

Chapter Five: Accusations and Confessions

1. Lawson, *Brief and True Narrative* in Burr, *Narratives,* 160.

2. Morgan, *Puritan Family,* 92.

3. I am grateful to Eben Moglen for suggesting this point to me. The ministers in Andover, Beverly, and Salem had known one another for a long time. The Putnams and their clients in the village had grown up together. Parris was the odd man out.

4. *SWP,* 3:745; Robinson, *Devil Discovered,* 58–77.

5. Compare, for example, the testimony of Ann Putnam Jr. and Elizabeth Hubbard against Sarah Good: that Good both pinched and pricked them, and that they each saw Good fly at the other the day of the examination, March 1, 1692. *SWP,* 2:372–73.

6. For example, *SWP,* 2:602 (Thomas and Edward Putnam depose that Ann Putnam Jr. named as the cause of her afflictions Rebecca Nurse).

7. Fowler, *Samuel Parris,* 8. Sewall's house was a block away from the courthouse in Salem. Betty was still close to the shrieks of the girls and the moans of the defendants. Joseph Putnam kept notes of the first two days' hearings. *SWP,* 2:361.

8. *SWP*, 2:598.

9. Karlsen, *Devil in the Shape of a Woman*, 140–41.

10. Here different from many of the continental European cases, but not the English cases, which were rarely overtly sensual. See Kern, "Eros, the Devil, and the Cunning Woman," 3–38. Mather, *Illustrious Providences*, 138, could only find one case in which a suspected witch admitted to sexual union with the Devil.

11. Demos, *Entertaining Satan*, 346.

12. Mather, *Illustrious Providences*, 140. Elizabeth Reis believes that those who confessed to conversation with Satan were in reality confessing to other sins, which amounted, in their minds, to such a conversation. See Reis, "Witches, Sinners, and the Underside of Covenant Theology," *EIHC* 129 (1993)" 110 ff.

13. Gragg, *Salem Witch Crisis*, 54.

14. Ulrich, *Good Wives*, 157; Morgan, *Puritan Family*, 66.

15. The displacement thesis that is the cornerstone of Demos, "Underlying Themes," 1324–25: girls angry at their mothers cannot vent their anger on its cause and so choose a substitute, another older woman, as target. What if the cause was real abuse but the abuser could not be accused?

16. Boyer and Nissenbaum, *Salem Possessed*, 204–5; *SWP*, 2:351–53.

17. *SWP*, 1:80

18. See, for example, Wendell, "Were the Salem Witches Guiltless?" 17.

19. Ulrich, *Good Wives*, 158.

20. Indeed, many at one time or another were indebted to Corwin and Hathorne. Konig, *Law and Society*, 79.

21. See, for example, *SVW*, 152–53.

22. Robinson, *Devil Discovered*, 33; Gildrie, *Salem*, 161–62; Young, *"Good Order,"* 168.

23. What, then, were the magistrates to do? The issue is still unresolved; we can take no comfort from our "modern" professional advances—for courts remain at a loss when they deal with children's evidence. See, for example, Veronica Serrato, "Expert Testimony in Child Abuse Cases: A Spectrum of Uses," *Boston University Law Review* 68 (1988): 155–64; J. Bulkley, ed., *Child Sexual Abuse and the Law* (Chicago, 1982); Wakefield and Underwager, *Accusations of Child Sexual Abuse*; Steven I. Friedland, "On Common Sense and the Evaluation of Witness Credibility," *Case Western Reserve Law Review* 40 (1990): 165–87; Jean Montoya, "On Truth and Shielding in Child Abuse Trials," *Hastings Law Journal* 43 (1992): 1259–88. The key Supreme Court case is *Maryland v. Craig*, 110 S Ct 3157 (1990), which in effect ruled that children did not have to face the cross-examination required of

adults in open court. The children accusers at Salem were protected in ways similar to this, for the only challenge to them came from the defendants, themselves under duress and already placed in compromising positions.

24. The warrants to the sheriff to bring Good, Osborn, and Tituba to the hearing specified that it would take place at Ingersoll's, but the locale was immediately shifted when the crowd and the noise made examination impossible. *SWP*, 2:355; Brown, *Guide*, 12.

25. As with so many surmises we make, I thought this insight was my own, until I happened across an Oxford University Press paperback edition of John Demos's *Entertaining Satan* and looked closely at the cover illustration. The credit line thanks the Granger Collection, New York, for the wood engraving from which the illustration was reproduced. In it, the girls sit in a pew; the accused stand. Behind the accused to the left is what must be a pulpit, raised, with a large book on it. To the right, the magistrates and the clerk sit behind a low, solid, wide table. The magistrate in the center is a dead ringer for Nathaniel Hawthorne and must have been modeled upon him—thus John Hathorne came to resemble his descendant. If the scene is the meeting house, then the table must be the communion table.

26. I have used the term *impatience* deliberately, for I just do not think that the Putnams had decided to use witchcraft accusations to bring down their village rivals. But *impatience* may be too diffuse. Boyer and Nissenbaum attribute stronger emotions to the Putnam clan: "Viewed thus schematically, the residential profile of the accused offers a vivid geographic metaphor for the anxieties of the 'Pro-Parris' [literally, the Putnam family] group: the regions beyond the Village bounds are dangerous 'enemy territory.' . . . The true Salem village has been driven westward and confined to a small enclave from which, back to the wall (or more literally, to the Ipswich River), it lashes out at the encircling enemy." Boyer and Nissenbaum, *Salem Possessed*, 192.

27. *SWP*, 1:113–14.

28. Ibid., 1:80.

29. Ibid. 2:356–57. All exorcists knew that sudden inability to speak was a symptom of possession. Fernando Cervantes, *The Devil in the New World: The Impact of Diabolism in New Spain* (New Haven, 1994), 116. On invisible props, see Michael Issachoroff, *Discourse as Performance* (Stanford, Calif., 1989), 9, 11.

30. *SVW*, 6.

31. *SWP*, 1:122.

32. The forms by which "speech criminals" confessed in Massachusetts are discussed in Jane Kamensky, "Words, Witches, and Woman Trouble:

Witchcraft, Disorderly Speech, and Gender Boundaries in Puritan New England," *EIHC* 128 (1992): 288–89, and Jane Kamensky, "Saying and Unsaying," paper read to the Philadelphia Center for Early American Studies/Institute of Early American History and Culture Conference, Philadelphia, June 4, 1994.

33. Konig, *Law and Society,* 147, 149–50.

34. Hall, *Witch-Hunting,* 49–50.

35. Joseph H. Smith, ed., *Colonial Justice in Western Massachusetts (1639–1702): The Pynchon Court Record* (Cambridge, Mass., 1961), 220.

36. *Essex County Court Records,* 1:108–9, 204.

37. Weisman, *Witchcraft, Magic, and Religion,* app. B, 204–7.

38. *Essex County Court Records,* 1:265.

39. Carlo Ginsburg, *The Night Battles: Witchcraft and Agrarian Cults in the Sixteenth and Seventeenth Centuries* (Baltimore, 1983), 139–40; Mary Elizabeth Perry, *Gender and Disorder in Early Modern Seville* (Princeton, 1990), 113. When a twenty-seven-year-old Mexican spinster confessed to making a pact with the Devil in order to have carnal relations with him, the inquisitors in New Spain concluded that she was "full of 'mad fantasies' peculiar to the unfortunate members of the 'fragile sex.'" Cervantes, *Devil in the New World,* 126.

40. There is no evidence of such suits in the docket books, file papers, waste books, and other records of the quarterly courts or later the county courts of Essex which I examined at the Essex Institute Library.

41. Smith, *Colonial Justice,* 145.

42. *SWP,* 2:355–78. When the girls began to accuse people of higher station, merchants such as Philip English, ministers such as Samuel Willard, and eventually the magnates of the colony, Governor William Phips began to look for a way to terminate the proceedings. English and others like him were allowed to escape from custody (although the rich were not the only ones to flee), and Phips adjourned the court. Did social and economic status play a role in causing the crisis? I think not. Did social and economic status have some impact upon the fate of the accused: an emphatic yes.

43. Gragg, *Salem Witch Crisis,* 51.

44. John Winthrop, *History of New England,* ed. James Savage (Boston, 1826), 47. I am grateful to Eben Moglen for calling this reference to my attention.

45. Gildrie, *Salem,* 135; John Murrin, "Magistrates, Sinners, and a Precarious Liberty: Trial by Jury in Seventeenth-Century New England," in Hall, Murrin, and Tate, *Saints and Revolutionaries,* 199; Wakefield and Underwager, *Accusations of Child Sexual Abuse,* 31.

46. *SWP,* 2:358.

47. Fischer, *Albion's Seed,* 103–11.

48. *SWP,* 2:609–13. The alternative was to take sureties for her good behavior and examine her again, later, if she was well enough. Witchcraft, a felony, was not a bailable offense.

49. Robinson, *Devil Discovered,* 267; Boyer and Nissenbaum, *Salem Possessed,* 193–94.

50. Hale, *Modest Inquiry,* in Burr, *Narratives,* 415.

51. Ibid., 414.

52. Hansen, *Witchcraft at Salem,* 38, regards Tituba as a genuine hysteric who may have had the power to go into trances. In this he follows Allen Putnam, who in *Witchcraft of New England Explained by Modern Spiritualism* (Boston, 1880) argued that Tituba must have been a spirit medium who could leave her body and fly to other regions (280). Without intending to, Tituba must have altered the girls' mental state (282). For the same reason—her powers as a medium—she was made dumb in the latter stages of her testimony.

53. Pierre Verger, "Trance and Convention in Nago-Yoruba Spirit Mediumship," in *Spirit Mediumship and Society in Africa,* ed. John Beattie and John Middleton (New York, 1969), 50–56.

54. Compare *SWP* 3:747 with 3:750. Tituba, if Yoruba, would believe in supernatural powers, specters flying through the air, and other spiritual manifestations of the other world, but she would not believe in a Devil. Yoruba belief systems involve a plenum of deities, but none of them is purely evil. See Philip John Niemark, *The Way of the Orisa* (San Francisco, 1993), 7 ff.

55. Starkey's version, in *Devil in Massachusetts,* 58: "[W]ith her slave's adaptability, her only weapon, she caught at every cue the magistrates offered her and enlarged on it." This trembling obsequiousness, combined with her "slurred, Southern voice," carried her through. Starkey, writing in the late 1940s, attributed the derogatory "sambo" image of the antebellum slave to Tituba.

56. When the magistrates submitted the indictment of Tituba to the grand jury, they returned it "ignoramus" instead of "billa vera"—the true bill needed to bring a defendant to trial. Tituba was safe, more or less. *SWP,* 3:755.

57. In a real way, she had forced her inquisitors to join her on a "middle ground" in which "people try to persuade others who are different from themselves by appealing to what they perceive to be the values and practices of those others. They often misinterpret and distort both the values and the

247

practices of those they deal with, but from these misunderstandings arise new meanings and through them new practices—the shared meanings and practices of the middle ground." White, *Middle Ground,* x.

58. How much of this was African, how much English? In other words, to what extent was this confession another "pidgin" account? Or did it fully integrate the African, West Indian, and English stories—making it a Creole confession? For example, Yoruba witches could fly, and did, but only at night, and then in their spectral form. They could also take the form of animals. See Awolalu, *Yoruba Beliefs,* 85.

59. *SWP,* 1:65. Hale noticed this transformation as well and featured it in his *Modest Inquiry,* Burr, *Narrative,* 420.

60. Jordan, *White over Black,* 3–43, 66–70.

61. ECCR (MS), 49: 57-2; Konig, *Law and Society,* 167.

62. See, for example, Kawashima, *Puritan Justice and the Indian,* 130–31.

63. *SWP,* 3:753–55.

64. My informant is a Nigerian Ife diviner, Joseph Olusola Faludon.

65. The Corys had the reputation of testing the honesty and the patience of their neighbors. It was Giles who had informed on John Proctor for selling liquor to the Indians in 1678, and the Corys often brought or defended slander suits. See, for example, *Essex County Court Records,* 7:123, 132.

66. *SWP,* 1:248–54; Parris, Sermon, March 27, 1692, in Cooper and Minkema, *Sermon Notebook,* 194–98.

67. Another reason a family might have for "putting out" a preteenager was that child's persistent misconduct. Wall, *Fierce Communion,* 103–4. Was Abigail assigned to the Parris's as a disciplinary measure?

68. Girls under the age of sixteen were still too young to give full account of themselves or to be full members of the church. Foster, *Long Argument,* 181. Abigail violated that norm, or rather hurdled it, by speaking out as she did.

69. Lawson, *Brief and True Narrative,* in Burr, *Narratives,* 154–55.

70. Deodat Lawson, *Christ's Fidelity the Only Shield Against Satan's Malignity* (Boston, 1693), 10–11, 46–47, 48, 49, 61, 63–64, 73. An earlier version was delivered on March 24, 1692, to the congregation of the Salem Village church. The published version is so obviously recut to conform to the post-trial pattern, with references to the Devil appearing in the shape of the innocent and calls for charity to those accused, that I cannot be sure what was said in Salem.

71. *SVW,* 19.

72. *SWP,* 3:839–40.

73. Lawson, *Brief and True Narrative,* in Burr, *Narratives,* 160–61.

74. See, for example, Joan Jacobs Brumberg, *Fasting Girls: The History of Anorexia as a Modern Disease* (Cambridge, Mass., 1988), 48.

75. Lawson, *Brief and True Narrative*, in Burr, *Narratives*, 160; *SWP*, 2:351–52; 3:994.

76. In one recent California case of alleged child abuse, the supposed victim's mother not only seconded her son's claims but later charged that he had been molested by three witches and a member of the Los Angeles School Board. McGough, *Child Witnesses*, 15.

77. *SWP*, 2:584–87.

78. Mather, *Illustrious Providences*, 269.

79. *SWP*, 2:587.

80. Parris, Sermon, March 27, 1692, in Cooper and Minkema, *Sermon Notebook*, 194–98.

81. *SWP*, 1:207–10.

82. Upham, *Salem Witchcraft*, 2:101–11; *SWP*, 2:657–90.

83. Mather, *Illustrious Providences*, 140–41.

84. *SWP*, 1:145, 146.

85. Ibid., 1:125–27.

86. I would guess that this might be true of little Dorcas Good, age four, who informed on her mother, Sarah, even if the latter was abusive. Dorcas Good confessed a week before she was scheduled to be executed. Much as those times differed from our own, I know of no other case of a small child hanged for such a crime, and surmise that the judges were eager to avoid that extremity, though I have no evidence for my surmise.

87. Robinson, *Devil Discovered*, 259–364, provides short biographies of all the accused witches.

88. See, for example, William Nelson, *Dispute and Conflict Resolution in Plymouth County, Massachusetts, 1725–1825* (Chapel Hill, 1981).

89. I should note that this is my reading of the way the system worked, much influenced by a rudimentary sociology of criminal law approach. A similar approach appears in the now classic study of deviance (including witchcraft) in the Bay Colony, Erikson, *Wayward Puritans*, 137–59, but I do not mean to adopt the cynical pose of those who condemn the magistrates or the judges as simple woman haters, as in Koehler, *Search for Power*, 389–411.

90. Demos, *Entertaining Satan*, 309.

91. The modernist protests that such could not happen today, but the Ingram case in Olympia, and increasing numbers of child abuse cases elsewhere, contradict that smug confidence. Paul Ingram, unable to remember any of the incidents his daughters recalled, came to believe under stress and

duress that he must have simply repressed the events and confessed to the charges. When this book was written, he was still serving a twenty-year sentence in a state penitentiary, although in a quieter time he recanted his confession. Wright, *Remembering Satan*, 193.

92. *SWP*, 2:405.

93. Ibid., 2:411–12.

94. Ibid., 2:413.

95. Ibid., 3:793–804.

96. Morgan, *Puritan Family*, 88; *The Diary of Michael Wigglesworth, 1653–1657: The Conscience of a Puritan*, ed. Edmund S. Morgan (New York, 1965), 17.

97. *Lawes and Liberties*, 35, 6.

98. *SWP*, 3:705.

99. Perry Miller, *The New England Mind: The Seventeenth Century* (Cambridge, Mass., 1938), 26–27; Darrett Rutman, *American Puritanism: Faith and Practice* (Philadelphia, 1970), 15, 26, 99–100.

100. *SWP*, 1:211–12.

101. The literature on cognitive dissonance as applied to historical subjects is rehearsed in Robert Jervis, *Perception and Misperception in International Politics* (Princeton, 1976).

102. Was it also good because it conformed to Puritan expectations of contrition? Gragg, *Salem Witch Crisis*, 132, believes that confession might have spared the accused witches through the intercession of the ministry, for a contrite heart was a heart open to reformation.

103. *SWP*, 1:63–76.

104. Mather, *Magnalia*, 329.

105. Alice Lounsberry, *Sir William Phips: Treasure Fisherman and Governor of the Massachusetts Bay Colony* (New York, 1941), 265–80.

Chapter Six: The Diviners

1. Fischer, *Albion's Seed*, 120.

2. Mather, *Wonders*, in Drake, *Witchcraft Delusion*, 1:17.

3. Mather's *Memorable Providences*, in Burr, *Narratives*, 91–143, proved that there were witches and that they had swooped down on the Bay Colony.

4. Mather, *Wonders*, in Drake, *Witchcraft Delusion*, 1:1. Mather published this in late 1692 but wrote it and delivered it as a sermon to his flock in early August 1692. It seems reasonable to me that, given his earlier close contact with the Devil, Mather expected the blows even before the Salem crisis erupted.

5. Powers, *Crime and Punishment*, 100–162.

6. Murrin, "Magistrates, Sinners, and a Precarious Liberty," 191–92; Bradley Chapin, *Criminal Justice in Colonial America, 1606–1660* (Athens, Ga., 1983), 5–15.

7. The uncertainties of the end of apartheid in South Africa brought a spate of accusations of witchcraft. The pattern was common: "Somebody in a village dies, or suffers a setback of some kind. The villagers conclude that the person must have been bewitched. . . . So the villagers try to divine a culprit, often seeking guidance from the local *sangoma* ('good' witch doctor)." The end result is the death of the supposed witch, "who is usually old, defenseless, and female." Paul Taylor, "As South African Blacks Gain Freedom, 'Witch' Killings Rise Sharply," *Washington Post,* October 22, 1994, A21. By the end of 1994, more than one hundred supposed witches had been stoned, burned, or drowned. Bob Drogin, "In South Africa, a Resurgence of Witchcraft Fears," *Philadelphia Inquirer,* December 31, 1994, A1.

8. John H. Langbein, "The Law of Evidence in the Eighteenth Century," paper read to the New York University Law School legal history colloquium, September 15, 1993. John Baker seems to agree: "There was little of the care and deliberation of a modern [criminal] trial before the last century. . . . [I]ndeed there were few if any rules of evidence before the eighteenth century." John H. Baker, *An Introduction to English Legal History,* 3d ed. (London, 1990), 582.

9. Thomas Starkie, *Practical Treatise on the Law of Evidence* (London, 1833), 1:478, used the phrase "to the entire exclusion of every reasonable doubt," but as Judge Jon O. Newman makes clear in his "Beyond 'Reasonable Doubt,'" *New York University Law Review* 68 (1993): 981–85, some modern courts have even shied away from explaining what the phrase means, for fear of misleading jurors.

10. Shapiro, *"Beyond Reasonable Doubt"*; Barbara J. Shapiro, *Probability and Certainty in Seventeenth-Century England: A Study of the Relationships between Natural Science, Religion, History, Law, and Literature* (Princeton, 1983).

11. *Colonial Laws of Massachusetts* [1672], ed. William H. Whitmore (Boston, 1887), 13, 16, 31, 52, 55, 59, 83, 131, 145.

12. Thomas Andrew Green, *Verdict According to Conscience: Perspectives on the English Criminal Trial Jury, 1200–1800* (Chicago, 1985), 247; Baker, *Introduction to English Legal History,* 89.

13. Mather, *Wonders,* 365 ff. Simon Greenleaf, *A Treatise on the Law of Evidence* (Boston, 1842), 1:148 n. 2, reported that, as of its date of publication, "the rule excluding hearsay [was] not of great antiquity." In England

there were a good many exceptions in the seventeenth century, for example, the death-bed confession.

14. Gaule, *Select Cases,* 46.

15. The diviner was consulted by the family, a form of private healing which corresponded to the praying cures of the ministers. See, for example, Alison Redmayne, "Chikanga: An African Diviner with an International Reputation," in *Witchcraft Confessions and Accusations,* ed. Mary Douglas (London, 1970), 103–26; Eugene L. Mendonsa, *The Politics of Divination: A Processal View of Reactions to Illness and Deviance among the Sisale of Northern Ghana* (Berkeley, Calif., 1982); M. G. Marwick, *Sorcery in Its Social Setting: A Study of the Northern Rhodesian Cewa* (Manchester, England, 1965), 89 ff.; Victor W. Turner, *The Drums of Affliction: A Study of Religious Processes among the Ndembu of Zambia* (Oxford, 1968), 27 ff. The Christian and Islamic among the African people might dismiss witchcraft accusations, as, for example, the Hausa of northern Nigeria and Akan-speaking Christians in Ghana do today (see L. Lewis Wall, *Hausa Medicine: Illness and Well Being in a West African Culture* [Durham, N.C., 1988], 130–201, and Kofi Appiah-Kubi, *Man Cures, God Heals: Religion and Medical Practice among the Akans of Ghana* [Totowa, N.J., 1981], 12–15), but they believe that people do practice witchcraft and such practices may bring harm to others. The comparison between African and English is not far fetched, or even original with me. See Geoffrey Parrinder, *Witchcraft: European and African* (London, 1958), although I do not subscribe to Parrinder's conclusions.

16. Fischer, *Albion's Seed,* 109, 189–96, 202–3.

17. Perkins, *Discourse,* 54; Gaule, *Select Cases,* 93, 97, 92, 98; Brinley, *Discovery of the Impostures,* preface.

18. Hoffer, *Law and People,* 27–28.

19. Russell K. Osgood, "The Supreme Judicial Court, 1692–1992: An Overview," in *The History of the Law in Massachusetts: The Supreme Judicial Court, 1692–1992,* ed. Russell K. Osgood (Boston, 1992), 12–13; Hutchinson, *Massachusets Bay,* 2:11–12.

20. John Evelyn, diary entry for February 3, quoted in Kittredge, *Witchcraft in Old and New England,* 338.

21. "Commission for a Court of Oyer and Terminer," reproduced in Hansen, *Witchcraft at Salem,* 122. But see Daniel G. Payne, "Defending against the Indefensible: Spectral Evidence at the Salem Witchcraft Trials," *EIHC* 129 (1993): 62–83, proposing that the overthrow of Andros in the colony and the absence of the new charter did not prevent the regular courts from functioning and that the witchcraft trials, which took place after the new charter arrived on May 14, 1692, were conducted under the old code rather

than the Statute of James I. This, Payne argues, can be inferred from the charter provision that those laws not in conflict with English law remained in effect. This may be so, but when the General Court tried to codify colonial practice, including the re-creation of the pre–Dominion-period Court of Assistants, the Privy Council in England disallowed the acts on the grounds that they conflicted with English law. *Acts and Resolves of . . . Massachusetts* (Boston, 1869), 1:55. From the English side of the Atlantic, at least, the code of 1648 was no longer law in 1692. Whether the magistrates and later the judges in Massachusetts considered the *Lawes and Liberties* to be reinstated with the fall of Andros remains an unanswerable question.

253

22. Hutchinson, *Massachusets Bay,* 2:11–12.

23. Foster, *Long Argument,* 214–15; John L. Sibley, *Biographical Sketches of the Graduates of Harvard College* (Cambridge, Mass., 1873), 1:197–203; Everett Kimball, *The Public Life of Joseph Dudley* (New York, 1911), 11, 29, 38, 44; Emory Washburn, *Sketches of the Judicial History of Massachusetts from 1630 to the Revolution in 1775* (Boston, 1840), 81, 85, 103, 114, 132; Michael G. Hall, *The Last American Puritan: The Life of Increase Mather, 1639–1723* (Middletown, Conn., 1988), 251.

24. Robert Earle Moody and Richard Clive Simmons, eds., *The Glorious Revolution in Massachusetts: Selected Documents, 1688–1692* (Boston, 1988), 323 ff.

25. Young, *"Good Order,"* 168.

26. An important point, David Konig informs us, for the Salem people had no love for outsiders on the bench. During the Dominion period, "the presence of appointed officials beyond local control [on the courts] combined with strict insistence of common law forms to make the once familiar and accessible system of local justice unrecognizable in Essex." Konig, *Law and Society,* 164. These anxieties continued into the period of the restoration of the charter.

27. Richard Dunn, *Puritans and Yankees: The Winthrop Dynasty of New England, 1630–1717* (Princeton, 1962), 206, 219, 230, 238, 239, 244, 251, 254, 259, 264–68.

28. Silverman, *Life and Times,* 101.

29. Mather, *Memorable Providences,* in Burr, *Narratives,* 93–94; John Noble and John F. Cronin, eds., *Records of the Court of Assistants of the Colony of Massachusetts Bay, 1630–1692* (Boston, 1901), 1:321, 322.

30. For example, *Essex County Court Records,* 8:394.

31. Sibley, *Graduates of Harvard College,* 2:1–6; Washburn, *Sketches,* 85, 141–45. David Konig reminds me that around this time Saltonstall began drinking heavily. Personal correspondence from Konig, October 17, 1994.

32. Sibley, *Graduates of Harvard College,* 2:345–50; Ola Elizabeth Winslow, *Samuel Sewall of Boston* (New York, 1964), 112–36.

33. David H. Flaherty, "Criminal Practice in Provincial Massachusetts," in *Law in Colonial Massachusetts, 1630–1800,* ed. Daniel R. Coquillette (Boston, 1984), 194.

34. Hansen, *Witchcraft At Salem,* 122; Konig, *Law and Society,* 171.

35. A handful of indictments still came to the courts of assize, marked "billa vera" by the grand juries, but these did not result in convictions. A straggler from the first year of the new century told the tale: Sarah Moredike was indicted for bewitching Richard Hathaway, who was "wasted and consumed," but Moredike was acquitted, and Hathaway, "having falsely accused Sarah Moredike of witchcraft without any reason or colour for the same and pretending himself to be bewitched," was to remain in jail until he found sureties for his good behavior. Ewen, *Witch Hunting,* 264–65. False accusations were routinely uncovered. Even James I, who feared witches and led a campaign against them, tried his hand at foiling fakes and succeeded. MacDonald, *Witchcraft and Hysteria,* xlix–l. But now there were no convictions, or conviction, to balance the exposés.

36. Mather, *Illustrious Providences,* 187.

37. Miller, *New England Mind from Colony to Province,* 200.

38. As in Darren Marcus Staloff, "Intellectual History Naturalized: Materialism and the 'Thinking Class,'" *WMQ,* 3d ser., 50 (1993): 406–17.

39. Michael P. Winship, "Prodigies, Puritanism, and the Perils of Natural Philosophy: The Example of Cotton Mather," *WMQ,* 3d ser., 51 (1994): 92–105.

40. I take my account of these events from Silverman, *Life and Times,* 59–137; Hall, *Last American Puritan,* 212–64; T. H. Breen, *The Character of the Good Ruler: A Study of Puritan Political Ideas in New England, 1630–1730* (New Haven, 1970), 180–202; David D. Hall, *The Faithful Shepherd: A History of the New England Ministry in the Seventeenth Century* (Chapel Hill, 1972), 238–69; and Robert Middlekauf, *The Mathers: Three Generations of Puritan Intellectuals, 1596–1728* (New York, 1971), 148–61.

41. Ford, *Diary of Cotton Mather,* 1:144.

42. I am grateful to Michael Winship for letting me see his soon-to-be published *Seers of God: Puritan Providentialism in the Restoration and Early Enlightenment* (Baltimore, 1996), which traces the Mathers' joint interest in the project.

43. Silverman, *Life and Times,* 97.

44. Reginald Scot, *The Discoverie of Witchcraft* [1584], in *Witchcraft in Europe, 1100–1700: A Documentary History,* ed. Alan C. Kors and Edward

Peters (Philadelphia, 1972), 328. But see Christina Larner, *Enemies of God: The Witch-Hunt in Scotland* (Baltimore, 1981), 157–91, arguing that the belief system that dominated both popular and elite cultures accepted the idea of witchcraft.

45. Mather, *Wonders,* in Drake, *Witchcraft Delusion,* 1:3, 17, 25 (an army of devils had descended upon New England); 37–42 (a summary of Perkins). 255

46. John H. Langbein, *Prosecuting Crime in the Renaissance* (Cambridge, Mass., 1974), 38–43, argues that the justices of the peace were also prosecutors.

47. William Perkins, *A Discourse on the Damned Art of Witchcraft* [1610], in *The Works of William Perkins,* ed. Ian Breward (Appleford, England, 1970), 587, 602, 604, 605.

48. Michael Dalton, *The Country Justice* [1622] (London, 1697), 383.

49. Bernard, *Guide,* 4, 6, 11, 21, 28, 38, 39, 75, 126, 163, 165, 169, 180, 249.

50. Gaule, *Select Cases,* 151–53; MacFarlane, *Witchcraft,* 141.

51. Robert Filmer, *An Advertisement to the Jury-men of England Touching Witches* [1653], reprinted in Filmer, *The Free-holder's Grand Inquest* (London, 1680), 318, 321; Bostridge, "Debates about Witchcraft," 44–47, 60, 65. Peter Laslett attributed Filmer's disgust at Perkins' methods to Filmer's attendance at the Maidstone assizes in 1652, where six suspected witches were tried and executed. Laslett, ed., *Patriarcha and Other Political Works of Sir Robert Filmer* (Oxford, 1949), 9. This may have been so, but Filmer's work fits perfectly into the genre of anti-Puritan exorcism developed in the 1590s and early 1600s. MacDonald, *Witchcraft and Hysteria,* xxii–xxxiii.

52. Joseph Glanvill, *Saducismus Triumphatus: Or Full and Plain Evidence Concerning Witches and Apparitions* (London, 1682), Appendage to the First Part, 136, 156–57; John Webster, *The Displaying of Supposed Witchcraft* (London, 1677), preface. For who not a party to the accusation had actually seen the Devil make a pact with a witch? Webster, *Displaying,* 65

53. See, for a convenient summary, Thomas Harmon Jobe, "The Devil in Restoration Science: The Glanvill-Webster Debate," *Isis* 72 (1981): 343–56.

54. Cotton Mather to John Richards, May 31, 1692, in Kenneth Silverman, ed., *Selected Letters of Cotton Mather* (Baton Rouge, 1971), 35–40; Bovet, *Pandaemonium,* 21, 71; Baxter, *Certainty of the Worlds of Spirits,* 123; Lovejoy, *Glorious Revolution,* 281.

55. Jonathan Swift, *The Battle of the Books* [1697], in *Gulliver's Travels and Other Writings by Jonathan Swift,* ed. Miriam Kosh Starkman (New York, 1981), 409.

56. Silverman, *Life and Times,* 245–54.

57. Greenleaf, *Law of Evidence,* 3:31.

58. Middlekauf, *The Mathers,* 202.

59. Ewen, *Witch Hunting,* 62.

60. Mather, *Wonders,* in Drake, *Witchcraft Delusion,* 1:141–51; Edmund Heward, *Matthew Hale* (London, 1972), 71–83; Notestein, *Witchcraft in England,* 272.

61. Ginsburg, *Night Battles,* 38, 140, 142; Perry, *Gender and Disorder,* 31.

62. Mather, *Illustrious Providences,* 187.

63. Again, as Mather later wrote in *Wonders,* Hale had allowed a search of Cullender and Duny for witches' teats and ordered the defendants to touch the victims.

64. *Essex County Court Records,* 7:329–30.

65. Greenleaf, *Law of Evidence,* 1:137: "The introduction of a falsehood into his defense is a strong presumption against the prisoner."

66. *SWP,* 1:84.

67. Ibid., 1:84, 92, 103, 94, 96, 87–91. By limiting the indictment in this (and later cases) to what had happened at the pre-trial hearings, the prosecution satisfied the "two-witness" rule for capital offenses.

68. Mather, *Wonders,* in Burr, *Narratives,* 174.

69. *SWP,* 1:109.

70. Text quoted from Hansen, *Witchcraft at Salem,* 123–25.

71. Silverman, *Life and Times,* 98–100, argues that Mather wanted no part of spectral evidence, but that is just not convincing in the light of his strong belief in wondrous events, including the appearance of specters. He credited them and collected evidence of them, and the letter to Richards makes clear Mather's conviction that specters could act on real people. I think that my reading of Mather makes more sense of his preaching the "Wonders of the Invisible World" sermon in the middle of the trials, and the way in which he defended the trials in the later, published version of *Wonders.* See, in accord, David Levin, "Did the Mathers Disagree about the Salem Witchcraft Trials?" *Proceedings of the American Antiquarian Society* 95 (1985): 19–37.

72. The very argument in Patricia Howery Davis, "Siding with the Judges: A Psychohistorical Analysis of Cotton Mather's Role in the Salem Witchcraft Trials" (Ph.D. diss., Princeton University, 1991), 185–86, but Davis concludes that this need to please arose only after the summer was almost over.

73. See Brown, "Salem Witchcraft Trials: Samuel Willard's *Some Miscellany Observations,*" 207–36; Stephen L. Robbins, "Samuel Willard and the

Specters of God's Wrathful Lion," *New England Quarterly* 60 (1987): 596–603.

74. Thomas Brattle, "Letter to ————," October 8, 1692, in Burr, *Narratives,* 180–81; Gragg, *Salem Witch Crisis,* 142.

75. Silverman, *Life and Times,* 106, gives the Andover outbreak as a turning point of Mather's thinking, proving his worst fears correct.

76. Mather to John Cotton, August 5, 1692, in Silverman, *Selected Letters,* 40.

77. Silverman, *Life and Times,* 108.

78. Ibid., 114–36. See also David Watters, "The Spectral Identity of Sir William Phips," *Early American Literature* 18 (1983–84): 219–32 (Mather continues to lionize Phips after the latter's death in 1697). Political flattery, here obsequiousness, was much better served and easier stomached in the late seventeenth century than it is today, but Mather's eagerness to get right with the authorities went far beyond what other Puritan divines wrote in their first-hand accounts. John Hale, for example, and Increase Mather took pains not to accuse the judges of doing evil, but they did not flatter the way Cotton did. What are we to make of it? The most obvious surmise is that Mather was insecure and needed parental or surrogate parental approval. He was, however, by this time a father with a family of his own, well established in his pulpit, well known in England, and the man that the politicians consulted. It is still difficult for me to sort out the personal and the political motives behind Mather's combination of paranoia and adulatory excess, but I think the "narcissism" theories that Demos propounds in *Entertaining Satan* would work perfectly on the younger Mather.

79. Mather to John Foster, August 17, 1692, in Silverman, *Selected Letters,* 41–43.

80. Thomas, *Diary of Samuel Sewall,* 1:294; Calef, *More Wonders,* in Burr, *Narratives,* 360–61.

81. Calef, *More Wonders,* in Burr, *Narratives,* 364–65.

82. *SWP,* 2:490–92.

83. I am sure that I cannot improve upon the account given of the Knapp episode in Demos, *Entertaining Satan,* 97–131. Demos attributes Elizabeth's fits to her wrestling with narcissism and reads Willard to have come to the same conclusion. Narcissistic injury had brought forth narcissistic rage (122). Perhaps also Elizabeth had conceived a fancy for the young minister, felt guilt and shame, had no mother at hand to share with or model herself on (for she was evidently not reared in the home of her own parents [114]), and so acted out her conflicts in this bizarre way, but Demos finds no evidence of "erotic aims" (119).

84. Mark A. Peterson, "'Ordinary' Preaching and the Interpretation of the Salem Witchcraft Crisis by the Boston Clergy," *EIHC* 129 (1993): 94–100.

Chapter Seven: Trials

1. Of thirty-one earlier cases in which verdicts were given, only eight ended in verdict that the defendant was guilty of witchcraft. The majority of the twenty-three remaining verdicts were not guilty; some of the other defendants were suspected of lying or misconduct (such as abusing their neighbors or making threats) and bound to their good behavior by sureties. The list appears in app. A of Weisman, *Witchcraft, Magic, and Religion,* 192–203.

2. Bearing in mind that a case that comes to trial has already passed though several filters screening out suspects against whom there is little evidence, one finds that colonial judges and juries convicted about 65 percent of those who came to trial for serious crimes. See Peter Charles Hoffer, introduction to *Criminal Proceedings in Colonial Virginia,* ed. Peter Charles Hoffer and William B. Scott, American Legal Records, vol. 10 (Athens, Ga., and Washington, D.C., 1984), lxix–lxx. In all of colonial Massachusetts's history, women were convicted of capital offenses in 39 of 132 cases. N. E. H. Hull, *Female Felons: Women and Serious Crime in Colonial Massachusetts* (Urbana, Ill., 1987), 105. This figure includes all the accused, not just those who were actually brought to trial. Murrin, "Magistrates, Sinners, and a Precarious Liberty," 202, gives a 75 percent conviction rate for Salem in the years 1660–86 for noncapital crimes. The rate would be lower if it included grand jury "no bills."

3. Demos, *Entertaining Satan,* 66, offers a selected list of the defendants to illustrate their ages, which proves to me that the older the women were, the more likely they were to have been accused of witchcraft at some time previous to 1692. Bishop, Carrier, and others—the "usual suspects"—are included, but so was Bradbury.

4. *SWP,* 3:755, 873. The grand jury's finding of "ignoramus," quashing the bill of indictment, is a technical point of great importance but one easily missed. Tituba was not tried for the crime because she was not indicted by the grand jury. For examples of errors arising from misreading of the record, see, for example, Rosenthal, *Salem Story,* 28–29 (erroneously stating that the Ipswich courts indicted her when courts do not indict anyone, and missing the fact that the bill of indictment in Tituba's case was indorsed "ignoramus"); Hansen, *Witchcraft at Salem,* 123 (Tituba not brought to trial because Puritans saw her confession as evidence of regeneration); Karlsen,

Devil in the Shape of a Woman, 263 (Tituba escaped execution by confessing).

5. Marilynne K. Roach, *Map of Salem Village and Vicinity* (Watertown, Mass., 1985); map of Salem town in Roach, *Time Traveler's Maps.*

6. Hutchinson, *Massachusets Bay,* 2:27.

7. Cockburn, *History of the English Assizes,* 122.

8. Green, *Verdict,* 135.

9. SWP, 3:903–44; Edgar J. McManus, *Law and Liberty in Early New England: Criminal Justice and Due Process, 1620–1692* (Amherst, Mass., 1993), 98–103; Powers, *Crime and Punishment,* 554.

10. Haskins, *Law and Authority,* 213–14. The special verdicts I have found in Salem were in civil cases. See, for example, *Essex County Court Records,* 8:189, 244, 263.

11. Mary Rhinelander McCarl, "Spreading the News of Satan's Malignity in Salem: Benjamin Harris, Printer and Publisher of the Witchcraft Narratives," EIHC 129 (1993): 55. Mather begged Stoughton and then Sewall for their help. Mather to Stoughton, September 2, 1692; Mather to Sewall, September 20, 1692, in Silverman, *Selected Letters,* 43–45.

12. Mather, *Wonders,* in Burr, *Narratives,* 212–13.

13. Calef, *More Wonders,* in Burr, *Narratives,* 299–300.

14. SVW, 34.

15. Victor, *Satanic Panic,* 40–56.

16. McManus, *Law and Liberty,* 148; Green, *Verdict,* 249–53.

17. Baker, *Introduction to English Legal History,* 189–93.

18. Hansen, *Witchcraft at Salem,* 122: "No more experienced or distinguished a court could have been assembled anywhere in English America." Brown, "Forfeitures at Salem," 86, agrees, citing as authority Weisman, *Witchcraft, Magic, and Religion,* 179. Brown writes, "[T]he judges conscientiously 'organized the most cautiously empirical and systematic investigation into witchcraft ever to occur in new England.'" The internal quote is from Weisman, true, but Weisman does not use the word conscientiously—that is Brown's own contribution. Nor does Weisman write "the judges." Instead, he wrote "the court." In fact there is no evidence that the judges set themselves a course of close reading of English tracts and precedents. Rather, in court, according to Weisman, they looked for witches' marks and forced suspects to look upon and touch their accusers. These tactics did reflect a systematic recovery of old, customary witch-finding devices but did not represent contemporary legal standards or empirical findings, and they hardly establish the legal acumen of the judges.

19. See, for example, Fiss, "Objectivity and Interpretation," 739, 744.

20. A nice recent summary is J. M. Beattie, "Scales of Justice: Defense Counsel and the English Criminal Trial in the Eighteenth and Nineteenth Centuries," *Law and History Review* 9 (1991): 221–67. There is no evidence that seventeenth-century Massachusetts procedure differed from this. See Flaherty, "Criminal Practice in Provincial Massachusetts," 191–242.

21. Notestein, *Witchcraft in England,* 320.

22. See, for example, John Langbein, "The Criminal Trial before the Lawyers," *University of Chicago Law Review* 45 (1978): 263–316.

23. *SWP,* 1:302.

24. John Langbein, "The Historic Origins of the Privilege against Self-Incrimination at Common Law," *University of Michigan Law Review* 92 (1994): 1050–52.

25. *SWP,* 2:607–8. The story is taken from Robert Calef's *More Wonders,* in Burr, *Narratives,* 358–59. What reason might Calef have had for structuring the story in this way? Surely it makes Stoughton look like a bully at best and a demon at worst.

26. Thomas Newton to Isaac Addington, May 31, 1692, in *SWP,* 3:867.

27. Flaherty, "Criminal Practice in Provincial Massachusetts," 194, 240–41; Alexander H. Shapiro, "Political Theory and the Growth of Defensive Safeguards in Criminal Procedure: The Origins of the Treason Trials Act of 1696," *Law and History Review* 11 (1993): 222, 235.

28. Konig, *Law and Society,* 140; for example, *Essex County Court Records,* 8:12 ("Mr. Nicholas Shapley or his attorney v. Samuel Seward").

29. Konig, *Law and Society,* 188.

30. For example, Noble and Cronin, *Court of Assistants,* 1:229, 233 (Mary Webster indicted on May 22, 1683, for making a pact with the Devil and allowing a familiar to suckle, but acquitted on September 4 by the trial jury). On the clerks, see Russell K. Osgood, "John Clark, Esq., Justice of the Peace, 1667–1728," in Coquillette, *Law in Colonial Massachusetts,* 107–52. Little has changed in the past two hundred years, at least in western Massachusetts; see Barbara Yngvesson, "Making Law at the Doorway: The Clerk, the Court, and the Construction of Community in a New England Town," *Law and Society Review* 22 (1988): 421–22.

31. *SWP,* 1:210, 147, 66, 59.

32. Ibid., 1:303–4.

33. Compare Hall, *Worlds of Wonder,* 164, 194–95.

34. *SWP,* 1:53. On July 23, John Proctor complained of "the enmity" of the judges in a letter he wrote from jail to the ministers. *SWP,* 2:689.

35. Ibid., 3:938.

36. Ibid., 2:607.

37. Ibid., 2:603.

38. Matthew Hale, *History of the Common Law of England* [1677], ed. Charles M. Grey (Chicago, 1971), 164.

39. William Lambard, *Eirenarcha* (London, 1582), 218; Greenleaf, *Law of Evidence,* 147.

40. Demos, *Entertaining Satan,* 301.

41. *SWP,* 2:592–93.

42. Mather, *Wonders,* 161, 165.

43. Lawson, *Brief and True Narrative,* in Burr, *Narratives,* 162.

44. Upham, *Salem Witchcraft,* 530; Mather, *Illustrious Providences,* 280; Perkins, *Discourse,* 208; Cotta, *Triall,* 115.

45. Powers, *Crime and Punishment,* 400–416.

46. *SWP,* 1:221–23.

47. Green, *Verdict,* 25.

48. Young, "Salem Witch Trials," 235 ff.

49. William E. Nelson, *Americanization of the Common Law: The Impact of Legal Change on Massachusetts Society, 1760–1830* (Cambridge, Mass., 1975), 21–31; J. R. Pole, "Reflections on American Law and the American Revolution," *WMQ,* 3d ser., 50 (1993): 132. Nelson and Pole could cite U.S. Supreme Court Chief Justice John Jay as authority. *Georgia v. Brailsford,* 3 U.S. (3 Dallas) 1, 4 (1794), but today the issue is far cloudier. Attempts to add an item on jury lawmaking to the instructions judges give to juries in state criminal trials has met opposition from the bench itself, according to one professor who wrote model jury instructions for the Michigan courts. Dorean Marguerite Koenig, Thomas M. Cooley Law School, communication to H-Law, Internet, September 28, 1994.

50. A survey of the "local knowledge" theories appears in Barbara Yngvesson, "Popular Legal Culture: Inventing Law in Local Settings," *Yale Law Journal* 98 (1989): 1690–91.

51. Green, *Verdict,* 257.

52. Ibid., 283–85; McManus, *Law and Liberty,* 101; Hull, *Female Felons,* 98.

53. Hall, *Witch-Hunting,* 128, 183–84, 253, 255; Mather *Wonders,* 365. Godbeer, *Devil's Dominion,* 170, 176, finds this to be evidence that the elite, legal culture was distinct from and could prevent the operation of popular credulity and hostility.

54. *SWP,* 1:83–109.

55. *Lawes and Liberties,* 35.

56. Dalton, *Country Justice,* 271; Hawkins, *Pleas of the Crown,* 172.

57. *Lawes and Liberties,* 6.

58. Ann Pudeator, executed on September 22, challenged the motives of the witnesses against her, begging that her life "not be taken away by such false evidence" as that given by convicted liars with grudges against her. *SWP,* 3:710.

59. Morgan, *Puritan Family,* 88; or at least they were supposed to know the capital laws, according to the edicts of the General Court.

60. Summary in Brown, *Guide,* 94–95. Minkema and Cooper, *Sermon Notebook,* 199, 204. Parris returned to the themes of anti–Roman Catholicism exercised by Baxter in his 1691 essay, linking together the dangers of Catholic worship and witchcraft.

61. Gragg, *Salem Witch Crisis,* 125–40.

62. Adam J. Hirsch, *The Rise of the Penitentiary: Prisons and Punishment in Early America* (New Haven, 1992), 6–9.

63. *Essex County Court Records,* 8:31–32.

64. Brown, "Forfeitures at Salem," 98–99. Brown argues that Massachusetts law, at least as interpreted by previous General Courts, refused to follow the English practice of "escheat"—the confiscation of a convict's property by the Crown. During the witchcraft crisis, the sheriff and the court reverted to the English practice. George Jacobs Sr., the Proctors, the Corys, Dorcas Hoar, Mary Parker, and the Wardwells forfeited personal property (92–95). Escape and jail breaking were also punishable by forfeiture (98–99), but flight to avoid indictment was not. Corwin ignored this distinction.

65. Peter Irons, *Justice at War: The Story of the Japanese American Internment Cases,* rev. ed. (Berkeley, Calif., 1993), 356.

66. Barstow, *Witchcraze,* 16.

67. *SWP,* 2:403–4. An act of some kindness on his part as well, for she had received the goods his maid, Margaret Lord, stole from him and his wife some years before. *Essex County Court Records,* 7:43.

68. A crime for which "benefit of clergy" was allowed. Originally, this was a way to insure that men in lay orders were not punished by the civil courts. They read the 51st Psalm. By the seventeenth century, reading was not necessary, for benefit of clergy had been extended to all first-time offenders in manslaughter and some property offenses.

69. "In the opinion of many unprejudiced, considerate, and considerable spectators, some of the condemned went out of the world with as great protestations, but also with as good shows of innocency, as men could do." Brattle, "Letter," in Burr, *Narratives,* 177.

70. According to Calef, *More Wonders,* in Burr, *Narratives,* 360–61.

71. Ibid., 369.

72. Higginson, preface to Hale, *Modest Inquiry,* in Burr, *Narratives,* 400–401.

73. Louis P. Masur, *Rites of Execution: Capital Punishment and the Transformation of American Culture, 1776–1865* (New York, 1989), 41. The same point is made in Hull, *Female Felons,* 109.

74. Boyer and Nissenbaum, Karlsen, and others agree that the court intended to try, convict, and execute those who confessed. *SWP,* 1:24 (it was never their intent to spare those who confessed); Karlsen, *Devil in the Shape of a Woman,* 278 n. 125 (delay in execution was "a temporary expedient"). Gragg, *Salem Witch Crisis,* 132, disagrees, arguing that the magistrates and ministers thought confession was a sign of a regenerate heart.

75. *Lawes and Liberties,* 8. John Proctor alleged the torture of suspects, including his son, William. *SWP,* 2:689–90.

76. Brattle, "Letter," in Burr, *Narratives,* 189.

Chapter Eight: Pardon

1. Hansen, *Witchcraft at Salem,* 136, believes that John Proctor's petition for redress spurred the ministers to review the way in which the court had heard (and ignored) their animadversions on spectral evidence.

2. McCarl, "Spreading the News of Satan's Malignity," 57.

3. Samuel Willard, *Some Miscellany Observations Respecting Witchcraft in a Dialogue Between S and B . . . Printed in Philadelphia in 1692* (reprinted Boston, 1869), 8. All things considered, Cotton Mather may have been closer to the spirit of Perkins and Bernard than Willard was, however.

4. Calef, *More Wonders,* in Burr, *Narratives,* 360.

5. Willard, *Observations,* 16, 21.

6. Ernest Benson Lowrie, *The Shape of the Puritan Mind: The Thought of Samuel Willard* (New Haven, 1974), 117, 127.

7. Hall, *Last American Puritan,* 261.

8. Lovejoy, *Glorious Revolution,* 371.

9. Hall, *Last American Puritan,* 261–62; McCarl, "Spreading the News of Satan's Malignity," 54.

10. Mather, *Magnalia,* 335.

11. *Victor v. Nebraska* joined with *Sandoval v. California,* 128 L. ED. 2d 583, 593, 594, 496 (1994).

12. Increase Mather, *Cases of Conscience Concerning Evil Spirits Personating Men* (Boston, 1693), preface.

13. Ibid., 283.

14. In what may be a final irony for the Mathers' part of the story, the

Salem trials marked the high point and the end of the trials the beginning of the decline of their influence. Foster, *Long Argument,* 264–66.

15. Print wars were typical of Puritan ministers, going back in Massachusetts to John Cotton and Roger Williams in the 1630s and 1640s, although I cannot find another example of a father-son battle like this.

16. Mather, *Wonders,* in Drake, *Witchcraft Delusion,* 1:2. By the time this passage appeared in print, Cotton had already seen his father's *Cases of Conscience* and knew that some would attribute an open breach to the apparent discrepancy in their views. He denied this, as would his father, but the distance between the works is still perceptible, even though the two had collaborated throughout the crisis.

17. Cotton Mather to John Cotton, October 20, 1692, in Silverman, *Selected Letters,* 45–46.

18. On September 22, 1692, Cotton dined with Stephen Sewall and Stoughton at Samuel Sewall's house. There Cotton again urged the two judges to support his planned account of the trials. Thomas, *Diary of Samuel Sewall,* 1:297.

19. Mather, *Wonders,* in Drake, *Witchcraft Delusion,* 1:4, 95, 104–5.

20. Ibid., 106–7.

21. Demos, *Entertaining Satan,* 122–23.

22. They are not the same, even though both men tried to present a united front to the outside world. Here I prefer Middlekauf, *The Mathers,* 153, and my own reading of *Cases of Conscience* to Levin, "Did the Mathers Disagree."

23. Gragg, *Salem Witch Crisis,* 164.

24. Ford, *Diary of Cotton Mather,* 150–51.

25. Mather to Robert Calef, January 15, 1694, in Burr, *Narratives,* 335.

26. Again the issue of cognitive dissonance. The shift in public opinion is mentioned in Thomas, *Diary of Samuel Sewall,* 1:298.

27. Mather, *Magnalia,* 331.

28. Mather, *Brand Pluck'd Out of the Burning,* in Burr, *Narratives,* 261. Notice again how identity shifts from black to red.

29. Ibid., 287.

30. Ford, *Diary of Cotton Mather,* 171–72.

31. Calef, *More Wonders,* in Burr, *Narratives,* 320.

32. Phips to Lords of Trade, October 12, 1692, in Burr, *Narratives,* 196–98.

33. Phips to Lords of Trade, February 21, 1693, in Burr, *Narratives,* 198–202.

34. Ibid., 201 n. 2.

35. McManus, *Law and Liberty*, 76–77; Haskins, *Law and Authority*, 34–35 ff.

36. *SWP*, 3:875–76.

37. Ibid., 3:880–81.

38. Ibid., 3:882–83.

39. Ibid., 3:865–903.

40. Phips to King William, February 21, 1693, in Burr, *Narratives*, 201.

41. Calef, *More Wonders*, in Burr, *Narratives*, 382–83.

42. *SWP*, 3:903–44.

43. Calef, *More Wonders*, in Drake, *Witchcraft Delusion*, 3:127. Duston was what Weisman, *Witchcraft, Magic, and Religion*, 184–85, regards as a traditional witch, a longstanding problem to her neighbors for her quarrelsome and uncharitable nature. Yet before Salem these suspected witches and known miscreants were not often tried, much less convicted or executed. Thus with Duston one has the return of the pre-Salem or traditional pattern. The pattern did not last long after Salem, however, for with a few exceptions, accusations did not even get to grand juries after 1693.

44. *SWP*, 3:791–92.

45. Ibid., 2:645.

46. Ibid., 3:924. Even Calef reported that she was one of the most "senseless and ignorant creatures that could be found." Calef, *More Wonders*, in Drake, *Witchcraft Delusion*, 2:125.

47. *SWP*, 3:938.

48. Cotton Mather, *Theopolis Americana* (Boston, 1710), 29.

49. *SWP*, 3:971–1046.

50. Brown, "Forfeitures at Salem," explains this issue. Lawful orders of courts must be obeyed, even if a later superior court finds those orders at fault. The same rule applies today, for example, in the issuance of temporary restraining orders.

51. Brattle, "Letter," in Burr, *Narratives*, 169–70, 171, 175, 176, 184.

52. Robert Calef to B[rattle], March 1, 1694, in Calef, *More Wonders*, in Drake, *Witchcraft Delusion*, 2:86.

53. Calef was aware of these, and of the fact that some of the accused were Quakers or had relatives who were Quakers. On the mythology of the Whig martyrs in the uprising of 1684, see Melinda Zook, "The Bloody Assizes: Whig Martyrologies and the Manipulation of Memory," paper read to the American Society for Legal History, Washington, D.C., October 21, 1994.

54. Calef to Samuel Willard, September 20, 1695, in Drake, *Witchcraft Delusion*, 2:102–5.

55. Calef, *More Wonders,* in Burr, *Narratives,* 296, 297.

56. Ibid., 336.

57. Ibid., 298, 299.

58. Ibid., 300, 301.

59. Ibid., 302, 299.

60. Ibid., 327, 328.

61. Ibid., 320, 321.

62. Ibid., 355.

63. Essex County General Sessions of the Peace Docket Book, 1692–95, Essex Institute, Salem Sessions, September 27, 1692; *SWP,* 3:789.

64. ECCR (MS), 52: 126-1.

65. Cooper and Minkema, *Sermon Notebook,* 23–24.

66. Boyer and Nissenbaum, *Salem Possessed,* 69–73.

67. Ibid., 74–75; *SVW,* 297–99.

68. *SVW,* 202, 222–23.

69. Boyer and Nissenbaum, *Salem Possessed,* 217–20.

70. *SWP,* 3:810.

71. Hale, *Modest Inquiry,* in Burr, *Narratives,* 404, 408–10, 427.

72. Winslow, *Sewall,* 134–35.

73. Thomas, *Diary of Samuel Sewall,* 1:366–67.

Conclusion

1. After reading an early version of this book, a good friend asked, "What is your thesis?" I could not answer him then and still cannot. I suppose I might argue that the novelties of the story as I have told it are its theses, but that was not what he wanted to know. After much thought, I concluded that some stories do not have theses. They have plot and character, setting and moral. I hope that is enough here.

2. As in Conrad Russell, *The Causes of the English Civil War* (Oxford, 1990), 24–25.

3. Herbert Leventhal, *In the Shadow of the Enlightenment: Occultism and Renaissance Science in Eighteenth-Century America* (New York, 1976), 85–103. The legal rules developed first in civil cases (William E. Nelson, *Americanization of the Common Law: The Impact of Legal Change on Massachusetts Society, 1760–1830,* 2d ed. [Athens, Ga., 1994], 23–26), but to some extent they were foreshadowed by new ways of looking at the world at large. See, for example, Demos, *Entertaining Satan,* 393–96.

4. Cotton Mather's sea changes I take from Winship, *Seers of God,* although again his father, Increase, was there first. Hall, *Worlds of Wonder,* 107. For both Mathers' parishioners, a new book of omens and prodigies

had been opened, no longer chronicling the malice of the Devil. Instead, its entries celebrated the piety of children. Sommerville, *Discovery of Childhood,* 64–65.

5. Thomas J. Davis, *A Rumor of Revolt: The "Great Negro Plot" in Colonial New York* (New York, 1985), 50–53, 236–37, 250–63

6. As in the examination of little Jemmy, six, on April 7, 1742: "[T]hen the boy was asked some questions by the recorder and town-clerk, tending to the same purpose, Concerning the actions of [two of the convicts]." Daniel Horsmanden, *The New-York Conspiracy, or a History of the Negro Plot . . . 1741–1742* [1810], ed. Thomas J. Davis (Boston, 1971), 465.

7. "Salem Revisited," *Economist* 320, August 31, 1991, 23; Richard Ofshe and Ethan Watters, *Making Monsters* (New York, 1994), 177–204.

8. Rosenthal, *Salem Story,* 204.

9. See, for example, *Los Angeles Times* Travel Section, September 26, 1993, 24; *Boston Globe,* July 11, 1993, B41.

10. But in Barbados, people who practice any "subtle craft" or tell fortunes are still subject to prosecution under the Vagrancy Act of 1897, Warren Alleyne of Christ Church, Barbados, tells me, and Joseph Faludon of Ibandan, Nigeria, has reminded me that authorities there are hostile to witches and their craft.

Appendix: What's in a Name?

1. Thinking about—struggling with is more accurate—this question, I came upon Jesse Lemisch's reflections on his famous and controversial "Jack Tar in the Streets" article (*WMQ,* 3d ser., 25 [1968]: 371–407). Lemisch recalled ruefully how his advisor at Yale, Edmund Morgan, remarked: "There are no sources." See Ronald Hoffman and Michael McGiffert, eds., *In Search of Early America* (Williamsburg, Va., 1993), 136.

2. *SWP,* 3:746, 747; 2:361; Calef, *More Wonders,* in Burr, *Narratives,* 343; Hale, *Modest Inquiry,* in Burr, *Narratives,* 413.

3. *SVW,* 10.

4. A musing following a conversation with Professor Mary Schweitzer, of Villanova University, at the Conference on Possible Pasts sponsored by the Institute of Early American History and Culture and the Philadelphia Center for Early American Studies, June 5, 1994. On the Spanish and English uses of Indian and Negro, see Jack D. Forbes, *Africans and Native Americans: The Language of Race and the Evolution of Red-Black Peoples,* 2d ed. (Urbana, Ill., 1993), 39–45, 62, 63, 84.

5. Almon Wheeler Lauber, *Indian Slavery in Colonial Times within the*

Present Limits of the United States (New York, 1913), 109, 126–27, 128, 131, 141–45, 148, 161, 164, 166–67, 202–4.

6. Daniel Mandell, "'Habits of Industry and Good Morals': Indians in Southern New England from the Encounter to the Industrial Age," paper read to the Second Mashantucket Pequot History Conference, October 1993, 5–6; quoted by permission of the author.

7. Joseph Willard, communicator, "Indian Children Put to Service, 1676," *New England Journal of Genealogy* (July 1854): 270–73.

8. Conversations with Neal Salisbury, Smith College, February 21, 1994, and Ives Goddard, Smithsonian Institution, February 24, 1994. I am grateful to both of them for their time and shared expertise.

9. See *SWP*, 3:746, 747; 2:361; Calef, *More Wonders*, in Burr, *Narratives*, 343; Hale, *Modest Inquiry*, in Burr, *Narratives*, 413. Hansen, *Witchcraft at Salem*, 31, and "The Metamorphosis of Tituba: Or Why American Intellectuals Can't Tell an Indian Witch from a Negro," *New England Quarterly* 47 (1974): 3–12, insists that Tituba must have been a Carib Indian from the Spanish Main or one of the islands near Barbados. Breslaw, "Salem Witch from Barbados," 217–38, opined that Tituba must have been Carib, but has changed her mind.

10. Upham, *Salem Witchcraft*, 2:2.

11. See, for example, Samuel Eliot Morison, *The Puritan Pronaos* (New York, 1936), 252.

12. Starkey, *Devil in Massachusetts*, 43.

13. Arthur Miller, *The Crucible*, act 1, scene 1: Tituba is dancing in the woods, waving her arms over a fire and muttering "gibberish."

14. Demos, "Underlying Themes," 1316.

15. Jerome S. Handler, "The Amerindian Slave Population of Barbados in the Seventeenth and Eighteenth Centuries," *Caribbean Studies* 8 (April 1968): 38–64.

16. Nancie L. Solien Gonzalez, *Black Carib Household Structure: A Study of Migration and Modernization* (Seattle, 1969), 17–19.

17. See Michael Craton, "From Caribs to Black Caribs: The Amerindian Roots of Servile Resistance in the Caribbean," in *In Resistance: Studies in African, Caribbean, and Afro-American History*, ed. Gary Y. Okihiro (Amherst, Mass., 1986), 110–12, and Philip P. Boucher, *Cannibal Encounters: Europeans and Island Caribs, 1492–1763* (Baltimore, 1992), 61–92.

18. Breslaw, "Salem Witch from Barbados," 227–36.

19. Breslaw, letter to the author, February 14, 1994, enclosing two pages of manuscript to be included in her forthcoming *Tituba: Reluctant Witch of Salem* (New York, 1996).

20. Breslaw, "Salem Witch from Barbados," 225.

21. Bennett, *Bondsmen and Bishops,* 34; Bridenbaugh and Bridenbaugh, *No Peace,* 356.

22. Craton, *Searching for the Invisible Man,* 55, 58, 156.

23. Lewis, "African Impact on Language and Literature," 104.

24. *SWP,* 1:179.

25. See Peter H. Wood, *Black Majority: Negroes in Colonial South Carolina from 1670 through the Stono Rebellion* (New York, 1974), 181–86, and Charles Joyner, *Down by the Riverside: A South Carolina Slave Community* (Urbana, Ill., 1984), 217–22.

26. *SWP,* 1:179, 180.

27. I am indebted to Ann Plane and Daniel Mandell for discussing the intermarriage question with me, and N. E. H. Hull for suggesting that it might explain why Tituba became an "Indian."

Index

273

Library of Congress Cataloging-in-Publication Data

Hoffer, Peter Charles, 1944–
     The devil's disciples : makers of the Salem witchcraft trials / Peter Charles Hoffer.
     p.   cm.
Includes bibliographical references and index.
ISBN 0-8018-5200-5 (alk. paper).
     1. Trials (Witchcraft)—Massachusetts—Salem.   2. Witchcraft—Massachusetts—
Salem—History—17th century.   3. Salem (Massachusetts)—Social conditions.
I. Title.
     KFM2478.8.W5H64   1996
     345.744'50288—dc20
     [317.505288]   95-31432

ISBN 0-8018-5201-3 (pbk.)